Economic Impacts of Intellectual Property-Conditioned Government Incentives

Dan Prud'homme · Hefa Song
Editors

Economic Impacts of Intellectual Property-Conditioned Government Incentives

IPKey

Springer

Editors
Dan Prud'homme
IP Key project, European Union Intellectual Property Office
Beijing
China

Hefa Song
Chinese Academy of Sciences, Institute of Policy and Management
Beijing
China

ISBN 978-981-10-1117-7 ISBN 978-981-10-1119-1 (eBook)
DOI 10.1007/978-981-10-1119-1

Library of Congress Control Number: 2016939107

Printed on acid-free paper

This Springer imprint is published by Springer Nature
The registered company is Springer Science+Business Media Singapore Pte Ltd.

Acknowledgements

This book was produced under the IP Key project (IP Key), which is funded by the European Union (EU) and co-financed and implemented by the European Union Intellectual Property Office (EUIPO) (previously, called "OHIM"), in cooperation with the European Patent Office (EPO). IP Key provided partial financial support for the completion of a few chapters in this book that were received in response to a public notice for the submission of papers and then judged in a competitive review process. IP Key also provided financial support to both editors of the book to substantively edit its chapters, and financial support to employ an external English editing firm to polish the language of the chapters.

Disclaimer: The opinions expressed in this book are those of the authors of each chapter and do not necessarily represent, in any way, those of the EU/European Commission; EUIPO or EPO; IP Key as an entity per se; nor any Chinese institution or other institutions with which IP Key has cooperated.

IPKey

EUIPO
EUROPEAN UNION
INTELLECTUAL PROPERTY OI

Contents

Contributors

Yi-jie Cheng School of Management and Economics, Beijing Institute of Technology, Beijing, China

Xu Dawei Sino-Danish Center for Education and Research, Beijing, China; School of Management, University of Chinese Academy of Sciences, Beijing, China

Alan Garcia KPMG China Centre of Excellence for R&D Incentives, Beijing, China

Johannes Holzer German Patent and Trade Mark Office, Munich, Germany

Josephine Jiang KPMG China, Beijing, China

Zongzhen Jin China National Institute of Standardization, Beijing, China; Center for IPR Research and Training, Institute of Policy and Management, Chinese Academy of Sciences, Beijing, China

Vinod Kalloe KPMG Meijburg & Co, Amsterdam, The Netherlands

Haibo Liu Center for IPR Research and Training, Institute of Policy and Management, Chinese Academy of Sciences, Beijing, China

Yun Liu School of Management and Economics, Beijing Institute of Technology, Beijing, China

Cheryl Xiaoning Long WISE and School of Economics, Xiamen University, Xiamen, China; Colgate University, Hamilton, USA

Oliver Lutze Spruson & Ferguson (Asia) PTE LTD, Shanghai, China

Federico Munari CIEG—Dipartimento di Scienze Aziendali, Università di Bologna, Bologna, Italy

Dan Prud'homme IP Key project, European Union Intellectual Property Office, Beijing, China

Hefa Song Center for IPR Research and Training, Institute of Policy and Management, Chinese Academy of Sciences, Beijing, China

Long Tan School of Management and Economics, Beijing Institute of Technology, Beijing, China

Conrad Turley KPMG China, Beijing, China

Jun Wang Intellectual Property Research Institute, Xiamen University, Xiamen, China

Mimi Wang KPMG China, Beijing, China

Liang Xu School of International Business, Sichuan International Studies University, Chongqing, China

Yafeng Zhang Center for IPR Research and Training, Institute of Policy and Management, Chinese Academy of Sciences, Beijing, China

Li Zhenxing Chinese Academy of Sciences Institute of Policy and Management, Beijing, China; Sino-Danish Center for Education and Research, Beijing, China

Chapter 1
Introduction

Dan Prud'homme and Hefa Song

Various countries' governments have employed incentives in an attempt to stimulate firm-level, sectoral, and/or nationwide competitiveness. Incentives are one instrument of industrial policy, which broadly includes policies directed at affecting the structure of the economy in favor of more dynamic activities (Rodrik 2004). Government intervention via industrial policy is an important tool in many countries to stimulate economic growth and competitiveness (Stiglitz et al. 2013; Greenwald and Stiglitz 2013; Lee 2013). Such policies may also be used to enhance national security, including physical security as well as energy and food security, social welfare, and/or environmental sustainability.

Among the many different incentives used as part of industrial policies, a particular branch with requirements specifically related to intellectual property (IP) [used interchangeably hereafter with the term "intellectual property rights" (IPR)], appear to be increasingly popular among governments. We call these "IP-conditioned" incentives, which, in the absence of a common definition thereof, we define as *measures imposed by the state that are intended to change economic behavior and are conditioned on meeting IP-related requirements*. IP-conditioned

Dan Prud'homme: Technical Expert, IP Key project, implemented by the European Union Intellectual Property Office, Beijing, China.

Hefa Song: Professor and Deputy Director of the Center for IPR Research and Training, Chinese Academy of Sciences Institute of Policy and Management, Beijing, China.

D. Prud'homme (✉)
IP Key project, European Union Intellectual Property Office, #2480 Sunflower Tower,
No. 37 Maizidian West Street, Beijing 100125, China
e-mail: dan.prudhomme@ipkey.org

H. Song
Center for IPR Research and Training, Institute of Policy and Management, Chinese
Academy of Sciences, No. 15 Zhongguancun Beiyitiao Alley, Haidian District, Beijing
100190, People's Republic of China

D. Prud'homme and H. Song (eds.), *Economic Impacts of Intellectual Property-Conditioned Government Incentives*, DOI 10.1007/978-981-10-1119-1_1

government incentives can take a variety of forms: they can be found in the areas of tax, subsidies and grants, public/government procurement, financing and loans, inventor remuneration and rewards, targets tied to work performance evaluations, non-monetary/"soft" awards, amongst other areas. They differ in structure, scope, and the amount of resources spent on creating and implementing them depending on their type and the country employing them.

One objective of some of these IP-conditioned incentives is to encourage innovation. One of the main methods to boost competitiveness and growth is through innovation (Schumpeter 1942). However, while social returns to innovation in the form of knowledge diffusion can be substantial, the private returns to firms on innovation investment are not always as positive. Herein, the public nature of innovation spillovers means that firms cannot appropriate all returns from their R&D investment (Arrow 1962). This creates an incentive for firms to in some cases spend below the socially optimal level of R&D (Bloom et al. 2013), which can hamper innovation. As such, government incentives and investment are needed to ensure more optimal innovation investment (Martin and Scott 2000). Some IP-conditioned incentives are intended to meet these ends.

Alternatively, as explained in chapter two of this book, there are various other, often even more prominent, rationales for the usage of IP-conditioned government incentives. Sometimes the incentives are intended to enable technological catch-up by latecomers through strategies not necessarily meant to stimulate valuable innovations in the near-term. And, in many cases, the incentives are simply meant to support small- and-medium-sized enterprises (SMEs) and individual inventors who have relatively few resources to expend on obtaining, maintaining, and enforcing IP. Yet other strategic objectives drive IP-conditioned government incentives.

There is useful recent literature investigating some aspects of some IP-conditioned government incentives. For example, de Rassenfosse and van Pottelsberghe de la Potterie (2013) discuss how differing patent fees can act as incentives or disincentives for patent filing. Evers et al. (2015) and Griffith et al. (2014) analyze the workings of patent box regimes in Europe and the types of incentives they create. Li (2012) suggests that provincial patent subsidies in China have significantly contributed to the country's patent explosion, and provides one type of assessment as to how these subsidies have impacted patent quality. Harhoff and Hoisl (2007) analyze the functioning and the types of incentives created by inventor remuneration schemes in Europe, focusing specifically on the German system. Prud'homme (2012) analyzes the impacts of government-set patent targets and linked performance evaluations, among other IP-conditioned incentives, on patent quality and innovation in China. WIPO (2006) notes how some countries, as part of their IP-based economic growth strategies, have employed government incentives with IP requirements.

Although the current body of literature provides some insights into the structure, objectives, legalities, and economic impacts of some IP-conditioned government incentives, there appears to be substantial room for further research into these areas. Currently available works typically are rather ad hoc in their treatment of these subjects: each focus on only a few of the aforementioned aspects, per one or two types of IP-conditioned government incentives, per one or just a few countries. There does not appear to be any single currently available work attempting to analyze what we call “IP-conditioned government incentives” from the perspective that they share the important commonality of being conditioned on IP requirements, nor analyzing their economic impacts, strategic objectives, and legalities across the many different types of such incentives employed by governments in both developed and developing countries. The need for more holistic research in this regard marks the point of departure for this book.

Moreover, further research into IP-conditioned government incentives is not just useful to bridge a gap in the literature, but is particularly exigent for several reasons. First, the increasingly globalized nature of business, and therein value chains and technology, makes study of the impacts of IP-conditioned incentives perhaps more important today than ever before. As economies become more interconnected, IP is an increasingly important asset determining firms’ competitiveness (Maskus 1997; WIPO 2011). Given this landscape, from a growth strategy perspective, IP is an important tool of firm competitiveness in high-income/developed countries (Ginarte and Park 1997; Ahn et al. 2014). And, although foreign incumbent holdings of IP can hamper catch-up in latecomer/less developed economies (Odagiri et al. 2010), if IP is developed strategically it can enable catch-up by middle-income economies (Song 2013).

Second, governments are increasingly learning from and experimenting based on one another’s experiences with IP-related policies and laws. In many cases this takes the form of developing countries transplanting IP legal instruments from developed countries (Morin and Gold 2014; Lee 2015). Yet there also appears to be some cross-directional policy learning occurring among countries at different levels of development. And there is governmental industrial policy learning among regions within countries (Chu 2011). These diffusion trends appear directly relevant to state-provided IP-conditioned incentives, whereby, as discussed throughout this book, such incentives seem to be proliferating in scale and scope within and across several countries around the world.

Given these dynamics, it is exigent to critically assess the economic impacts of IP-conditioned government incentives and the effectiveness of the government strategies they intend to implement. This book is an attempt to shed light on this area in a way that is useful to scholars, policymakers, and practitioners. In particular, we aim to provide insights to the following questions:

- How are IP-conditioned government incentives structured, and how do they compare among countries?
- What are the strategic objectives of these incentives and reasons for these objectives?
- What economic impacts have the incentives had? How effective have they been at meeting their objectives? What factors impact the ability of the incentives to meet their objectives?

- Do the incentives conflict with national or international economic laws, and if so how?
- What are the implications of research into the aforementioned questions for policymakers?

This book analyzes these research questions via analysis of empirical data and in-depth studies from the European Union (EU) and China. Our focus is on the EU and China in particular because, as discussed throughout this book, these are locations where IP-conditioned incentives appear to be both heavily utilized and increasingly criticized. Also, these locations are chosen given the book draws on an activity under the IP Key Project, which is financially supported by the European Union and implemented by the European Intellectual Property Office (EUIPO) (formerly "OHIM") with support from the European Patent Office (EPO). The IP Key activity on IP-conditioned government incentives was conducted in partnership with the Chinese Academy of Sciences Institute of Policy and Management (CAS IPM), and included a conference held at CAS IPM in Beijing, China on December 4th 2014. Preliminary versions of some of the chapters featured in this book were presented at that conference.

Although not exclusively focusing on *monetary* IP-conditioned government incentives, most chapters in this book focus on this particular branch of the incentives. Although not all possible types of IP-conditioned incentives are investigated in detail, the book does investigate examples of most of the different types of these incentives that appear to exist in the EU and China. A brief outline of each chapter of the book is provided below.

1.1 Outline of Book

In the next (second) chapter, within Part I, which focuses on inter-country comparative analyses and studies from the EU, Dan Prud'homme uses typological analysis to identify the strategies behind more than 70 IP-conditioned government incentive programs in China and 21 EU Member States. The chapter then compares these strategies and uses policy case studies to analyze the effects of patent subsidy programs in particular on patent quality. The chapter finds that China and the EU both attempt to localize benefits of knowledge investment and discourage off-shoring of taxable assets through controversial IP-conditioned tax incentives. At the same time, China appears to use IP-conditioned incentives on a larger scale, and more techno-nationalistically, than EU Member States; and although this strategy can be explained by China's position as a latecomer, some of these incentives nonetheless appear questionably effective at enabling catch-up. The chapter notes that while IP-conditioned incentives in the EU are most commonly intended to provide needs-based commercial support to SMEs, it is not uncommon for such types of incentives to be provided to large firms/other entities in China. Additionally, it is shown how IP-conditioned incentives lowering costs of utility model patents, when combined with lack of Substantive Examination for such rights, can lower patent quality—a situation Chinese policymakers have sought to address by adopting a strategy for reforming such incentives that evolves with the country's technological development trajectory.

In chapter three, Johannes Holzer provides an analysis of the workings of a range of IP-conditioned incentives in Germany. Based upon an analysis of legal texts, court decisions, a review of the literature, and practitioner/government administrator perspectives, he analyzes whether various German IP-conditioned support programs relating to patent applications, tax, and other State and private support programs for inventors constitute 'subsidies' according to the EU definition of the concept. Furthermore, the chapter makes general observations about the ability of these programs to meet their intended objectives. It is concluded that although such German policies generally work to meet their objectives and do not usually conflict with EU rules governing subsidies, some improvements could be made.

In chapter four, Federico Munari and Xu Liang provide an empirical analysis of the impact of patent subsidies in Italy on the quality of patents from Italian SMEs. The authors first analyze patent subsidies implemented in Italy from 2002 to 2012 and classify them according to four different typologies, based on their rationale and objectives. They then use data from a sample of 222 patents subsidized by the Chamber of Commerce of Milan in Northern Italy, and a control group of non-subsidized patents, to assess the impact of patent subsidies on patent value and firms' turnover growth.

In chapter five, Vinod Kalloe discusses the EU's strategy to try and incentivize R&D. Part of this strategy has been to develop specific tax incentives for R&D expenditure. In recent years, many EU Member States have also developed specific tax incentives concerning income derived from intellectual property. The chapter finds that the effects of IP-conditioned tax incentives, insofar as they have been evaluated, are not fully clear, although there is some indication they may not be optimally meeting their objectives. On the one hand, in practice it seems that certain R&D tax incentives do indeed lead to opportunities for companies resulting in observable incremental increases in additional R&D. However, on the other hand, certain IP-conditioned tax incentives may lead to aggressive international tax planning where there is no real nexus with actual ongoing or additional R&D.

In chapter six, Oliver Lutze conducts a comparative analysis of state-mandated inventor remuneration and reward schemes in Germany and the current draft Chinese Service Invention Regulation (SIR). He finds that the draft SIR follows a methodology similar in some aspects to Germany's principles of defining statutory remuneration rewards. However, the simplification of the procedure in China together with fewer possibilities to make deductions will, in effect, require that employed inventors are paid especially high remuneration. As a result, the SIR may conflict with the interests of existing research-based companies with sizable R&D activities in China. These companies will undoubtedly attempt to legally define and affirm their own remuneration schemes, but potentially face uncertainty concerning the validity of their schemes, and regular disputes with employed inventors could follow. The chapter finds the unpredictability of the requirements for remuneration could become a negative factor for companies contemplating R&D investments in China. And the chapter finds that it remains to be seen whether China's proposed rewards and remuneration incentives will have the desired effect of stimulating innovation by individual employed inventors working outside of large, well-established research companies.

Within Part II, which focuses on studies from China, in chapter seven, Hefa Song, Li Zhenxing, and Xu Dawei study the impact of government policies on the upsurge of domestic patent applications in China. They find that the explosion in the number of patent applications in China is significantly correlated with increased expenditure on R&D by companies, universities and other entities. However, based on regression modeling, they find that provincial government subsidy programs have also played a crucial role in the upsurge in domestic applications since 2010. Disconcertingly, patent quality is diminished by these subsidy programs due to the distorted incentive structure that they create for filing patent applications. The authors find that the Chinese experience has important policy implications for other countries.

In chapter eight, Alan Garcia, Josephine Jiang, Conrad Turley, and Mimi Wang provide an overview of existing Chinese tax law provisions having an impact on the conduct of R&D and IP in China, including the licensing of IP by foreign multinational enterprises to their Chinese operating subsidiaries. The tax challenges for companies, and consequent issues for the attention of policymakers, are organized according to a three-part framework for evaluating IP tax management. Likely future trends in Chinese and international tax policy are also discussed.

In chapter nine, Cheryl Long and Wang Jun study the quality of patents resulting from China's patent explosion. Using patent data at the provincial level for 1985–2010, they find that the average quality of Chinese patents has declined; thus, the dramatic rise in the number of patents during that time most likely has not produced a proportionate increase in the country's total innovation capacity. In addition, the authors find evidence that the patent promotion policies (PPPs: namely preferential tax policies, subsidies, and subsidies for patent filing and maintenance fees) adopted by various government agencies in China can explain both the quantity increase and the quality fall in Chinese patents.

In chapter ten, Liu Yun, Tan Long, and Cheng Yijie examine how Chinese universities, including those supported by government programs aimed at developing science and technology, and patents, contribute to China's national innovation system (NIS) through patent licensing. To do this, the authors develop a composite dataset from multiple information sources and use a combination of research methods such as text mining, scientometrics, and social network analysis, to analyze the structural features of patent licensing activities by Chinese universities. They find that universities that are part of Project 211, which is a government program to support technological development in certain Chinese universities, play an important role in patent licensing. The authors suggest that increased patent licensing between entities in lesser-developed regions and universities in relatively more developed regions—particularly those with more capabilities to develop patented technologies worth out-licensing—could be useful to better diffuse technology throughout China's NIS. Furthermore, this may be feasible since geographic distance itself does not appear to significantly inhibit patent licensing by universities in China. Considering these findings, the authors discuss ways in which the Project 211, and some other Chinese policies, could be improved in order to better contribute to technology transfer in China's NIS.

In chapter eleven, Zhang Yafeng, Liu Haibo, and Jin Zongzhen introduce and analyze the IP Demonstration City (IPDC) Program in China. Following interviews with government officers from local IP offices in various IPDCs, they identify the effects of the IPDC Program, which include an increase in IP creation, the growth of IP-related industries, the improvement of both companies' IP awareness and the governments' IP administrative system, and potentially an increase in the inflow of foreign direct investment. However, at the same time, the authors find that the effect of the program within many provinces appears to be relatively limited, although it may be stronger in less developed provinces. Furthermore, the marginal economic return of the current IPDC Program decreases as more IPDCs are introduced, although in the long term a greater number of IPDCs may eventually generate more general nationwide economic returns. In order to understand how different localities implement and benefit from central-level IP-conditioned government programs in China, the authors conduct brief case studies of the cities of Changji and Quanzhou and analyze the policies implemented by local governments there to achieve and maintain IPDC status.

In the last chapter, chapter twelve, Jin Zongzhen and Liu Haibo discuss the usefulness of a strategy to develop 'light IP' in certain regions in China. They note that invention patents have a significant influence on industrialized regions, especially new product and technological development in heavier industries. However, the cultivation of 'light IP' (designs, trademarks, copyrights, geographical indications, trade secrets, utility models, and new plant varieties) may be preferred over invention patents in regions rich in environmental resources and traditional culture, and where there is a desire to protect natural resources. Taking the green economic development of Lishui Prefecture in Zhejiang Province as a case study, the authors analyze how policies to encourage development and utilization of light IP enable the regional protection of the environment as well as economic growth. The approach of Lishui Prefecture is shown as an alternative development strategy to simply following central government-level advice to stimulate invention patents, and one that is useful for regions in China that are less industrialized but have rich natural resources.

1.2 Abridged Policy Recommendations

All of the chapters in this book provide practical recommendations to policymakers on how to maximize potential benefits of certain IP-conditioned government incentives or mitigate potentially negative impacts of such incentives. The following is a selection of abridged and merged recommendations, only meant to provide a flavor of the recommendations in the book. These recommendations are elaborated upon and supplemented with other recommendations in the individual chapters.

Cross-cutting recommendations

- Strong, well thought-out qualification criteria are essential components of all IP-conditioned incentives.
- Strong institutional coordination mechanisms are necessary to optimize the effectiveness of IP-conditioned government incentive policymaking and implementation. This requires that different localities within a country, and different countries within a region, craft IP-conditioned incentives that are catered to their local needs and capabilities, rather than merely copying incentives developed elsewhere. It also requires clear delineation of responsibilities among government bodies at different levels (national, provincial, and county) in countries implementing such incentives.
- Monitoring and evaluation (M&E) of IP-conditioned incentive schemes is essential. As necessary, systems should be revised to mitigate negative effects identified in the M&E.
- Countries with IP-conditioned incentives should collate information on all such programs on an Internet platform that is easily accessible by the public.

Instrument-specific recommendations

- Patent fees
  - Annual maintenance/renewal fees for patents should increase incrementally over time.
- Patent subsidies
  - The underlying quality of patent applications potentially being supported by the incentives should be assessed ex ante to determine if they are indeed worth supporting.
  - Subsidies should only be provided to patents that are ultimately granted.
  - As a rule of thumb, invention patents that require a Substantive Examination in order to be granted are more deserving of patent subsidies than utility models that do not undergo a Substantive Examination in order to be granted. Policymakers should consider this when crafting patent subsidies.
  - Subsidies for utility model patents should only be awarded when a positive Search Report is provided, although it may be reasonable to allow government subsidies to cover the costs of conducting a Search Report.
  - Patent renewal/maintenance fees should be very cautiously subsidized, if at all.
  - It can sometimes be useful to cover the costs of official patent application fees and costs of drafting patent applications. But it can sometimes be even

more useful to cover services related to patent their use and commercialization (such as costs for services related to patent evaluation and due diligence, marketing studies, license drafting, feasibility studies, and proofs of concept).

- Tax schemes
  - Governments should carefully consider different tax incentives to incentivize the different stages of innovation, ranging from R&D capital investments to R&D operational costs and from patent acquisition to other aspects of IP management.
  - The basis and scope of IP-conditioned tax incentives should not change too frequently in order to enhance the predictability of eligible R&D activities and expenditure.
  - The evaluation of IP-conditioned tax incentives should focus on identifying how much additional R&D activity is to be attributed to such tax incentives.
  - The EU and OECD have produced useful guidance on how to craft and manage IP-conditioned tax incentives, which can serve as a model for designing and revising such incentives.
- Patent targets
  - Simplistic quantitative patent targets linked to performance evaluations should not be overemphasized by the government.
- Inventor remuneration and rewards
  - State-mandated inventor remuneration and reward schemes should clearly specify that remuneration systems established by firms can only be rendered invalid under the law in exceptional circumstances.
  - Excessive remuneration claims should be avoided in state-mandated inventor remuneration and reward schemes by disallowing high turnovers to be used for blockbuster inventions, for example by using the 'scaling down' method used in Germany.

References

Ahn S, Hall BH, Lee K (2014) Introduction. In: Ahn S, Hall BH, Lee K (eds) Intellectual property for economic development. Edward Elgar and Korean Development Institute, Northampton, pp 1–10

Arrow K (1962) Economic welfare and the allocation of resources for invention. In: Nelson R (ed) The rate and direction of inventive activity: economic and social factors. Princeton, New Jersey, pp 609–25

Bloom N, Schankerman M, Reenen JV (2013) Identifying technology spillovers and product market rivalry. Econometrica 81:1347–1393

Chu WW (2011) How the Chinese government promoted a global automobile industry. Ind Corp Change 20:1235–1276

de Rassenfosse G, van Pottelsberghe de la Potterie B (2013) The role of fees in patent systems: theory and evidence. J Econ Surv 27(4):696–716
Evers L, Miller H, Spengel C (2015) Intellectual property box regimes: effective tax rates and tax policy considerations. Int Tax Public Finance 22:502–530
Ginarte J, Park WG (1997) Determinants of patent rights: a cross-national study. Res Policy 26:283–301
Greenwald B, Stiglitz J (2013) Industrial policy, creation of a learning society and economic development. In: Stiglitz J, Lin JY (eds) The industrial policy revolution I: the role of government beyond ideology. Palgrave Macmillan, New York, pp 43–71
Griffith R, Miller H, O'Connell M (2014) Ownership of intellectual property and corporate taxation. J Public Econ 112(1):12–23
Harhoff D, Hoisl K (2007) Institutionalized incentives for ingenuity: patent value and the German Employees' Inventions Act. Res Policy 36(8):1143–1162
Lee K (2013) Capability failure and industrial policy to move beyond the middle-income trap: from trade-based to technology-based specialization. In: Stiglitz J, Lin JY (eds) The industrial policy revolution I: the role of government beyond ideology. Palgrave Macmillan, New York, pp 244–272
Lee N (2015) Intellectual property law in China—from legal transplant to governance. In: Lee N, Bruun N, Li M (eds) Governance of intellectual property rights in China and Europe. Edward Elgar, Cheltenham, pp 5–19
Li X (2012) Behind the recent surge of Chinese patenting: an institutional view. Res Policy 41:236–249
Martin S, Scott J (2000) The nature of innovation market failure and the design of public support for private innovation. Res Policy 29:437–447
Maskus K (1997) The role of intellectual property rights in encouraging foreign direct investment and technology transfer. Prepared for the Conference Public-Private Initiatives After TRIPS: Designing a Global Agenda
Morin JF, Gold R (2014) An integrated model of legal transplantation: the diffusion of intellectual property law in developing countries. Int Stud Q 58:781–792
Odagiri H, Goto A, Sunami A, Nelson R (2010) Introduction. In: Odagiri H, Goto A, Sunami A, Nelson R (eds) Intellectual property rights, development, and catch-up. Oxford University Press, Oxford, pp 1–28
Prud'homme D (2012) Dulling the cutting edge: how patent-related policies and practices hamper innovation in China. European Chamber, Beijing
Rodrik D (2004) Industrial policy for the twenty-first century. John F. Kennedy School of Government Faculty Research Working Paper Series, Cambridge, Mass
Schumpeter J (1942) Capitalism, socialism, and democracy. Harper & Brothers, New York
Song H (2013) Zizhu chuangxin nengli jianshe yu zhishi chanquan fazhan (Indigenous innovation capability-building and the development of intellectual property rights) (in Mandarin Chinese). Chinese Academy of Sciences Intellectual Property Rights Press, Beijing
Stiglitz J, Lin JY, Monga C (2013) The rejuvenation of industrial policy. In: Stiglitz J, Lin JY (eds) The industrial policy revolution I: the role of government beyond ideology. Palgrave Macmillan, New York, pp 1–15
WIPO (2006) IP asset development and management: a key strategy for economic growth. Available from http://www.wipo.int/edocs/pubdocs/en/intproperty/896/wipo_pub_896.pdf
WIPO (2011) The changing face of innovation. Available from http://www.wipo.int/edocs/pubdocs/en/intproperty/944/wipo_pub_944_2011.pdf

Part I
Inter-country Comparative Analyses and Studies From the EU

Chapter 2
IP-Conditioned Government Incentives in China and the EU: A Comparative Analysis of Strategies and Impacts on Patent Quality

Dan Prud'homme

Abstract This paper uses typological analysis to identify the strategies behind more than 70 IP-conditioned government incentive programs in China and 21 EU Member States, compares these strategies, and uses policy case studies to analyze the effects of patent subsidy programs in particular on patent quality. It finds that China and the EU both attempt to localize benefits of knowledge investment and discourage offshoring of taxable assets through controversial IP-conditioned tax incentives. At the same time, China appears to use IP-conditioned incentives on a larger scale, and more techno-nationalistically, than EU Member States; and although this strategy can be explained by China's position as a latecomer, some of these incentives nonetheless appear questionably effective at enabling catch-up. The analysis notes that while IP-conditioned incentives in the EU are most commonly intended to provide needs-based commercial support to SMEs, it is not uncommon for such types of incentives to be provided to large firms/other entities in China. Additionally, it is shown how IP-conditioned incentives lowering costs of utility model patents, when combined with lack of Substantive Examination for such rights, can lower patent quality—a situation Chinese policymakers have sought to address by adopting a strategy for reforming such incentives that evolves with the country's technological development trajectory.

Keywords Intellectual property · IP-conditioned incentives · Patent subsidies · China · EU · Typological analysis · Case study · Strategy · Patent quality · Catch-up

---

Dan Prud'homme: Technical Expert, IP Key project, implemented by the European Union Intellectual Property Office, Beijing, China.

D. Prud'homme (✉)
IP Key project, European Union Intellectual Property Office, #2480 Sunflower Tower, No. 37 Maizidian West Street, Beijing 100125, China
e-mail: dan.prudhomme@ipkey.org

D. Prud'homme and H. Song (eds.), *Economic Impacts of Intellectual Property-Conditioned Government Incentives*, DOI 10.1007/978-981-10-1119-1_2

2.1 Introduction

As mentioned in the introduction to this book, the study of the economic impacts of intellectual property (IP)-conditioned government incentives (hereafter referred to simply as "IP-conditioned incentives") is perhaps more relevant today than ever before. As economies become more interconnected, IP is an increasingly important asset determining firms' competitiveness (Maskus 1997; WIPO 2011). Also, governments are increasingly learning from one another's experiences with IP-related policies and laws, and experimenting based on these experiences. Driven by these factors, state-provided IP-conditioned incentives seem to be proliferating in scale and scope in countries around the world.

As also mentioned in the introduction to this book, there is some useful recent literature investigating some aspects of some IP-conditioned incentives in Europe and China, the focus regions of this book. For example, de Rassenfosse and van Pottelsberghe de la Potterie (2013) discuss how differing patent fees can act as incentives or disincentives for patent filing. Evers et al. (2015) and Griffith et al. (2014) analyze the workings of patent box regimes in Europe and the types of incentives they create. Li (2012) suggests that provincial patent subsidies in China have significantly contributed to the country's patent filing explosion, and provides a preliminary assessment as to how these subsidies have impacted patent quality. Forfas (2014) analyzes the impacts of various government incentives in Ireland for stimulating R&D and innovation, including several IP-conditioned incentives like patent subsidies. Harhoff and Hoisl (2007) analyze the functioning and the types of incentives created by inventor remuneration schemes in Europe, focusing specifically on the German system. Prud'homme (2012) analyzes the impacts of government-set patent targets and linked performance evaluations, among other IP-conditioned incentives, on patent quality and innovation in China.

Although current literature provides some insights into the strategies and economic impacts of some IP-conditioned incentives, a comparative analysis of the strategies and impacts of various IP-conditioned incentives in Europe, including the EU in particular, and China does not appear available. This gap in the literature is exigent to bridge to more fully understand how the strategies driving IP-conditioned incentives and the economic impacts of the programs compare and contrast among countries, and why. This leads to the following questions: ***(1) How do China's and EU Member States (MS)' IP-conditioned incentives compare in terms of their underlying strategic objectives and impacts on patent quality? (2) If there are major differences, why is this the case? (3) What are the implications of these findings for policymakers?*** This chapter's preliminary investigation of these questions is intended as a starting point for contextualizing the other chapters in this book.

The chapter aims to contribute to the literature in several ways. First, it provides a typological analysis of the strategies behind a diverse range of more than 70

IP-conditioned incentives in the EU and China, based on a review of primary and secondary resources. Second, it provides a qualitative, as well as basic quantitative, comparative analysis of these strategies. Third, it provides mini policy case studies on the economic impacts of two incentive programs (patent subsidy programs from China and Italy) in terms of patent quality. Fourth, it fleshes out policy implications and recommendations from this analysis. This being said, the chapter attempts to only provide very preliminary insights to the research questions posed, as fully assessing them would require a much more extensive analysis.

The remainder of this chapter is structured as follows: the next section (Sect. 2.2) provides a brief conceptual framework to guide the comparative analysis performed, Sect. 2.3 outlines the methodological approach used to conduct the analysis, Sect. 2.4 presents the results and discusses their significance relative to the research questions posed, and Sect. 2.5 concludes and makes some policy recommendations.

2.2 Conceptual Framework

A multi-faceted conceptual framework is needed to ground a comparative analysis on strategies underlying IP-conditioned incentives in China and the EU and their economic impacts. The framework in Sect. 2.2.1 focuses foremost on concepts/factors potentially explaining similarities and differences in strategies behind IP-conditioned incentives in the EU and China. Although all of the IP-conditioned incentives reviewed do not exclusively focus on patenting, the vast majority of them do, and thus this conceptual framework focuses primarily on patent-relevant concepts. The framework is not intended to cover all possible factors determining strategic objectives behind IP-conditioned incentives, rather it is kept relatively straightforward to keep the subsequent analysis manageable. Some of the objectives may be inter-related, although were deemed worthwhile to distinguish. An effort was made to distinguish rationales behind IP-conditioned incentives were not overly narrow but also not overly broad (and thus quite broad rationales like encouraging firm competitiveness and jobs, although clearly overall objectives of the incentives, are not individually singled out).

The brief framework in the second part of this section focuses specifically on one key indicator of the economic impacts of IP-conditioned incentives: "patent quality." In line with the scope of the research question set-forth in the introduction, this focus is intended to keep the research manageable (although other indicators of the economic impacts of such incentives, e.g. in terms of number of and revenue-generating significance of new products to market, could be investigated in future research).

2.2.1 Factors/Concepts Explaining Strategic Objectives of IP-Conditioned Incentives

2.2.1.1 Broadest Factor: Latecomer Catch-up

The most fundamental factor for distinguishing the strategic objectives behind IP-conditioned incentives in China and EU Member States (MS) is the fact that China is a latecomer nation (i.e. it began developing later than forerunner nations) economically and technologically seeking to catch up with forerunners, like those in the EU. Latecomers can benefit from state support in the form of development policies to catch up with forerunners (Gerschekron 1962; Johnson 1982; Abramovitz 1986).

Given that lack of core indigenous IP rights is a pervasive problem limiting China's catch-up ability at present, whereby the IP landscape in many high-tech industries continues to be dominated by foreign incumbents (Song et al. 2010; Song 2013), IP-conditioned incentives may seem like an attractive tool to help domestic entities compete in this environment. Amidst this landscape, in addition to struggling to maintain freedom-to-operate in various technological fields, given their latecomer starting point, Chinese firms will likely have a more difficult time breaking into and growing in industries with strong foreign incumbent patent thickets (Song et al. 2010; Song 2013; Xiao et al. 2013), including those created by EU MS firms.[1] Latecomer nations like China with proactive state intervention may see IP-conditioned incentives as one way to navigate these patent minefields.

Of course, the pro-activeness of the government determines the extent to which catch-up goals are actually prioritized in strategies and targeted via policies. In China, both central-level and provincial-level government bodies are active in driving policy, forming a "catch-up consensus" (Chu 2011). This being said, China's system of economic decentralization, whereby the central-level government sets forth industrial policy guidance aimed at catch-up and this guidance is fleshed out and implemented by provincial and local governments, can complicate this process (Naughton 2007). It seems likely that the strategy behind China's IP-conditioned incentives aligns closely with this overall desire and buy-into catch up via state intervention. Although the governments of EU MS themselves face varying pressures to enhance their own technological and economic capabilities vis-à-vis each other and other nations, they are not driven by a catch-up consensus like in China, although it is the goal of the EU to further align MS to build an innovative EU.

[1]As such, there may be an industry-specific element within the strategic objectives of countries that use IP-conditioned incentives. Specifically, in IP-intensive technological areas (e.g., in information and communication (ICT) technologies) (Hall and Ziedonis 2001; Hall 2009), the incentives may be seen as particularly important. However, because the IP requirements uncovered in the incentives presented in Table 2.1 in the Annex do not clearly focus on such industries (although, judging from the research performed, there is some indication that in practice some incentives are concentrated on patenting in certain industries, including ICT), this conceptual element is not discussed at length in this paper.

2.2.1.2 Other Major Factors

Stimulating Spending Enabling Research and/or Commercialization

Some IP-conditioned incentives are likely intended to encourage spending enabling research and/or commercialization, which collectively create innovation.[2] The public nature of knowledge spillovers means that firms cannot appropriate all returns from their research and development (R&D) investment, although an IP rights system can provide a method of appropriability (Arrow 1962). This market failure creates an incentive for firms to in some cases spend below the socially-optimal level of R&D (Bloom et al. 2013), which can hamper innovation. As such, government incentives and investment is needed to ensure more optimal knowledge investment (Martin and Scott 2000), and some IP-conditioned incentives may be intended to meet these ends.

Needs-Based Commercial Support

For individual inventors and small and medium-sized enterprises (SMEs) in particular, they may need support to stimulate their competitiveness in ways related to innovation as well as aspects of IP management not immediately related to innovation. SMEs often identify lack of access to financial resources as their topmost obstacle to growth (OECD 2004). Some of these entities may have limited financial and other resources to expend on innovation activities (although some in fact devote a significant portion of their resources to R&D and other innovation activities, and even more so, proportionally, than multinationals). These entities may have less financial resources and other resources to spend on managing IP—including IP acquisition, IP exploitation, IP maintenance (including renewing IP rights), and IP enforcement (WIPO 2004). In such circumstances, some IP-conditioned incentives may be intended to meet the commercial needs of individual inventors and SMEs.

Given their latecomer starting point, it is possible that individual inventors and SMEs in China in particular will have an even higher need for support for innovation activities and IP management potentially provided via IP-conditioned incentives than their counterparts in the advanced economies of the EU MS. In reaction to this need, and given the Chinese government generally pursues a highly active role in promoting technological catch-up, there may be more extensive IP-conditioned incentives offered in China than any individual EU MS.

Information Failure

Lack of IP awareness among newcomer individual inventors and SMEs may broadly constitute a type of "information failure" (Greenwald and Stiglitz 1986),

---

[2]As innovation encompasses the full process of research and inventing, as well as developing and commercializing the inventions (Schumpeter 1942), research (and invention) without commercialization is not tantamount to innovation.

which includes information asymmetry, a type of market failure. Many newcomers may have less perfect information (internally within the firm, or via external patent agents or other external advisors) than that available to a range of incumbents benefitting from advanced information tools and aggregation services developed through years of experience. Also, newcomers may enter into transactions with incumbents who black-box technology and/or adopt other information-withholding methods to provide incumbents with certain advantages, which limit spillovers. Encouraging development of IP via IP-conditioned incentives may be seen as one potential method to correct these market failures. Considering these dynamics and those previously mentioned regarding provision of needs-based commercial support, there may be more extensive IP-conditioned incentives offered in China than in any individual EU MS.

Localizing Benefits of Knowledge Investment

Geographic localization policies can play an important role in the generation and distribution of knowledge (Keller 2010). Such policies can encourage geographical concentrations of knowledge diffusion, which creates a virtuous circle/cycle by strengthening the knowledge base of the location, in turn attracting other innovating firms and leading to increase knowledge inflows in the future (Iammarino and McCann 2006). Some IP-conditioned incentives may aim to localize knowledge investment in order to facilitate the evolutionary processes mentioned.

Also, some IP-conditioned incentives may aim to localize the benefits of knowledge investment in order to avoid it being lost to other regions with stronger pull (or push) policies. The existence of IP-conditioned incentives in one jurisdiction may pressure another to develop similar or even more significant incentives in order to attract or retain R&D investments, technology transfer, and other forms of knowledge investment (UN 2005; OECD 2010, 2011). And similar pressure may be created to attract and retain R&D jobs (UN 2005; OECD 2010, 2011).

Discouraging Offshoring of Taxable IP Assets

Tax incentives in different jurisdictions have led to tax planning that has eroded the taxable revenue base for many countries (OECD 2014a, 2015). IP-conditioned incentives may be partially to blame for these trends (see the chapters by Kalloe 2016; Garcia et al. 2016, in this book). At the same time, the threat of offshoring of taxable assets per se is likely one factor guiding the strategic objectives of IP-conditioned incentives, whereby some tax incentives are meant to discourage offshoring of taxable IP assets by encouraging them to be held locally. It is worth noting that the existence of IP-conditioned tax incentives in one jurisdiction, especially if close geographically, may pressure another to develop similar or more significant policies in order to keep IP assets based in the jurisdiction—a concept in line with competition and emulation-based policy diffusion theories (Graham et al.

2013; Morin and Gold 2014). It is worth also noting that the objectives of IP-conditioned tax incentives appear particularly closely intertwined with those discussed in the "localize benefits of knowledge investment" section above.

Techno-Nationalism

Some countries may seek to implement IP-conditioned incentives meant to "techno-nationalistically" build domestic industry. The term "techno-nationalism" refers to state intervention to replicate aspects of the technology development process using domestic (rather than foreign) capabilities as part of a strategy to compete internationally in high-tech industries (Hart and Prakash 2000). Generally, in situations where this ideology is at odds with foreign-domestic cooperation generating healthy growth, ardent techno-nationalism is often criticized as not necessarily economically prudent (Ostry and Nelson 1995).[3] Various scholars have suggested that many of China's technology policies, including those with IP requirements, are techno-nationalist in nature (Suttmeier and Yao 2011; Ernst 2011). At the same time, it is possible that techno-nationalist motives also guides some IP-conditioned incentives in some places in Europe (as well as in the US and other advanced nations), as such motives have driven high-tech industry development policies in the past (Ostry and Nelson 1995). Various factors, including polarizing historical events and changing economic landscapes, contribute to techno-nationalism (Ostry and Nelson 1995).

2.2.2 Importance of Patent Quality, and the Impacts of Policies on Patent Quality

Scholars have identified that valuable patents can enable technological advancement and other economic benefits in some industries and in some countries (Fink and Maskus 2005; Falvey and Foster 2006; Lopez 2009; Hall 2014). However, poor "quality" patents can create significant negative economic impacts. The definition of "quality" patents used herein follows the one in Prud'homme (2012), namely patents that meet the statutory requirements for patentability and contribute to economic, social, and/or environmental progress; and low-quality patents do not

[3]This is certainly not meant to say that it is not economically prudent for economies to adopt policies that enrich their own national economic interests. Nor does it ignore the fact that techno-nationalism can also refer to technology policy specifically meant to meet national security goals (Samuels 1994), which governments sometimes consider to be outside the scope of immediate economic policy considerations.

meet these criteria.[4] Specifically, the self-reinforcing nature of an economy rife with low-quality patents leads rational firms to seek more low-quality patents rather than higher-quality patents (Wagner 2009). And poor patent quality generates uncertainty, which leads to lower incentives to innovate, which stifles technological development, entrepreneurship, employment, and ultimately growth and consumer welfare (Guellec and van Pottelsberghe de la Potterie 2007; Hall et al. 2003).

Even well-intentioned government IP policies meant to develop the domestic economy can drag down patent quality (OECD 2014b). Overly low costs of obtaining and maintaining patents, lack of legal safeguards for granting and enabling efficient invalidation of patents, among other legal, policy and institution-related factors can hamper patent quality (Prud'homme 2012; de Saint-Georges and van Pottelsberghe de la Potterie 2013). As such, poorly calibrated government policies can waste government resources better used in different ways to meet their strategic objectives. This axiomatically applies to IP-conditioned incentives as well.

2.3 Methodology

2.3.1 Main Research Sources and Approach

As a first step to investigating the research questions posed in this chapter, secondary sources were located that provided an overview of what countries throughout the world have IP-conditioned incentives. Key reports used in this regard include KPMG (2014), Deloitte (2014), Ernst and Young (2014), PWC (2014), Jaiya and Kalanje (2006), Harhoff and Hoisl (2007), and Lutze (2015). The research then focused on detailing the IP-conditioned incentives in China and EU MS specifically, and EU MS were chosen according to which ones had most readily available information from primary sources and secondary sources (often from government or consulting companies) available online. This ultimately resulted in a focus on policies/programs in China and 21 out of 28 EU MS: Austria, Belgium, Croatia, Cyprus, the Czech Republic, Denmark, Finland, France, Germany, Hungary, Italy, Ireland, Latvia, Lithuania, Luxembourg, Malta, the Netherlands, Spain, Poland, Portugal, and the UK. The research on Chinese policies and their effects draws primarily on the research conducted in Prud'homme (2012, 2015). Best efforts were made to ensure the details of the programs researched were up-to-date, although given the often fast changing nature of such programs it is possible that at the time of publication of this chapter some details of the programs have already changed.

[4] It is possible to draw a distinction between "quality" and "value" when evaluating patents; however, for simplicity, the two are used interchangeably hereafter.

A skeleton typology of the main structural elements of the policies/programs was created, including the name of the promulgating country, IP requirements, other major requirements, and benefits. And each policy/program per country was reviewed and relevant information was added to flesh out this typology.

2.3.2 Analysis

2.3.2.1 Identifying and Analyzing Trends in Strategies

A multi-step analytical process was undertaken fitting within the broad three-part framework for qualitative analysis proposed by Miles and Huberman (1994): data reduction, data display, and conclusions. First, where readily available, secondary sources and the text of the policy documents (including the preamble, among other sections) were reviewed in an attempt to understand the strategic objectives behind the policies. Second, the literature was searched to understand the strategic objectives behind the policies; however, robust relevant literature was usually not readily available and thus some degree of inductive analysis was typically required to identify these strategies.

Third, typological analysis incorporating inductive analysis, which, according to Hatch (2002), is particularly fitting for research with a strong focus on artifact data (such as text of policies and laws), was used to identify potential strategic objectives of the policies/plans reviewed; these objectives were divided into the policies' "immediate IP-related objective" and "wider objectives." This basic inductive analysis was carried out based upon a juxtaposition of the structural elements of each policy (i.e. the main IP requirements, other major requirements per each policy/program, and benefits) vis-à-vis elements formative of the concepts behind IP-conditioned incentives. Herein, "immediate IP-related objectives" were chosen from the typology of IP management presented in WIPO (2004). The "wider objectives" came from the concepts discussed in Sects. 2.2.1.1 and 2.2.1.2; whereby relevant keywords were identified in the structural elements of each policy (e.g. requirements for SMEs, requirements to localize IP usage, fees for consulting/information services, etc.) that had a clear direct relationship with such concepts. Fourth, a few consultations with academics and lawyers familiar with the workings of certain IP-conditioned incentives were used to triangulate the results of the inductive analysis. Collectively, this analysis resulted in the creation of a typological chart (see Table 2.1 in the Annex).

Fifth, trends were then deciphered in the typological analysis by counting (using a function in word processing software) the occurrence of each strategic objective and categorization of IP-conditioned incentives depicted in the typology in Table 2.1 in the Annex per the clearest latecomer countries (i.e. China) and more advanced economies (i.e. EU MS). Conclusions were then drawn based upon these occurrences. This coding and counting approach to data analysis generally follows that prescribed in Miles and Huberman (1994).

2.3.2.2 Limitations of the Methodology

There are several limitations of the abovementioned methodology. First, the list of policies in Table 2.1 in the Annex is not necessarily an exhaustive list of all IP-conditioned incentives in the countries studied, although it is a list of the programs that could be readily identified. Second, for the analysis of China's IP-conditioned incentives in particular, given often differing non-IP-specific requirements (e.g. among provinces) in several IP-conditioned incentives in China, such incentives may have more main wider objectives than those explicitly identified in Table 2.1 in the Annex. Third, sometimes, given the limited information available on some of the incentives in the EU and China, some degree of supposition was required to identify their main immediate and wider objectives. Considering these limitations, it is important to note that there may be some IP-conditioned incentives existent in the EU and China that are unintentionally overlooked in the analysis, and the occurrences of the objectives identified by the counting analysis in this chapter are likely only lower bound estimates.

This being said, the counting analysis identifies general trends that appear to be distinct enough so that it seems unlikely they would be significantly altered even if some incentive programs were missing from the analysis. Further, considering the methodological limitations mentioned, special care was taken to cautiously word the findings. As such, it appears that the results based upon analysis of Table 2.1 in the Annex can be said to be reasonably robust.

2.3.2.3 Assessing Impacts on Patent Quality

Three main steps were followed to investigate the economic impact of IP-conditioned incentives on patent quality. First, patent subsidy policies in China and Italy were chosen for analysis. These countries and programs were chosen for several reasons: in order to make the analysis manageable, only two programs were chosen; one specific policy/program was chosen from China because it is the clearest latecomer among the countries studied, and Italy was chosen given it is a more economically advanced country than China, thus useful point of comparison; patent subsidy programs were chosen from both countries in an attempt to allow comparability in the cross-case analysis; and the programs were chosen given the ready availability of information to the author on the programs.

Second, mini case studies were then compiled on each of these policy programs and cross-case analysis was performed. These mini studies were formed primarily by summarizing existing literature on the effectiveness of the patent subsidy programs in China and Italy, and supplemented with a few consultations with experts from government and academia closely familiar with the programs. Case studies are valuable methods to investigate research questions that provide more context to the analysis than is often available in strictly quantitative studies (Yin 2003). Third, basic cross-cases analysis was performed by comparing and contrasting information from the cases in order to identify major determinants of IP-conditioned incentive effects on patent quality, and the corresponding direction of such effects. Cross-case analysis is useful for comparing and contrasting multiple cases (Schwandt 2001; Creswell 2007; Yin 2003).

2.3.3 *Policy Recommendations*

Based on the findings generated from the aforementioned analysis, several policy recommendations were formulated. The recommendations were selected upon the condition that they were relatively intuitive to the reader based on the analysis. Also, they were selected upon the condition that they were important for policy-makers in China, the EU, and potentially elsewhere to consider when seeking if and how to create IP-conditioned incentives.

2.4 Results and Discussion

2.4.1 *Comparison of Strategies Behind IP-Conditioned Incentives in EU and China*

Table 2.1 in the Annex provides a typology of policy mechanisms and strategic objectives behind over 70 IP-conditioned government incentive programs in the EU and China. As noted in Sect. 2.3.2, despite several methodological limitations, it appears the main findings discussed in this section based upon analysis of Table 2.1 in the Annex are still reasonable. To keep the analysis concise, the objectives of the incentives are purposefully confined to what appear to be the *main* relevant objectives (drawn from the list in Sect. 2.2.1), although they may less so/more indirectly also aim to achieve other objectives. Assignment of an objective within the typology of course does not necessarily indicate the proposed policy mechanisms will actually be effective at meeting such an objective.

Using the counting approach to analyzing data in Table 2.1 in the Annex described in the methodology, a number of useful findings surface about how China's and EU MS' IP-conditioned incentives compare in terms of their underlying strategic objectives, and why there are some key differences. These are discussed below, as well as relevant implications for policymakers.

First, tax incentives are a highly prevalent type of IP-conditioned government incentive program used in EU MS.[5] This seems likely explained by the competition

[5]Based on the counting analysis, the following categories of IP-conditioned incentives in the EU occurred with the following frequency (frequency in parenthesis): tax incentives (20), patent subsidy/patent and design subsidy programs (14), grants (10), service invention remuneration and

and emulation drivers behind policy diffusion, whereby tax incentives in one jurisdiction in the EU pressure another to develop similar or more significant policies in order to attract IP assets and/or otherwise keep IP assets based in the jurisdiction. Geographical proximity itself among EU MS may also lead to quick cross-border diffusion of such policies in the EU.

This indicates that European Commission policymakers should pay particularly close attention to the effects of these tax incentives. Even if the policies have negative economic effects, unless actually reviewed and properly overseen, they still may rapidly diffuse to other EU MS and/or further entrench themselves in the EU MS presently maintaining the policies. Realizing these issues, the European Commission is closely considering recent OECD initiatives to harmonize and better regulate IP-conditioned tax incentives (OECD 2014a, 2015; also see the chapter by Kalloe 2016, in this book). And the European Commission (at the time of writing of this chapter) is also specifically considering proposals brought by some EU MS to prohibit any EU MS to newly establish a patent-box after June 2016 and to also phase out all existing patent-box programs by 2021 (see the chapter by Kalloe (2016), in this book).

Second, it is noteworthy that several countries in the EU, and not just China, institute IP-conditioned grants and patent subsidy programs. It is worthwhile for EU policymakers to keep this in mind, if only to avoid blindly criticizing the Chinese policy environment for its heavy usage of grants and patent subsidy programs (among various other incentives) to stimulate patenting.

At the same time, as explained in the cross-case analysis in Sect. 2.4.2, until recently, many regions in China have not instituted safeguards (i.e. quality-ensuring requirements and sufficient institutional oversight mechanisms) in their patent subsidy programs to ensure patent quality. Also, the scale of China's IP-conditioned incentives at large and grants and patent subsidies in particular appears to be far greater than those of individual EU MS—in part because of the *de minimis* rules on subsidies within the EU (see Johannes Holzer's chapter in this book), but also given China's strong state intervention to enable latecomer catch-up as mentioned below. Accordingly, this indicates policymakers view safeguards as integral to avoid instituting IP-conditioned incentives that foster low-quality patents. It also indicates that policymakers in the EU cap legally-allowed subsidy amounts in all EU MS in an effort to support SMEs but limit distortions of competition that might significantly harm firm growth and consumer welfare. These principles are relevant to both the EU and China given that both regions have a great deal of decentralized economic governance and many diverse regions with a propensity to adopt diverse approaches to state aid.

Third, China clearly has the most sizeable and diverse IP-conditioned incentives out of any country studied, ranging from patent targets tied to performance

(Footnote 5 continued)

rewards (4), loans and financing (5), and other (4). The methodological limitations mentioned in Sect. 2.3.2 should be considered alongside these figures.

evaluations and non-monetary awards to service inventor remuneration and awards regulations. This finding represents the comparative aggressiveness of state intervention in China's economy in order to facilitate latecomer catch-up. Also, the large size of China's economy and sometimes dramatically different levels of development of industries and geographical regions therein may also contribute to the need to have sizeable and diverse incentives.

Fourth, IP acquisition is clearly the most common immediate objective of IP-conditioned government incentive programs in the EU and China, and grants and patent fee subsidies appear to be the most common policy vehicles for meeting these objectives.[6] Several of these policies are intended to facilitate patenting abroad, others domestically, others both. Interestingly, some EU MS have IP-conditioned incentives reserved for IP acquisition in China in particular or provide larger amounts of funding for IP acquisition in China in particular than otherwise offered.

These findings show that IP-conditioned incentives are clearly more focused on enabling firms and other entities to acquire IP than other policies, like typical R&D subsidies, which are more focused on inputs into invention. This reinforces the idea that governments in both developed and developing countries view acquisition of IP in an increasingly inter-connected world as an important end in itself for government policy, although whether this is an optimal strategy deserves further research to better inform policymaking in China and the EU.

Fifth, IP exploitation is a relatively common immediate objective of many IP-conditioned incentives in the EU and China, and tax incentives appear to be the most common, although not only, policy vehicle for meeting this objective. And some countries have policies intended to facilitate both IP acquisition and IP exploitation, which respectively cover the intermediate and end outputs of the innovation process. IP maintenance and IP enforcement are much less common immediate objectives, although are objectives of some policies. Interestingly, some EU MS provide IP-conditioned incentives reserved for IP enforcement in China in particular. This finding shows that different types of policies are viewed by policymakers in the EU and China as better than others to immediately support different aspects of the IP management process.

Sixth, needs-based commercial support is the most common wider strategic objective behind IP-conditioned incentives in the EU.[7] This is clearly exhibited in

[6]Based on the counting analysis, the following main immediate objectives of IP-conditioned incentives occurred with the following frequency (frequency in parenthesis): IP acquisition (53), IP exploitation (38), IP maintenance (13), and IP enforcement (7). For at least one program, although the main objectives appear to be counted, other objectives may in fact apply. The methodological limitations mentioned in Sect. 2.3.2 should be considered alongside these figures.

[7]Based on the counting analysis, the following main wider objectives of IP-conditioned incentives in the EU occurred with the following frequency (first figure in parenthesis is the frequency for all 21 Member States, and average frequency is the second figure): needs-based commercial support (35, 1.67), localizing benefits of knowledge investment (21, 1), stimulate spending enabling research and/or commercialization (15, 0.71), discourage offshoring of taxable assets (14, 0.67), latecomer catch-up (N/A for the purposes of this analysis), information failure (9, 0.43), and

the requirements that many of the incentives can only be utilized by SMEs. Given that over 99 % of firms in the EU are SMEs (which include microenterprises for the purposes of this chapter), and the under-resourced nature of SMEs mentioned in the conceptual framework, this should not be surprising. Interestingly, in several cases, needs-based commercial support provided by IP-conditioned incentives (e.g. subsidized costs for consulting services to identify infringement risks) appears intended to mitigate information failure experienced by SMEs, allowing them to better manage their intangible assets.

Seventh, it is noteworthy that a range of IP-conditioned incentives in China are not always clearly designed to provide/reserved for needs-based commercial support for individuals or SMEs. As such, comparatively well-resourced entities in China (including large Chinese firms) can take advantage of at least some of the IP-conditioned support provided. This point is also mentioned in Song et al.'s (2016), chapter in this book, which specifically focuses on patent subsidies, whereby the authors note this strategy may divert government resources away from entities needing them the most to catch up. And a similar point is raised in Long et al. (2013). At the same time, a number of Chinese IP-conditioned incentives, for example grants from some provincial technology development funds, appear targeted at SMEs. This represents a multi-faceted strategy behind China's current approach to IP-conditioned incentives: not only stimulating growth of the most needy latecomer enterprises, but also encouraging large firms to develop and exploit IP-intensive technologies in China. Further research is needed to determine if this strategy should evolve, and do so at a different pace in different provinces in China depending on their technological capabilities, and/or considering differences in industrial organization, and how exactly policies implementing the strategy should be designed in order to best facilitate catch-up.

Eighth, another common objective of IP-conditioned incentives in the EU appears to be localizing the benefits of knowledge investment within the EU MS making the policy. Tax incentives are the most common vehicle for meeting these objectives (and often also appear intended to discourage offshoring of taxable IP assets), although other types of policies, like patent fee subsidies are sometimes used. Some of these incentives require that the (a) IP be "self-developed"/developed in-house within the entity applying for the incentives, (b) the R&D behind the IP be conducted in the country providing the incentives, (c) the IP be registered in the country providing the incentives, and/or (d) the IP be commercially exploited in the country providing the incentives. These are relatively restrictive requirements, and

(Footnote 7 continued)

techno-nationalism (1, 0.05). The counting analysis for China yielded the following results: needs-based commercial support (3), localizing benefits of knowledge investment (7), stimulate spending enabling research and/or commercialization (7), discourage offshoring of taxable assets (1), latecomer catch-up (20), information failure (3), and techno-nationalism (4). For at least five programs in China and three in the EU, although the main objectives appear to be counted, other objectives may in fact apply. The methodological limitations mentioned in Sect. 2.3.2 should be considered alongside these figures.

there is controversy about how useful they are in meeting their objectives (see OECD 2014a, 2015; and the chapters by Kalloe 2016; Garcia et al. 2016, in this book). As such, these types of incentives deserve to be particularly closely studied by policymakers.

Ninth, China has a number of IP-conditioned incentives to localize the benefits of knowledge investment, some of which, although similar in some ways to the most restrictive incentive qualification requirements in the EU, appear even more restrictive and techno-nationalist. Although some EU MS have perhaps surprisingly restrictive requirements in their IP-conditioned tax incentives, there do not appear to be any requirements in any EU MS, as there are in China (at least from some provincial governments in the recent past), that IP from *foreign affiliates* in the country cannot qualify for incentives/monetary support from the government for innovation, but instead must meet restrictive "自主知识产权/*zizhu zhishi chanquan*" ("indigenous intellectual property") requirements (i.e. IP held by domestically-registered firms without foreign-majority ownership).[8] Also, it does not appear that EU MS require "core" IP to be owned or exclusively licensed by entities in the country providing the IP-conditioned tax incentives in order to enjoy the benefits of the incentive, which, at the time of writing this chapter, is a requirement of China's High and New Technology Enterprise (HNTE) tax deduction scheme.[9]

These comparatively more restrictive requirements in China are part of a state effort to enable domestic Chinese firms to catch up in a world where the IP landscape is dominated by foreign incumbents often inclined to avoid developing or transferring core technology in/to China in order to maintain their competitive advantages, avoid potential appropriability-loss given fears over China's IP protection environment, and perhaps to minimize tax burdens. These are understandable strategic objectives. However, the extent to which these requirements actually meet policymakers' objectives is not fully clear and deserves further empirical research; and, in fact, there may be negative economic impacts of the policies (see Prud'homme 2012, 2013; and the chapter by Garcia et al. 2016, in this book). Considering these findings, EU policymakers can better understand the rationale for restrictive Chinese IP-conditioned incentives, and Chinese policymakers can see that some of their policies are comparatively quite restrictive, potentially even to the detriment of meeting their underlying objectives.

---

[8]The sometimes differing definitions of "自主" intellectual property among different regions in China (whereby some are more restrictive than others) is likely owed to China's policymaking system of economic decentralization which provides the different provinces notable autonomy in how they interpret and implement policy advice from the central level. (These dynamics of course also allow central-level policymakers to blame individual provinces for unpopular policies and encourage them to reform.).

[9]At the time of writing this chapter, there were ongoing discussions about potentially revising the qualification requirements in China's HNTE tax scheme.

2.4.2 Comparison of Economic Impacts of the Patent Subsidy Programs in China and Italy

2.4.2.1 Mini Case-Study 1: Patent Subsidies in China

In an attempt to reach the ambitious innovation-related goals and quantitative patent targets set by China's central government,[10] Chinese policymakers have developed a range of IP-conditioned incentives over the past decade. This has resulted in the promulgation of over 10 national-level quantitative patent targets and over 150 provincial/municipal quantitative patent targets, mostly to be met by 2015, linked to performance evaluations for government officials, managers of state-owned enterprises (SOEs), publically-funded research institutes, among others (Prud'homme 2012). And China has developed a massive system for subsidizing patents as one tool to meet these targets. At the provincial level, Shanghai was the first, in 1999, to institute a patent subsidy scheme, and by 2007, 29 of the 31 provinces/municipalities in Mainland China had launched a patent subsidy scheme (Li 2012). The provincial subsidies differ in their amounts and what they cover, although generally cover the costs of filing patents domestically at China's State Intellectual Property Office (SIPO) including patent application and examination fees, sometimes include annual maintenance/renewal fees,[11] and occasionally include patent attorney fees. They sometimes also cover the costs of filing patents abroad. Further, some Chinese subsidies related to IP, patents included, are given as grants or rewards not specifically linked to, and/or covering costs far beyond, official patenting fees (see Prud'homme 2012, and Table 2.1 in the Annex hereto). When the term "patent subsidies" is used hereafter in this section it refers to all these types of incentives.

---

[10]China's National Medium and Long-term Science & Technology Plan (2006–2020) (S&T MLP) sets the goals to become an "innovation-oriented" country by 2020 and a "leading science power" by 2050; the 12th Five Year Plan on National Social and Economic Development sets the target of 3.3 patents "owned" (note: the Chinese term here "拥有" is best translated as "owned" and is different from the term SIPO uses for "in force" [有效]) per 10,000 people; the National Patent Development Strategy (2011–2020) promulgated on November 11, 2010 prescribes that 2 million patents should be filed annually by 2015; and the National IP Strategy (2014–2020) promulgated on December 29th 2013 sets the target of 14 invention patents per 10,000 people. For more information on other central-level patent targets and all provincial-level patent targets see Prud'homme (2012, 2015).

[11]Although not explored at length in this paper, it is important to note there are risks of subsidizing renewal/maintenance fees of patents (see Prud'homme 2014a) for one brief discussion in the context of China's subsidization of patent maintenance/renewal fees). Subsidizing renewal/maintenance costs of a patent, at least throughout the entire life of the patent, relieves the patentee of any post-filing financial responsibility to ensure that the patents are valuable to their business. For the very reason that patent renewal/maintenance rates are validated in the literature to be a useful measure of patent quality (because they represent that patentees are willing to spend their money to maintain only valuable patents), it would seem potentially unwise to remove this incentive. Also, removing this incentive could potentially clog the system with patents that are not "cleared" by normal market-based mechanisms, in turn inflating restrictions on firms' freedom-to-operate thus potentially stifling innovation.

These provincial patent subsidies have contributed to China's recent domestic patent explosion (Li 2012), as has intensifying R&D, competitive-threat driven foreign investment, and legal and institutional reforms (Hu and Jefferson 2009). (Additionally, the central-level government at one point offered subsidies for filing patents abroad, although sources indicate the Ministry of Finance has, in practice, discontinued this program.[12]) On one hand, some scholars have not been particularly concerned about the potentially negative bi-products on patent quality of China's recent drive to stimulate patenting—instead suggesting that China's technological catch-up strategy has intentionally been geared towards first focusing on quantity of outputs and then eventually shifting towards ensuring the quality of outputs. The rationale behind this approach is that without first building awareness of the importance of inventing and filing IP rights on such inventions, there will be an insufficient amount of domestic/indigenous innovations in China, continued domination of innovation trajectories by foreign incumbents, and thus limited technological catch-up (Zhu 2012). Indeed, in the early stages of China's technological development catch-up path, this approach seems to have its merits. On the other hand, there does not seem to be clear consensus on exactly when and how the state-led shift from patent quantity to quality should take place; and more concerning, the discussion has not always focused enough on dynamics related to IP-conditioned incentives and the utility model patent legal framework in particular.

In addition to increasing invention patent numbers, provincial patents subsidies, in combination with other incentive policies in China also appear to have contributed to the rise in domestic utility model filings. This finding is relatively well acknowledged in government, academic, and practitioner circles in China, and is confirmed by the empirical analysis by Long and Wang (2016), in this book. There has been so much of an explosion in utility model filings in China that from 2010 to 2013 utility model filings actually outnumbered invention patent filings (see Chart 2.1).

Amidst this surge, China's patent subsidies, in combination with other IP-conditioned government incentive policies, appear to have generated low-quality patents in a way jeopardizing the optimality of the country's catch-up trajectory. According to Lee and Kim (2010), the ratio of utility models to invention patents can be an indicator of the level of technological advancement (particularly catch-up) of a country—whereby more advanced countries prefer to patent more sophisticated technologies that are better (or can only be) protected by invention patents. Considering this basic metric and the relatively short lifespans of utility models in China, it appears that some of China's patent-related policies and practices (including patent incentives) contributed to a patent quality trajectory that has not kept up with the country's patent quantity upsurge (Prud'homme 2012). In effect, this has recently made China's technological development trajectory less than optimal (Prud'homme 2012, 2015).

More specifically, a combination of factors has directly contributed to this situation. In China, no Substantive Examination is conducted before utility models are

[12]Consultations with Song Hefa, December 2015.

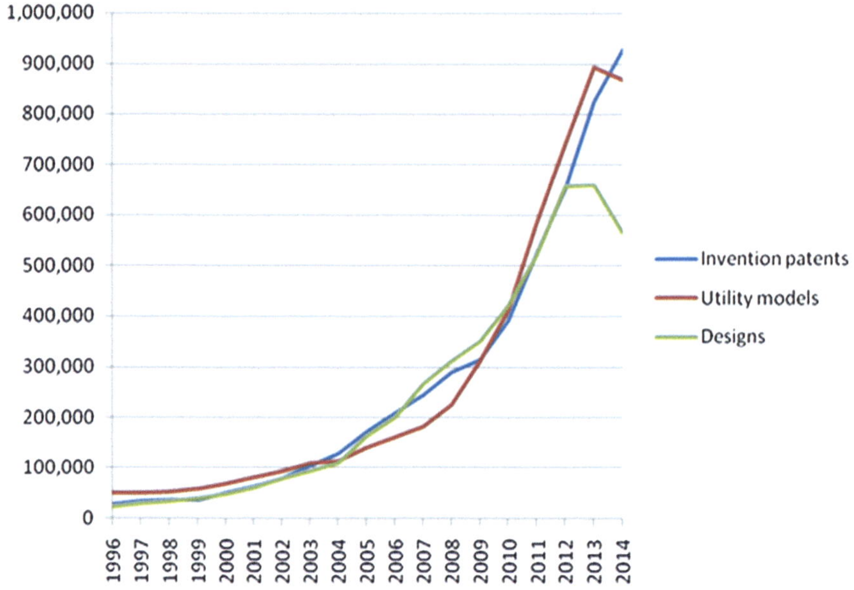

Chart 2.1 Patent filings in China, by type (1996–2014). *Source* Based on SIPO statistics

granted to ensure that they actually fully meet the statutory requirements for patentability (although a Preliminary Examination is conducted on formalities and "obvious" defects in utility model applications). And statute stipulates a lower inventiveness threshold for utility models than for invention patents. And the patent office only issues an administrative decision about whether a utility model fully meets statutory patentability requirements if a formal invalidation procedure is initiated (not via Substantive Examination prior to grant, nor upon pre-grant oppositions or observations, which do not exist for utility models in China). This system, which is shared by a number of other countries, per se does not create patent quality problems for all such countries. However, given that invention patents face a relatively higher threshold for patentability and a relatively more rigorous process (i.e. a Substantive Examination) to ensure they meet this threshold, there is a higher chance that, on average, granted invention patents are of higher quality (and perhaps value) than granted utility model patents (Prud'homme 2012).

Further, the criteria for qualifying for provincial subsidies in China have not been rigorous enough to safeguard against low-quality, unexamined utility models being awarded patent fee subsidies. For example, in the past, in many places in China, only a utility model application number was needed to claim subsidies. This environment was easy for entities to exploit to claim government-provided incentives on IP rights—namely utility models and registered designs—that technically did not even meet statutory patentability requirements.[13]

Further, consultations with Chinese IP scholars indicate that in different provinces/municipalities, patentees have exploited the lack of coordination between local and provincial/municipal governments to make significant money from the patent subsidy scheme in a way not intended by policymakers. For example, in the past (prior to recent reforms) it was possible to separately apply and receive subsidies from the Haidian district government in Beijing and Beijing municipal government for patent-related costs, ultimately resulting in applicants receiving "double" subsidies from the government sometimes far exceeding the total costs of obtaining patents—even low-quality patents. This was not the intention of the government.

Recent research supports the idea that China's patent subsidy policies have indeed contributed to a decrease in the quality of China's patent stock. Gao et al. (2011) finds that the subsidies have encouraged behavior that maximizes patent quantity at the cost of quality, namely repeated patent applications; splitting inventions into smaller inventions just to boost the number of applications; filings for products that are already published or otherwise disclosed (in some cases for a significant amount of time) and thus are not patentable; and filing applications only to get an application number in order to claim subsidies but not even paying official patent fees. Dang and Motohashi (2013) empirically show that patent subsidies have encouraged patents with a particularly narrow claim breadth, an indicator of low-quality patents. Lei et al. (2013) empirically show that China's patent subsidy system has encouraged firms to break-up inventions in an attempt to capture a greater amount of patent subsidies. Boeing and Mueller (2015) find that while China's subsidies for PCT patent filings contributes to a rise in PCT applications, based on an analysis of International Search Report citations, the policies also contribute to Chinese PCT applications achieving only 34 % of the quality level of international PCT applications.

Most recently, the chapter by Song et al. (2016), in this book empirically shows that provincial subsidy policies issued from 2010 onwards encouraged patenting in China at a much faster pace than the subsidies from prior years, while at the same time also likely created a decline in patent quality. And the chapter by Long and Wang (2016) in this book empirically shows that China's patent promotion incentives (including certain patent subsidies, as well as tax policies) have created a decline in the quality of domestic utility models and designs.

In reaction to these negative effects of Chinese patent subsidies and other incentives, various sub-central governments in China have recently instituted key initiatives to move away from a fixation on quantity of any type of patents at any

[13]Design rights in China, even though not dealing with technical inventions, are considered "patents" in China. They are not substantively examined.

cost. Many provinces now require that patent fee subsidies only be awarded to owners of a granted IP right. Shanghai, one of the richest sub-central regions in China (a municipality), revised its patent subsidy program several years ago so that it only provides subsidies for invention patents. Other provinces have followed in reforming some aspects of their IP-conditioned incentives, although questions remain about the extent to which lesser developed regions in China have reformed their IP-conditioned incentives to focus more on patent quality.

At the central level, measures implementing China's Patent Law were reformed to create better safeguards to limit low-quality utility models, including those spurred by IP-conditioned provincial government incentives (but certainly not intended to only limit subsidized low-quality utility models). Article 44 of the Implementing Regulations of the Patent Law was amended on January 9th 2010 to expand the scope of Preliminary Examination for utility models to assess "obvious" lack of novelty (and the same provision was also extended to designs) and "obvious" non-compliance with industrial applicability requirements. Also, the Patent Examination Guidelines were amended on September 16th 2013 to expand, albeit just slightly, the novelty assessment for utility models and designs.

Perhaps the most notable recent initiative to move away from IP-conditioned incentives that stimulate quantity of any type of patents at any cost is SIPO's Several Opinions on Further Improving Quality of Patent Applications promulgated on December 18th 2013 (hereafter "the Opinions"), which is also discussed in a brief January 21st 2014 SIPO interpretation of the Opinions.[14] The Opinions recommend a number of important initiatives, for example that funding should only be given to granted utility models; Search Reports (or more substantive Patent Evaluation Reports) should be provided along with applications for utility model subsidies (if negative reports are actually used as a basis for rejecting subsidy applications, this in effect makes the threshold for awarding subsidies more rigorous than the SIPO examination undertaken to grant utility models); that the level of funding a subsidy recipient can obtain is not higher than the sum of all official charges and patent agency service fees that the recipient pays; that patent targets and performance evaluation systems better reflect patent quality; and that bad faith disincentives should be strengthened. Although there is some uncertainty as to exactly how the Opinions have been diffused from the central level down through the provincial and local levels due to China's sometimes disjointed system of economically decentralized governance, they constitute one of the most specific pieces of guidance in recent years to improve patent quality in China.

By way of another example, SIPO has recently started to view the higher ratio of utility model to invention patent filings in China as an indicator of a less-than-optimal innovation trajectory, and thus recently has targeted a ratio of

[14]Opinions available here (in Chinese) http://www.sipo.gov.cn/yw/2013/201312/t20131225_891833.html; Interpretation available here (in Chinese) http://www.sipo.gov.cn/zcfg/zcjd/201401/t20140121_899716.html.

more invention patents to utility models (Xinhua 2014a, b; Fu 2014). Also, the targets in the National IP Strategy (2014–2020) generally reflect a more sophisticated approach to state-led patenting than that of the past, namely one with greater emphasis on the need to stimulate patents that are actually commercialized and thus have value (Prud'homme 2015).

2.4.2.2 Mini Case Study 2: Patent Fee Subsidies in Italy

As illustrated in Table 2.1 in the Annex, Italy has a range of IP-conditioned incentives, including various patent fee subsidies.[15] Some of these programs are administered directly by government departments, while others are administered by chambers of commerce or other private/quasi-private/non-governmental entities. The patent fee subsidies appear available only for SMEs (see Table 2.1 in the Annex for details).

Italy's patent subsidy programs do not seem to be significantly increasing domestic filings of utility models and designs, which are more prone than invention patents to be of low quality given that in Italy these rights do not undergo a Substantive Examination. As depicted in Chart 2.2, for over fifteen years the filings of utility model applications in Italy have come nowhere near to surpassing those of invention patents. And based on the rate of utility model filings in Chart 2.2, although this of course is very prima facie evidence per se, patent subsidy programs in Italy do not seem to have given rise to a significant increase in utility model patent filings in the country. This indicates that Italy's patent subsidy programs are likely having a less pronounced negative impact on patent quality than those in China.

Still, one useful assessment conducted by Xu and Federico (2016), featured in this book, of a sample of Italian patent fee subsidies from a major regional subsidy program (in Milan province) finds that those subsidies do not appear to have significantly improved or harmed patent quality. One reason that subsidized patents in Milan were not found to be of particularly high quality could be because of the lack of stringency of the requirements and procedures for granting the subsidies (although could also be related to the methodology used in the paper). The first edition of the patent subsidy program in Milan, administered by the local chamber of commerce, did not have stringent requirements for granting: in fact, the subsidies were automatically assigned in the order in which subsidy applications were received, with no real ex-ante assessment of the quality of the patents.[16]

---

[15]Information on a range of patent subsidy programs in Italy can be found here: http://www.uibm.gov.it/index.php/incentivi; and information on the IP box program in particular can be found here: http://www.mise.gov.it/index.php/it/per-i-media/notizie/2033226-patent-box-ecco-il-decreto-attuativo.

[16]Consultations with Federico Munari, January 26th 2016.

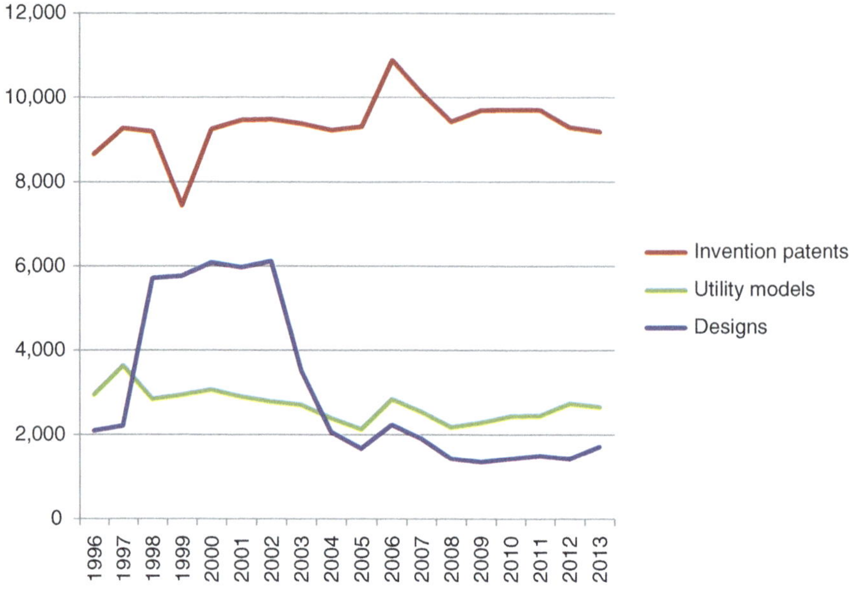

Chart 2.2 Patent and design filings in Italy (at UIBM), by type (1996–2013). *Source* Based on WIPO statistics for total applications (direct and PCT national phase entries) by filing office. Figures for 2014 not available at time of research

Fortunately, the current requirements for being granted patent fee subsidies from major patent programs in Italy are relatively strict. For example, the Brevetti+ patent subsidy program funded by the Italian Ministry of Economy and administered by the Italian Patent Office (UIBM) considers the outcome of the Search Report before awarding patent fee subsidies.[17] Consultations with UIBM officials indicate that UIBM prides itself on instituting a strict set of qualification criteria and oversight process for a range of different programs for subsidizing patent costs.[18]

This being said, there is a lack of comprehensive assessments of the impacts of all of Italy's patent subsidy programs on patent quality. As such, significantly more research is warranted in this area, especially as new Italian government programs, like the Brevetti+ 2 program, which started on October 6th 2015, are rolled out in an attempt to improve competitiveness of Italian firms.[19]

[17]ibid.

[18]Consultations with Giovanni de Sanctis, UIBM on May 22nd 2014 at IP Key-SIPO roundtable on utility model patents at SIPO in Beijing, China; Prud'homme (2014b).

[19]Consultations with a representative of UIBM on October 13th 2015. See more information on the Brevetti+ 2 program here: http://www.uibm.gov.it/index.php/06-10-2015-brevetti-2-invia-la-domanda.

2.4.2.3 Cross-Case Analysis

Several findings can be drawn from the abovementioned cases studies. First, in the short-to-mid-term, governments in latecomer nations like China may adopt the strategy of using IP-conditioned incentives (e.g. patent subsidies) largely to build awareness of the importance of patenting and increase quantity of patents, and in the process willingly sacrifice some quality of the patent stock. This strategy appears intent on first and foremost addressing the dynamics particularly relevant to latecomers mentioned in Sect. 2.2, namely the need to catch up, lack of IP awareness and perfect information, and perhaps the challenge of cutting through incumbent patent thickets.

Second, after reaching a critical point, pressure will arise to shift the strategy to focus more on quality of patents, and in the process attempt to also meet other potential objectives, including stimulating innovation, discussed in Sect. 2.2. Amongst other modes, this evolution may take place via reforms to IP-conditioned incentives and/or institutional mechanisms governing them to ensure they have stricter requirements that better filter out low-quality patents and only promote higher-quality patents. As such, it appears important to very carefully monitor and quickly calibrate IP-conditioned incentives to ensure that the shift to a higher-quality patent stock is not overly delayed thus potentially slowing the catch-up process. Herein, there may be different "crossing-over" points for different regions in China whereby IP laws and institutions change based on local abilities to shift from being IP imitators to innovators (Yu 2009, 2013, 2015); and this may mean that regions that are more economically and technologically advanced in China should move especially quickly to ensure their IP-conditioned incentives stimulate higher quality patents.

Third, the qualification requirements within IP-conditioned incentives are important safeguards of patent quality. In the past, there were relatively few qualification requirements in some provinces in China for entities seeking to claim subsidies for patenting costs—sometimes all that was required was an application number for a utility model or design application. More recently, Chinese provincial governments, guided by detailed advice from SIPO, have realized the need to strengthen their qualification requirements for patent subsidies and have already or are currently undertaking initiatives to do so. In Italy, a number of programs have rather stringent qualification requirements, which may ensure a minimum level of quality of patents subsidized by such programs; however, more research is warranted into how the quality of patents resulting from the various Italian patent subsidy programs may differ depending on qualification criteria for, institutional oversight of, and amount and type of support offered by such programs.

Fourth, IP-conditioned incentives afforded to utility models and designs are particularly prone to have negative effects on patent quality, especially if lacking sufficiently stringent qualification requirements. As clearly illustrated in the case of China, the costs of utility models have a significant impact on the propensity of entities to file and maintain utility models, and IP-conditioned incentives that lower these costs and even provide monetary support/awards beyond these actual costs can have a very significant impact on the ultimate filing and usage of these rights. This created a significant patent quality problem when combined with the statutorily-mandated lack of a Substantive Examination of utility models prior to grant, lack of pre-grant oppositions or observations to challenge the granting of utility models, and lower inventive step for utility models. And this situation was exacerbated in areas with insufficiently stringent qualification requirements in IP-conditioned incentives. This particular mix of lack of legal and policy safeguards resulted in the stimulation of low-quality IP rights in China—which, in the worst cases, included subsidizing rights that (paradoxically, even if granted) did not technically meet statutory patentability requirements.

There does not appear to be as compelling evidence that the low costs and IP-conditioned incentives for patents (sometimes including utility models) in Italy are having a significant negative impact on the quality of the country's patent stock. This is likely owned to a combination of factors in China that collectively do not exist in Italy in the same way, namely: widespread government pressure on some Chinese entities to file IP (often without specifications on the quality of this IP) in order to meet performance review requirements; existence of different types of significant patent-related IP-conditioned incentives all over China without significant patent quality-related qualification requirements; and willingness of Chinese entities to file low-quality utility models (and designs) primarily to meet the aforementioned performance requirements, to acquire a very low cost or cost-free IP right (which, even if low quality, could provide some benefits as a commercial negotiation tool, especially for latecomer firms), and/or to shrewdly make money from the government from filing such rights.[20] This being said, the exact extent to which such programs have impacted patent quality in Italy is worth further study.

Fifth, institutional coordination and oversight can play an important role in determining the impact of IP-conditioned incentives on patent quality. For example, less-than-optimal coordination between some district and municipal/provincial governments in instituting patent subsidies lead to abuse of the program in China that likely wasted government resources better spent on encouraging higher-quality patents. There may be a benefit of administering patent subsidy programs through non-government or quasi-government entities, but only if they have more management expertise than government departments. Further, in Italy, past experiences indicate that even if leaving patent subsidy programs to an external body to

[20]It is also possible that, on average, the technological advancement of utility model filers in China is lower than those in Italy, therefore contributing to this situation. However, in the absence of an empirical comparison, this is speculation.

implement, the government should ensure that the qualification requirements in the programs are stringent enough to avoid subsidizing low-quality patents.

2.5 Conclusions and Policy Recommendations

2.5.1 Conclusions

This chapter provides insights into how China's and EU MS' IP-conditioned incentives compare in terms of their underlying strategic objectives and impacts on patent quality, and some key differences among these incentives and reasons for the differences. It also highlights implications of these insights for policymakers.

The first set of findings in the chapter is drawn from typological analysis of the policy mechanisms and strategic objectives behind IP-conditioned incentives in the EU and China. First, IP-conditioned tax incentives are the most prevalent type of IP-conditioned incentive in EU MS and there are some indications they are having negative economic effects. Second, unbeknownst to some, both EU MS and China institute IP-conditioned grants and patent subsidy programs, and policymakers in both regions can learn from each other's experiences with these particular policies. Third, in order to facilitate catch-up, China clearly has more sizeable and diverse IP-conditioned incentives than any EU MS.

Fourth, IP acquisition is the most common immediate objective of IP-conditioned government incentive programs in the EU and China, and grants and patent fee subsidies appear to be the most common policy vehicles for meeting these objectives. These trends reinforce the idea that governments in both developed and developing countries view acquisition of IP in an increasingly inter-connected world as an important end in itself for government policy, although whether this is an optimal strategy deserves further research to better inform policymaking. Fifth, different types of policies are viewed by policymakers in the EU and China as better than others to support different aspects of the IP management process.

Sixth, needs-based commercial support is clearly the most common wider strategic objective behind IP-conditioned incentives in the EU. Seventh, a range of IP-conditioned incentives in China are not always clearly designed to provide needs-based commercial support for individuals or SMEs; and further research is needed on whether China's strategy and implementing policies in this regard should evolve, and perhaps evolve differently among regions and industries in China, to best facilitate catch-up. Eighth, the second most common objective of IP-conditioned incentives in the EU appears to be localizing the benefits of knowledge investment within the EU MS making the policy. Ninth, China has a number of IP-conditioned incentives to localize the benefits of knowledge investment, some of which, although similar in some ways to the most restrictive incentive qualification requirements in the EU, appear even more restrictive and techno-nationalist—potentially even to the detriment of meeting their underlying objectives.

The next set of findings in the chapter is drawn from analysis of the patent subsidy programs in China and Italy in particular. First, in the short-to-mid-term, governments in latecomer nations like China may adopt the strategy of using IP-conditioned incentives largely to build awareness of the importance of patenting and increase the quantity of patents, and in the process willingly sacrifice some quality of the patent stock. Second, after reaching a critical point, pressure will arise to shift the strategy to focus more on quality of patents, and in the process attempt to also meet other long-term objectives such as stimulating innovation. Third, the qualification requirements within IP-conditioned incentives are important safeguards of patent quality. Fourth, IP-conditioned incentives afforded to utility models (and possibly designs) are particularly susceptible to creating negative effects on patent quality given the often relatively low statutory and procedural requirements for granting these rights. And if incentives lacking sufficiently stringent qualification requirements are provided for these rights, they can significantly hamper patent quality. Fifth, institutional coordination and oversight can play an important role in determining the ultimate impact of IP-conditioned incentives on patent quality.

2.5.2 Recommendations

Based on the aforementioned conclusions, several policy recommendations appear both intuitive and important for policymakers to consider in China, the EU, and potentially elsewhere, when seeking if and how to create IP-conditioned incentives:

- Patent subsidies (including patent fee subsidies, among others) should only be paid to patents that are eventually granted.
- Generally speaking, IP-conditioned incentives should have stringent enough qualification requirements to ensure they do not create a significant drag on the quality of a country's patent stock. While there can be strategic differences in these requirements among economies pending their levels of technological development, latecomer economies need to ensure they are not overly lax with their requirements because this may hamper catch-up.
- In jurisdictions providing IP-conditioned incentives for unexamined utility models and/or utility models with low (or no) inventive step requirements, the qualification requirements for such incentives should be especially carefully calibrated because they may notably affect patent quality.

- The qualification requirements for IP-conditioned incentives for design rights should be carefully calibrated to avoid providing state support to designs with little economic or social value.
- Requiring a positive Search Report as a precondition for receiving patent subsidies for utility models serves as a useful patent quality safeguard.
- Patent renewal/maintenance fees should be very cautiously subsidized, if at all.
- Institutional oversight/administration mechanisms must be carefully calibrated in order to prevent abuse of IP-conditioned incentives. Private or quasi-private entities may sometimes be useful for administering IP-conditioned incentives but still require some oversight by the government.
- Further studies should be conducted on the impacts of restricting certain types of IP-conditioned incentives to SMEs as an industrial development strategy.
- Oversight of IP-conditioned incentives should be more centralized in China to the extent possible, including via strict monitoring and evaluation of provincial and county implementation of SIPO's December 2013 Opinions on Further Improving Quality of Patent Applications.
- Further study is required into the impacts, including the potentially negative ones, of restrictions on the support provided by some Chinese IP-conditioned incentives to only support "自主/indigenous" IP (i.e. only IP held by domestic entities without foreign-majority ownership), and requiring "core" IP ownership or worldwide exclusive licenses.
- EU policymakers should adopt new restrictions, possibly like those proposed by the OECD and several EU MS at the time of writing this chapter, on IP-conditioned tax incentives currently proliferating among EU MS.
- Chinese policymakers should familiarize themselves with EU MS' approaches to IP-conditioned incentives, including *de minimis* rules related to subsidies which are relevant to economically decentralized economies like China.
- In order to most constructively engage with China, foreign policymakers can benefit from understanding why China strategizes the way it does and that some often-criticized IP-conditioned incentives are not completely unique to China.

Acknowledgements The author would like to thank the managers of IP Key for allowing him to write this chapter (as well as edit the book in which this chapter is published) as part of his work responsibilities. This being said, the opinions expressed in the chapter are those of the author and do not necessarily represent those of the IP Key project or any institutions with which it has cooperated in any way. The author would also like to thank Gao Xintong of IP Key for helping with the research of IP-conditioned incentives in the EU featured in the Annex of this chapter.

Annex: Typological Analysis

See Table 2.1.

Table 2.1 Strategies behind and details of IP-conditioned government incentives in the EU and China

Country	Policy mechanisms				Strategic objectives	
	Benefits category	Brief description of benefits	IP requirements	Other major requirements of recipients	Immediate objective(s)	Wider objective(s)
Austria	Grants	Grants and counseling services. Up to 50 % of eligible costs are covered. Eligible costs include those for translations and legal fees amounting to 5000–10,000 EUR. (May also cover litigation costs in cases of infringement.)	IP in emerging markets, especially China	SMEs	IP enforcement (abroad)	Needs-based commercial support; Information failure
	Grants	Can cover costs related to patent registration, maintenance, marketing, and enforcement. For registration, covers up to 100 % of eligible costs, capped at 18,000 EUR. For marketing, up to 100 % of eligible costs funded. For the identification of intellectual property violations and for enforcement of existing intellectual property rights whereby 50 % of eligible costs are covered, capped at 100,000 EUR	Must involve costs related to patents and other IP fitting into one of the following categories: costs for registering/granting patents in emerging markets outside Europe; consultancy services for patenting in China, India, and Russia; patent marketing, identification, licensing and exploitation and enforcement of IPR nationally or internationally	SMEs	IP acquisition (abroad); IP maintenance; IP exploitation; IP enforcement	Needs-based commercial support; Information failure; Stimulate spending enabling research and/or commercialization
	Grants	Up to 50 % of IP enforcement costs covered, capped at 100,000 EUR	Costs for legal services for IP infringement identification and enforcement	SMEs except for those in the tourism/leisure industries	IP enforcement	Needs-based commercial support; Information failure

(continued)

Table 2.1 (continued)

Country	Policy mechanisms				Strategic objectives	
	Benefits category	Brief description of benefits	IP requirements	Other major requirements of recipients	Immediate objective(s)	Wider objective(s)
Belgium	Grants	Grants for industrial research or repayable grants for experimental development. Covers costs of acquiring patents from outside sources	Patents must be in-licensed or ownership transferred from outside sources	Young innovative companies	IP exploitation	Needs-based commercial support; Localize benefits of knowledge investment
	Patent subsidy	Subsidies range from 15 to 50 % of costs of registering and maintaining patents	Patents should ultimately be commercially exploited in the Walloon region. Patents registered abroad also eligible	SMEs registered in the Wallonia Region	IP acquisition; IP maintenance; IP exploitation	Needs-based commercial support; Localize benefits of knowledge investment
	Patent subsidy	Costs of filing and maintaining patents. Benefits range from 35 to 70 % of eligible costs, depending on nature of project and entity. A 15 % increase in costs covered when involving patents resulting from collaborations with research institutes	Patents	SMEs who undertake part of their commercial activities in the Brussels-Capital Region	IP acquisition; IP maintenance	Needs-based commercial support; Localize benefits of knowledge investment
	Tax incentives (patent box)	80 % reduction of qualified income from exploited patents, with a maximum effective tax rate of 6.8 %	Eligible IP includes patents, supplementary protection certificates, or know-how closely related to the patents. Patents should be self-developed or acquired and registered in Belgium under the	All Belgian-resident entities subject to Belgian corporate income tax. Belgian branches of nonresident entities subject to nonresident	IP exploitation	Discourage offshoring of taxable IP assets; localize benefits of knowledge investment

(continued)

Table 2.1 (continued)

Country	Policy mechanisms				Strategic objectives	
	Benefits category	Brief description of benefits	IP requirements	Other major requirements of recipients	Immediate objective(s)	Wider objective(s)
			EPC or PCT regime. Eligible income includes that from licensing patents or sale of patented products	Belgian corporate income tax		
China[b]	Grants	Provincial and/or local subsidies/grants from science and technology-related government funds (e.g. Technology Invention Fund for SMEs, Key Technology Invention Project Fund)	Entities newly develop自主知识产权 (*zizhu zhishi chanquan*) (hereafter "indigenous IP") or obtain the rights to indigenous IP. Note on definitions: some provinces and localities in China have—at least in the recent past—defined 自主知识产权as only IP developed by and owned by (or sometimes in-licensed from) a wholly-Chinese-owned entity. Definitions of the term may differ among regions in China, and may differ from the central-level government's definition of the concept. See Prud'homme (2012, 2013) for more details`	Requirements vary, offered to SMEs but often not only SMEs	IP acquisition	Needs-based commercial support; latecomer catch-up; techno-nationalism

(continued)

Table 2.1 (continued)

Country	Policy mechanisms				Strategic objectives	
	Benefits category	Brief description of benefits	IP requirements	Other major requirements of recipients	Immediate objective(s)	Wider objective(s)
	Grants	Grants/subsidies from the Central Foreign Trade Development Fund (CFTDF) (itself composed of over 37 billion RMB) and/or other funds	Indigenous IP requirements on products being exported	Exporting certain volume of products; other requirements vary	IP exploitation	Latecomer catch-up; (likely some) techno-nationalism
	Grants	Subsidies/grants (e.g. of 1 million RMB)	Indigenous patents incorporated into technical standards	Requirements vary	IP acquisition; IP maintenance; IP exploitation	Latecomer catch-up; (likely some) techno-nationalism; stimulate spending enabling research and/or commercialization
	Grants	Funding from national S&T programs (e.g. the Key Technologies Program, 863 Program, 973 Program, Torch Program, National Key Laboratories program)	Newly developed and owned IP or the rights to IP otherwise obtained (can include indigenous IP requirements)	Requirements vary	IP acquisition	Stimulate spending enabling research and/or commercialization; Latecomer catch-up
	Government procurement	Government procurement contracts awarded	Indigenous IP requirements Note: In 2011, central government officially stated that indigenous IP requirements should be delinked from government procurement preferences	Requirements vary	IP exploitation	Latecomer catch-up; techno-nationalism; other objectives may apply

(continued)

Table 2.1 (continued)

Country	Policy mechanisms				Strategic objectives	
	Benefits category	Brief description of benefits	IP requirements	Other major requirements of recipients	Immediate objective(s)	Wider objective(s)
	Reduced patent fees and delayed payment[a]	Various programs. Reduced or delayed payments allowed for official filings fees and/or maintenance and renewal fees. Sometimes provided at flat rate	Pending the program, can be allowed for utility models, designs, and/or invention patents	Requirements may vary	IP acquisition (domestically); IP maintenance	Needs-based commercial support; latecomer catch-up
	Patent subsidy	Various programs. Covers costs of official fees for filing patents abroad; sometimes includes attorney costs for preparing filings, and maintenance and renewal costs; can potentially cover other generally related costs. Sometimes provided at flat rate Note: some sources indicate that central-level subsidies are no longer offered for international filings, although provinces still offer subsidies for international filings	PCT or other international patents. In some cases, allowed for utility models and designs in addition to invention patents	Requirements may vary	IP acquisition (abroad); IP maintenance	Latecomer catch-up
	Patent subsidy	Various programs in different regions in China. Covers costs of official fees for filing patents in China; sometimes includes attorney costs for preparing filings and maintenance and renewal costs; can potentially cover other generally related costs. Sometimes provided at flat rate	Patent requirements vary. In some cases, allowed for utility models and designs in addition to invention patents	Requirements vary	IP acquisition (domestically); IP maintenance	Latecomer catch-up

(continued)

Table 2.1 (continued)

Country	Policy mechanisms				Strategic objectives	
	Benefits category	Brief description of benefits	IP requirements	Other major requirements of recipients	Immediate objective(s)	Wider objective(s)
	Patent targets	Tied to work performance reviews	Patent requirements vary	Government officials, state-owned enterprise managers, university and public research institute managers, etc.	IP acquisition	Latecomer catch-up; Information failure
	Risk assessments/FTO analysis	Various types of support (financial or otherwise) for risk assessments/freedom-to-operate analysis for filing and exploitation of IP	Often for patents, although can cover resources needed for risk assessments for other IP, filed in China and/or abroad	Requirements may vary	IP acquisition; IP exploitation	Information failure; latecomer catch-up
	Financing	Funding from venture capital and other financing entities (via pledge financing, Patent Banks, etc.) directly affiliated with the government	At least sometimes set indigenous IP requirements	Requirements vary	IP acquisition; other objectives may apply	Latecomer catch-up; other objectives may apply
	Tax incentives	High and New Technology Enterprise (HNTE) tax scheme, which affords a 10 % reduction of the Enterprise Income Tax, 150 % super deduction for R&D expenses, and a potential business tax deduction	Utility models, designs for which the pattern and shape of a product is changed in a "non-simple" manner, software copyrights, proprietary integrated layout design rights, and	10 % of employees must engage in R&D; at least 30 % must be technology personnel holding college diplomas or higher degrees; certain ratio required of qualifying	IP acquisition; IP exploitation	Discourage offshoring of taxable IP assets; localize benefits of knowledge investment; latecomer catch-up

(continued)

Table 2.1 (continued)

Country	Policy mechanisms				Strategic objectives	
	Benefits category	Brief description of benefits	IP requirements	Other major requirements of recipients	Immediate objective(s)	Wider objective(s)
			new plant varieties. Applicant should own "core" IP independently-developed in China or the applicant should obtain worldwide exclusive rights to such IP for 5 years or more Note: potential changes to these requirements were being discussed at the time of drafting this chapter	R&D expenditures to sales revenue for the most recent three financial years		
	Tax incentives	Benefits vary among regions	IP requirements vary among regions	Requirements vary among regions	IP acquisition; IP exploitation	Localize benefits of knowledge investment; latecomer catch-up
	IP insurance	Patent enforcement insurance, patent infringement liability insurance, or other IP insurance provided by government-affiliated entities	IP requirements vary	Requirements vary	IP enforcement	Information failure; other objectives may apply
	Monetary awards	Monetary awards (e.g. Worker Inventor Award, Women Inventor Award, Juvenile	Often for patents, but may be provided for other types of IP (can have	Requirements vary	IP acquisition	Latecomer catch-up; (can include) needs-based commercial support;

(continued)

Table 2.1 (continued)

Country	Policy mechanisms				Strategic objectives	
	Benefits category	Brief description of benefits	IP requirements	Other major requirements of recipients	Immediate objective(s)	Wider objective(s)
		Inventor Award) given by the government	indigenous IP requirements)			(can include) stimulate spending enabling research and/or commercialization
	Monetary awards	Patent-specific awards (outside of normal patent subsidies), for example, the Gold Award for China Patents and China Patent Excellence Award	Patents (can have indigenous IP requirements)	Requirements vary	IP acquisition	Stimulate spending enabling research and/or commercialization; (can include) latecomer catch-up
	Non-monetary awards	Non-monetary awards (plaques, etc.) from the government	Various types of IP (can have indigenous IP requirements)	Requirements vary	IP acquisition	Stimulate spending enabling research and/or commercialization; (can include) latecomer catch-up
	Administrative recognition	Administrative recognition Note: at least previously, monetary benefits were also provided for qualifying trademarks. The status of “local famous trademark” is distinct from the legal recognition/protection that is	Trademarks with a certain regional reputation	Requirements vary. Appear to be concentrated on domestic Chinese entities	IP exploitation	Latecomer catch-up; other objectives likely apply

(continued)

Table 2.1 (continued)

Country	Policy mechanisms				Strategic objectives	
	Benefits category	Brief description of benefits	IP requirements	Other major requirements of recipients	Immediate objective(s)	Wider objective(s)
		associated with "well known" trademarks				
	Large-scale experimental IP programs	IP Demonstration Enterprises, IP Demonstration Cities, Patent Navigation Programs, and various other programs	IP requirements vary pending the program	Requirements vary pending the program	IP acquisition; IP maintenance; IP exploitation; IP enforcement (may vary among programs)	Latecomer catch-up; other objectives likely apply
	Service invention remuneration and rewards	Specific statutory remuneration and rewards need to be paid unless a "reasonable" remuneration and reward agreement between the entity and its service inventor is reached Note: as specified by 2015 draft regulation	Creative achievements made in China on subject matter that can be protected by patents (invention patents, utility models, designs), plant varieties, integrated circuits layout designs Note: as specified by 2015 draft regulation	Entities with service inventors	IP acquisition; IP exploitation	Stimulate spending enabling research and/or commercialization; Latecomer catch-up
	Laws on S&T development	Government rules on types of support required specified in the Law on S&T Progress, as well as the Law on Promoting the Transformation of S&T Achievements	Patents and other types of intellectual property. Restrictions on foreign ownership and exclusive licensing of IP if resulting from state-funded research	Various requirements, particularly applicable to universities and public research institutes but also firms using government funding	IP exploitation	Latecomer catch-up; stimulate spending enabling research and/or commercialization

(continued)

Table 2.1 (continued)

Country	Policy mechanisms				Strategic objectives	
	Benefits category	Brief description of benefits	IP requirements	Other major requirements of recipients	Immediate objective(s)	Wider objective(s)
Croatia	Patent subsidy	Subsidize patent registration costs up to a maximum of two patents at 120,000 HRK per patent in Croatia and 180,000 HRK for international applications	Patents	Privately owned, knowledge-based SMEs located in Croatia	IP acquisition (domestically and abroad)	Needs-based commercial support
	Tax incentives	Super tax deduction of between 175–250 %, depending on the type of research activities, for costs including depreciation of costs to buy patents, or licensing fees of technologies used for research activities	Patents	Engage in projects involving basic research, applied research, development research, or technical feasibility studies	IP acquisition	Stimulate spending enabling research and/or commercialization
Cyprus	Tax incentives (patent box)	80 % deduction and a maximum effective tax rate of 2 % for royalties from licensing of IP and capital gains from the sale of IP	Self-owned (not sub-licensed) patents, trademarks, industrial designs and copyrights	Entity is subject to the company tax regime of Cyprus	IP exploitation	Discourage offshoring of taxable IP assets; localize benefits of knowledge investment
	Tax incentives	Annual capital allowance deduction of 20 % of cost of developing and acquiring IP. Capital allowance is tax deductible over 5 years including the year of IP acquisition	Intangible assets as defined under the Patent Rights Law, Intellectual Property Law, and Trademarks Law	Entity is subject to the company tax regime of Cyprus	IP acquisition	Discourage offshoring of taxable IP assets; other objectives may apply

(continued)

Table 2.1 (continued)

Country	Policy mechanisms				Strategic objectives	
	Benefits category	Brief description of benefits	IP requirements	Other major requirements of recipients	Immediate objective(s)	Wider objective(s)
Czech Republic	Reduced patent fees[a]	50 % reduction of the application fee	Utility models	For individual inventors	IP acquisition	Needs-based commercial support
Denmark	Tax incentives	Eligible costs related to IP can be fully expensed in the year of acquisition or amortized over a seven-year period	Patents and know-how (including purchasing rights and licenses to utilize patents or know-how)	Entities subject to Danish tax code	IP acquisition	Discourage offshoring of taxable IP assets; other objectives may apply
	Service inventor remuneration and rewards	(Required by government, but paid by employer.) Specific statutory remuneration and rewards need to be paid unless the value of the invention does not exceed what the employee, in view of his working conditions as a whole, may reasonably be assumed to produce	Inventions that are patentable as invention patents or as utility models in Denmark	Public or private entities which employ the service inventor	IP acquisition; IP exploitation	Stimulate spending enabling research and/or commercialization
Finland	Grants	Covers 50 % of eligible costs for obtaining all rights to inventions through purchasing or licensing, and procuring analyses related to protecting the product or service (e.g. via patenting)	Can cover patents	Micro-enterprises	IP acquisition	Needs-based commercial support; Information failure
	Service inventor remuneration and rewards	(Required by government, but paid by employer.)	Inventions patentable in Finland	Public or private entities which employ the service inventor	IP acquisition; IP exploitation	Stimulate spending enabling research

(continued)

Table 2.1 (continued)

Country	Policy mechanisms				Strategic objectives	
	Benefits category	Brief description of benefits	IP requirements	Other major requirements of recipients	Immediate objective(s)	Wider objective(s)
		Specific statutory remuneration and rewards need to be paid unless it was agreed otherwise before the invention was made				and/or commercialization
France	Loans	Covers expenses for protecting IP by applying for registration ranging from 50,000 to 5 million EUR (note: some sources alternatively indicate the cap is 3 million EUR)	Patents	SMEs established for over 3 years, which have filed a patent or a digital creation, have assisted in the R&/or D/innovation, or have incurred significant expenditures for R&D within the last 24 months	IP acquisition	Needs-based commercial support
	Loans	Loans (ADI) repayable with a zero interest rate, whereby 25–65 % of eligible costs can be covered. Eligible costs include those for patent filing and maintenance, and acquisition of technical knowledge	Patents, technical knowledge	SMEs	IP acquisition; IP maintenance	Needs-based commercial support
	Loans	Loans (ADICI) for 65 % of eligible costs for firms with fewer than 250 people, 50 % for firms with 250–2000 people.	Can cover patents	SMEs collaborating with foreign partners	IP acquisition; IP maintenance	Needs-based commercial support

(continued)

Table 2.1 (continued)

Country	Policy mechanisms				Strategic objectives	
	Benefits category	Brief description of benefits	IP requirements	Other major requirements of recipients	Immediate objective(s)	Wider objective(s)
		Eligible costs include those for patent filing and maintenance				
	Support for patents in standards	Patents bought by Fonds souverain de propriété intellectuelle (FSPI) (administrated by Caisse des Dépôts et Consignations, entrusted by the French government) are licensed to businesses; advocacy of inclusion of patents of French or European origin in international standards and patent pools	Patents resulting from French research	Focus on SMEs	IP acquisition; IP exploitation	Needs-based commercial support; (possibly some) techno-nationalism; localize benefits of knowledge investment
	Reduced patent fees	50 % discount of patent application, examination, and maintenance costs	Patents	SMEs	IP acquisition; IP maintenance	Needs-based commercial support
	Patent subsidy	50 % of costs for preparing and filing an entity's first patent, capped at 10,000 Euros	First patent application of the SME	SMEs	IP acquisition	Needs-based commercial support
	Tax incentives	Tax credit covering 30 % of first 100 million Euros of qualifying R&D expenses, plus 5 % for any amount exceeding 100 million	Patents stemming from the R&D conducted	Qualifying activities must occur fully in the EU	General (IP acquisition and IP exploitation appear most relevant)	Stimulate spending enabling research and/or commercialization; Localize benefits of knowledge investment

(continued)

Table 2.1 (continued)

Country	Policy mechanisms				Strategic objectives	
	Benefits category	Brief description of benefits	IP requirements	Other major requirements of recipients	Immediate objective(s)	Wider objective(s)
	Tax incentives	Full exemption from CIT for first profitable year and 50 % exemption for the second profitable year	Qualifying companies that file patents	"Innovative Company" (Jeune Entreprise Innovante) status, which is granted for SMEs no more than 8 years old with R&D spending that accounts for at least 15 % of expenses	General (IP acquisition and IP exploitation appear most relevant)	Needs-based commercial support; stimulate spending enabling research and/or commercialization
	Tax incentives (patent box)	Reduced tax rate of 15 % including social tax contributions, with a maximum effective tax rate of 16.245 %, for royalties and capital gains from disposal of IP (except where the sale takes place between a firm's affiliates)	Patents, utility model certificates, associated industrial/manufacturing processes that can be viewed as an essential element of a patent, and plant right certificates. Must be for patents recorded or eligible to be recorded in France Acquired IP is subject to a two-year holding period (no such requirement if IP results from the R&D activities conducted by the company/is self-developed)	Entities subject to tax code in France	IP exploitation	Discourage offshoring of taxable IP assets; localize benefits of knowledge investment

(continued)

Table 2.1 (continued)

Country	Policy mechanisms				Strategic objectives	
	Benefits category	Brief description of benefits	IP requirements	Other major requirements of recipients	Immediate objective(s)	Wider objective(s)
Germany	Patent subsidy	Eligible costs include prior art search, cost-benefit analysis, patent and utility model registration in Germany; and application fees in other countries; and preparation for exploiting the rights. 50 % of eligible costs funded, capped at 8000 EUR per firm. Provided under the SIGNO program Note: the SIGNO program ended at the end of 2015 and has since been replaced by the WIPANO initiative designed by BMWi	Patents or utility models developed through in-house process within 18 month before application	Firms with up to 250 employees and under a certain ceiling for turnover (i.e. SMEs) who have headquarters or production facilities in Germany, and no patent or utility model registrations in the last five years	IP acquisition; IP exploitation	Needs-based commercial support; information failure; stimulate spending enabling research and/or commercialization
	Patent subsidy	Eligible costs include the fees for preliminary examination of the invention (fixed at 375 EU), substantive examination of the invention (including prior art search) (1200 EU), strategy consultation and coordination for patent application preparation (2000 EU), patent application fees (official fees and expenses for patent attorneys) (10,000 EUR) and activities for exploiting an invention (3000 EUR)	Patents and utility models	SMEs which operate exclusively in principal industries with a subsidiary or permanent establishment in Germany, and have no patent or utility model registrations in the five years prior to applying for support	IP acquisition; IP exploitation	Needs-based commercial support; information failure; stimulate spending enabling research and/or commercialization

(continued)

Table 2.1 (continued)

Country	Policy mechanisms				Strategic objectives	
	Benefits category	Brief description of benefits	IP requirements	Other major requirements of recipients	Immediate objective(s)	Wider objective(s)
	Service inventor remuneration and rewards	Employee is entitled to reasonable compensation from the employer, payment of which is due no later than three months after the IP rights to the invention have been granted (required by government, but paid by employer) The specific amount of the remuneration depends on the value of the invention, and the share factor of the inventor, which represents the expected contribution of the inventor	Inventions made during the course of the employment contract and are either the result of the activity of the employee in the company or are mainly based on the company's experience or work Note: Non-exploited patents, including "defensive patents" (preventing competitors to enter with equivalent products) and "storage patents" (patents withheld for future developments) are also remunerable under the German law. The former is seldom remunerated in practice as the criteria are too difficult to meet. The latter is usually remunerated	See columns to left	IP acquisition; IP exploitation	Stimulate spending enabling research and/or commercialization

(continued)

Table 2.1 (continued)

Country	Policy mechanisms				Strategic objectives	
	Benefits category	Brief description of benefits	IP requirements	Other major requirements of recipients	Immediate objective(s)	Wider objective(s)
Hungary	Patent subsidy	Up to 90 % of costs relating to international patent applications are funded under the VICACE Programme	Patents filed abroad	SMEs	IP acquisition (abroad)	Needs-based commercial support
	Tax incentives (patent box)	50 % deduction with a maximum effective tax rate of 9.5 % (deduction capped at 50 % of total pre-tax profits) for royalties and capital gains from disposal of IP	Self-developed or purchased IP including patents, industrial designs, know-how, trademarks, trade names, trade secrets, and authentic works protected by copyright. Some incentive programs require that the IP is registered and owned locally	Entities subject to tax code in Hungary	IP exploitation	Discourage offshoring of taxable IP assets; localize benefits from knowledge investment
Italy	Grants	Incentives for maximizing the economic value of patents. 80 % of eligible costs funded, capped at 70,000 EUR. Eligible costs include consultation fees for patent industrialization, management, and/or transfer	Patents already filed with UIBM, EPO or WIPO and subject to substantive examination	Micro-enterprises and SMEs with a registered and operating office in Italy	IP exploitation	Needs-based commercial support; information failure; stimulate spending enabling research and/or commercialization
	Grants	1000 EUR for design applications in Italy or an EU country; 1000 EUR for a design application in one non-EU country; 3000 EUR for a design application in 1–5 non-EU	Application for registration of a design in Italy, EU countries, or non-EU countries	Micro-enterprises and SMES with a registered and operating office in Italy	IP acquisition (domestically and abroad)	Needs-based commercial support

(continued)

Table 2.1 (continued)

Country	Policy mechanisms				Strategic objectives	
	Benefits category	Brief description of benefits	IP requirements	Other major requirements of recipients	Immediate objective(s)	Wider objective(s)
		countries; 4000 EUR for design applications in more than 5 countries. An additional 1500 EUR provided for design applications filed in the US or China				
	Patent subsidy	Awards for patenting. Up to 5 applications per award type, total award capped at 30,000 EUR Note: incentive discontinued as of December 3rd 2015	Patent applications filed at UIBM, or extension (of one or more applications) of a national patent with the EPO or WIPO (via the UIBM) and subject to substantive examination	Micro-enterprises and SMES with a registered and operating office in Italy	IP acquisition (domestically and abroad)	Needs-based commercial support
	Financing	Risk capital (IPGest) from National Innovation Fund for investments up to 1.5 million EUR over a 12-month period per firm	Self-owned or licensed patents	Micro enterprises and SMEs incorporated as join-stock firms with operating offices in Italy	IP exploitation	Needs-based commercial support; localize benefits of knowledge investment
	Loans	Debt capital from National Innovation Fund in the form of bank loans of a maximum of 3 million EUR per firm and a maximum duration of between 36 months and 10 years. Eligible costs include investments in tangible and intangible assets and costs of consultancy services supplied by external consultants	Patents, designs or utility models, registered and valid in Italy, or patent applications with a negative search report issued by the EPO	Micro enterprises and SMEs located in Italy	IP exploitation	Needs-based commercial support; information failure

(continued)

Table 2.1 (continued)

Country	Policy mechanisms				Strategic objectives	
	Benefits category	Brief description of benefits	IP requirements	Other major requirements of recipients	Immediate objective(s)	Wider objective(s)
	Tax incentives (patent box)	Tax exemption from corporate income tax or local tax of 50 %, making the effective tax rate 15.7 %; the exemption is reduced to 30 % for 2015 and 40 % for 2016 respectively	Patents (granted or in granting process, including invention patents and utility models, patents for plant varieties and semiconductors' topographies), trademarks (registered or in registering process, including collective marks), legally protected models and designs, and software protected by copyrights. Also business, commercial, industrial and scientific information and know-how which can be held as secret and whose protection can be legally enforced can be eligible. Licensing or the direct exploitation of IP required	Individuals that carry out business activities. Italian resident firms or Italian affiliates of non-resident/foreign firms	IP exploitation	Stimulate spending enabling research and/or commercialization; discourage offshoring of taxable IP assets; localize benefits of knowledge investment

(continued)

Table 2.1 (continued)

Country	Policy mechanisms				Strategic objectives	
	Benefits category	Brief description of benefits	IP requirements	Other major requirements of recipients	Immediate objective(s)	Wider objective(s)
	Tax incentives	Tax credit for up to 50 % of incremental eligible expenses with cap of 2.5 million EUR. Eligible costs include those for purchasing technical knowledge and patents	Purchases of technical knowledge and patents	Minimum annual investment of 50,000 EUR but yearly turnover not exceeding 500 million EUR	IP acquisition	Needs-based commercial support
	Trademark subsidy	Trademarks+ program for international trademarks: 80 % of eligible costs covered, capped at 4000 EUR for each application designated in a single country, or 5000 for two or more countries. If the designation is in Russia or China, an amount 10 % + 1000 EUR higher than the aforementioned amount will be provided. A maximum of 15,000 EUR is available per firm under the program. Eligible costs include trademark creation, priority searches, costs of trademark acquisition and licensing in WIPO countries, and WIPO application and registration fees.	Trademarks filed abroad	Micro enterprises and SMEs registered and with operating offices in Italy which are holders or applicants on a national or EU trademark	IP acquisition (abroad); IP exploitation	Needs-based commercial support

(continued)

Table 2.1 (continued)

Country	Policy mechanisms				Strategic objectives	
	Benefits category	Brief description of benefits	IP requirements	Other major requirements of recipients	Immediate objective(s)	Wider objective(s)
		For Community Trademarks registered at OHIM (now EUIPO): 80 % of eligible expenses incurred, capped at 4000 EUR for each trade mark application filed at OHIM (now EUIPO). The facility can be granted up to the maximum of 15,000 EUR per company. Eligible costs include designing the new brand, trademark search and assistance for filing, assistance for the acquisition of the trademark or registered nationally, support for the licensing of the trademark and filing fees. Note: Incentive discontinued as of March 2015				
Ireland	Grants	Enterprise Ireland RDI Fund: up to 50 % of total cost of R&D project funded, with maximum grant of 650,000 EUR for standard projects and 150,000 EUR for small projects, with patent costs not exceeding 20 % of eligible project costs. Eligible	IP granted in Ireland or abroad	Irish firms, particularly SMEs	IP acquisition (domestically or abroad)	Needs-based commercial support

(continued)

Table 2.1 (continued)

Country	Policy mechanisms				Strategic objectives	
	Benefits category	Brief description of benefits	IP requirements	Other major requirements of recipients	Immediate objective(s)	Wider objective(s)
		patent costs include those for preparing, filing, reviewing, validation, and translating the application, among potential others				
	Grants	Commercial case feasibility grant: grants from 10,000 to 15,000 EUR	Foreground IP generated in the project owned by the designated institution	Higher education institutions and research-performing organizations in Ireland	IP exploitation	Stimulate spending enabling research and/or commercialization; localize benefits of knowledge investment
	Patent subsidy	HEI Patent Fund—grants usually capped at 20,000 EUR at second stage filing with initial costs covered by firm; Industry Patent Fund Administration of these funds appear to now be handled by relevant Technology Transfer Offices with support from Enterprise Ireland under the technology transfer strengthening initiative	Patent filing fees	Patents from higher education institutions for HEI Patent Fund; etc.	IP acquisition	Several objectives may apply

(continued)

Table 2.1 (continued)

Country	Policy mechanisms				Strategic objectives	
	Benefits category	Brief description of benefits	IP requirements	Other major requirements of recipients	Immediate objective(s)	Wider objective(s)
	Tax incentives (patent box)	Maximum effective corporate tax rate of 12.5 % but can be reduced to 2.5 %, capped at 80 % of total taxable IP trading profits in any given period Note: new changes proposed in October 2015 to this tax scheme, including reducing tax rate to 6.25 % of overall expenditure and income from qualifying IP	Income arising from the exploitation of IP is eligible. Eligible IP includes: copyrights, trademarks, trade names, brands, brand names, domain names, service marks, patents, registered designs, software and the right to use or deal with software, secret processes or formula, and know-how. Patents should be self-developed, and acquired patents subject to arm's length restrictions for "connected party" acquisitions (see Sect. 10 (6) of Ireland's Taxes Consolidation Act for a definition)	Companies subject to corporate income tax regime	IP exploitation	Discourage offshoring of taxable IP assets; localize benefits of knowledge investment
Latvia	Grants	Micro enterprise and SME new product development program: up to 60 % of eligible costs covered, capped at 14,300 EUR. Eligible costs include those incurred by enforcing IPR	Patents, industrial designs, topographies of semiconductor products	Micro enterprises and SMEs	IP enforcement	Needs-based commercial support

(continued)

Table 2.1 (continued)

Country	Policy mechanisms				Strategic objectives	
	Benefits category	Brief description of benefits	IP requirements	Other major requirements of recipients	Immediate objective(s)	Wider objective(s)
Lithuania	Patent and design fee subsidies	Up to 95 % of eligible costs covered, capped at 100,000 LTL per patent/design registration. Eligible costs included those for filing, use of attorney, search, examination, translation, and maintenance of PCT patent applications in Europe; prior art search with the EPO; and registration, publication, deferment, translation and use of attorney for design registration	European or PCT patent registrations, OHIM's (now EUIPO's) Registered Community Design or international design registrations	SMEs and science and research institutions registered in Lithuania	IP acquisition; IP maintenance	Needs-based commercial support; Information failure
Luxembourg	Tax incentives (patent box)	80 % tax exemption for net income, with a maximum effective tax rate of 5.84 % on royalties and capital gains from exploited IP Note: tax scheme to be abolished as of July 1st 2016	Patents, software, designs, models, trademarks, and domain names. IP registered/owned locally, developed or acquired after December 31st 2007. IP should not be acquired from an affiliated company/eligible IP should be developed in-house.	Entities subject to corporate income tax law in Luxembourg	IP exploitation	Discourage offshoring of taxable IP assets; localize benefits of knowledge investment

(continued)

Table 2.1 (continued)

Country	Policy mechanisms				Strategic objectives	
	Benefits category	Brief description of benefits	IP requirements	Other major requirements of recipients	Immediate objective(s)	Wider objective(s)
Malta	Tax incentives (patent box)	Full tax exemption of royalty payments, advances or similar income from qualifying IP	Owned patents, trademarks, and copyrights (including software). Individual owners of patents must have engaged in the development process	Entity subject to Malta's corporate income tax regime	IP exploitation	Discourage offshoring of taxable IP assets; localize benefits of knowledge investment
	Tax incentives	Tax deductions for R&D expenditures including those for patents (up to 25 % of total project costs)	Costs for registering intellectual property, or R&D related to personnel, instruments and equipment, etc.	Registration of Industrial Property Rights by SMEs attained from the qualified R&D activities carried out from Malta Eligible projects completed within 36 months from the date of approval	IP acquisition	Needs-based commercial support; localize benefits of knowledge investment; stimulate spending enabling research and/or commercialization
	Tax incentives	Tax credit for costs incurred for IP registration, including those for application preparation, translation, and filing and prosecution; and those for defending the validity of the right during opposition proceedings	Patents as well as other industrial property rights	Registration (obtaining and validating) of Industrial Property Rights by SMEs attained from the qualified R&D activities carried out in Malta. Expenses	IP acquisition; IP maintenance	Needs-based commercial support; localize benefits of knowledge investment; stimulate spending enabling research and/or commercialization

(continued)

Table 2.1 (continued)

Country	Policy mechanisms				Strategic objectives	
	Benefits category	Brief description of benefits	IP requirements	Other major requirements of recipients	Immediate objective(s)	Wider objective(s)
		For small-sized enterprises, 70 % of IP costs incurred by industrial research and 45 % of those incurred by experimental development. For medium-sized enterprises, 60 and 35 % respectively Eligible costs include: costs preceding grant of IP rights, translation costs, costs incurred in defending the validity of the right		can be covered within 24 months from the date when the R&D project is finalized		
Netherlands	Tax incentives (patent box)	75–80 % deductions of corporate income tax on royalties and capital gains from exploited patents	Self-developed IP for which a patent or intangible asset resulted from research and development work formally recognized by a Research and Development Certificate. IP owned in the Netherlands	Entities subject to the corporate tax code of the Netherlands	IP exploitation	Discourage offshoring of taxable IP assets; localize benefits of knowledge investment
Spain	Patent subsidy	Up to 80 % of expenses covered, capped at 60,000 EUR per application. For individuals and SMEs, up to 90 % of expenses covered, capped at 65,000 EUR. Eligible costs	Patents and utility models	Private sector, especially individuals and SMEs	IP acquisition	Needs-based commercial support

(continued)

Table 2.1 (continued)

Country	Policy mechanisms				Strategic objectives	
	Benefits category	Brief description of benefits	IP requirements	Other major requirements of recipients	Immediate objective(s)	Wider objective(s)
		include those for filing and translating applications under the EPC or PCT regime. Also can include costs of prior art searches				
	Tax incentives (patent box)	Maximum effective tax rate of 15 % and a 60 % deduction on income from licensing and transfer of IP	Patents, secret formula or processes, designs or models, plans; rights on information of industrial, commercial or scientific nature. Self-developed or acquired IP	Entities subject to the Corporate Taxation Act of Spain	IP exploitation	Discourage offshoring of taxable IP assets; localize benefits of knowledge investment
Sweden	Service inventor remuneration and rewards	(Required by government, but paid by employer.) The employee is entitled to obtain a "reasonable remuneration" even if it is otherwise agreed upon before the coming into existence of the invention	Patentable inventions	Public or private entities that employ the service inventor	IP acquisition; IP exploitation	Stimulate spending enabling research and/or commercialization
Poland	Patent and design fee subsidies	35–75 % of eligible costs covered depending on the size of the entity and nature of project. Subsidies available range from 2000 to 400,000 ZL.	Patents, utility models, and industrial designs	SMEs established in Poland	IP acquisition	Needs-based commercial support

(continued)

Table 2.1 (continued)

Country	Policy mechanisms				Strategic objectives	
	Benefits category	Brief description of benefits	IP requirements	Other major requirements of recipients	Immediate objective(s)	Wider objective(s)
		Eligible costs include those for preparation and filing of IP applications				
	Patent subsidy	Patents+ program: up to 90 % of eligible costs funded, capped at 800,000 ZL per project. Eligible costs include operational costs for patent applications and market research, wages, subcontracting costs and overheads	Patent applications under the EPC or PCT regime in countries other than Poland	SMEs, higher educational institutions and research institutions	IP acquisition (abroad)	Needs-based commercial support
Portugal	Tax incentives (patent box)	50 % deduction with effective tax rate of 15 % for royalties, capital gains and compensations derived from certain IP	Patents, utility models, and industrial designs. Self-developed IP from activities performed in Portugal	Entities subject to corporate tax code of Portugal	IP exploitation	Discourage offshoring of taxable IP assets; localize benefits of knowledge investment
UK	Tax incentives (patent box)	56.5 % deduction with effective tax rate of 10 % for royalties, capital gains from exploiting IP, and damages for IP infringement and insurance payments	UK or European patents and supplementary protection certificates. Patents should be self-developed or exclusively licensed. Eligible entities should be taxpayers actively involved in the patent development cycle	Entities subject to the corporate tax code of the UK	IP exploitation; IP enforcement	Discourage offshoring of taxable IP assets; localize benefits of knowledge investment

(continued)

Table 2.1 (continued)

Country	Policy mechanisms				Strategic objectives	
	Benefits category	Brief description of benefits	IP requirements	Other major requirements of recipients	Immediate objective(s)	Wider objective(s)
	Patent subsidy	Smart offered by innovate UK: the incentive consists of 3 categories: Proof of Market, Proof of Concept, and Development of Prototype. The eligible costs include that for patent filing and maintenance. Patent filing costs for new IP generated by eligible projects, capped at £7500 per project. Patent maintenance is eligible as part of the overhead, the cap of which depends on the category the project belongs to. For Proof of Market, the maximum grant is £25 k, and up to 60 % of total project costs. For Proof of Concept, up to £100 k and 60 % of total project costs. For Development of Prototype, £250 k, up to 35 % of total project costs for medium enterprises and 45 % for small and micro enterprises	Patents	UK-based SMEs engaging in R&D activities	IP acquisition	Needs-based commercial support

Sources various IP and commerce-related laws and other measures of the different countries; Ernst and Young (2014), Deloitte (2014), KPMG (2014), PWC (2014); Erawatch portal (http://erawatch.jrc.ec.europa.eu/); Austria Wirtschaftsservice (http://www.asg.at/); Innoviris (http://www.irsib.irisnet.be/); Wallonia Region incentives/DG06 platform (http://www.ncpwallonie.be/en/ and https://recherche-technologie.wallonie.be/); Ecofunding Platform EU (http://www.ecofundingplatform.eu/); Jaiya and Kalanje (2006), Prud'homme (2012, 2013), Harhoff and Hoisl (2007); Tuotevayla Product Track (http://tuotevayla.fi/en/keksinn%C3%B6n-rahoitus);

Forfas (2014); French INPI (http://www.inpi.fr); Prestation Technologique Réseau (PTR) (http://les-aides.fr.html); Patent France (http://www.francebrevets.com/); Legifrance (http://www.legifrance.gouv.fr/); Bpifrance (http://www.bpifrance.fr/); WIPO (2006), European Commission (2014); German Federal Ministry of Economics and Technology (www.signo-deutschland.de); Lutze (2015, 2016); Irish Finance Bill No. 95 of 2015; Ireland's Taxes Consolidations Act of 1997; Hungarian IP Office (http://www.hipo.gov.hu); Italian Patent and Trademark Office (http://www.uibm.gov.it); Technopolis (2007). Enterprise Ireland (http://www.enterprise-ireland.com/en/); Latvia Investment and Development Agency (http://www.liaa.gov.lv); Lithuanian Science, Innovation and Technology Agency (http://www.mita.lt); MaltaEnterprise (http://www.maltaenterprise.com/en); Polish Agency for Enterprise Development (http://larr.pl/); and National Center for Research and Development of Poland (http://www.ncbir.pl/); House of Commons (2001). Ekos (2007); Scottish Enterprise (http://www.scottish-enterprise.com/); and Innovation UK Technology Strategy Board (https://interact.innovateuk.org/)

Notes

Table 2.1 is not necessarily an exhaustive list of all IP-conditioned government incentives provided in the countries listed, although it is a listing of the incentives for which information was most readily accessible during the research for this chapter. Tax deductions for IP-derived personal income were excluded from the chart given difficultly in confidently identifying the most up-to-date information on these programs for all countries analyzed. Service inventor remuneration rules are only listed when governed by a special legal measure outside the patent law (some EU countries, for example, Austria, France, Italy, and the UK, have service inventor remuneration and reward requirements embedded in their patent laws—see Table 2 in Lutze (2015) for details of inventor remuneration programs in EU countries)

The "wider objectives" column in Table 2.1 attempts to identify the *main wider objectives* of the policies, but other objectives may still apply. See Sect. 2.3.2 in the methodology for a discussion on these and other limitations of the counting analysis used in this chapter based on Table 2.1

Assignment of an objective (immediate or wider) within Table 2.1 of course does not necessarily indicate the proposed policy mechanisms will actually be effective at meeting such objective(s)

[a]Other countries listed in Table 2.1, outside the Czech Republic and China, very well may have programs reducing IP fees for certain entities, but these are not discussed in the table given difficultly in confidentially identifying the most up-to-date information on such programs

[b]Given often differing non-IP-specific requirements (e.g. among provinces) in several IP-conditioned incentives in China, such incentives may have more main wider objectives than those explicitly identified in Table 2.1

References

Abramovitz M (1986) Catching-up, forging ahead, and falling behind. J Econ Hist 46:385–406

Arrow K (1962) Economic welfare and the allocation of resources for invention. In: Nelson R (ed) The rate and direction of inventive activity, economic and social factors. Princeton, NJ, pp 609–625

Bloom N, Schankerman M, Reenen JV (2013) Identifying technology spillovers and product market rivalry. Econometrica 81:1347–1393

Boeing P, Mueller E (2015) Measuring patent quality in international comparison—index development and application to China. Centre for European Economic Research Discussion Paper No. 15-051. Available from http://ftp.zew.de/pub/zew-docs/dp/dp15051.pdf

Chu WW (2011) How the Chinese government promoted a global automobile industry. Industrial and Corporate Change 20(5):1235–1276

Creswell JW (2007) Qualitative inquiry and research method: choosing among five approaches. Sage Publications, Thousand Oaks

Dang J, Motohashi Z (2013) Patent statistics: a good indicator for innovation in China? Patent subsidies program impacts on patent quality. IAM discussion paper series #029. Available from http://pari.u-tokyo.ac.jp/unit/iam/outcomes/pdf/papers_131118.pdf

Deloitte (2014) 2014 Global survey of R&D tax incentives. Deloitte Publications. Available from http://www2.deloitte.com/content/dam/Deloitte/global/Documents/Tax/dttl-tax-global-rd-survey-aug-2014.pdf

de Rassenfosse G, van Pottelsberghe de la Potterie B (2013) The role of fees in patent systems: theory and evidence. J Econ Surv 27(4):696–716

de Saint-Georges M, van Pottelsberghe de la Potterie B (2013) A quality index for patent systems. Res Policy 42:704–719

Ekos (2007) Evaluation of Scottish Enterprise large company R&D Plus scheme. Final report for Scottish Enterprise. Available from http://www.evaluationsonline.org.uk/evaluations/Documents.do?action=download&id=130&ui=browse

Ernst D (2011) Indigenous innovation and globalization: the challenge for China's standardization strategy. UC Institute on Global Conflict and Cooperation and East-West Center Joint Publication. Available from http://www.eastwestcenter.org/sites/default/files/private/ernstindigenousinnovation.pdf

Ernst and Young (2014) Worldwide R&D incentives reference guide. Ernst & Young Publication. Available from http://www.ey.com/Publication/vwLUAssets/EY-worldwide-randd-incentives-reference-guide/$FILE/EY-worldwide-randd-incentives-reference-guide.pdf

European Commission (2014) A study on R&D tax incentives: final report. Available from http://ec.europa.eu/taxation_customs/resources/documents/taxation/gen_info/economic_analysis/tax_papers/taxation_paper_52.pdf

Evers L, Miller H, Spengel C (2015) Intellectual property box regimes: effective tax rates and tax policy considerations. Int Tax Public Finance 22:502–530

Falvey R, Foster N (2006) The role of intellectual property rights in technology transfer and economic growth: theory and evidence. UNIDO Publication. Available from http://www.unido.org/fileadmin/import/60030_05_IPR_rights_in_technology_transfer.pdf

Fink C, Maskus K (2005) Intellectual property and development: lessons from recent economic research. World Bank, Washington, D.C.

Forfas (2014) Evaluation of enterprise supports for research development and innovation [in Ireland]. Report commissioned by the Department of Jobs, Enterprise, and Innovation of Ireland. Available from http://edepositireland.ie/bitstream/handle/2262/69460/17042014-Evaluation_of_Enterprise_Supports_for_Research_Development_and_Innovation-Publication.pdf?sequence=1&isAllowed=y

Fu G (2014) Patent quality control mechanisms at SIPO. Presentation (in Chinese) at IP Key-SIPO experience-sharing roundtable on utility model systems in Europe and China, State Intellectual Property Office of China, Beijing, China, 22 May 2014

Gao L, Li M, Cheng Y (2011) Report on the quality of patents for invention in China. Unpublished report commissioned under the "IPR2" Project
Garcia A, Jiang J, Turley C, Wang M (2016) The evolving environment for intellectual property tax management in China. In: Prud'homme D, Song H (eds) Economic impacts of intellectual property-conditioned government incentives. Springer, Singapore
Gerschenkron A (1962) Economic backwardness in historical perspective. Harvard University Press, Cambridge, Mass
Graham E, Shipan C, Volden C (2013) The diffusion of policy diffusion research in political science. Br J Polit Sci 43:673–701
Greenwald BC, Stiglitz JE (1986) Externalities in economies with imperfect information and incomplete markets. Quart J Econ 101:229–264
Griffith R, Miller H, O'Connell M (2014) Ownership of intellectual property and corporate taxation. J Public Econ 112(1):12–23
Guellec D, van Pottelsberghe de la Potterie B (2007) The economics of the European patent system: IP policy for innovation and competition. Oxford University Press, New York
Hall BH (2009) The use and value of patent rights. Research Paper for UK Economic Value of Intellectual Property Forum, Strategic Advisory Board for Intellectual Property Policy, London
Hall BH (2014) Does patent protection help or hinder technology transfer? In: Ahn S, Hall BH, Lee K (eds) Intellectual property for economic development. Edward Elgar and Korean Development Institute, Northhampton, Mass, pp 11–32
Hall BH, Ziedonis R (2001) The patent paradox revisited: an empirical study of patenting in the US semiconductor industry, 1975–1995. RAND J Econ 32:101–128
Hall BH, Graham S, Harhoff D (2003) Prospects for improving U.S. Patent quality via post-grant opposition. NBER working papers no. 9731. Cambridge, Mass: National Bureau of Economic Research. Available from www.nber.org/papers/w9731
Harhoff D, Hoisl K (2007) Institutionalized incentives for ingenuity: patent value and the German Employees' Inventions Act. Res Policy 36(8):1143–1162
Hart J, Prakash A (2000) Coping with globalization. Routledge, London
Hatch JA (2002) Doing qualitative research in education settings. State University of New York Press, New York
House of Commons (2001) Annual Report on the Industrial Development Act of 192. Government report, Available from https://www.gov.uk/government/uploads/system/uploads/attachment_data/file/235521/0083.pdf
Hu AG, Jefferson GH (2009) A great wall of patents: what is behind China's recent patent explosion? J Dev Econ 90:57–68
Iammarino S, McCann P (2006) The structure and evolution of industrial clusters: transactions, technology and knowledge spillovers. Res Policy 25(7):1018–1036
Jaiya GS, Kalanje CM (2006) Managing patent costs: an overview. WIPO Working Paper. Available from http://www.wipo.int/export/sites/www/sme/en/documents/pdf/managing_patent_costs.pdf
Johnson C (1982) MITI and the Japanese miracle: the growth of industrial policy, 1925–1975. Stanford University Press, Palo Alto
Kalloe V (2016) IP-conditioned tax incentives: the right approach to stimulate innovation and R&D in the European Union? In: Prud'homme D, Song H (eds) Economic impacts of intellectual property-conditioned government incentives. Springer, Singapore
Keller W (2010) International trade, foreign direct investment, and technology spillovers. In: Hall BH, Rosenberg N (eds) Handbook of the economics of innovation, vol 2. North-Holland/Elsevier, Oxford, pp 794–829
KPMG (2014) R&D incentives—adding value across ASPAC. KPMG Publications. Available from https://assets.kpmg.com/content/dam/kpmg/pdf/2015/03/aspac-rd-incentives-guide-overview.pdf
Lee K, Kim YK (2010) IPR and technological catch-up in Korea. In: Odagiri H, Goto A, Sunami A, Nelson R (eds) Intellectual property rights, development, and catch-up: an international comparative study. Oxford University Press, UK, pp 133–167

Lei Z, Sun Z, Wright B (2013) Are Chinese patent applications politically driven? Evidence from China's domestic patent applications. OECD Published Working Paper. Available from http://www.oecd.org/site/stipatents/4-3-Lei-Sun-Wright.pdf

Li X (2012) Behind the recent surge of Chinese patenting: an institutional view. Res Policy 41:236–249

Long C, Wang J (2016) Evaluating patent promotion policies in China: consequences for patent quantity and quality. In: Prud'homme D, Song H (eds) Economic impacts of intellectual property-conditioned government incentives. Springer, Singapore

Long T, Yun L, Fangjuan Y (2013) Subsidy policy that supports coordinated development of patent quality and application quantity. Sci Technol Prog Policy 30:99–104

Lopez A (2009) Innovation and appropriability, empirical evidence and research agenda. In: The economics of intellectual property. WIPO, Geneva. Available from http://www.wipo.int/edocs/pubdocs/en/economics/1012/wipo_pub_1012.pdf

Lutze O (2015) Comparison on employee invention laws and regulations—Germany vs. China. Report for IP key project. Available from http://www.ipkey.org/en/resources/ip-information-centre/38-resource-type/3735-comparison-on-employee-invention-laws-and-regulations-germany-vs-china

Lutze O (2016) Incentives for Chinese inventors: a proposal for a new inventor remuneration scheme with German elements. In: Prud'homme D, Song H (eds) Economic impacts of intellectual property-conditioned government incentives. Springer, Singapore

Martin S, Scott J (2000) The nature of innovation market failure and the design of public support for private innovation. Res Policy 29:437–447

Maskus K (1997) The role of intellectual property rights in encouraging foreign direct investment and technology transfer. Prepared for the conference public-private initiatives after TRIPS: designing a global Agenda. Available from http://siteresources.worldbank.org/INTRANETTRADE/Resources/maskus2.pdf

Miles MM, Huberman AM (1994) Qualitative data analysis. Sage Publications, Thousand Oaks

Morin JF, Gold E (2014) An integrated model of legal transplantation: the diffusion of intellectual property law in developing countries. Int Stud Quart 58:781–792

Naughton B (2007) The Chinese economy: transitions and growth. MIT Press, Cambridge

OECD (2004) Promoting SMEs for development. Second OECD conference of ministers responsible for SMEs. Available from http://www.oecd.org/cfe/smes/31919278.pdf

OECD (2010) R&D tax incentives: rationale, design, evaluation. OECD Publishing. Available from http://www.oecd.org/sti/ind/46352862.pdf

OECD (2011) Attractiveness for innovation: location factors for international investment. OECD Publishing. Available from http://dx.doi.org/10.1787/9789264104815-en

OECD (2014a) BEPS action 7: preventing the artificial avoidance of PE status. OECD Publishing revised discussion draft. Available from http://www.oecd.org/tax/treaties/revised-discussion-draft-beps-action-7-pe-status.pdf

OECD (2014b) National intellectual property systems, innovation and economic development: with perspectives on Colombia and Indonesia. OECD Publications. Available from http://www.oecd-ilibrary.org/science-and-technology/national-intellectual-property-systems-innovation-and-economic-development_9789264204485-en

OECD (2015) Countering harmful tax practices more effectively, taking into account transparency and substance. OECD/G20 base erosion and project shifting project paper. Available from http://www.oecd-ilibrary.org/docserver/download/2314271e.pdf?expires=1443166889&id=id&accname=guest&checksum=2BB95B69C8AA1A6B0FB0D975573988CC

Ostry S, Nelson R (1995) Techno-nationalism and techno-globalism: conflict and cooperation. Brookings Institution, Washington D.C

Prud'homme D (2012) Dulling the cutting edge: how patent-related policies and practices hamper innovation in China. European Chamber, Beijing, China

Prud'homme D (2013) China's indigenous IP policies—here to stay? Managing Intellect Prop 233:24–27

Prud'homme D (2014a) Rethinking what international patenting data really says about Chinese innovation. J Intellect Prop Law Pract 9:986–992
Prud'homme D (2014b) Creating a "model" utility model system: a comparative analysis of the utility model patent systems in Europe and China. IP Key project working paper series 2014. Available from http://www.ipkey.org/en/ip-law-document/item/3275-creating-a-model-utility-model-system-a-comparative-analysis-of-the-utility-model-systems-in-europe-and-china
Prud'homme D (2015) China's shifting patent landscape and State-led patenting strategy. J Intellect Prop Law Pract 10:619–625
PWC (2014) Global tax accounting services—patent box and technology incentives: tax and financial reporting considerations. PWC Publications. Available from https://www.pwc.com/gx/en/tax/publications/assets/pwc-patent-box-and-technology-incentives-tax-and-financial-reporting-considerations.pdf
Samuels R (1994) "Rich Nation, Strong Army": national security and the technological transformation of Japan. Cornell University Press, Ithaca, New York
Schumpeter J (1942) Capitalism, socialism, and democracy. Harper & Brothers, New York
Schwandt TA (2001) Dictionary of qualitative inquiry. Sage Publications, Thousand Oaks
Song H (2013) Zizhu chuangxin nengli jianshe yu zhishi chanquan fazhan (Indigenous innovation capability-building and the development of intellectual property rights) (in Chinese). Chinese Academy of Sciences Intellectual Property Rights Press, Beijing
Song H, Wan J, Reng Z (2010) Woguo zhanlue xing xinxing chanye neihan tezheng, chanye xuanze yu fazhan zhengce yanjiu (Characteristics of China's strategic emerging industries, industry selection, and development policy research) (in Chinese). Sci Technol Develop 5 (9):1–14
Song H, Li Z, Xu D (2016) The upsurge of domestic patent applications in China: is R&D expenditure or patent subsidy policy responsible?. In: Prud'homme D, Song H (eds) Economic impacts of intellectual property-conditioned government incentives. Springer, Singapore
Suttmeier R, Yao X (2011) China's IP transition: rethinking intellectual property rights in a rising China. NBR Special Report #29. Available from http://china-us.uoregon.edu/pdf/IP_report.pdf
Technopolis (2007) Effects of counterfeiting on EU SMEs and the review of public and private IPR enforcement initiatives and resources. Report for the European Commission
UN (2005) Taxation and technology transfer: Key issues. UNCDTAD/ITE/IPC/2005/9. Available from http://unctad.org/en/Docs/iteipc20059_en.pdf
Wagner PR (2009) Understanding patent quality mechanisms. Federal Trade Commission. Available from http://www.ftc.gov/bc/workshops/ipmarketplace/apr17/docs/rwagner2.pdf
WIPO (2004) Intellectual property for business. WIPO manual. Available from www.wipo.int/export/sites/www/sme/en/ip_business/…/ip_business.doc
WIPO (2006) IP asset development and management: a key strategy for economic growth. Available from http://www.wipo.int/edocs/pubdocs/en/intproperty/896/wipo_pub_896.pdf
WIPO (2011) The changing face of innovation. Available from http://www.wipo.int/edocs/pubdocs/en/intproperty/944/wipo_pub_944_2011.pdf
Xiao Y, Tylecote A, Liu J (2013) Why not greater catch-up by Chinese firms? The impact of IPR, corporate governance and technology intensity on late-comer strategies. Res Policy 42:749–764
Xinhua (2014a) April 22. China sees larger proportion of invention patent applications. Xinhua. Available from http://news.xinhuanet.com/english/china/2014-04/22/c_133281638.htm
Xinhua (2014b) April 24. China eyes quality patent amid application surge. Xinhua. Available from http://www.chinaipr.gov.cn/newsarticle/news/government/201404/1810614_1.html
Xu L, Munari F (2016) The impact of public support for SMEs' patenting activity: empirical evidence from Italy. In: Prud'homme D, Song H (eds) Economic impacts of intellectual property-conditioned government incentives. Springer, Singapore
Yin RK (2003) Case study research: design and methods. Sage Publications, Thousand Oaks
Yu P (2009) Global intellectual property order and its undetermined future. WIPO J 1(1):1–15

Yu P (2013) Five oft-repeated questions about China's rise as a patent power. Cardozo Law Rev De Novo 78:81–88

Yu P (2015) The Chinese intellectual property system at 35: transplant, transformation and what's next. Presentation at Hanken school of economics conference on legal transplant for innovation and creativity: China and the evolution of IP norms, Helsinki, Finland, 4 Dec 2015

Zhu X (2012) A dialectical understanding of the quality and quantity of patents in China (in Chinese). Paper presented at the 7th Bayer-Tongji University IPR Forum, Shanghai, China, 9 Nov 2012

Chapter 3
IP-Conditioned Subsidies in Germany and the EU: Operation, Dangers, and Recommendations

Johannes Holzer

Abstract If crafted correctly and in compliance with international laws, IP-conditioned monetary support policies for the development and legal protection of inventions may encourage technological development. Based upon an analysis of legal texts, court decisions, a review of the literature, and practitioner/government administrator perspectives, this chapter analyzes whether various German IP-conditioned support programs relating to patent applications, tax, and other State and private support programs for inventors constitute 'subsidies', according to the EU definition of the concept. Furthermore, this chapter makes general observations as to the ability of these programs to meet their intended objectives. In conclusion, although such German policies generally work to meet their objectives and do not usually conflict with EU rules governing subsidies, some improvements could be made.

Keywords Patent application fees · European union · IP protection · Subsidies · Subsidies control · Tax law

3.1 Introduction

3.1.1 Improving Conditions for IP Development

Many countries seek to improve IP protection in order to create a better environment for the development of technology. In this regard, IP protection can be a powerful driving force for the overall economy (Idris 2003; Owczarczuk 2012; Qu 2012; Wang and Sallet 2013).

Johannes Holzer: Director of Government, German Patent and Trade Mark Office in Munich (and former Head of the Utility Model and Topography Section, German Patent and Trade Mark Office)

J. Holzer (✉)
German Patent and Trade Mark Office, Munich, Germany
e-mail: johannes.holzer@ymail.com

D. Prud'homme and H. Song (eds.), *Economic Impacts of Intellectual Property-Conditioned Government Incentives*, DOI 10.1007/978-981-10-1119-1_3

However, IP protection is only one aspect of a comprehensive approach to create higher quality inventions in order to potentially drive the economy forward to further technological development. In this regard, the improvement of the working conditions of inventors appears to be at least as important as the protection of IP rights. IP filing fees can be expensive and can be an important factor in the choice of IP right, or whether to file for an IP right at all. A common goal of inventors is to license their IP rights, but at the same time it is necessary to pay taxes on related profits. If crafted correctly and in compliance with international laws, policies lowering the taxes on license fees may promote inventive activity, and subsidies from the State and further support from private organizations related to the innovation process may also encourage innovation. The aim of this chapter is to evaluate if these policies can be improved in Germany and to provide general recommendations to policy makers.

3.1.2 Policies to Improve IP Development

Improved conditions for inventors can lead to more and higher quality inventions. For example, certain countries have policies to encourage the filing of patents, which include subsidies, tax policies, and governmental procurement and standard-making processes (Wang and Sallet 2013).

The literature concerning these policies is quite limited, although it appears that some policies relate to inventive activities from the conception of the idea to the development of the invention and its usage. If inventors want to obtain a protected IP right, they have to file an application at the Patent Office. Several policies aimed at enhancing IP development are directed at improving the filing procedure and application process. The support provided to inventors by the State or private organizations intended to stimulate inventive activity, including inventive-friendly tax systems, reimbursements for employee inventors, and promotional activities, can be considered by governments to be useful tools for improving the conditions for inventors and companies.

However, at the same time, certain studies have identified problems with a number of IP-related government programs intended to encourage inventive activity. For example, one study discussed possible improvements to the European patent system concerning the correlation of low application fees for patents and the increasing annual renewal fees. The assistance provided to applicants of limited financial means during the patent application procedure has also been criticized, as it is argued that there is no correlation between the assistance provided and the quality of the resulting IP right (Blind et al. 2009). The organization of institutions providing patent information to applicants has also been criticized and it has been proposed that more cooperation between the State and independent promotional programs could be beneficial (Blind et al. 2009).

Another study has argued that taxation policy in Germany is not beneficial for inventors because their research efforts and creativity are not adequately rewarded (Zacher 2011). It has also been proposed to reduce the individual tax rate of the inventor by spreading income from qualifying inventive activity over several years (Kunzmann 2012).

Others have contended that some patent applications may only be being filed for the purpose of receiving government subsidies, and as such these subsidies are only weakly correlated to break-through innovation (Prud'homme 2012; Wang and Sallet 2013). The authors propose that subsidies should be better tailored to boost high quality innovation, rather than preferentially supporting low quality innovation. It is important to note that the number of patents alone does not directly correlate with the quality of innovation. However, several studies suggest that there may be a correlation between subsidies for patent application fees and other subsidies and the low quality of granted IP rights, and that low application fees and other subsidies may encourage the filing of IP rights if there is no adequate control over the quality of the IP right finally granted (Prud'homme 2012, 2014; Dang and Motohashi 2013; Radauer et al. 2015; Song et al. 2016).

3.1.3 Germany as a Model Country for IP Development

Germany is often looked upon as a global leader in innovation, and as a pioneer of various IP laws and policies. Germany is also a Member State of the EU, with its strong supranational subsidies control, which demonstrates the limit of State subsidies within a common market.

As previously discussed, literature concerning IP-conditioned incentives is limited, and this is also true of German IP-conditioned incentives. Therefore, this chapter seeks to close some of the gaps in the literature by providing answers to the following questions. Firstly, does Germany's support of invention, including IP-conditioned government incentives, conflict with EU rules? Secondly, notwithstanding any potential legal challenges, what key challenges do these programs face in meeting their objectives? Finally, what are the policy implications of these findings?

Several countries within the EU and indeed around the world may have laws and policies similar to those present in Germany. Therefore, an analysis of the advantages and disadvantages of the German system may be useful as a basis to provide general recommendations for policymakers and to demonstrate the possible economic impact of IP-conditioned government incentives. This chapter makes a useful contribution concerning how the application procedure and associated fees of the German Patent and Trade Mark Office, in addition to the taxation system and available subsidies in Germany, affects inventive activity and how these policies align with relevant EU regulations. Following this introduction and an overview of the methodology used, this chapter will consider EU restrictions on subsidies and observations on the effectiveness of IP-conditioned incentives. The chapter will also consider the legal and economic challenges of programs supporting inventions and IP in Germany. Finally, concluding remarks and policy recommendations will be given.

3.2 EU Restrictions on Subsidies and Observations on the Effectiveness of IP-Conditioned Incentives

In this section the basic framework for assessing whether different German IP-conditioned support programs conflict with supranational legal obligations will be outlined. This will include discussion of EU subsidy regulations that are applicable to all State-given subsidies. The drafting of IP-conditioned incentives in a form that does not optimally allow them to meet their objectives will also be considered.

3.2.1 EU Rules on Subsidies

3.2.1.1 Principles of the EU Related to Subsidies

Despite political renewals of both foreign and security policy provided by the Treaty of Maastricht (1991), the concept of the Common Market remains an important key principle of the EU. Section 107(1) of the European Community Treaty (in the form of the Treaty of Lisbon) determines that all State subsidies, which can undermine the competition in the Common Market by promoting certain enterprises or production branches, are forbidden. The first form of this rule, the former Section 87 of the European Community Treaty, provided only a few exceptions. However, following various insolvencies, where enterprises had been required to pay back certain subsidies, this rule and restriction was reviewed by the European Commission and subsequently approved in the Treaty of Lisbon.

The driving rationale behind these regulations is to achieve equal economic working conditions between all EU Member States. For example, if economic support is provided in only one or several Member States, then an imbalance between various regions within the EU could occur. Such an imbalance may disturb the stable economic growth of all Member States and could affect the free transfer of goods, competition and trade within the EU (Schwarze 2007). Only those subsidies with the potential to affect these principles are forbidden. Therefore, subsidies directed at promoting culture and cultural heritage are permissible.

EU regulations do not define the term ‘subsidies’ (Schwarze 2007). However, Section 107(1) of the European Community Treaty the European Court interprets ‘subsidies’ as any and all State measures with the aim of promoting enterprises in either a direct or indirect way, or to give economic advantage, which the enterprise would not have achieved under regular and normal market conditions (Möhlenkamp 2014).[1] However, it is necessary to examine this interpretation of ‘subsidy’ on a case-by-case basis (Montag and Bonin 2012). In this context, only

[1]European Court, 2003/07/24—C-280/00 (Altmark Trans).

the real working of the measures and not the intention of the promoting State is relevant.[2] Consequentially, all direct subsidies provided by Member States, including those for inventions and start-ups, are to be considered subsidies in the sense of the definition, whereas other subsidies not provided by the State cannot violate the regulations of the EU. Subsidies that fall below the threshold of EUR 7.5 million per undertaking, project or feasibility study are not to be considered subsidies according to the aforementioned definition (Jaensch 2013). However, this limit has to be considered on a case-by-case basis because it forms the *de minimis* rule of the EU subsidy regulations.

The concept of a subsidy creates a very unique problem in the taxation system. If tax advantages are compared with 'classic' subsidies, clearly there is no direct transfer of money from the State to the taxpayer. Nevertheless, tax exemptions can resemble subsidies in the sense of Section 107(1) of the European Community Treaty, if they privilege a taxpayer and provide an exemption from paying certain taxes in comparison to all other taxpayers. The European Court will examine on a case-by-case basis whether a tax regulation provides a 'selective' tax advantage in comparison to the 'normal' tax regulations, the so-called 'reference system' (Seer 2014). A 'selective' advantage will be found if the tax regulation in question is different to the Member State's common taxation system, and provides a distinction between taxpayers who are, in respect of the aim of the national Tax Law, in a comparative real and legal situation.[3] Therefore, unjustified tax exemptions for only a group of taxpayers are prohibited by EU regulations. In contrast, no 'selective' advantage will be found if the provided advantage is justified by the common aim of the national Tax Law.[4] This common aim could include influencing certain taxpayer behavior. For example, a reduction of taxes for electric cars would lead to increase in sales of those cars.

3.2.1.2 Legal Exceptions from Forbidden Subsidies

Exceptions to the general rule concerning subsidies are provided by Section 107(2) of the European Community Treaty for the 'New Countries' in Germany, to equalize structural disadvantages due to the reunification of Germany. The European Commission can also assume that no violation of Section 107(1) of the European Community Treaty has occurred if the subsidies provided serve only to promote economic growth in areas with exceptionally low income or high unemployment, or to promote projects with a common European interest or to correct considerable disturbances in the economic life of a Member State (see Section 107 (3) of the European Community Treaty). This exception also concerns subsidies for the promotion of the development of certain economic activities that do not change

[2]European Court, 2012/06/05—C-124/10 (Eléctricitë de France).

[3]European Court, 2013/07/18—C-6/12 (P-Oy).

[4]European Court, 2011/11/15—C-106, 107/09 (Gibraltar).

trading conditions in a manner that is not in the common interest of the EU. As previously stated, this rule is in accordance with the fundamental principles of the EU and the Common Market (Schwarze 2007). Section 107(3) of the European Community Treaty further stipulates that any subsidies directed at the promotion of culture and cultural heritage should not work against the principles of the Common Market, and therefore should be approved by the European Commission (Schwarze 2007). The European Commission's standpoint is that an enterprise promoted by such subsidies can only rely on their duration if the procedure set out in Section 108 of the European Community Treaty has been complied with.

3.2.1.3 Consequences of Forbidden Subsidies

In general, any promoting State (in Germany this may be the Federal Republic of Germany itself, or one of the German Federal States such as Bavaria) is not allowed to pay subsidies unless the European Commission has approved the payment in accordance with Section 108(3) of the European Community Treaty (Möhlenkamp 2014; Soltész 2014),[5] or if the payment is permitted by Section 107(2) of the European Community Treaty.[6] The procedure for repayment is regulated by the 'Procedure Code in Subsidies Cases', following Section 109 of the European Community Treaty (Soltész 2014).[7] If the European Commission detects any non-permissible subsidies, it will apply a 'negative decision' against the State in non-compliance with the rules of the European Community Treaty and will require the State to obtain repayment from the promoted enterprise. As a consequence, the violating State will in effect act like a private creditor, and is not permitted to disclaim or write-off the repayment. This is because from the viewpoint of the European Community the immediate repayment of subsidies with interest,[8] usually within a two-month period, is a logical and powerful mechanism to restore the market to the position before any subsidies were paid to the promoted enterprise.[9]

Furthermore, European law does not permit the application of any national laws that would aggravate the requirement for repayment of the subsidies, nor does European law permit any national law from having the effect of making the repayment 'practically impossible' (Schwarze 2007). Instead, the promoting State is

[5]European Court, 2004/06/21—Rs C-110/02.

[6]European Court, 2013/11/21—Rs C-284/12 (Lufthansa).

[7]Decree No. 659/1999 from 1999/03/27 about special orders for the application of Sec. 93 (now Sec. 88) European Community Treaty, Office Journal L 83/1.

[8]European Court, 2006/10/05—Rs C-232/05.

[9]European Court, 1999/06/17—Rs C-75/97; European Court, 2003/06/26—Rs C-404/00; European Court, 2004/06/21—Rs C-110/02.

required to undertake all appropriate measures to secure the repayment and to ensure that the subsidies are in reality returned.[10] As a consequence, the promoting State is not permitted to give any further new subsidies in an effort to compensate the repayment order of the European Commission.[11] The State is also required to obtain repayment, even in the event of an insolvency procedure, or from any third parties such as a succession enterprise who may have profited from the subsidies (Ehricke 2003). Please refer to the Annex for further discussion on the EU's regulation of subsidies.

3.2.2 *The Effectiveness of IP-Conditioned Incentives*

As previously mentioned, government support programs directed at inventions and inventive activity can be constructed and drafted in a way that does not optimally enable them to meet their stated objectives. This principle forms the basis of the general observations set out and discussed in the remainder of this chapter concerning the ability of various Germany IP-conditioned incentives to meet their objectives.

3.3 Methodology

The research presented in this chapter attempts to describe the structure of law in relation to the IP-right application procedure, taxes and the law of subsidies. Sources of research include legal texts in addition to practitioner and academic literature. Certain aspects are explained by reference to Court decisions concerning tax law, and the law of the EU. In addition to a review of relevant literature and Court decisions, the professional experience of the author, including 25 years as a judge and administration officer, contributes to the basis for the multifaceted analysis of the application procedure of the German Patent and Trade Mark Office, the operation of German tax law, and any possible conflicts between German support programs and EU rules for subsidies. This is both useful and necessary in order to examine the promotional conditions of State and non-State programs, and to explain how these programs work in practice. Analysis conducted on this basis will demonstrate how different German support programs for inventions, including IP rights, meet their objectives and/or face challenges in meeting those objectives.

[10]European Court, 2006/10/05—Rs C-232/05; see also European Court, 2005/05/12—Rs C-415/03 (Olympic Airways).

[11]European Court, 2004/06/21—Rs C-110/02; European Court, 2004/06/21—Rs C-110/02.

3.4 Analysis of the Legal and Economic Challenges of Programs Supporting Inventions and IP in Germany

3.4.1 Subsidies Concerning the Patent Application Procedure

Overview and assessment of conflicts with EU rules on subsidies

It is often quite expensive to file a patent application. The inventor has to pay the costs of the application procedure itself, annual renewal fees, and applicable fees for scientific research and patent attorneys. The following overview seeks to identify if there are any subsidies available for applicants to assist with the costs associated within the patent application procedure.

The costs associated with the application procedure of the German Patent and Trade Mark Office, including protection for the first year, are relatively low compared with the costs in other countries. The cost of filing a patent application is EUR 60 and includes up to ten claims, and the cost of a utility model application is EUR 40. A reduction of EUR 10 is also applied when the electronic filing procedure is used. The low fees are intended to provide easy access to the protection of IP for all inventors. Although the intentions of the legislator are not explicitly stated, it can be assumed that hidden subsidies of sorts are in operation, because the low application fees do not cover the actual costs of the examination procedure conducted by the German Patent and Trade Mark Office. The perception that the low application fees are intended to promote inventive activity is correct because the real examination costs are only partly covered by year-on-year increases to the annual renewal fee (Böhm et al. 2007).

The annual renewal fees for IP rights increase year-on-year. For example, the renewal fee for utility models increases from EUR 250 after three years and then increases to EUR 530 after eight years. The legal and policy reasoning for these increases is not to give subsidies to the inventor during the early years, but rather to request the inventor to verify his IP right and to provide an opportunity for considering a withdrawal or a non-maintenance action in the situation that the right becomes worthless. Therefore, the rules concerning the annual renewal fees have the prime function of protecting the German Patent and Trade Mark Office, with its limited staff and resourcing, from unnecessary evaluation and administrative work for inventions of minor economic value.[12] No subsidies are intended or implicated by the operation of the renewal in this system, and so therefore there are no conflicts with any applicable EU rules or regulations.

[12]Reasons to the amendment of the Patent Law, in: Journal for Patent and Trade Mark Law (original title: Blatt für Patent-, Muster- und Zeichenwesen), 1967, p. 251.

Practical experience demonstrates that due to the way they are structured, annual renewal fees work in practice like subsidies in the first years following grant of the patent, during which time the inventor is usually starting to commercialize his invention. Practice also shows that initially the inventor usually requires some time to license his IP right, and so following an initial period it is to be expected that the hidden subsidies will decrease and the cost of renewal fees increase during the lifetime of patent protection.

In Germany, patent attorneys fees are comparatively high and are usually between EUR 2000 and EUR 4500 depending on the complexity of the patent application. The fees for other IP rights, such as utility models, are a little lower. There are no subsidies available within the fee structure arrangement for patent attorneys, and therefore there is no conflict with EU subsidies regulations.

If an applicant is of limited financial means, provisions under Section 129 of the Patent Law and Section 21(2) of the Utility Model Law provide the applicant with financial assistance to cover legal expenses, in accordance with civil procedure rules. Such financial assistance includes payment of patent attorney fees and the associated costs of filing the application, but no other costs are covered, including costs incurred to obtain technical drawings and costs concerning research of the patent examiner. It is important to note that young inventors below a certain age do not automatically receive financial assistance, as the financial status of their parents will be taken into account. Therefore, parents above a certain financial worth are required to pay application fees on behalf of their children, whereas young inventors from families assessed to have a lower financial worth may receive financial assistance.

The financial assistance potentially available to poorer applicants is not primarily aimed at promoting inventiveness, but rather to ensure participation of such applicants in a procedure before a public office. Therefore, the rules concerning assistance for poorer applicants can be viewed as the implementation of the principles of constitutional democracy according to Section 20(3) of the German Constitution. Such assistance has been criticized in the literature, mainly due to the fact that there appears to be no correlation between financial assistance and the quality of the IP right eventually granted (Blind et al. 2009). Nevertheless, such a provision of subsidies can be successful in certain situations and may help lift some inventors out of poverty due to the eventual commercialization of their invention. This may be particularly true in the field of utility models that are comparatively inexpensive to apply for and provide a quick IP right of high validity.

The law also provides assistance for the maintenance of IP rights. Such assistance is only available if there is a real prospect that the invention will be commercially exploited. Therefore, it is necessary for the inventor to sell a license of his IP right to at least a few interested parties, and to be able to demonstrate that he has carried out this action by letters of intent or acceptance.[13]

[13]Federal Patent Court, 2014/5/20–35 W (pat) 23/13; 2014/5/20–35 W (pat) 20/13; 2013/12/19—35 W (pat) 24/13.

The German Patent and Trade Mark Office operates a technical information center (TIZ) from its Berlin office. Similar information is provided by 23 patent information centers (PIZ) that are located in larger German cities. The organization of these centers is very different: some centers are part of a University, for example the library, or of a regional IP support agency, a technical examination agency (TÜV), a Chamber of Commerce, or even part of the administration of a German Federal State (Blind et al. 2009). These centers offer different forms of assistance to inventors. For example, they may provide a technical overview of the invention and some practical assistance concerning the application procedure, but no financial assistance is available. Further, due to the fact that these centers are organized outside the general concept of the State, it is unlikely that the State intended subsidies to be provided by the establishment of these centers. Rather, it is likely that the intended aim of these centers is to provide assistance for applicants and the German Patent and Trade Mark Office by promoting the submission of pre-checked patent applications. Therefore, EU subsidies regulations do not affect this structure.

Nevertheless, these centers are very helpful to private inventors and are working in practice as subsidies (Idris 2003). Similar assistance and incentives are also provided by the private sector (see Sect. 3.4.5).

Other observations on effectiveness

Although there are no official State-sponsored subsidies, patent application fees and maintenance fees for granted patents are relatively low in Germany. In this regard, no change to the current system appears to be necessary. This is because the way application and annual renewal fees are structured ensures that they have the same effect as subsidies in practice. It is noted that the situation is similar in other countries with low patent application fees (see Sect. 3.4.1). In countries where application fees are relatively high, policymakers may consider reducing fees in order to promote inventive activity. Nevertheless, application fees should stay within reasonable limits because a reduction to a very low level may promote very low quality patent and utility model applications (Dang and Motohashi 2013; Prud'homme 2014; Radauer et al. 2015; Song et al. 2016). A further study has discussed the effect of providing patent application subsidies without controlling the quality of IP rights eventually granted (Wang and Sallet 2013). The application fee system can be improved by increasing annual renewal fees over time. Such an incremental increase will support the quality of granted IP rights because inventors are unlikely to continue to pay such fees for their non-licensable inventions year-on-year, and so these IP rights are likely to lapse.

A critical issue concerns the fees of patent attorneys, as these are difficult for policymakers to change. Nevertheless, policymakers may consider offering assistance to inventors with limited financial means for the payment of necessary patent attorney fees. Although such assistance is often criticized because it may lead to patent applications of lower quality, they can be justified according to constitutional principles, and in practice they do operate as subsidies. Policymakers in countries with legal systems that do not have these provisions may consider recommending them.

3.4.2 Deductions in the Costs of Filing for Certain Types of Entities

Overview and assessment of conflicts with EU rules on subsidies

As for every procedure of the Courts and official offices, the Federal Republic of Germany and federal corporations are exempt from the costs of the German Patent and Trade Mark Office according to Section 4(1) of the Regulation of the Administrative Costs of the German Patent and Trade Mark Office. This rule is also effective not only for the German Federal States and its federal corporations, but also for communities and international legal associations, including WIPO (Prud'homme 2014). However, applications from private legal entities, such as limited companies whose principal shareholder is the Federal Republic of Germany or a German Federal State, are not exempted.

Applications by the German Federal States and related communities are very rare. Therefore, the rules concerning fee exemptions are in practice only effective in the field of military inventions of the German Federal Armed Forces. Information concerning these inventions is rarely in the public domain as it is usually protected by information security legislation, according to Section 50 of the Patent Law, and such applications are reviewed and processed by a special unit of the German Patent and Trade Mark Office ('Office 99'). Nevertheless, it can be assumed that the reason for such fee exemptions for State or State-related institutions are that they are all State structures, as is the German Patent and Trade Mark Office. Therefore, exempting a fee payment from one State body to another is merely an administrative simplification and cannot be seen as an application fee subsidy. Therefore, these provisions do not violate EU subsidies regulations.

Other observations on effectiveness

Exemptions from the payment of application fees for the State or State-related entities are reasonable because they can be justified as a simplification of the system which is itself administered by staff employed by the State. Legal systems that do not have such exemptions for State bodies and institutions may consider adopting such regulations on the premise that the State should not be liable to pay on its own costs.

3.4.3 Tax Law and Inventive Activity

Overview and assessment of conflicts with EU rules on subsidies

Unfortunately, the German taxation system is probably one of the most complicated systems in the world. Therefore, it comes as no surprise that over 90 % of world literature concerning tax has been written in Germany. Individual personal income tax is comparatively high with rates of up to 33 % of taxable income. The only opportunity for inventors to reduce their effective tax rate in respect of the commercialization of their invention is to claim deductions from their taxable income for expenses related to their inventive activity. In general, this principle is also applicable to companies (refer to end of this section concerning corporate taxation). However, before tax deductions are considered, it is necessary to evaluate whether the inventor should pay any tax at all in relation to his invention.

An inventor is not required to pay tax on license fees received from a unique invention, because taxation on income is only possible if the taxpayer has the intention to generate sustained profit from his invention from the beginning of the inventive activity. An example of such income tax relief is provided by a case decided by the Münster Financial Court.[14] A group of engineers for communication and security techniques invented a new method for labeling optical data storage devices. However, the engineers had not originally set out to invent a new method, as the idea had simply arisen during a discussion over dinner. Nevertheless, the engineers took the opportunity to sell their idea. The Financial Court decided that in general the engineers did not have the necessary intention to generate sustained profit from inventions but had instead made the discovery and invented the new method by chance. Therefore, they were not required to pay tax on any of the generated income.

The decision of the Financial Court demonstrates that exemptions from paying income tax are the consequence of the theoretical basis of the German income tax system, which follows the theory of 'net worth growth of assets'.[15] According to this principle, tax is only payable on the growth of assets, which is achieved by the ongoing effort and intention of the taxpayer and not by a single asset growth event, even if it leads to a registered IP right and the payment of license fees. Although this can result in an inventor benefiting from non-taxed profit for a single invention created by chance, there are no subsidies involved.

The inventor's income will be the basis for taxation (taxable income), if he is a freelancer or generates the income from his business enterprise, according to Sections 15 and 18 of the Income Tax Law (Zacher 2011). In both situations, claiming allowable deductions from income can reduce the amount of income tax payable. Deducting all allowable costs involved in creating and registering the invention can reduce taxable income. For example, patent attorney and German or foreign Patent Office fees, the costs for technical drawings and technical or scientific research for development of the invention in a very wide sense, can be deducted. Expenses can also be deducted for the employment of assistants, obtaining literature, travel, research, and the negotiation or drafting of licenses. The costs incurred in creating inventions can also be utilized in the tax balance, if the inventor is obliged to prepare an annual balance statement, according to Section 5 of the Income Tax Law.

Certain provisions of taxation law can resemble subsidies if the State seeks to direct economic behavior by offering a reduced rate of tax or tax exemptions (Jarrass 1980). For example, a reduced rate of tax for cars directed at the promotion

[14]Financial Court Münster, 2011/05/03—1 K 2214/08.

[15]Financial Court Cologne, 1995/05/11—7 K 762/88.

of the development of cleaner, less polluting technology. Tax deductions are not intended to direct the behavior of the taxpayer, as they are only the consequence of expenses arising from inventive activity. Therefore, they are not to be considered subsidies for creating inventions (Jaensch 2013). Nevertheless, tax subsidies do in practice have the function of subsidies, since they can reduce the cost of creating an invention and indirectly promote inventive activity (Owczarczuk 2012; Stewart 2007).

Despite the elaborate German tax laws, there are some exceptions to what an inventor can deduct from his taxable income. For example, if an inventor does not intend to make use of his granted IP right, and does not license his invention, he is required to pay tax on all income derived from the inventive activity and is not permitted to make tax deductions for expenses related to the invention. If the Financial Office wants to consider that an inventive activity without the aim of generating sustained profit has taken place, it has to consider the individual nature of the inventive activity, and that even an extended period without profit does not automatically mean that the activity is not inventive under the provisions of the Income Tax Law.

In a case decided by the Federal Fiscal Court,[16] a taxpayer worked as an employed inventor for nearly 20 years and as a freelancer for approximately 18 years. The inventor was granted several patents for his inventions and received no financing from third parties. Despite receiving some small license fees for his inventions, he conducted his inventive activity at a loss over a long period. The losses significantly reduced his and his spouse's taxable income, and some years later the Tax Office presumed that there was no ongoing inventive activity, in the sense of the Income Tax Law. Consequently, the inventor was no longer allowed to claim tax deductions. In the appeal against the decision of the Tax Office, the Federal Fiscal Court disagreed with the opinion of the Tax Office and ruled that even after an extended period it is usually not possible to decide if an inventive activity has led to a sustained profit for the inventor. Following the findings of the Court, it is possible to achieve license fees for only 10 % of all inventions, and the time during which profit can be generated can seldom be overlooked due to the length of the patent application procedure and the further work necessary to develop the invention and bring it to commercial production. The Court's decision means that the Tax Office will observe the inventive activity over a period of several years until it becomes possible to decide if the inventive activity can be recognized under the Income Tax Law.

This particular case also demonstrates that the fiscal treatment of inventors is in some ways different from that of other professions. However, despite these circumstances, in general the fiscal treatment of inventors does not benefit from exceptions to the rules under the Income Tax Law. Neither the literature nor Court rulings consider that tax deductions are direct subsidies for inventors: they are instead simply the consequences of the Income Tax Law.

---

[16]Federal Fiscal Court, 1985/03/14—V R 8/84, Federal Tax Journal 1985 part II page 424 ff.

Before 1990 proper subsidies for inventions did exist in Germany. During this time the Income Tax Law allowed for a reduction of the tax rate to 10 % for scientific activities, and it was also possible for income tax reporting purposes to spread the income derived from licensing the invention over the duration of patent protection, according to Section 34(1) and (3) of the Income Tax Law, 1949. This led to a steady but reduced annual income over time, and a moderate rate of tax instead of a high rate of tax being applied during the years when a high level of income was generated due to the payment of license fees. As an alternative, an inventor could apply for his personal rate of income tax to be reduced to 50 %, which was attractive because the maximum rate during this period was 56 %.[17] It is interesting to note that these reductions to the tax rate were only available with respect to granted patents, and not utility models, as they are not substantially examined.

Unfortunately the German legislator eventually abolished these subsidies, because they were considered to disturb the equality of the taxation system. Following the constitutional principle set out in Section 3(1) of the German Constitution, all individuals and companies are to be taxed equally, depending on their economic status.[18] In principle, this requires that tax rates should be lower on low income and higher on high income, and that taxpayers with the very lowest income are exempt from paying income tax. Although this is the theory, in practice the legislator does not obey this rule at all times. For example, there is a maximum tax rate of 25 % for interest income. Therefore, the German Constitution would not hinder the legislator if it decided to create a reduced tax rate concerning inventions.

A remaining provision from this former law is the fact that the tax rate for all kinds of compensation, for example damages, can be reduced on demand of the taxpayer, according to Section 34(2) of the Income Tax Law. However, this is not applicable to license fees, which are paid as a lump sum (Holzer 2015), or to fees relating to employee inventions because they are considered part of the employee's regular income and not compensation[19] (please refer to Sect. 3.4.6.). Therefore, an inventor should aim to avoid single payments for license fees and should negotiate for their annual payment.

Nevertheless, a reduced tax rate could be a useful incentive to stimulate inventive activity. Despite the fact that an inventor is permitted to claim deductions from his taxable income, it can be argued that the former tax subsidies available in Germany made inventive activity a more attractive proposition than it is today. The reduction of tax rates for private inventors and companies does not work as a selective advantage for these taxpayers in the sense of the EU regulations, because a reduced tax rate for all inventing persons or companies is applied equally and does not depend on any typical or specific characteristics of a certain group of taxpayers.

---

[17]Decree for the treatment of income taxation of free inventors, 1951/05/30, Federal Law Journal (original title: Bundesgesetzblatt) 1950, 387.

[18]Federal Constitutional Court, 2008/02/13—2 BvL 1/06.

[19]Federal Fiscal Court, 2012/02/29—IX R 28/11.

EU regulations would be violated if tax reductions would be given only for certain types of inventions, in some geographical areas of the country, or for only a limited group of taxpayers. In contrast, the decision of the legislator to provide tax reductions only in respect of granted patents and not for utility models would be within the common aim of the Tax Law to influence a certain type of taxpayer behavior, which in this case is to encourage the filing of full patent applications instead of utility model applications.

Legal entities recognized under German Company Law are required to pay tax according to the provisions of the Corporate Tax Law. The rules are similar to those for natural persons who are required to pay tax on taxable income under the rules of the Income Tax Law. Legal entities are entitled to deduct expenses following the rules of the Income Tax Law, according to Sections 7 and 8 of the Company Tax Law, although the tax rate is relatively low at 15 %.

Section 5 of the Corporate Tax Law provides many tax exemptions for entities working in the public interest such as the German Federal Bank, political parties, insurance companies or entities providing apartments for accommodation, agricultural assistance or research by order of the State or State-related entities. These tax exemptions are direct subsidies directed at entities engaged in reasonable activities in the public interest. Usually, these entities are not inventors in the context of the current research project. Even if the aforementioned research entities are inventors, they will be required to pay corporate tax in respect of their inventions, if they intend to use the inventions in a professional manner or did not create the invention on the basis of a State or State-related order, according to Section 5 (No. 23) of the Company Tax Law.

The Tax Law does not therefore provide subsidies for private persons or companies, so that EU regulations are not violated.

Other observations on effectiveness

In summary, the situation in Germany is not ideal for inventors because they cannot claim special tax reductions. Every tax system can aim to change the behavior of the taxpayers. Therefore, the promotion of inventive activity due to incentive provisions in tax law can increase inventive activity, and lead to more applications for IP rights. Furthermore, provisions under tax law are generally less expensive for the State than providing direct subsidies (Takalo 2009). This indicates that a government should in general reduce the tax burden of inventing enterprises and private inventors instead of providing direct subsidies. In this regard, no modifications appear to be necessary to German tax law since all expenses relating to inventive activity are already deductible. Other countries may also consider introducing tax deductions for the costs associated with inventive activity, including research, development and the filing of applications at the Patent Office, (Owczarczuk 2012; Stewart 2007). Even super deductions over 100 % of the expenses are possible (Ernst & Young 2010). As an alternative, tax rates may be reduced for income derived from the receipt of IP license fees. This is a simple yet effective mechanism to promote inventors and inventive activity and could be incorporated into every taxation system in the world.

The former German Tax Law demonstrates very well how the taxation system can be used to incentivize inventors. However, legislators need to act cautiously. Tax rate reductions should be directed at patent license fees and should not apply to utility model license fees, if there has been no substantial examination of the application like under the German Utility Model Law. In general, the focus on invention patents may assist in discouraging the filing of low-quality utility model applications without substantial examination (Moga 2012; Prud'homme 2012, 2014; Radauer et al. 2015).

3.4.4 State Subsidies

Overview and assessment of conflicts with EU rules on subsidies

The issue of State subsidies for IP is large and complicated. In the Federal Republic of Germany, the granting of subsidies is centralized under the management of the Federal Ministry for Economy and Energy, whereas the individual German Federal States play a very minor role. Only a few Federal States provide IP subsidies, such as the 'Bavarian Technology Support Program' operating in Bavaria.[20] However, as discussed in the literature, better organization and coordination between these programs is required in order for them to be more effective in promoting invention (Blind et al. 2009).

The Federal Republic of Germany provides special programs for inventors (Jaensch 2013) and business start-ups. The programs and subsidies available are easy to navigate because an official website maintained by the Federal Republic of Germany (www.foerderinfo.bund.de) provides clear information and documentation concerning all federal research subsidies, and provides links to the subsidy programs of the German Federal States and the European Commission (www.foerderdatenbank.de).

It is necessary to detail the legal structure and mechanism of the decision-making process under which subsidies may be provided. Usually two steps are involved. The first step in the process is an administrative decision under public law, of the office intending to provide the subsidy, for example the Federal Ministry of Economy and Energy. If it should become necessary, the office intending to provide the subsidy can be sued before the Administrative Court. In the second step, payment of the subsidy occurs following a decision, in accordance with private law, of the bank involved. The bank is usually one specializing in the payment of subsidies, for example the Credit Office for Reconstruction or the Reconstruction Bank of Saxony.[21] The bank receives the subsidies from the State and subsequently provides loans or donations to the inventor in accordance with the regulations of the

[20] Bayerisches Technologieförderprogramm (BayTP).

[21] Kreditanstalt für Wiederaufbau (KfW), www.kfw.de; Sächsische Aufbaubank (SAB), www.sab.sachsen.de.

approving office. The bank supervises the repayments and transfers them back to the State. Legal proceedings concerning any irregularities associated with the payment of subsidies can be brought before the Civil Courts.[22] State subsidies are usually provided for special intended purposes, and in most cases this is to encourage and achieve a certain economic behavior of the subsided person or entity (Jarrass 1980).[23]

The SIGNO[24] program is probably the most important federal subsidy program for inventions (www.signo-deutschland.de) conducted by the Federal Ministry of Economy (Blind et al. 2009; Federal Ministry of Economy 2012). This program is designed to help universities, small and middle-sized entities, as well as private inventors to secure and license their inventions. The program is divided into three specialized sections: a section for universities aimed at improving the flow of information between science and technology; a section for enterprises aimed at promoting small and middle-sized entities with assistance in protecting their inventions as industrial property rights; and a section for private inventors aimed at supporting creativity and providing advice to inventors.

The SIGNO homepage provides a good overview of the possible subsidies available, so that every inventor can make a quick pre-check of what may be available for his invention. The information provided by SIGNO and private SIGNO partners is sufficient to enable inventors to file for subsidies without the need to instruct a lawyer. Through the homepage it is possible to access documents, application forms and arrange meetings with experts. However, for the second step of the process that involves payment, access to a personal bank adviser can be useful. The subsidies provided by SIGNO for IP rights are for an average EUR 4000 per invention and are focused on achieving a successful IP right registration (Blind et al. 2009) and are conducted in five steps (search report, analysis of licensing possibilities, patent or utility model applications in Germany, commercial usage of IP, and patent applications in other countries). Over 80 % of SIGNO-promoted patent applications are approved by the German Patent and Trade Mark Office which may indicate the significant quality of the subsidized inventions (Belling et al. 2010), and correlates with the aim of the SIGNO program to not only increase the number of IP applications but to also improve the quality of the invention itself (Blind et al. 2009). Therefore, the SIGNO program appears to fulfill the requirement often promoted in the literature that subsidies should be well tailored to high-quality inventions (Prud'homme 2012; Wang and Sallet 2013), and that subsidies in the absence of sufficient control over inventive quality may have negative consequences (Radauer et al. 2015).

All of the subsidies provided by the SIGNO program are direct and indirect subsidies for the purpose of the EU subsidies regulations. The risk of SIGNO

[22]Federal High Court, 1971/10/12—VI ZR 87/69.

[23]Federal High Court, 2010/04/16—V ZR 175/09; 2006/07/21—V ZR 252/05.

[24]'Schutz von Ideen für die Gewerbliche Nutzung' (protection of ideas for commercial use).

program subsidies violating EU regulations does not differ from section to section. The support available for private inventors, universities and small and middle-sized entities, does in most cases cover the costs for patent research, economic analysis, patent application fees and licensing. On average, these costs will total up to EUR 4000 (Blind et al. 2009) so that the critical threshold sum of EUR 7.5 million will not be reached. Therefore, it can safely be assumed that the SIGNO program does not conflict with the EU subsidy regulations.

Other State programs provide subsidies for fundamental research, industrial research, experimental development and demonstration activities. It is often a requirement that projects run for a certain period of time, usually between 18 and 36 months, and normally conclude with a pilot or laboratory prototype although a marketable product is usually not necessary. Normally, subsidies will cover between 25 and 75 % of project-related costs including personnel costs, materials, equipment and costs for subcontractors, amortization and overheads. The applicant has to respect the deadlines for the submission of interim reports detailed in the letter of approval, and the final payment will only be made at the end of the project following the verification of the final report by the office providing the subsidy. Although the enterprise receiving subsidies can be situated outside of Germany, it does at least have to have a branch in Germany (Jaensch 2013).

Germany prefers to provide subsidies to SMEs involved in the development of key technologies that act as drivers of innovation (Brandkamp 2006), for example in the field of information and communication technologies, optical technologies, production, materials technologies, biotechnology, nanotechnology, micro systems technology and innovative services (Jaensch 2013).

In addition to special subsidies for inventions or inventors, State subsidies are also available for start-up businesses, or for special research projects that are not focused on a particular type of invention. Nevertheless, these subsidies are also intended to promote inventive activity and IP rights, and so they are mentioned here (Belling et al. 2010).

Subsidies for capital requirements are, for example, given by the 'ERP-Startfonds'[25] (Belling et al. 2010) or the 'High-Tech-Gründerfonds'[26] (Federal Ministry of Economy 2012), and paid out by the Credit Office for Reconstruction (www.kfw.de). There are also subsidies provided by the 'EIF/ERP-Dachfonds' (www.eif.org) for technology transfer and post-financing for technology-based entities (Federal Ministry of Economy 2012). Subsidies directed at supporting post-competition research, 'Joint Research on the Industrial Sector'[27] (www.aif.de), or public-interested industrial research in Eastern Germany (www.fue-foerderung.de) are also available. Subsidies for key technologies are widespread (Jaensch 2013), and may include air traffic (www.dlr.de), maritime technology (www.ptj.de), space research and electromobility (Federal Ministry of Economy 2012).

[25]Start-up-funds.

[26]High-tech start-up funds.

[27]'Förderung der industriellen Gemeinschaftsforschung—IGF'.

These subsidies can also cover the costs associated with inventions including IP protection, if they are connected with a business start-up, and are ideal for inventors with a small number of inventions that can be the basis for a specialized type of business. In comparison with standalone subsidies for inventions, these subsidies provide a package that effectively covers both the invention itself and the corporate enterprise. In practice, these subsidies do not play a leading role in promoting inventions.

In general, it is a requirement that the subsidized activities are performed in Germany, and that costs are incurred within Germany. Many other nations offering subsidies also require subsidized activities to take place in their respective countries (Kalloe 2016). As a consequence, it is a requirement that any results obtained from subsidized projects, such as registered IP rights, remain within Germany for a certain period of time after the finalization of the project. This is usually for a period of two to three years during which the transfer of IP rights to third parties is not permitted (Jaensch 2013).

Nevertheless, these requirements can be problematic, as subsidies provided to support the generation of IP that then remains in the home country for a certain period of time can undermine the rules of the Common Market, since they could create an imbalance between the promoting state and neighboring countries within the EU (Kriegel 2012). This has the consequence that the EU subsidy regulations are applicable, and that in general view such subsidies as operating against the principles of the Common Market. In contrast to subsidies given under the SIGNO program, it is more likely that the subsidies described above could exceed the threshold limit of EUR 7.5 million, whereas most other programs are designed to remain under this limit. For example 'High-Tech-Gründerfonds' provides subsidies up to EUR 0.5 million (Federal Ministry of Economy 2012).

If subsidies exceed the threshold limit of EUR 7.5 million, it is not safe to assume that subsidies do not violate the principles of the Common Market. The promoting State cannot give a guarantee that no repayment will take place, and so only a positive decision of the European Commission can give absolute security. Consequentially, in these situations good legal advice is essential and backup financing is an important aspect of good risk management.

Other observations on effectiveness

In the large field of State subsidies, the German government provides a very good overview of what is available, so that all inventors can obtain appropriate information and application forms relevant to their inventive and financial situation. Valuable State subsidies are available in Germany for creating IP and for enterprise start-ups. Due to the federal structure of the country, subsidy programs are provided by the Federal Republic of Germany and by the German Federal States, all of which could benefit from better coordination. For example, coordination could be improved by integration of the Patent Information Centers and private SIGNO partners (Blind et al. 2009).

Although the legal system for assessing and paying subsidies in Germany is reliable and detailed information is provided, some insecurity remains in respect of the EU regulations concerning the Common Market. In this environment, the greatest risk is not to be subsided by the State in the first place, but the possibility of being required to repay the subsidies at an unexpected time in the future. If there is a likelihood that the threshold sum of EUR 7.5 million will be exceeded, the promoting State should make statements in the national regulations governing the subsidies, or in any advertising of the subsidies, to state the conformity of the subsidies to the rules and regulations of the EU. The promoting State should also make clear, as appropriate, if the European Commission has checked and pre-approved the regulations. In case of any doubt, a positive decision of the European Commission should be requested.

If a repayment is ordered, it is likely that companies will require back-up financing. Such financing cannot be provided by the promoting State because this would in itself be a violation of forbidden subsidies (please refer to the section above). In all German States the assistance can only be provided by banks specializing in loan guarantees.[28] These loan guarantees can cover a demand order for immediate repayment of the subsidies and can help companies avoid serious problems, such as insolvency.

3.4.5 Private Support

Overview and assessment of conflicts with EU rules on subsidies

Alongside State subsidies, many private incentives are available in Germany to support private inventors or legal entities to create, file and license their inventions. The structure of private incentives and the application procedure are quite similar to those for State subsidies.

The promoting enterprise is usually a private law foundation, very often founded by a financial legacy and with a special purpose. This purpose can be focused on inventions of a particular type or on a special group of inventors, for example, young people, private inventors, or engineers. Support can only be granted if the inventor files and describes the invention and its purpose according to the rules in the regulations. After filing an application for support, the invention will be examined by an expert or a team of experts, and following a positive review the support can be granted.

In most cases, the support consists of the fees of the patent attorney and the German Patent and Trade Mark Office, and sometimes includes the annual renewal fees for the first years. Financial assistance is also sometimes provided for the costs of drawing, research or construction of the invention. Some foundations provide

[28] Bürgschaftsbanken (loan guarantee banks) Baden-Württemberg (www.buergschaftsbank.de), Bayern (Bavaria) (www.bb-bayern), Nordrhein-Westfalen (Northrhine-Westfalia) (www.bb-nrw.de).

assistance for the development and negotiation of license agreements or to support the filing of applications for State or other private support. In some cases a coach is hired to give special advice to the enterprise (Brandkamp 2006). In the private sector there is financial support for almost every purpose. It can be assumed that the scope of private support is wider than that of State subsidies and more focused on special measures to support the inventor. In contrast to the State, private organizations tend to provide financial assistance only for a part of the inventive activity and process, such as the application fees of the German Patent and Trade Mark Office. This is demonstrated by the following examples.

A very old and famous initiative in Germany is 'Youth Invents'[29], which has been supported by schools for several decades. Young people aged between 15 and 21 can participate in this contest of ideas in the field of natural science and technology. Prizes are awarded to the best participants and patent application can also be paid. However, this program does not cover the expenses of a search report, which are relatively expensive at EUR 250.

Another example of private support is the patent initiative of the 'Fraunhofer Foundation' in Munich (www.fraunhofer.de) for freelancers from universities, small entities and the private sector. This foundation offers loans to inventors without any interest. If the invention is not ultimately successful, no repayment of the loan is necessary. If the invention is commercialized, the foundation will receive 25 % of the license fees to cover expenses.

The 'ISUS foundation' in Deisenhofen (www.isus-stiftung.de), which provides information about public subsidies for private inventors, and small and middle-sized entities at the annual 'Night of the Inventor' event, awards prizes for the five best inventions and research projects with the best prospects, in cooperation with the University of the German Federal Armed Forces in Neubiberg. In contrast, the 'Hans Sauer Foundation' (www.hanssauerstiftung.de) provides support for new ideas and inventions in the environment and health sectors, as well as providing an inventor workshop. Finally, the 'High-Tech Gründerfonds' (www.high-tech-gruenderfonds.de) is a cooperation between the Federal Ministries of Economy and Industry, and provides risk capital for innovative technology, as well providing coaching to the subsided enterprises (Brandkamp 2006).

All monetary support programs provided by private entities do not conflict with EU subsidy regulations since the regulations are applicable only to State subsidies.

Other observations on effectiveness

Private companies and entities provide assistance and support for nearly every kind of invention and for almost all categories of inventors. A private inventor or an inventing enterprise may experience difficulties in searching for and identifying the most appropriate private subsidy, but there are no concerns regarding the EU subsidy regulations. Therefore, it is necessary and desirable for the State to provide a comprehensive overview of all the forms of private monetary support available, so

[29]'Jugend forscht', www.jugend-forscht.de.

that all interested parties can obtain accurate information and the relevant application forms according to their specific situation. This may lead to better support and promotion of private inventors and may reduce the requirement for State subsidies and the potential crowding-out effects of state subsidies on private monetary support.

3.4.6 The Employee Invention Law

Overview and assessment of conflicts with EU rules on subsidies

The Employee Invention Law provides for the payment of fees for inventor employees of private entities or of the State if the employee creates and develops the inventions as part of his duties to the employer, and not as a private person. This law has its origins in a wartime order of 1942 that was intended to promote employee inventions in the military sector. The Employee Invention Law provides a reliable set of rules and a special Chamber at the German Patent and Trade Mark Office for employee complaints concerning low fees. Although the current law was modeled on the 1942 order, the underlying intention of the law has changed. The present law is directed at giving employees fair compensation for their inventions and at encouraging the further creation of industrial property rights that can be used by the employer. No direct subsidies are provided and so therefore there is no violation of the EU subsidies regulations. Nevertheless, the possibility of receiving fees from their employer can incentivize and stimulate employee creativity and lead to more and perhaps higher quality inventions.

Other observations on effectiveness

Although fees for employed inventors are not considered subsidies, the possibility of obtaining fees from the employer can promote creativity. This incentive can only work successfully because there is sufficient control over the fees by the Federal Patent Court or a Chamber of the German Patent and Trade Mark Office. Legislators should keep this in mind when considering the issue of fees for inventor employees.

3.5 Conclusions and Policy Recommendations

Inventive activity and inventions are the motor of industrial production and a crucial factor for the growth of many national economies, including the German economy. If crafted correctly and in compliance with international laws, economic support for the development and legal protection of inventions may be a useful and powerful tool to further enable development. The current research is directed at what lessons government policymakers in Germany, and in other countries, may learn when crafting new or revising old incentive schemes and legislation.

The promotion of inventive activity and inventions in Germany is very highly rated, to the extent that the German subsidy system can be considered 'best practice' from an international perspective. There are no direct subsidies in the patent application system, or under Tax Law or the Employee Invention Law. However, state-given subsidies can violate EU subsidies regulations if sums in excess of EUR 7.5 million are provided. All of the subsidy programs reviewed in this chapter, including the well-known SIGNO program, do not reach this threshold and so no conflict with EU rules occurs. Furthermore, private support and subsidies do not violate EU subsidies regulations.

Considering these and other aspects of the analysis in this chapter, the following points could form the basis for policy recommendations to support patent policy (Idris 2003):

- Application fees of the patent office should be low enough to stimulate patenting but not too low.
- Annual renewal fees for patents should increase incrementally over time.
- IP law should provide assistance to poor applicants.
- Tax rates for income derived from patent licensing (but not utility models) should be reduced.
- Tax deductions for inventive activities should be permissible if the national Tax Law allows deductions as a general concept.
- Laws concerning employee inventions should provide the possibility to control the fees of the employee.
- The conditions relating to State subsidies, including repayment conditions, should be clearly defined.
- Information concerning all available State and private subsidies should be collated and provided as an internet-based resource.

If policymakers in Germany and elsewhere implement these recommendations, it is possible that they could strengthen their respective environments for innovation and improve the efficiency of their economies at large.

Acknowledgements The author would like to thank Major Anthony Holland (retired), Army Air Corps (UK), for critical remarks and useful suggestions.

Annex: Additional Notes on the Framework Governing Subsidies in the EU

All EU Member States have learned that the common interest of the European Community in maintaining an undisturbed market needs to be considered in all circumstances,[30] even if the consequences are the insolvency or liquidation of the

[30]European Court, 1997/03/20—Rs C-24/95 (Alcan).

promoted enterprise.[31] Therefore, the European Commission very rarely allows exceptions or a stay from the duty to repay unlawful subsidies.[32] Due to the European Community Treaty, the Member States have a duty to work together with the European Commission in a collaborative and loyal manner, and so can seldom claim that it is impossible for the subsided enterprise to repay the subsidy.[33] National Courts are also required to obey the rules of section 107(1) of the European Community Treaty and are obliged to stop payments to the subsided enterprise[34] because otherwise the decision of the European Commission could be undermined. Therefore, the subsided enterprise is not allowed to claim in a national procedure that the decision of the European Commission is unlawful.[35]

Demands for repayment made by the Federal Republic of Germany have led in some cases to the issuance of high repayment orders and have even resulted in insolvency, such as occurred with 'Graf Henneberg Porcelain GmbH'[36] and 'CDA Compact Disc Albrecht GmbH',[37] where the companies were unable to repay the subsidies (Koenig 2000)[38] and became insolvent (Holzer 2007). Both of these examples demonstrate the severe consequences of violating European Law in the field of subsidies, and that the inappropriate receipt of subsidies in the EU can be very dangerous and even threaten the existence of the promoted company. These risks are not due to the national German law, whose integrated structure between public and private law operates well together, but to the consequent realization of the principles of the European Common Market, even at the price of insolvency of the subsided enterprise.

Despite the severe consequences for violations of the EU subsidy regulations, the regulations are important because they are designed to protect the Common Market and are therefore part of one of the main principles of the EU. Due to their background and importance, EU subsidy regulations are seldom criticized in the literature. However, one particular article criticized the regulations (Paulus 2014).

[31]European Court, 1990/03/21—Rs C-142/87 (Tubemeuse); 2004/04/29—Rs C-277/00 (SMI); German Federal High Court, 2007/07/05—IX ZR 221/05 and IX ZR 256/06.

[32]European Court, 1999/06/7—Rs C-75/09.

[33]European Court, 2003/06/26—Rs C-404/00.

[34]European Court, 2013/11/21—Rs C-284/12 (Lufthansa).

[35]European Court, 2006/10/05—Rs C-232/05.

[36]European Commission, 2000/09/23—2000/C 272/05, ABl. C 272/30; "GmbH" means limited liability company.

[37]European Commission, 2000/06/21, Economy Law Review 2000, 1953.

[38]Further to CDA case see District Court Meiningen, 1998/03/31—2 O 534/91, Economy Law Review 1998, 991 ff.

References

Belling U, Kössler S, Krey K (2010) With the patent for success, businesses get support for innovation (original title: Mit dem Patent zum Erfolg, Innovationsförderung für Unternehmen). Available from http://www.bmwi.de/Dateien/Patentserver/PDF/mit-dem-patent-zum-erfolg,property=pdf,bereich=bmwi2012,sprache=de,rwb=true.pdf

Blind K, Cuntz A, Köhler F, Radauer A (2009) The economic significance of intellectual property and its protection, with a focus on SMEs (original title: Die volkswirtschaftliche Bedeutung geistigen Eigentums und dessen Schutzes mit Fokus auf den Mittelstand). Available from http://www.bmwi.de/Dateien/Patentserver/PDF/volkswirtschaftliche-bedeutung-geistigen-eigentums-endbericht,property=pdf,bereich=bmwi2012,sprache=de,rwb=true.pdf

Böhm F, Eucken W, Hoffmann G, Kromphardt W, Lampe A, Liefmann-Keil E, Müller-Armack A, v Nell-Bräuning O, Nölting E, Peter H, Preiser E, Raiser L, Sauermann H, Schiller K, Veit O, Weisser G, Wessels T (2007) Patent protection and innovation (original title: Patentschutz und Innovation). Available from http://www.bmwi.de/Dateien/Patentserver/PDF/patentschutz-und-innovation,property=pdf,bereich=bmwi2012,sprache=de,rwb=true.pdf

Brandkamp M (2006) Venture capital for innovative technology start-ups: the high-tech foundation fund (original title: Risikokapital für innovative Technologiegründungen, The High-Tech Foundation Fonds). In: Garn M, Kalt G (eds) Innovation drivers in Germany: companies taking responsibility (original title: Innovationstreiber am Standort Deutschland, Unternehmen übernehmen Verantwortung), pp 86–87

Dang J, Motohashi Z (2013) Patent statistics: a good indicator for innovation in China? Patent subsidies program impacts on patent quality. IAM discussion paper series #029. Available from http://pari.u-tokyo.ac.jp/unit/iam/outcomes/pdf/papers_131118.pdf

Ehricke U (2003) Insolvency and subsidies control—newest developments (original title: Insolvenz und Beihilfekontrolle—Neueste Entwicklungen). In: Breitenbücher B, Ehricke U (eds) Insolvency Law. RWS Publishers, Cologne, pp 58–117

Ernst & Young (2010) R&D incentives in the new tax landscape. E&Y, UK

Federal Ministry of the Economy (2012) Economic support, help for investments and innovations (original title: Wirtschaftliche Förderung, Hilfen für Investitionen und Innovationen). Downloaded on 12 March 2016 from http://www.bmwi.de/DE/Mediathek/publikationen,did=718016.html

Holzer J (2007) Commentary on sec. 39 of the insolvency code (original title: Kommentierung § 39 Insolvenzordnung). In: Kübler B, Prütting H (eds) Commentary on the insolvency code. RWS Publishers, Cologne, pp 1–15

Holzer J (2015) Copyright law in insolvency (original title: Urheberrecht in der Insolvenz). In: Limper J, Musiol C (eds) Handbook of intellectual property and media law. Carl Heymanns Publishers, Cologne, pp 863–874

Idris K (2003) Intellectual property, a power tool for economic growth (downloaded on 12 September 2015 from www.wipo.int/

Jaensch M (2013) Germany. In: EYGM Limited Worldwide, R&D incentives reference guide 2013–2014, pp 67–72 (downloaded on 12 September 2015 from www.ey.com)

Jarrass H (1980) The law of economic subsidies (original title: Das Recht der Wirtschaftssubventionen), Juridical Training (original Title: Juristische Schulung), pp 115–120

Kalloe V (2016) IP-conditioned tax incentives: the right approach to stimulate innovation and R&D in the European Union? In: Prud'homme D, Song H (eds) Economic impacts of intellectual property-conditioned government incentives. Springer, Singapore

Koenig C (2000) Subsidies in insolvency (original title: Beihilfen in der Insolvenz). In: Bork R, Kübler B (eds) Insolvency law 2000. RWS Publishers Cologne, Germany, pp 155–175

Kriegel J (2012) Strategies to leverage Chinese patent subsidies. Intellect Prop Mag July/August 2012:78–79

Kunzmann J (2012) Federal tax court—tax benefiting invention fees, reduced tax rate for prospective fees (original title: BFH—Steuerbegünstigte Erfindervergütung, Ermäßigter

Steuersatz für zukunftsbezogene Pauschalvergütung), IP compact (original title: IP kompakt), vol 7, pp 7–8
Moga T (2012) China's utility model patent system: innovation driver or deterrent (downloaded on 14 April 2015 from https://www.uschamber.com/sites/default/files/legacy/reports/1211_china_patent_paper.pdf)
Möhlenkamp A (2014) Guidelines 2014 of EU commission for state subsidies for rescuing and restructuring non-financial enterprises in trouble (original title: Leitlinien 2014 der EU-Kommission für staatliche Beihilfen zur Rettung und Umstrukturierung nichtfinanzieller Unternehmen in Schwierigkeiten), economy law review (original title: Zeitschrift für Wirtschaftrecht), Supplement to vol 44/2014, pp 1–26
Montag F, Bonin A (2012) The development of the union law until the middle of 2012 (original title: Die Entwicklung des Unionsrechts bis Mitte 2012). New Legal Wkly J (original title: Neue Juristische Wochenschrift), pp 3553–3557
Owczarczuk M (2012) Government incentives and FDI inflow into R&D—the case of visegard countries. Entrepreneurial Bus Econ Rev, 2013, 1(2), 74–85
Paulus C (2014) European competition law and its relationship to national insolvency law (original title: Europäisches Wettbewerbsrecht und sein Verhältnis zum nationalen Insolvenzrecht), Economy Law Review (original title: Zeitschrift für Wirtschaftsrecht), pp 905–909
Prud'homme D (2012) Dulling the cutting edge: how patent-related policies and pracices hamper innovation in China. European Union Chamber of Commerce in China, China
Prud'homme D (2014) Creating a "model" utility model patent system, a comparative analysis of the utility model patent systems in Europe and China (downloaded on 14 April 2015 from http://www.ipkey.org/en/activities/past-activities/item/2956-peer-to-peer-exchange-on-utility-model-systems)
Qu S (2012) Intellectual property law in China. Kluwer Law International, Alphen aan den Rijn
Radauer A, Rosemberg C, Cassagneau-Francis O, Goddar H, Haarmann C (2015) Study on the economic impact of the utility model legislation in selected Member States, final report, a study tendered by the European Commission (downloaded on 22 September 2015 from http://bookshop.europa.eu/en/study-on-the-economic-impact-of-the-utility-model-legislation-in-selected-member-states-pbET0415184/?AllPersonalAuthorNames=true)
Schwarze J (2007) European economy law. Basics, composition, limits (original title: Europäisches Wirtschaftsrecht. Grundlagen, Gestaltungsformen, Grenzen), Nomos Publishers Baden-Baden, Germany
Seer R (2014) Final report of the commission for the harmonization of insolvency and tax law (original title: Abschlussbericht der Kommission zur Harmonisierung von Insolvenz- und Steuerrecht). Econ Law Rev (original title: Zeitschrift für Wirtschaftsrecht) 42/2014:1–17
Soltész U (2014) The new european subsidies regulations (original title: Das neue europäische Beihilferecht). New Legal Wkly J (original title: Neue Juristische Wochenschrift), pp 3128–3132
Song H, Li Z, Xu D (2016) The upsurge of domestic patent applications in China: is R&D expenditure or patent subsidy policy responsible? In Prud'homme D, Song H (eds) Economic impacts of intellectual property-conditioned government incentives. Springer, Singapore
Stewart T (2007) China's industrial subsidies study, high technology (downloaded on 12 September 2015 from http://origin.www.uscc.gov/sites/default/files/Research/China's%20Industrial%20Subsidies%20High%20Technology.pdf
Takalo T (2009) Rationales and instruments for public innovation policies, (downloaded on 12 September 2015 from https://www.etla.fi/wp-content/uploads/…/dp1185.p)
Wang C, Sallet J (2013) Collaborative innovation and economic growth: a comment on China's innovation policies. Cardozo Law Rev, 148–166
Zacher T (2011) Reimbursements for inventors and limited tax duty—typical questions (of design) in practice (original title: Erfindervergütungen und beschränkte Steuerpflicht – typische (Gestaltungs-) Fragen in der Praxis, Magazine for the tax lawyer (original title: Steueranwaltsmagazin), pp 125–128

Chapter 4
The Impact of Public Support for SMEs' Patenting Activity: Empirical Evidence from Italy

Liang Xu and Federico Munari

Abstract Over the last decade, public patent subsidies have played an important role in several countries in enhancing international filings by domestic companies, especially SMEs. In this paper, we first analyze patent subsidies implemented in Italy from 2002 to 2012 and classify them according to four different typologies, based on their rationale and objectives. We then use data from a sample of 222 patents subsidized by the Chamber of Commerce of Milan in Northern Italy, and a control group of non-subsidized patents, to assess the impact of patent subsidies on patent value and firms' turnover growth. We conclude by discussing policy recommendations for the optimal design of patent subsidy schemes.

Keywords Patents · Subsidy · Turnover growth · Forward citations · Italy

Liang Xu is Associate Professor at the Research Center for International Business and Economy in School of International Business of Sichuan International Studies University. She received a Ph.D. in Management at Chongqing University, China. She has been a Post-doctor researcher at University of Bologna, Italy. Her research interests are in the fields of technological innovation and strategic management.

Federico Munari is the author for correspondence. He is Professor of Technology and Innovation Management at the Department of Management of the University of Bologna. He was the Director of the Ph.D. Program in General Management of the University of Bologna. He is the author of several published articles and books on issues related to entrepreneurial finance, intellectual property management, technology transfer, and R&D management.

L. Xu
School of International Business, Sichuan International Studies University, Chongqing, China

F. Munari (✉)
CIEG—Dipartimento di Scienze Aziendali, Università di Bologna, Via Terracini 28, 40123 Bologna, Italy
e-mail: federico.munari@unibo.it

D. Prud'homme and H. Song (eds.), *Economic Impacts of Intellectual Property-Conditioned Government Incentives*, DOI 10.1007/978-981-10-1119-1_4

4.1 Introduction

Over the last decade, patent subsidies have played an important role in several countries in enhancing international filings by domestic companies, especially SMEs. Patent subsidies refer to a series of policies, undertaken at the national or local level, aimed at financing firms' patent applications, examination, and maintenance (Li 2012). They are intended to stimulate firms' patenting activities (in particular those undertaken at the international level) by lowering the financial burden, something that tends to be particularly relevant for SMEs. Significant policy actions centered on public subsidies for SMEs have been launched over the last decade in a number of countries (i.e. Italy, Spain, Belgium, Japan, China, India, and the United Kingdom), with the aim of fostering the innovation capabilities of domestic inventors.

However, in spite of a rich literature addressing the rationale and effectiveness of R&D subsidies programs (Klette et al. 2000; Gonzalez and Pazo 2008; Colombo et al. 2011), very limited attention has been paid to the mapping and assessing of patent subsidies (Dang and Motohashi 2013; Lei et al. 2013; Li 2012), and only a small number of empirical exercises have been undertaken to evaluate their impact, especially in countries outside China. We have, therefore, a limited understanding of how to design these types of schemes optimally in order to encourage innovation and competition. Regarding this latter point, a critical issue surrounding this type of policy measure relates to patent quality. A debate involving government insiders, legal experts, and academic scholars (Dang and Motohashi 2013; Li 2012; Prud'homme 2012), and reflected in the financial press (Financial Times 2008; The Economist 2010, 2014), has raised concerns about the possibility that subsidization by public bodies leads to an increase in the number of patents of low quality.[1] According to more sharply critical views, reducing or eliminating initial fees and costs to be paid by applicants could in fact lead to an inflation of patent filings that do not meet statutory requirements (and whose legal validity can therefore be challenged) and that are characterized by limited economic value for the applicants.

Building on such debate, our study intends therefore to fill a gap in the literature, by analyzing policy actions based on patent subsidies implemented in Italy from 2002 to 2012. It also assesses in more depth the impact on patent value of the first and largest of such programs, the one promoted by the Chamber of Commerce of Milan (in collaboration with the province of Milan and the region of Lombardy) in Northern Italy. The case of Italy is particularly interesting given that numerous and diversified schemes centered on patent subsidies and specifically oriented to SMEs have been established there over the last decade, promoted by local, regional, or national authorities. In particular, the measure promoted in the province of Milan in

[1]For instance, referring to subsidized patents in China, an article from The Economist (2014) states: "The quality of many of these patents is in doubt. Of the desired 2m filings, many will be for 'utility' or 'design' patents, which are less substantial than 'invention' patents. Critics suggest that even in the latter category, many Chinese filings fall short of global standards.".

Northern Italy has funded, since its inception in 2002, hundreds of SMEs by covering some of the expenses related to their international patent filings. Based on this empirical evidence, this study addresses the following three research questions: (1) What are the design characteristics of patent subsidies programs for SMEs? (2) What is the impact of such programs on the quality of subsidized patents (as compared to a control group of non-subsidized ones)? (3) What is the impact of such programs on the growth of target companies?

The objective of the first part of the study is therefore to investigate the characteristics of all the policy measures established in Italy at various levels (national, regional and local) in order to promote patent filings and their exploitation by domestic firms. At this stage, we first identify and map 35 patent subsidies measures implemented in Italy since 2002 and analyze them in terms of several dimensions relevant to the program design: main objectives; promoting institutions; geographical scope of the measure; eligible expenses; eligible companies; amount of funding; and ex-ante and ex-post evaluation. We are therefore able to identify four different categories of measures, based on their ultimate objectives: measures promoting *patent-filings*; measures promoting *patented technology maturation*; measures promoting *patent exploitation;* and measures promoting patent leverage to *access external financing*.

The second part of the study focuses on a specific measure, namely that implemented by the Chamber of Commerce of Milan. It aims to assess the impact of this policy action on patent value and turnover growth, by analyzing, in a regression framework, differences in patent value between two groups of patents: a group of 111 patents that were subsidized over the period 2002–2007 in the province of Milan, and a control group of 111 non-subsidized patents. The control group was created using a matched-paired research design, identifying, for each subsidized patent, a corresponding patent with the same priority year and filed by an SME located in the province of Milan. In order to measure patent value, we adopted measures based on patent information, identified and validated in the literature, resorting in particular to the number of forward citations and the legal status of the patents (Lanjouw and Schankerman 2004; Munari and Sobrero 2011; Pakes and Schankerman 1984; Reitzig 2003, 2004; Trajtenberg 1990).

We therefore aim to contribute to the empirical literature that evaluates the effects of public support of R&D and innovation activities (Klette et al. 2000; Gonzalez and Pazo 2008), by focusing on the design and impact of patent subsidies programs, a topic that, despite its increasing relevance for policymaking, has been overlooked until now by empirical studies. In terms of policy implications, our study intends to shed light on the role of public intervention in fostering SME patents, in order to stimulate innovation, promote markets for new ideas and products, and enhance economic development. Ultimately, we intend to provide policy guidelines for the design and implementation of effective patent policies for SMEs.

The rest of the chapter is organized as follows. In the first section, we review the relevant literature and provide an overview of the different actions centered on patent subsidies implemented around the world. We then focus on the Italian experience, by mapping and analyzing the different actions realized at the national, regional, and provincial levels. We then describe in more detail our sample and variables, related to a group of patents filed by SMEs in the province of Milan. We finally report the results of our regression analyses and conclude by discussing policy implications.

4.2 Literature Review

4.2.1 Patenting by SMEs: Is There a Market Failure?

Endogenous-growth theory claims that technological change is a major factor driving economic growth (Arrow 1962; Grossman and Helpman 1994; Davidson and Segerstrom 1998). Moreover, the growing body of literature on the importance of spillovers in R&D and innovative activities (Honore et al. 2014; Klette et al. 2000; Munari and Oriani 2005) has recognized the existence of market failures as one of the main justifications for policy measures subsidizing R&D and innovation programs. Subsidies are thus intended to adjust market failures and to augment the supply of socially rewarding technologies. Such market failures tend to be particularly pronounced for small and medium-sized enterprises (SMEs) due to the limited financial resources available to support R&D, patent, and innovation expenditures (Gabriel and Florence 1993) and to the absence of scale and scope economies in R&D (Ortega-Argilés et al. 2009). As a consequence, extensive innovation support programs have explicitly targeted SMEs over the last decades across many countries (Hoffman et al. 1998).

The patent system itself can be viewed as a policy instrument originally aimed at encouraging the generation and diffusion of innovation. Similar to issues explored in the R&D subsidies literature, the design of effective patent systems represents a key area of attention for both scholars and policymakers (Guellec and van Pottelsberghe de la Potterie 2007). On this point, Encaoua et al. (2006), in an overview of the economics of patents and patent policy, suggest that economic research should focus more on how to design effective policies in the patents field, in order to lever the innovation process.

In particular, SMEs represent a very important and specific target for patent policies, since it is well documented that they are characterized by a low propensity to file for and use patents, for several reasons (Blind et al. 2006; Munari et al. 2012). An initial explanation deals with the high costs involved in patent filings and maintenance and with the honoraria of IP consultants, which can represent a significant financial burden for small enterprises. Moreover, IP rights are costly to enforce. Consider, for instance, the type of costs that an innovator has to undertake in case of infringement disputes. On the one hand, there are direct legal costs. In addition to that, there are business costs related to litigation, which can take several forms, going from the time devoted by managers and researchers to preparing documents and depositions to the court, to the blockage of cooperative relations with suppliers and customers, to the shut-down of production and sales activities during the litigation period. SMEs may not have the financial resources to fund such dispute resolution procedures and face the related risks, and hence may prefer to resort to informal protection mechanisms (such as trade secrets). Finally, an important organizational resource for exploiting IP strategies fully is represented by the availability of firm-level expertise in the areas of IP law and IP management. However, given the resource constraints that typically characterize SMEs, it is often very difficult for them to retain in-house the necessary expertise, either in terms of formalized IP departments or individual IP professionals.

Building on such premises, existing empirical evidence supports the view that a firm's size is a driving force behind patenting activity and that SMEs tend to be disadvantaged in comparison to large companies (Blind et al. 2006). It is therefore likely that a specific market failure will characterize patent activity by SMEs. To address this issue, policy actions centered on patent subsidies have been established in many countries around the world over the last few decades.

4.2.2 Patent Subsidies for SMEs: International Experiences

Over the last decade, an increasing number of countries and regions around the world have established subsidies or funds to support R&D/innovation activities for national enterprises, research institutes, and universities (OECD 2013; WIPO 2006). Among such measures, the use of patent subsidies, in particular those favoring SMEs, has recently gained increasing attention from policymakers (WIPO 2006). The most relevant experience in this area has probably been that of China, although many other countries have implemented similar programs.[2] Typically, patent subsidies measures take the form of direct financial support of some of the expenses related to national and, more often, international patent filings. Such schemes are generally intended to cover part of the filing costs, with a few of them also subsidizing maintenance fees or enforcement expenses. Such measures may be funded by the national government, through a ministry or a specialized agency. Patent subsidies may also be awarded by regional authorities, through a department or a specialized innovation agency. Domestic SMEs constitute the primary target of patent subsidies measures, even though there are also other beneficiaries, such as large enterprises, research institutes, and universities. Although the number of patent subsidies conferred to beneficiary firms varies widely from country to country, most are executed via the reimbursement of a certain proportion of costs incurred (typically with an upper limit), or through the awarding of a fixed amount for each subsidized patent.

[2]See Annex I for a presentation of a selected set of policies centered on patent subsidies from various countries outside China.

4.2.3 The Design and Impact of Patent Subsidies: Insights from the Literature on R&D Subsidies

Despite the growing diffusion and relevance of patent subsidies measures around the world, some of which we have partially documented here, to the best of our knowledge only a limited number of attempts have been made in the literature to assess their characteristics and effectiveness (Dang and Motohashi 2013; Li 2012; Lei et al. 2013; Prud'homme 2012). Most of the studies have analyzed the context of China, given the important diffusion of these measures in that country. Li's article (2012) examines a number of influential forces that may have contributed to the explosive growth of Chinese patenting in recent years, including regional patent subsidy programs. The empirical analyses in Li's article show that the launch of patent subsidy schemes has indeed stimulated the rapid upswing of patenting in China. The study also shows an increase in the ratio of patent applications granted by national patent office SIPO, although it does not perform more specific analyses of the dynamics of patent quality. The study by Dang and Motohashi (2013) analyzed a merged dataset of Chinese patent data and industrial survey data to assess the patenting and innovation activities of Chinese large and medium-sized enterprises. Their empirical results show that that patent count is correlated with R&D input and financial output, and that patent subsidy programs significantly increased patent counts more than 30 %. Finally, the paper by Lei et al. (2013) analyzes the seasonal trends of patent filing counts in China from 1986 to 2007, by comparing domestic and foreign filings. They show a strong monthly pattern of domestic filings, with peaks in December, which seems to suggest the existence of politically driven influences on domestic patent filings. They do not, however, find differences in the quality of domestic patents filed in December, as measured by grant rates.

Such initial analyses help to shed light on the influence exerted by patent subsidy measures on patenting and innovation activities, although they also present a series of limitations. First, they are largely focused on the experience of China, while similar analyses of other contexts are largely missing. Second, they tend to assess the impact on patent quality by adopting a limited set of quality measures (i.e. grant ratios). Third, they do not analyze the effectiveness of patent subsidies at the level of recipient companies, as might be revealed by, for instance, assessing the ultimate impact of such measures on the economic performance of awardees. We therefore rely on the established literature on R&D subsidies to infer some additional useful indications for the appropriate design, implementation, and assessment of patent subsidies measures. Several efforts have been dedicated to evaluating the effects of R&D subsidies on firms' R&D behavior and growth. A key area of attention concerned the balance between public and private R&D, in terms of complementarity or substitution. On one hand, the positive impact of R&D subsidies on firms' R&D expenditures has been suggested by works such as those by Leyden and Albert (1991), Busom (2000), Almus and Czarnitzki (2003), Koga (2005), Hussinger (2008), Aerts and Schmidt (2008), and among others. On the other hand, the substitutive effect of public R&D crowding out private R&D has been observed in studies by Lichtenberg (1984, 1987, 1988), Mamuneas and Nadiri (1996), and Wallsten (2000).

Previous studies have analyzed the allocation process of R&D subsidies. Blanes and Busom (2004), for instance, reveal the heterogeneity of projects and of firms' selection rules across different agencies and industries. They suggest that national and regional programs end up supporting different types of firms and that each agency may use R&D subsidies with different policy goals in each industry. Giebe et al. (2006) identify two sources of inefficiency in the selection rules for allocating R&D subsidies and propose an improved mechanism designed to correct this allocation inefficiency, including a form of auction in which applicants bid for subsidies. A recent study of Colombo et al. (2011), based on a sample of new technology-based firms in Italy, compares the effects of different types of subsidization schemes, distinguishing between 'automatic' and 'selective' subsidies, in which the latter provide financial support only to selected applicants based on substantive examination. Their results suggest that the receipt of selective R&D subsidies tends to have a greater impact on a firm's performance than do automatic subsidies, thus making the former more effective in terms of the economic success of target firms.

On a different level, Scherer and Harhoff (2000) suggest that technological policy should allocate government subsidies in order to support a sizeable array of projects, with the emphasis placed on a relatively small number of big successes, as a consequence of the highly skewed distribution of the value of innovations (i.e. the fact that a small minority of innovations yields the lion's share of all innovations' total economic value). This observation is particularly important when assessing the effectiveness of patent subsidies because of the tremendous heterogeneity in the value of patents, something that has been well documented in the literature (Munari and Sobrero 2011).

The rich literature on R&D subsidies thus provides several important indications on how to assess the effectiveness of patent subsidies for SMEs. First, as mentioned by Encaoua et al. (2006), more empirical testing of the economic effects of patent policies is required. Second, the debate on the additionality or crowding-out effects of R&D subsidies provides important methodological guidelines for the assessment of patent subsidies measures, particularly in terms of the application of a matching estimations method (Bérubé and Mohnen 2008). Third, the review highlights the need to assess the impact of policy measures not only in terms of the number of additional patent filings undertaken by SMEs, but also in terms of the value of subsidized patents.

This latter point appears of particular interest in light of the recent debate involving government insiders, legal experts, and academic scholars (Li 2012; Lei et al. 2013; Prud'homme 2012), and reflected in the financial press (Financial Times 2008; The Economist 2010, 2014), about the possibility that patent subsidization by public authorities may lead to an increase in the number of patents of low quality. More critical voices have argued that, by reducing or eliminating the initial fees and other costs to be paid by the applicants, such measures may inflate weak patents that may generate little or no economic value for their owners, and whose legal validity can ultimately be challenged (The Economist 2014). This concern would most often apply to types of patents that are not substantively examined, as is often the case for utility models and designs. However, this could also apply to invention patents if subsidies are awarded to invention patent filings prior to substantive examination by the responsible patent authorities.[3]

The economic literature has convincingly questioned the assumption that "more patents is better," arguing that a surge in the number of low-value patents can have, on the contrary, a detrimental effect on innovation and competition (Guellec and van Pottelsberghe de la Potterie 2007). One practical concern is related to the difficulties experienced by patent offices coping with an inflated workload, ultimately inducing a significant backlog that can cause delays in procedure (Encaoua et al. 2006). More importantly, a marked increase in the volume of patents of low quality, or in outright illegitimate patents (i.e. not novel or not sufficiently inventive), can raise uncertainties about the enforceability of property rights and give rise to overlapping patents (patent thickets), ultimately increasing patent disputes and discouraging innovation (Lemley and Shapiro 2005).

As to this point, Encaoua et al. (2006) highlight that patent application and renewal fees can act as "self-selection mechanisms" to encourage the patenting of highly valuable inventions and discourage that of the least valuable ones. Arguing this, it becomes important to assess whether or not the provision of public subsidies to SMEs has an impact on the value of patents, and in turn on the subsequent economic performance of the recipient company. In the empirical part of our work, we address such research questions by first mapping the characteristics of patent subsidy measures adopted in Italy. We then focus on a specific measure and assess its effectiveness in terms of patent value and in terms of the subsequent growth of the company by comparing a sample of subsidized and control patents. The analyses we perform are primarily oriented toward deriving lessons for policymakers that can be applied usefully in the design of patent policy measures, as discussed in the final part of our work.

4.3 Research Design

We focus our analysis on policy actions taken in Italy to foster patenting by SMEs. The case of Italy is of particular interest for several reasons. First, the Italian economic system is characterized by a strong diffusion of SMEs, which account for

[3]As mentioned above, such debate has been particularly centered on the experience of China, whose impressive growth in the number of patent filings over the last decade has been in part encouraged by a relevant program of patent subsidies administered by the central, provincial, and city governments (Lei et al. 2013). The fact that most Chinese patents over the period 2001–2008 were related to new design appearances or new models, thus not requiring great technical innovation, has been interpreted as a signal that public subsidies to cover patent application costs can artificially inflate the number of filings (Financial Times 2008; The Economist 2010).

the lion's share of persons employed and value-added generated in the country, with value considerably above average EU levels. As far as innovation is concerned, according to the European Innovation Scoreboard (EIS 2013), Italy lags behind its main European partners in many indicators of technology and innovation —and in particular in those indicators concerning European Patent Office (EPO) and United States Patent and Trademark Office (USPTO) patent applications. In order to address such issues, several policy actions have been taken over the last decade in Italy at different levels (national, regional, and local) in order to promote patent applications by domestic firms, in particular by SMEs. For all these reasons, Italy represents an ideal context in which to address our research interests.

4.3.1 The Research Context

We performed our data collection and analyses in two steps. We were first interested in identifying the main characteristics in the design of patent subsidies measures implemented in Italy. We thus initially conducted a detailed mapping of all such measures realized in Italy by national, regional, or provincial authorities. We then focused our attention on the experience of the Chamber of Commerce of Milan, in the Lombardy region of Northern Italy, in order to assess the impact of subsidies on patent value. We analyzed the different measures established by the Chamber of Commerce of Milan (in collaboration with the province of Milan and the region of Lombardy) in order to support European and international patent filings by SMEs located in the province of Milan. Such measures started in 2002, with total available funding of EUR 2 million that year.

In this policy measure, the subsidy was assigned automatically, based on the chronological order of applications, after a check of formal requirements related to the satisfaction of eligibility criteria for the applicant and the expenses incurred for patent filings.[4] However, no substantive examination was conducted of applications for the subsidies. The subsidy covered up to 50 % of expenses incurred by an SME for an international patent filing (including drafting expenses), up to a maximum amount of EUR 15,000. The policy was renewed annually up to and including 2011 (with the exception of 2004), funding hundreds of companies. Until August 2011 it was by far the most important measure of this kind in Italy, in terms of amount of funding and number of companies involved.[5] In this section we first present the

[4]The eligibility criteria referred, for instance, to compliance with the EU definition of SME on the part of the applicant, and the compliance of incurred expenses with those specified in the call.

[5]In August 2011 the Italian Ministry of Economic Development launched an ambitious subsidy scheme with the objective of boosting the number of patent filings by SMEs and of their economic exploitation, allocating a budget of EUR 40 million to this measure. This is, however, too recent to be included in our assessment exercise, given that a significant time span is required to construct the patent quality measures we adopt in the analyses. In addition, information on patents subsidized through such policies is not publicly available.

sources we used to collect the data, and then describe in more detail the sample and variables we adopted in our analyses of how subsidies affect patent value.

4.3.2 Data Sources

In order to identify all the patent subsidies measures promoted in Italy over the last decade, we first analyzed the web pages of all the chambers of commerce in Italy, since they are responsible, through local offices, for patent filing registrations, in collaboration with the Italian Patent and Trademark Office (UIBM).[6] In addition to this role, the local chamber of commerce is typically responsible for a series of activities aimed at promoting the diffusion of a patent culture. We then complemented this initial search by performing a more general web search using keywords related to patent subsidies.[7] In order to complement this initial search, we then performed five further interviews with, respectively, representatives of the patent offices of two major Italian chambers of commerce (Milan and Bologna); consultants with two leading IP consulting firms in Italy; and a consultant with a major Italian consulting firm specializing in enterprise and public funding. The interviews were intended to enrich our knowledge and understanding of the main measures implemented in Italy to promote patenting, to clarify their design and logic, and to give us feedback on their impact and effectiveness.

Based on this data collection, we were able to identify 35 patent subsidy actions implemented in Italy over the period 2002–2012: 25 actions were promoted by the local chamber of commerce, three by provincial authorities, three by regional authorities, and four at the national level by the Ministry of Economic Development (Ministero per lo Sviluppo Economico). We then focused on the patent subsidy measures established from 2002 onward by the Chamber of Commerce of Milan, the province of Milan, and the region of Lombardy, in Northern Italy.

4.3.3 Sample

In our study on the different measures established by the Chamber of Commerce of Milan, we decided to focus on the calls published in 2002, 2003, 2005, and 2006 (in 2004 the policy was not implemented), in order to have a time period sufficient to assess the final outcome of the patent application process (i.e. whether or not a grant

---

[6]Patent applications for industrial inventions in Italy can be filed with the chamber of commerce or directly with the Italian patent and trademark office. In the former case, the chamber sends the documents received to the central office.

[7]Patent applications for industrial inventions in Italy can be filed with the chamber of commerce or directly with the Italian patent and trademark office. In the former case, the chamber sends the documents received to the central office.

was received). We were able to identify all patents and companies receiving the subsidies in these years (as well as those companies that applied for a subsidy but were not selected), using information from the website of the Milanese Chamber of Commerce.

Our data gathering was structured in three phases. In the first phase, we identified all SMEs and the related patents that obtained a subsidy in 2002, 2003, 2005, and 2006. This initial sample consisted of 146 SMEs in the province of Milan, operating in industries ranging from biotechnologies and healthcare to electronics and ICT, as well as mechanics and materials. In the second phase, we collected information on patent applications for cases registered as EPO or PCT applications, using Espacenet as a data source.[8] From the initial sample we retained only those SMEs for which information on their subsidized patents was available in the patent database. After whittling down the initial sample following these criteria, we were left with a sample of 136 SMEs and 191 subsidized patents.

In the third and final phase of our data collection, we constructed a matched sample of SMEs (and related patents) located in the province of Milan that did not receive a patent subsidy over the period of analysis. In order to construct such a control group, for each subsidized patent we identified a corresponding patent satisfying the following three conditions: (1) having an SME as applicant; (2) having Milan as the applicant's address; (3) having the same priority date as the subsidized patent. We applied the SME definition of the European Commission in order to filter the patents in the control group. We thus checked whether the applicant's turnover (in the priority year of the subsidized patent) fell within the limits posed by the EC definition of SMEs, matching companies included in the same category of either micro, small, or medium-sized enterprises.[9] This means that a subsidized patent from a micro enterprise was matched to a corresponding unfunded patent, with the closest priority date, filed by another micro enterprise located in the province of Milan.[10] Following the same logic, we identified the control patents for the small and medium-sized companies included in our sample. Information on firms' turnover and addresses for the initial and matched samples came from the AIDA commercial database, including accounting information on both public and privately held companies in Italy.

[8]We did not collect information on domestic (Italian) patent applications, given that the website of the Italian IP Office (UIBM) did not allow the collection of information on forward citations.

[9]We use Recommendation 2003/361/EC, adopted by the European Commission, as a criterion here, categorizing micro enterprises as those with a turnover no greater than EUR 2 million, small enterprises as those with a turnover no greater than EUR 10 million, and medium-sized enterprises as those with a turnover no greater than EUR 50 million.

[10]We proceeded in the following way. First, we selected from the OECD Regpat database (a comprehensive database presenting patent data that have been linked to regions and provinces) all EP and PCT patents filed by applicants located in the province of Milan. We identified in this set of patents the patent with the nearest priority date. We used this patent as a control only if the company was included in the corresponding turnover category (micro, small, or medium). If this was not the case, we moved to the next patent with the nearest priority date, until we found a company in the same category of turnover level, and used such a patent as a control.

In this process, we were not able to find a corresponding match for some of the subsidized patents, since in some instances accounting information was not available on AIDA for either beneficiaries or target companies. Because of this, we were left with a final sample of 111 subsidized patents—including 60 EP patents and 51 PCT patents—applied for by SMEs in the province of Milan with priority years ranging from 2000 to 2007. Such patents were matched to a corresponding group of 111 control patents (including 60 EPO patents and 51 PCT patents) that did not receive a subsidy, identified through the procedure described above.

4.3.4 Methods and Variables

We employed two main regression models in order to evaluate the effects of subsidies on patent value. We first used the number of forward citations received by each patent as the dependent variable, since it represents the most frequently used proxy for the value of patents in the literature (for a review of this literature see Munari and Sobrero 2011; Omland 2011). As dependent variable in the second model, we used a dummy variable to capture whether or not the patent was granted up to March 2015. Because of the non-negative, discrete, and highly skewed nature of the first dependent variable ("Number of forward citations"), we adopted a Poisson regression model in the first equation. In the second equation, we used a logit specification to analyze the impact of patent subsidies on the likelihood of grant.

Dependent variables. As a measure of *patent value* we used the number of forward citations received by each patent from patents subsequently issued. Forward citations were identified and collected through Espacenet. Citations from later patents of the patent under examination (forward citations) represent a significant indicator of value, and have been analyzed, validated, and used in numerous scientific studies for several decades (Harhoff and Narin 1999; Reitzig 2003, 2004; Trajtenberg 1990). Several theoretical arguments explain this empirical fact (Omland 2011). The existence of citations from later patents indicates that patents on similar technology continued to be applied for, meaning that subsequent investments building on the initial invention were made and that the technology is perceived as attractive and useful. Moreover, citations indicate that the claims of the later patent may have been limited by what was already described in the earlier patents; this suggests that the newer invention might integrate aspects already protected by earlier patents. Hence, the 'old' patent claims appear to be still relevant in the newer technology space. For these reasons, the number of forward citations is probably the most commonly used proxy in the literature for the value of patents (Munari and Sobrero 2011; Sapsalis et al. 2006).

As an additional variable for patent quality, we used the legal status of the patent, constructing a dummy variable, *Patent grant,* that takes the value 1 if the patent was granted as of March 2015. This serves as another empirical indicator widely used in the literature to approximate the quality of a patent by indicating the probability of getting a patent granted (Guellec and van Pottelsberghe de la Potterie 2000, 2001). In addition to that, it has been generally employed by previous articles assessing the impact of patent subsidies (Li 2012; Lei et al. 2013).

As a measure of economic performance at the company level, we referred to *Turnover Growth*. This was computed as the growth (in percent) of turnover levels in the three years after receipt of the subsidy, for both subsidized and control companies. More precisely, for each company *i*, this variable is computed as:

$$Turnover\,Growth_i = [Turnover_i(+3) - Turnover_i(0)]/Turnover_i(0) * 100$$

where $\text{Turnover}_i(0)$ captures turnover level in the year of receipt of the subsidy (for control companies, this year is identified with reference to the corresponding subsidized company) and $\text{Turnover}_i(+3)$ is the third year after receipt of the subsidy. We were able to compute such variables only for a subset of sample companies, due to limited data availability on turnover levels.

Independent variable. In our regression models, we included a dummy variable, *Patent Subsidy,* taking the value 1 to indicate the beneficiary status of the subsidized patent in our sample, and 0 otherwise (for patents in the control group). We use this dummy as a key explanatory variable in order to evaluate the effectiveness of patent policy measures on patent value.

Control variables. The *number of inventors* for each patent was counted and collected as a potential determinant of patent value. It is established as an indicator of the number of researchers involved in a research project, and a proxy reflecting the importance of the research to the company and the potential profits expected (Sapsalis et al. 2006). Another variable used to determine the value of a patent in our study is the number of *co-assignees*, which indicates the level of collaboration with other knowledge-generating institutions or individuals (Sapsalis et al. 2006). We then built a *patent scope* variable, counting the number of IPC classes to which the patent is assigned. IPC classes encode and classify the technical content of patent documents, which is positively correlated with the patent's value (Lerner 1994; Harhoff and Reitzig 2004). We also counted the *number of backward citations* for each patent as another determinant of patent value. This measure could indicate the extent to which a patent is based on previous science or technological knowledge, and it is theorized to operationalize the technical novelty of a patent (Sapsalis et al. 2006; Reitzig 2004). We also included a dummy variable, *PCT,* to separate PCT patents from others. The choice of application route has been proposed as a potential value indicator (van Zeebroeck and van Pottelsberghe 2008). The observed choice of the applicant to use the PCT system has been tested as a value indicator by Harhoff and Reitzig (2004), and Harhoff and Hoisl (2007). We also constructed a dummy *Utility patent* to distinguish utility models from patents for technical inventions. The time effect of patents being cited or granted is taken into account through a set of time dummies (Sapsalis et al. 2006), corresponding to the priority year of each patent, from 2000 to 2007.

A variable *Firm's turnover* was adopted in order to capture size effects that might have an impact on the quality of the patent. For each firm, turnover levels were measured in the priority year of the patent, according to AIDA. Finally, to control for industry-level effects, we constructed four sector dummies, based on the main ATECO code of the company: *Manufacturing* takes the value 1 for companies in manufacturing sectors (ATECO codes from C10 to C19, and from C23 to C33); *Chemical and Pharma* takes the value 1 for companies in chemical and pharma sectors (ATECO codes from C20 to C22); *Scientific Sector* takes the value 1 for companies operating in scientific, technical and professional activities (ATECO codes M); *Other Sectors* takes the value 1 for the remaining sectors. In our regression analyses we used the Manufacturing sector as the baseline case (and excluded the related dummy in the models).

4.4 Analyses and Results

4.4.1 The Design of Patent Subsidies Measures in Italy

In the first step of our research, we identified all patent subsidies measures established in Italy from 2002 to 2012, for a total of 35 actions that we were able to map and analyze. Table 4.1 briefly analyzes these different measures in terms of dimensions that are relevant to the design of the scheme: (1) promoting institutions and geographic coverage; (2) rationale and objectives; (3) target beneficiaries of the measure; (4) eligible costs; (5) maximum amount of funding; (6) overall budget; (7) selection and evaluation criteria.

It is possible to classify such measures along the first two dimensions reported in Table 4.1, which are particularly relevant for their design and implementation: their geographic scope and their rationale and objectives. In terms of geographic scope, it is important to note that the greatest number of measures is promoted at the local (provincial) level, typically by provincial chambers of commerce, thus limiting the number of intended beneficiaries to the SMEs located in the province. A few measures have been implemented by regional authorities, and in more recent years (2011–2012), four major programs have been implemented at the national level, three of them by the Ministry of Economic Development (Measures Brevetti+ Premi, Measure Brevetti+ Incentivi valorizzazione, and Fondo Nazionale per l'Innovazione) and one by the Ministry of Education, Universities and Research (Proof of Concept Network). The second dimension of analysis deals with the rationale and objectives underlying such measures. In this sense, it is possible to identify four different types of measures: measures promoting *patent-filings*; measures promoting *patented technology maturation*; measures promoting *patent exploitation;* and measures promoting patent leverage to *access external financing*.

In the first and largest group are included those measures aiming to encourage SMEs to protect their IPRs at an international level, thus fostering innovation and internationalization activities, particularly by SMEs. Typically, they provide subsidies to cover patent filing fees and expenses for patent attorneys. This group

Table 4.1 The design of patent subsidies measures in Italy

Promoting institutions and geographic coverage	The vast majority of patent subsidy measures (25 cases) have been promoted and managed by local chambers of commerce, often with the financial support of provincial or regional authorities (11 cases out of 25). In three cases (Venice, Apulia, and Lazio), the measure was promoted, funded, and managed directly by a regional authority, in three cases by a provincial authority (Roma, Trento, and Parma), and in one case by a foundation (Fondazione Cassa di Risparmio di Imola in the case of Imola). Three recent measures were established at the national level in August 2011 by the Ministry for Economic Development, and one at the end of 2012 by the Ministry for University and Research. For measures promoted by chamber of commerce and provincial authorities, the scheme is oriented only toward companies located in the relevant province. For measures managed by regional authorities, the action is oriented toward companies located within the region
Rationale and objectives	All the calls we have analyzed present similar objectives oriented toward encouraging firms to protect their IPRs at an international level, in order to foster innovation and internationalization activities, particularly by SMEs. Only five calls report as their objective not just the granting of patents, but also their promotion and exploitation (two from the Italian Ministry for Economic Development, one from the Italian Ministry for University and Research, one from the Lazio region, and one from the province of Trento)
Target beneficiaries	In most of the cases, the target beneficiaries of the measures are small and medium enterprises (typically defined according to the EU classification). In all of the cases, only companies satisfying the requirements of the 'de minimis aid' rule are admitted to the calls, in order to comply with the state-aid regulations of the European Community.[a] Submissions presented by individual inventors are typically not admitted (with the exception of one measure that allows this). In some cases, patents from universities and public research centers are also admitted (the call for the Apulia region is specifically reserved for such institutions)
Eligible costs	Typically, subsidies are provided for invention patents and utility patents.[b] Coherent with this aim, the subsidies (awarded in the form of grant) cover all the costs incurred for submitting an application to the national office or the European Patent Office (including filing fees, costs for patent attorneys, costs for patentability search), and the costs for extensions of the patent in other territories[c]
Amount of funding awarded	The maximum amount of funding awarded for the measures oriented toward patent filings varies significantly across programs, ranging from a minimum amount of 500 EUR per applicant (Campobasso) up to EUR 70,000 (Italian Ministry of Economic Development). In the case of the Fondo Nazionale per l'Innovazione, a measure intended to promote access to external funding, beneficiary companies can receive from selected banks up to EUR 3 million in debt financing, leveraging the ministry's credit-risk guarantee fund

(continued)

Table 4.1 (continued)

Overall available budget	There is great variation in the overall budgets available for the measures, ranging from a minimum of EUR 5000 (Chamber of Commerce of Campobasso) to a maximum of EUR 1,200,000 for provincial measures (Milano), 3,000,000 for regional measures (Lombardy), and 75,000,000 for national measures (Italian Ministry of Economic Development)
Selection and evaluation criteria	In the vast majority of cases, no ex-ante evaluation of the submitted patent is made (except for a formal check of the satisfaction of eligibility criteria), and instead the subsidies are automatically awarded based on chronological order of submission, up to the consumption of the overall budget. In only eight cases (Ravenna, Imola, Venice, Roma, Trento, Trieste, Lazio, and the Italian Ministry for Economic Development) is the selection made by a selection committee based on predefined criteria (including degree of innovation; potential market size and scope; competences of the applicant; and collaborations with universities and public research centers)

Sources Data are related to 35 measures promoted by local chambers of commerce, provincial, regional or national authorities in Italy over the period 2002–2010

[a]According to the 'de minimis rule', aid of no more than EUR 200,000 granted over a period of three years is not regarded as state aid within the meaning of Article 87(1). The regulation does not apply to aid for fisheries and aquaculture, the primary production of agricultural products, export-related activities, the coal sector, the acquisition of road freight transport vehicles or firms in difficulty, or to aid tied to the use of domestic rather than imported goods. It applies to aid granted to firms in all other sectors, including transport and, under certain conditions, for the processing and marketing of agricultural products

[b]In a few cases these subsidies also address registered designs, whereas in only one case (the Chamber of Commerce of Mantua) are layout designs for integrated circuit and plant variety rights included. Generally, registered trademarks are not considered in such measures, with the exception of the measure implemented by the Chamber of Commerce of Avellino

[c]Generally, maintenance fees for the patent are excluded from eligible costs in such actions. In two cases (those of the Chambers of Commerce of Gorizia and Udine), the aid is also intended to cover legal expenses incurred for any litigation of the patent

includes the vast majority of the measures included in our sample (30 programs). In addition to that, all measures with a local geographic scope (with the exception of the one in the Province of Trento) have a strict focus on promoting patent filings. The remaining three types, on the other hand, in addition to promoting patent filings, also try to support beneficiary companies in their subsequent commercial exploitation and financial valorization.

The second type of measure intends to promote the *maturation of patented inventions* up to a stage at which they can attract the interest of external acquirers or investors. In this case, public subsidies are provided in order to cover, for instance, feasibility studies, realization of prototypes and demos, and market analyses. This measure is particularly suited for patents generated by universities and public research organizations, since they typically operate at the frontier of scientific advancements and involve considerable uncertainties regarding their market potential (Kochenkova et al. 2015). A recent example of this type of measure in Italy is the Proof of Concept Network, coordinated by Area Science Park in Trieste and funded in 2012 by the Ministry for Education, Universities and Research (see Annex II).

A third type of measure aims to promote *patent exploitation*, by providing funding to cover expenses related to drafting and finalization of licensing/sale agreements for patented technologies (such as technology marketing analyses, due diligence, patent valuation, and legal costs of licensing agreements). Examples of this type of measure include the Fund Brevetti+, established by the Italian Ministry for Economic Development, or the Fund Trentino Brevetti, established by the province of Trento in Northern Italy (see Annex II). The fourth and final type of measure supports SMEs in exploiting their patented invention in order to *access external financing,* either from banks or venture capital funds. An example of this innovative funding scheme is provided by the measure Fondo Nazionale per l'Innovazione, established with a budget of EUR 75 million by the Italian Ministry for Economic Development, through two different schemes: the first scheme acts as a credit risk guarantee fund to incentivize banks in providing credit to innovative SMEs with patented technologies; the second scheme acts as a public-private venture capital fund to provide risk capital to innovative IP-rich new ventures (see Annex II).

Looking at Table 4.1, it clearly emerges that most of the programs centered on patent subsides established in Italy are included in the first category, promoting patent filings, whereas measures in favor of patent exploitation are more limited in number, tend to be promoted at the national level, and are still largely pilots. Below, we present more specific comments related to the first set of subsidy measures, centered on patent filings, given their wider diffusion and more settled nature. From an analysis of Table 4.1, some critical issues that have characterized the design of patent subsidy schemes centered on patent filings in Italy are immediately evident. First is the marked fragmentation of the different programs, due to the activation of several schemes that are often geographically bounded to single provinces, have limited available budgets (in many cases of less than EUR 50,000), and award to beneficiary firms only a small amount of funding to cover a minimal amount of patent expenses. Therefore, such measures are often established with a mere signaling role, but it is unlikely that they will have real impact as an incentive for SMEs to file additional patents. Moreover, the emerging picture is that of limited coordination among the different institutional actors involved in the process (chambers of commerce, provinces, regions, foundations), which hinders the possibility of establishing sizeable programs with the critical mass needed to make a real contribution.

A second critical point relates to the definition of the measures' objectives. The vast majority of the schemes have a strong focus on supporting an increase in the number of patents filed by SMEs as a way to strengthen innovation and the internationalization process. In other words, the measures are centered on augmenting the number of patents filed, with limited or no attention to improving the quality of patents filed or fostering the economic valorization of intellectual property rights. No measure in our sample has been established with the declared objective of enhancing the number of "high-quality" patents.

A third critical issue, which stems directly from the previous one, is the lack of predefined criteria to guide the evaluation and selection of the patents to be subsidized. In the vast majority of the schemes under analysis, no ex-ante evaluation of the submitted patent was made, with the exception of a formal check on the satisfaction of eligibility criteria.[11] Typically, the subsidies were automatically awarded based on the chronological order of the submissions, up to the consumption of the overall budget. In only four cases were the programs managed as selective schemes providing financial support only to selected applicants. In such cases, a committee of experts was formed to make a selection based on predefined criteria (including the geographic and technological scope of the patent; the degree of innovation; potential market size and scope; the competences of the applicant; and collaborations with universities and public research centers). A direct consequence of three such shortcomings in the design of policy measures centered on patent filings is the risk of subsidizing patents of low quality and limited exploitation potential, thus limiting the effectiveness of the measure. This is essentially what we wanted to test in our next analyses, based on data from patents subsidized in the province of Milan.

4.4.2 The Impact of Subsidies on Patent Value and Turnover Growth: Descriptive Analyses

In the following sections, we report the results of our analyses designed to test whether the receipt of subsidies has an impact on patent value, based on data related to patent subsidy schemes implemented by the Chamber of Commerce of Milan. Table 4.2 reports descriptive statistics on our sample of 222 patents from SMEs located in the province of Milan, including 111 subsidized and 111 control patents with priority years ranging from 2000 to 2007.

Table 4.2 shows that the average patent in the sample receives less than 1 forward citations by subsequent patents (0.91), with a maximum number of 10 citations per patent. About 44 % of patents in our sample were granted by March 2015, with the remaining patents being either refused or withdrawn. The average breadth of patents, as measured by the number of four-digit IPC classes, is around 3. The average number of inventors and of applicants reaches nearly 2 per sample patent, with maximum levels of 8 and 9 respectively. The number of backward citations on average is nearly 5. Such descriptive statistics related to different

[11] Such formal checks typically regarded the following aspects: the nature of the participating company (i.e. correspondence with the EU definition of SME); the type of IP for which the grant was requested (i.e. correspondence with the eligible types of IP described in the call); and whether the expenses for which the company was requesting the grant corresponded with the eligible expenses described in the call.

Table 4.2 Descriptive statistics of patent applications by SMEs in the province of Milan

Variable	N	Mean	Std.	Min	Max
Number of forward citations	222	0.91	1.59	0.00	10.00
Dummy grant	222	0.38	0.49	0.00	1.00
Dummy of patent subsidy	222	0.50	0.50	0.00	1.00
Number of IPC class	222	3.07	3.34	1.00	39.00
Number of inventors	222	1.72	1.20	1.00	8.00
Number of applicants	222	1.97	1.49	1.00	9.00
Number of backward citations	222	4.96	2.82	0.00	20.00
Dummy PCT	222	0.46	0.50	0.00	1.00
Dummy utility	222	0.06	0.24	0.00	1.00
Turnover growth (in %)	157	35.84	90.67	−97.01	440.54
Turnover (in million Euro)	222	6.01	8.31	0.001	35.56

Sources AIDA database, Espacenet

measures of patent quality—such as the number of forward citations, the likelihood of grant, the number of IPC classes, the number of inventors, the number of applicants, and the number of backward citations—suggest high skewing in the value distributions, which are consistent with findings of previous studies demonstrating high heterogeneity in the value of patents (Munari and Sobrero 2011). The SMEs responsible for these international filings have, on average, an annual turnover of EUR 6 million.

We then used a corrected t-test to compare the mean values of different indicators of patent quality between the two samples of subsidized patents and control (i.e. non-subsidized) patents. Table 4.3 reports the results of this comparison, showing in general terms that no statistically significant differences in patent quality seem to emerge between the two samples.

The number of forward citations received by subsidized patents is indeed slightly higher than the matched sample, with average values of 0.94 citations as compared to 0.87 citations, even though the difference is not statistically significant at conventional levels. Similarly, subsidized patents have a higher likelihood of receiving a final patent grant as compared to control patents (more precisely, 49 % of them are granted as to March 2015, as compared to 39 % of control patents), but the difference is not statistically significant either. Moreover, the number of backward citations in the sample of patents with subsidies is greater than in the matched sample, with the average value of 5.1351 compared to 4.7838, but the difference is not significant. On the other hand, the patent's breadth, the number of inventors, and the number of applicants are all smaller for subsidized patents than for the matched sample, but only in the case of the number of inventors is such difference statistically significant, at the 10 percent level. Regarding turnover data, it is noteworthy that, as a consequence of the matching procedure we adopted in the construction of the control group of patents, average turnover levels are similar between subsidized firms and control firms. The average value of turnover growth

Table 4.3 Comparison of patent value indicators between the sample of patents with subsidies and the control group

	Patents with subsidies (mean value)	Control patents (mean value)	T-value	Sig. (2-tailed)
Number of forward citations	0.9369	0.8739	0.319	0.750
Dummy of grant	0.4954	0.3423	1.347	0.181
Number of IPC class	3.0360	3.1081	−0.171	0.865
Number of inventors	1.5856	1.8468	−1.740	0.085
Number of applicants	1.9640	1.9820	−0.129	0.898
Number of backward citations	5.1351	4.7838	0.890	0.375
Company turnover (000 Euro)	6205.99	5813.87	0.350	0.726
Turnover growth (in %)	28.83	43.12	0.987	0.325

Patent data refer to 111 patents with subsidies and 111 control patents. Data on company turnover growth refer to 80 patents with subsidies and 77 control patents for which information on turnover growth was available

results, however, is higher for companies included in the control group compared to those subsidized (43.12 % vs. 28.83 %), and such difference is statistically significant, at the 10 percent level.

4.4.3 *The Impact of Subsidies on Patent Value and Turnover Growth: Regression Analyses*

We then performed regression analyses in order to control for other factors that might influence patent value and turnover growth, in addition to the receipt of a subsidy. Table 4.4 first reports the correlation matrix for our main variables in the full sample. It shows that traditional patent value determinants, such as patent breadth, number of inventors, number of applicants, and number of backward citations tend to be positively correlated with each other. However, no significant evidence of multi-collinearity seems to emerge from the data.[12]

Turning to the regression models reported in Table 4.5, Model 1 adopts the total number of forward citations received by each patent as the dependent variable. We adopted a negative binomial regression model in order to estimate this, given the

[12]The strongest correlation levels regarded the variables Number of Inventors and Number of Applicants, and the variables PCT and Number of Applicants. We therefore decided not to include Number of Applicants as a control variable in our regression models.

Table 4.4 Correlation matrix among main variables in the full sample

	(1)	(2)	(3)	(4)	(5)	(6)	(7)	(8)
(1) Forward citations	1.00							
(2) Dummy grant	0.53	1.00						
(3) Dummy patent subsidy	0.02	0.08	1.00					
(4) IPC class	0.30***	0.06	−0.11	1.00				
(5) Inventors	0.09	−0.12*	−0.11	0.14**	1.00			
(6) Applicants	0.05	−0.11*	-0.01	0.20***	0.76***	1.00		
(7) Backward citations	0.09	−0.05	0.06	0.21***	0.09	0.14**	1.00	
(8) Dummy PCT	0.03	−0.08	0.00	0.19***	0.24***	0.68***	0.07	1.00

*$p < 10$ %, **$p < 5$ %, ***$p < 1$ %

Table 4.5 Regression models on the impact of patent subsidies on patent value and grant probability

	(1) Negative binomial regression model	(2) Poisson regression model	(3) Logit regression model
	Dependent variable: number of forward citations	Dependent variable: number of forward citations	Dependent variable: dummy granted patent
Dummy patent subsidy	0.157 (0.220)	0.178(0.151)	0.514 (0.298)*
Number of IPC classes	0.048 (0.025)*	0.054 (0.011)***	0.037 (0.049)
Number of inventors	0.199 (0.097)**	0.222 (0.059)***	0.005 (0.136)
Backward citations	0.008 (0.042)	0.020 (0.027)	−0.083 (0.055)*
Dummy PCT	−0.005 (0.259)	−0.057(0.179)	−0.143 (0.334)
Turnover	−0.001 (0.001)	−0.001 (0.001)	−0.001 (0.001)
Dummy utility patent	0.330 (0.318)	0.317(0.274)	−1.070 (0.658)
Scientific and technical	−0.132(0.304)	−0.220 (0.221)	−0.030 (0.402)
Chemical and pharma	−0.314 (0.355)	−0.331 (0.255)	0.675 (0.481)
Other sectors	0.577 (0.318)*	0.437 (0.204)**	0.471 (0.441)
Priority year dummies	Yes	Yes	Yes
Constant	−0.391 (0.333)	−0.474 (0.225)**	0.490 (0.477)
Log likelihood	−269.251	−296.753	−136.316
LR Chi^2	36.93	93.41	28.78
Prob > Chi^2	0.0013	0.001	0.011
Number of observations	222	222	220

*$p < 10$ %, **$p < 5$ %, ***$p < 1$ %; standard errors are in parentheses

count nature of the dependent variable.[13] As an additional check, we repeated such estimates using a Poisson regression model (Model 2). Both Models 1 and 2 include the dummy *Patent Subsidy* as the independent variable, and other value determinants as control variables. Model 3, on the other hand, adopts a Logit estimation, with the dummy *Patent Grant* used as dependent variable. It adopts the same explanatory variables used in the previous two models.

The results of the regression models largely confirm those of the t-test analyses. The evidence presented in Model 1 shows that obtaining a patent subsidy does not have a significant effect on patent value as measured in terms of subsequent forward citations. In this model, the coefficient of the dummy *Patent Subsidy* is positive, but not statistically significant at conventional levels. By looking at these results, we thus cannot conclude that the Milanese Chamber of Commerce's specific patent subsidy measure has provided incentives for developing low-quality patents, but neither can we support the assertion that it has had a positive impact on patent quality.

When examining the effect of other value determinants, in Model 1 we notice that the coefficient of the number of IPC classes is positive and significant, at the 10 percent level, signaling that patents with a larger scope are more likely to be cited subsequently. This is consistent with the findings of previous literature on the breadth of patents (Munari and Toschi 2014a), showing that broad patents are more likely to have a subsequent impact in different technical domains. Moreover, the number of inventors has a positive and significant impact (at 5 %) on patent value, as measured by forward citations. Indeed, the size of the research team can be linked to the quality of the underlying invention and its expected impact. A larger inventors' team would thus suggest a better patent quality with a higher expected value. The dummy variable Other Sectors is also positive and statistically significant, at the 10 percent level. Not surprisingly, the coefficient of the time dummies in this model suggests that more recent patents have a lower likelihood of receiving subsequent citations than do older ones. Finally, our results do not suggest that a firm's size has a significant effect on patent value, probably due to the fact that all firms in our sample are included in the SME category. The results of Model 2, adopting a Poisson specification, are largely in line with the findings of Model 1. In this case as well, the Patent Subsidy variable does not show a statistically significant relationship with the number of forward citations received by the patent.

If we move to Model 3, on the other hand, we notice that, after controlling for other influential factors, the dummy Patent Subsidy is positive and statistically significant, although only at the 10 percent level. In this specific case, therefore, it seems that receiving a subsidy increases the likelihood of having the patent granted.

[13]Poisson models and negative binomial models are typically used for count data. Poisson models assume that the conditional mean and variance of the distribution are equal. Given that forward citations data rarely satisfy this assumption, we decided to adopt a negative binomial regression model in our analyses. As a robustness check, we also tested the Poisson model, obtaining similar results.

This result is consistent with previous studies on the effects of patent subsidies on grant ratios (Li 2012; Dang and Motohashi 2013). It could suggest that the receipt of the subsidy may encourage applicants to proceed with the examination process, by reducing the likelihood of applicants withdrawing the patent request due to financial constraints. In this model, the control variables on the number of backward citations has a negative and statistically significant (at the 10 percent level) relationship with the grant likelihood. Since backward citations indicate the presence of a higher number of previous patents upon which the current patent builds, this can reduce the inventive step of the patent and ultimately result in a lower likelihood of obtaining the patent. We do not find statistically significant effects for other control variables in this model.

Finally, Model 1 in Table 4.6 reports the results of the OLS regression analyses using turnover growth as the dependent variable. The dummy Patent Subsidy is used as the main explanatory variable in this model, in addition to other control variables. Table 4.5 does not support the existence of significant differences between subsidized and matched patents in terms of assignees' turnover growth in the three years following the receipt of the subsidy, once one controls for additional influential factors. Indeed, the coefficient of the dummy Patent Subsidy is not significant at conventional statistical levels. Such findings therefore do not support the idea of a strong positive impact on companies' economic performance resulting from the receipt of patent subsidies. In this specification, the variable *Nr Inventors* is positive and statistically significant (at the 10 percent level). This is consistent with the idea that a larger team of inventors leads to innovation with a stronger commercial impact. The dummy variable for the Chemical and Pharma sector is also positive and statistically significant (at the 10 percent level) in this model.

4.5 Conclusions and Policy Implications

This chapter has investigated a series of issues related to the design and assessment of patent subsidies schemes to foster patent activities by SMEs. Such measures have gained increasing importance over the last few years in a number of countries as a way to address the market failures connected with innovation and patenting activities by small and medium enterprises. We thus contribute to an emerging literature that aims to investigate empirically the optimal design of such schemes and to evaluate their effectiveness (Prud'homme 2012). We were particularly interested in assessing the impact of public subsidies on the value of patents and on their ultimate impact on economic performance levels, inspired by a series of concerns related to a potential increase in low-quality patents following the adoption of these kinds of measures (Financial Times 2008; The Economist 2010, 2014).

From an empirical standpoint, we first mapped and analyzed a series of 35 policy programs centered on patent subsidy schemes activated in Italy by local, regional, or national authorities starting in 2002. We then studied a sample of 222 patents, including 111 subsidized and 111 control patents, from the province of Milan in

Northern Italy to test whether the receipt of a subsidy was associated with low patent value. Our mapping exercise highlights some limitations that seem to characterize the majority of patent subsidy measures activated in Italy: a strong fragmentation among the measures themselves, often resulting in a limited budget and a small amount of funding provided to beneficiary firms; a lack of coordination among actions undertaken at different levels (local, regional, national); a focus on increasing the number of patent fillings, but not on increasing the quality of patents; the predominant automatic assignment of the subsidies based purely on chronological order, and the consequent absence of ex-ante evaluation of the quality and economic potential of submitted inventions. All such shortcomings may have negative consequences, such as providing inadequate incentives for SMEs to apply or funding patents with limited economic potential, thus generating inefficiencies in the distribution of public financial resources.

We then assessed in a regression framework the impact of subsidies on patent quality in the specific case of the measure implemented by the Chamber of Commerce of Milan. The results from our regression analyses provide mixed evidence on this issue. Our results do not support the concern that the receipt of a subsidy may be associated with lower patent value. In one model, the receipt of the subsidy is significantly and positively related to the probability that the patent will be granted; we do not find any statistically significant effect, however, on the number of forward citations received by the patent as a proxy of its underlying value. Besides that, our analyses do not show the existence of statistically significant differences in a firm's turnover growth in the three years after the receipt of a subsidy when compared to the control group of non-subsidized companies. Based on such evidence, therefore, our findings do not show a strong economic impact resulting from the measure we analyzed.

Such results should be interpreted with caution, given our focus on a single policy measure and the relatively small number of patents we were able to analyze. The findings could be a direct consequence of the design of the specific measure we analyzed, based on the automatic awarding of subsidies to qualified applicants, following a mere check of the formal requirements, but with no substantial examination of the quality of the patent or the underlying technology. The findings could also be explained by the limited amount of financial support provided by this measure to recipient companies. In any case, our findings suggest that the effectiveness of policy measures centered on patent subsidies is likely to be reduced when these measures are characterized by limited funding and lack of ex-ante quality assessment in the selection process.

Our study therefore identifies some important lessons and implications for policymakers in designing and implementing effective patent policies for SMEs based on subsidies. A first issue concerns the size of the programs. Rather than fragmenting financial resources into narrowly designed schemes (often with rigid geographical limits) with limited budgets and small subsidies, the implementation of sizeable programs should be encouraged (Scherer and Harhoff 2000). Future research should address this issue more directly by assessing the influence not just of receiving a subsidy, but also of subsidy levels. Ideally, future studies should compare the effectiveness of different measures centered on patent subsidies in order to understand in greater depth the influence of specific design dimensions (including the amount of funding provided per project).

A second issue relates to the importance of jointly boosting the quantity *and* the quality of patents filed. It is well documented in the literature that the value of patents is extremely skewed, and the large majority of patents are of limited, if any, value to the applicants, since they are not subsequently exploited in downstream product developments or licensing agreements (Munari and Sobrero 2011). The twin challenges of patent quantity and quality should therefore be encouraged by policymakers, particularly in light of the explosion in both the number and volume of patent filings for all patent offices over the last two decades (Guellec and van Pottelsberghe de la Lotterie 2007).

A third issue, strongly linked to the previous one, relates to the selection and evaluation criteria used to identify beneficiaries of the scheme. It is doubtful whether the establishment of patent subsidy schemes that assign money via an automatic procedure based on chronological order, with no substantive examination of applications, would reach this goal, as suggested by our results. As to this point, previous research on the impact of public R&D subsidies has highlighted that when competition among applicants is tough and the support program is administered by a reputable government agency, selective schemes are likely to be more beneficial than automatic ones for fostering SMEs' value creation (Colombo et al. 2011).

Moreover, as suggested by Lerner (1999), selective schemes may provide certification of the quality of beneficiary firms (and the underlying patents) to uninformed third parties, such as external investors or potential licensees. In the case of patent subsidies, therefore, selective schemes providing financial support only to selected applicants, based on an ex-ante evaluation of the quality of the patent and the economic potential of the invention, could be more appropriate for reaching this goal. Our analysis of the measures implemented in Italy has suggested a series of criteria that can be used by a committee of experts to implement this kind of selection, including the geographic and technological scope of the filed patent; the degree of innovativeness of the technology; potential market size and scope; the applicant's competences and skills; and the existence of collaborations with universities and public research centers.

Finally, and as a direct consequence of the previous point, from a policy perspective, it appears important to encourage not only domestic and international patent filings by SMEs, but also their actual use to generate economic value. SMEs in particular can take advantage of their patents in a wide variety of ways, including the protection from imitation and freedom to operate, but also outward licensing, access to external financing, and reputation building (de Rassenfosse 2012; Giuri et al. 2013; Munari and Toschi 2014b). As we highlighted in the assessment of the patent measures implemented in Italy, an ideal extension of policy measures centered on patent filings is thus also the encouragement of the economic exploitation of patents through coverage not only of expenses related to patent fees and drafting, but also to services related to their use and commercialization (for instance, costs for services related to patent evaluation and due diligence, marketing studies, license drafting, feasibility studies, and proofs of concept). In this sense, the recent pilot initiatives implemented in Italy promoting maturation, exploitation, and financial leverage of patents appear extremely interesting, although it is too early to assess their actual impact.

A critical element that emerges in the implementation of this experience is the importance of methods and approaches to assess the value of the patent and the underlying technology. For this purpose, qualitative methods to assess the value of the patented technology have been developed (Munari and Oriani 2011), although their validation and effectiveness are still under scrutiny. Policy initiatives are therefore also required in this area, in order to favor the emergence of valuation approaches that are validated and mutually recognized. The evidence we have presented here provides several implications that are worth some reflection by policymakers, due to the increasing diffusion of public patent subsidies measures around the world.

Annex I

Example of public measures supporting the exploitation of patents in various countries

County/region	Funding scheme	Eligible costs relate to patenting	Agency responsible	Target company	Amount
Spain	The Foreign Promotion Initiation Plan	Registration of patents and trademarks abroad, including the professional fees of an Industrial Property Agent	The Spanish Institute for Foreign Trade, and the Higher Council of Chambers of Commerce	Spanish SMEs	The subsidy of up to 80 % of the expenses, up to a maximum of €46,000
Canada	The Atlantic Innovation Fund	Patent searches and filing fees	The Atlantic Canada Opportunities Agency, a federal government agency in Canada	Private sector firms	Actual cost
Ireland	R&D Fund	Costs of research, development and innovation projects in preceding the granting of the patent or other industrial property rights in Ireland and aboard	The government agency of Enterprise Ireland, coordinated by Department of Enterprise, Trade and Employment	Irish based companies, particularly SMEs	The maximum R&D grant of a company is €450,000, with the Patent costs no more than 20 % of the overall project cost

(continued)

(continued)

County/region	Funding scheme	Eligible costs relate to patenting	Agency responsible	Target company	Amount
Scotland, U.K.	The SMART, SPUR or SPUR^{PLUS} Grants	Essential project costs such as: labor, overheads, materials, subcontracting, consultancy and intellectual property	Scottish Executive Enterprise, Transport and Lifelong Learning Department of the Scottish Government	SMEs based in Scotland	75, 35, 35 % of eligible costs, with maximum grant of €35,000, €52,000, €351,000 for SMART, SPUR and SPRUR^{PLUS}
Wallonia, Belgium	Subsidy for Patent Registration and Extension	Patent application to national or European patent office with a search for previous patents; additional formalities and the extension to other territories	The Directorate General Operational for Economy, Employment and Research (DGO6) of the Ministry of the Walloon Region	Local SMEs	35 and 70 % of the costs incurred of patenting an innovation and all cost incurred for national validation
Gujarat, India	Patent Registration Assistance	Patent registration in India and abroad	Industries and Mines Department of the Government of Gujarat	Local small, medium and large company	50 % (maximum Rs. 5.00 Lakhs) of necessary expenditure incurred for obtaining the patent

Source WIPO (2006); Erawatch

Annex II

Example of public measures supporting the exploitation of patents in Italy

Name	Proof of Concept Network
Established	2012
Website	http://www.area.trieste.it/opencms/opencms/area/it/attivita/progetti_az/PoCN.html
Funding agency	Ministry of University and Research, through Area Science Park
Budget	EUR 1.974.000 (period 2012–2014)

(continued)

(continued)

Type of measure	Measure promoting the maturation of patented inventions
Description	The Proof of Concept Network (PoCN) is a pilot project funded by the Ministry of University and Research and managed by Area Science Park (a multi-sector science and technology park in Trieste), in collaboration with other Italian partners. The project aims to promote the commercial exploitation of the scientific research results of universities and public research organizations (PRO), through the validation and development of prototypes in collaboration with industry. In particular, PoCN involves the use of research results and patents available from universities for specific industrial activities through co-development with businesses in order to test their performance in real application contexts and generate prototypes of products/processes of practical interest to the company. The projects for industrial validation programs have a maximum term of nine months and are financially supported up to a maximum of EUR 30,000
Name	Fondo Brevetti Trentino Sviluppo (Patent Fund Trentino Sviluppo)
Founded	2006
Website	http://www.trentinosviluppo.it/
Responsible	Province of Trento, through the Innovation Agency Trentino Sviluppo
Budget	EUR 120.000 (for year 2011).
Type of measure	Measure promoting the commercialization of patented inventions
Description	Fondo Brevetti Trentino Sviluppo was set up by the Province of Trento in Northern Italy through the Innovation Agency Trentino Sviluppo in order to promote business initiatives in the local area by exploiting the findings of research funded by the province. It is a financial instrument for valorizing and commercializing research results by encouraging technology transfer between the research world and business. Fondo Brevetti Trentino Sviluppo can acquire and assign intellectual property rights (patents, trade-marks, know-how, software, etc.) resulting from research projects developed by local bodies with provincial financing. Fondo Brevetti Trentino Sviluppo is responsible for protecting assigned rights and promoting them in order to support the birth of business initiatives that may derive a competitive advantage from those rights. If the exploitation in the Trentino area is not possible, the rights may be granted under license or transferred to third parties, even if they operate in markets other than Trentino. Up to 2012, the Fund had backed 15 patents and four trademarks related to seven different technologies developed by researchers from nine different research centres
Name	Fondo Nazionale per l'Innovazione (National Innovation Fund)
Established	2011
Website	http://www.sviluppoeconomico.gov.it
Funding agency	Ministry of Economic Development

(continued)

(continued)

Budget	EUR 75 million (for both measures based on debt and equity financing)
Type of measure	Measure promoting the financial leverage of patented inventions
Description	The Ministry of Economic Development set up the National Innovation Fund, a tool for small and medium-sized enterprises, to support the development and financing of innovative projects based on the exploitation of patents and industrial designs. The ministry, through the fund, provides a guarantee that facilitates the granting of loans by selected banks in order to facilitate access to credit for small companies and reduce the costs of the loans. Funding is awarded up to a maximum amount of EUR 3 million per company, with a maturity of up to 10 years, and no real or personal guarantees are required of the company. Two banks, Mediocredito Italiano (group Intesa Sanpaolo) and Unicredit, have been selected to implement this initiative. A joint measure has been developed to provide risk capital to IP-rich new ventures, through a new seed fund jointly backed by the ministry and the VC firm Innogest

References

Aerts K, Schmidt T (2008) Two for the price of one? Additionality effects of R&D subsidies: a comparison between Flanders and Germany. Res Policy 37:806–822

Almus M, Czarnitzki D (2003) The effects of public R&D subsidies on firms' innovation activities: the case of Eastern Germany. J Bus Econ Stat 21:226–236

Arrow K (1962) Economic welfare and the allocation of resources for invention. In: Universities-National Bureau Committee for Economic Research, Committee on Economic Growth of the Social Science Research Council (eds) The rate and direction of inventive activity: economic and social factors. Princeton University Press, Princeton, NJ, pp 609–626

Bérubé C, Mohnen P (2008) Are firms that receive R&D subsidies more innovative? Can J Econ 42(1):206–225

Blanes JV, Busom I (2004) Who participates in R&D subsidies programs? The case of Spanish manufacturing firms. Res Policy 33:1459–1476

Blind K, Edler J, Frietsch R, Schmoch U (2006) Motives to patent: empirical evidence from Germany. Res Policy 35(5):655–672

Busom L (2000) An empirical evaluation of the effects of R&D subsidies. Econ Innov New Technol 9:111–148

Colombo M, Grilli L, Murtinu S (2011) R&D subsidies and the performance of high-tech start-ups. Econ Lett 112:97–99

Dang J, Motohashi K (2013) Patent statistics: a good indicator for innovation in China? Patent subsidies program impacts on patent quality. IAM Discussion Paper Series #029 Available from http://pari.u-tokyo.ac.jp/unit/iam/outcomes/pdf/papers_131118.pdf

Davidson C, Segerstrom P (1998) R&D subsidies and economic growth. Rand J Econ 29:548–577

de Rassenfosse G (2012) How SMEs exploit their intellectual property assets: Evidence from survey data. Small Bus Econ 39(2):437–452

EIS (2013) European innovation scoreboard. European Commission, Brussels (downloaded on 9 September 2014 from http://ec.europa.eu/enterprise/policies/innovation/policy/innovation-scoreboard/index_en.htm)

Encaoua D, Guellec D, Martínez C (2006) Patent systems for encouraging innovation: lessons from economic analysis. Res Policy 35:1423–1440

Financial Times (2008) The value of branding becomes patent. Financial Times, July 2 (downloaded on 10 September 2014 from http://www.ft.com/cms/s/0/3389c83a-4850-11dd-a851-000077b07658.html#axzz42XxZXogw)
Gabriel D, Florence EM (1993) Technology watch and the small firm. OECD Observer 182:31–34
Giebe T, Grebe T, Wolfstetter E (2006) How to allocate R&D (and other) subsidies: an experimentally tested policy recommendation. Res Policy 35:1261–1272
Giuri P, Munari F, Pasquini M (2013) What determines university patent commercialization? Empirical evidence on the role of IPR ownership. Ind Innov 20(5):488–502
Gonzalez G, Pazo G (2008) Do public subsidies stimulate private R&D spending? Res Policy 37:371–389
Grossman GM, Helpman E (1994) Endogenous innovation in the theory of growth. J Econ Perspect 8:23–44
Guellec D, van Pottelsberghe de la Potterie B (2000) Applications, grants and the value of patent. Econ Lett 69(1):109
Guellec D, van Pottelsberghe de la Potterie B (2001) The internationalization of technology analysed with patent data. Res Policy 30(8):1256–1266
Guellec D, van Pottelsberghe de la Potterie B (2007) The economics of the European patent system. IP Policy for Innovation and Competition. Oxford University Press, Oxford
Harhoff D, Hoisl K (2007) Institutionalized incentives for ingenuity—patent value and the German Employees' Inventions Act. Res Policy 36(8):1143–1162
Harhoff D, Narin F (1999) Citation frequency and the value of patented inventions. Rev Econ Stat 81(3):511–515
Harhoff D, Reitzig M (2004) Determinants of opposition against EPO patent grants: the case of pharmaceuticals and biotechnology. Int J Ind Organ 22:443–480
Hoffman K, Parejo M, Bessant J, Perren L (1998) Small firms, R&D, technology and innovation in the UK: a literature review. Technovation 18(1):39–55
Honore F, Munari F, Van Pottelsberghe de la Potterie B (2014) Corporate governance practices and companies' R&D orientation: evidence from European countries. Res Policy 44(2):533–543
Hussinger K (2008) R&D and subsidies at the firm level: an application of parametric and semiparametric two-step selection models. J Appl Econometrics 23:729–747
Klette TJ, Møen J, Griliches Z (2000) Do subsidies to commercial R&D reduce market failures? Microeconometric evaluation studies. Res Policy 29:471–495
Kochenkova A, Grimaldi R, Munari F (2015) Public policy measures in support of knowledge transfer activities: a review of academic literature. J Technol Transfer (forthcoming)
Koga T (2005) R&D subsidy and self-financed R&D: the case of Japanese high-technology start-ups. Small Bus Econ 24:53–62
Lanjouw JO, Schankerman M (2004) Patent quality and research productivity: measuring innovation with multiple indicators. Econ J 114(495):441–465
Lei Z, Sun Z, Wright B (2013) Are Chinese patent applications politically driven? Evidence from China's domestic patent applications. Fung Institute Berkley Innovation Seminar paper (downloaded on 12 Nov 2014 from http://www.funginstitute.berkeley.edu/research/spring-2013)
Lemley M, Shapiro C (2005) Probabilistic patents. J Econ Perspect 19:2, 75–98
Lerner J (1994) The importance of patent scope: an empirical analysis. RAND J Econ 25(2):319–333
Lerner J (1999) The government as venture capitalist: the long-run effects of the SBIR program. J Bus 72:285–318
Leyden DP, Albert LN (1991) Why are government R&D and private R&D complements? Appl Econ 23(10):1673–1681

Li X (2012) Behind the recent surge of Chinese patenting: an institutional view. Res Policy 41 (1):236–249
Lichtenberg FR (1984) The relationship between federal contract R&D and company R&D. Am Econ Rev 74(2):73–78
Lichtenberg FR (1987) The effect of government funding on private industrial research and development: a re-assessment. J Ind Econ 36(1):97–104
Lichtenberg FR (1988) The private R&D investment response to federal design and technical competitions. Am Econ Rev 78(3):550–559
Mamuneas TP, Nadiri IM (1996) Public R&D policies and cost behavior of the U.S. manufacturing industries. J Publ Econ 63(1):57–81
Munari F, Oriani R (2005) Privatization and economic returns to R&D activities. Ind Corp Change 14(1):61–91
Munari F, Oriani R (2011) Why, when and how to value patents. In: Munari F, Oriani R (eds) The economic valuation of patents: methods and applications. Edward Elgar Pub, Cheltenham, pp 3–24
Munari F, Sobrero M (2011) Economic and management perspectives on the value of patents. In: Munari F, Oriani R (eds) The economic valuation of patents. Methods and applications. Edward Elgar Pub, Cheltenham, pp 56–81
Munari F, Toschi L (2014a) Running ahead in the nanotechnology gold rush. Strategic patenting in emerging technologies. Technol Forecast Soc Chang 83(1):194–207
Munari F, Toschi L (2014b) Do patents affect VC financing? Empirical evidence from the nanotechnology sector. Int Entrepreneurship Manage J 11(3):623–644
Munari F, Sobrero M, Malipiero A (2012) Absorptive capacity and localized spillover: Focal firms as technological gatekeepers in industrial districts. Ind Corp Change 21(2):429–462
OECD (2013) Commercialising Public Research: new trends and strategies. Organization for Cooperation and Economic Development, Paris
Omland N (2011) Valuing patents through indicators. In: Munari F, Oriani R (eds) The economic valuation of patents. Methods and applications. Edward Elgar Pub, Cheltenham, pp 169–204
Ortega-Argilés R, Vivarelli M, Voigt P (2009) R&D in SMEs: a paradox? Small Bus Econ 33 (1):3–11
Pakes A, Schankerman M (1984) The rate of obsolescence of patents, research gestation lags, and the private rate of return to research resources. In: Griliches Z (ed) R&D, Patents and Productivity. University of Chicago Press for the NBER, Chicago
Prud'homme D (2012) Dulling the cutting edge: how patent-related policies and practices hamper innovation in China. European Chamber, Beijing
Reitzig M (2003) What determines patent value? Insights from the semiconductor industry. Res Policy 32:12–26
Reitzig M (2004) Improving patent valuations for management purposes—validating new indicators by analyzing application rationales. Res Policy 33:939–957
Sapsalis E, Van Pottelsberghe B, Navon R (2006) Academic versus Industry patenting: an in-depth analysis of what determines patent value. Res Policy 35:1631–1645
Scherer FM, Harhoff D (2000) Technology policy for a world of skew-distributed outcomes. Res Policy 29:559–566
The Economist (2010) Innovation in China: patents yes, ideas maybe. The Economist, 14 Oct (downloaded on 11 Sept 2014 from http://www.economist.com/node/17257940)
The Economist (2014) Patent fiction. Intellectual property in China. The Economist, 13 Dec (downloaded on 20 Dec 2014 from http://www.economist.com/)
Trajtenberg M (1990) A penny for your quotes: patent citations and the value of inventions. RAND J Econ 21:172–187
van Zeebroeck N, van Pottelsberghe B (2008) Filing strategies and patent value. CEPR discussion paper 6821
Wallsten SJ (2000) The effects of government-industry R&D programs on private R&D: the case of the Small Business Innovation Research Program. RAND J Econ 31:82–100
WIPO (2006) Managing patent costs: an overview. Working paper, World Intellectual Property Organization, Geneva

Chapter 5
IP-Conditioned Tax Incentives: The Right Approach to Stimulate Innovation and R&D in the European Union?

Vinod Kalloe

Abstract This chapter will outline the longstanding strategy of the EU to incentivize and foster R&D. Part of this strategy has been to develop tax policy recommendations concerning specific tax incentives for R&D expenditure. In recent years, many EU Member States have also developed specific tax incentives concerning income derived from intellectual property (so-called IP-conditioned tax incentives). The effect of IP-conditioned tax incentives, insofar as they have been evaluated, appear to be inconclusive. On the one hand, in practice it does seem that certain R&D tax incentives indeed lead to opportunities for companies resulting in observable incremental increases in additional R&D. However, on the other hand certain IP-conditioned tax incentives may lead to aggressive international tax planning where there is no real nexus with actual ongoing or additional R&D.

Keywords Tax incentives · IP-conditioned tax incentives · Increased R&D activity · State aid · Tax planning

5.1 Introduction and Methodology

During the past 25 years, many EU Member States have increased efforts to stimulate and drive innovation. The EU's effort to coordinate and streamline all of these national initiatives led to the so-called EU Lisbon Strategy, part of which included an EU-wide R&D action plan for the period between 2000 and 2010. The aim of this plan was to make the EU "*the most competitive and dynamic knowledge-based economy in the world capable of sustainable economic growth with more*

Vinod Kalloe: Head of International Tax Policy, KPMG Meijburg & Co Tax Lawyers Amsterdam, and former European Commission national expert.

V. Kalloe (✉)
KPMG Meijburg & Co, Laan van Langerhuize 9, P.O. Box 74600, 1070 DE Amsterdam, The Netherlands
e-mail: kalloe.vinod@kpmg.com

D. Prud'homme and H. Song (eds.), *Economic Impacts of Intellectual Property-Conditioned Government Incentives*, DOI 10.1007/978-981-10-1119-1_5

and better jobs and greater social cohesion" by 2010 (EU Council 2000). In this context, EU Member States aimed to increase overall EU R&D investment to approximately 3 % of GDP by 2010, two-thirds of which was intended to have been provided by the private sector. However, by 2010 these goals were unfortunately not sufficiently realized, and so the plan to incentivize R&D was continued and further developed in the EU's Europe 2020 Growth Strategy. The focus remains on developing an EU economy based on knowledge and innovation (European Commission 2010). Early on, the European Commission had already provided practical guidance to Member States through the publication of its communication 'Investing in research: an action plan for Europe', which focused on developing public support measures to increase private R&D investment by optimizing a combination of grants, tax incentives and risk-sharing mechanisms (European Commission 2003).

In practice, it appears that several EU Member States have struggled to find the most effective mix of tax policies to promote R&D activities within their jurisdictions. Furthermore, not all Member States are convinced that the use of R&D tax policies is the most effective way to incentivize innovation since some of the most innovative countries in the EU do not offer any, or at least no significant, R&D-related tax incentives.[1] Some observers claim that in principle, direct spending (i.e. subsidies through direct grants rather than through the tax system) should be the preferred approach to drive innovation and R&D as financial resources may be targeted more effectively, precisely and efficiently.

Nevertheless, in recent years, EU Member States have increasingly introduced so-called generic R&D tax incentives in combination with IP-conditioned tax incentives. The rationale for using R&D tax incentives is to incentivize expenditure on R&D (exploration), whereas IP-conditioned tax incentives enable companies to benefit from reduced corporate taxation of income derived from the commercialization of their IP (exploitation). In recent years and in particular from 2008 onwards, it is especially noticeable that EU Member States have engaged in fierce tax competition as they have sought to maintain and attract innovative companies, R&D activities and the R&D centers of multinational companies to their respective jurisdictions. A basic overview of both R&D and IP-conditioned incentives is provided in Box 1 below.

Box 1: An overview of the basic principles of R&D and IP-conditioned incentives

When categorizing all of the tax incentives relating to innovation that are currently in place in EU Member States, it is useful to distinguish between the different phases of innovation from a company's perspective. When

[1]See for example Bloomberg Innovation index 2015 where some of the top-ranked countries do not offer specific R&D and IP-conditioned tax incentives: http://www.bloomberg.com/graphics/2015-innovative-countries/.

multinational companies engage in the continuous process of innovation, the starting point will usually include capital expenditure and initial investment, followed by operational R&D expenditure. In principle, most EU Member States allow R&D costs and amortization of capital expenditure to be deductible for the purpose of calculating corporate income tax.

Moreover, many Member States have also introduced specific R&D tax incentives and IP-conditioned tax incentives which provide for corporate tax allowances in the form of:

- the ability to deduct more than 100 % of actual R&D expenditure for corporate tax purposes;
- tax credits as a percentage of R&D expenditure;
- specific incentives under wage tax legislation, and
- tax levied at a reduced rate of corporate tax, or on a reduced corporate tax base, for income derived from the exploitation of IP.

EU Member States typically define eligible R&D activities widely. These activities are usually defined as those which further R&D into new products, new processes and innovative technologies. These can include basic or fundamental research, applied research, experimental or ordinary R&D and construction, and the development and testing of a prototype, including the development of software.

From the perspective of a multinational company engaged in R&D and IP management, all these incentives will become relevant depending upon the specific phase of innovation. During the first phase, an R&D project is commenced and capital investments are often made, and during the second phase companies engage in day-to-day R&D operations. Throughout these phases companies are supported by R&D tax incentives that result in a lower payable amount of corporate tax. These incentives include:

- R&D corporate tax deductions at 100 % or 'super deductions' (at more than 100 %);
- R&D accelerated depreciation of capital expenditure;
- R&D corporate tax credits (preferably leading to cash refunds);
- R&D wage tax reductions and the possibility for corporate tax loss compensation in the form of 'carry forward' and 'carry back' techniques.[2]

Following the successful completion of R&D activities, during the third phase the company will need to consider its options for commercializing the IP that has been generated. In this context, EU Member States have focused on introducing IP-conditioned tax incentives resulting in a reduced effective

[2]'Carry forward' is an accounting technique that applies the current year's net operating losses to future years' profits in order to reduce future tax liability. 'Carry backward' is an accounting technique with which a company retroactively applies net operating losses to a preceding year's income in order to reduce tax liabilities present in that previous year.

rate of corporate tax on income derived from the commercialization of IP that has been generated by the research. Other issues that a company will need to consider in the context of IP management include the location of IP generation and the scope for IP protection and enforcement, and also the potential withholding taxes at source on cross-border license fees and royalties that are paid to the licensor.

However, an important question remains: are these tax incentives actually effective? This chapter highlights the finding that the majority of research and reports that have studied empirical literature on R&D tax incentives, have found that these incentives do indeed promote and increase R&D activity to a certain extent. Studies suggest that one euro of foregone tax revenue results in slightly less than one euro of additional private R&D investment (CPB 2015; Lokshin and Mohnen 2012; Mulkay and Mairesse 2013). More detailed research appears to indicate that R&D tax incentives stimulate the creation of new products and innovation but perhaps tend not to stimulate more radical innovations (Ernst and Spengel 2011; Westmore 2013; Ernst et al. 2014). However, most of the IP-conditioned tax incentives that have been introduced during the last ten years have not been adequately evaluated for their potential to promote additional R&D activity, their effect in determining the location of R&D activities, or on the impact they may have in terms of patenting applications and budgetary considerations.

This chapter will further elaborate on the recommendations made by the European Commission for more detailed research and evidence-based policy for R&D and IP-conditioned tax incentives, especially since most IP-conditioned tax incentives have been introduced in the years following 2008. This chapter will also share context on the current global and OECD debate concerning the aggressive international tax planning strategies of multinational companies and the impact of IP-conditioned tax incentives (OECD 2014). The objective of the chapter is to provide the building blocks for a more comprehensive approach for developing and evaluating IP-conditioned tax incentives in the ever more complex world of international tax policy. To this end, the chapter is based on a multidisciplinary literature review of international tax and economic impact analyses, combined with on-the-ground experiences of advising multinational companies on R&D and IP-conditioned tax incentives globally.

The remainder of the first section of this chapter will provide a brief overview of R&D tax incentives and IP-conditioned tax incentives in the EU. The second section contains a more detailed analysis of the European Commission guidance to Member States on designing and evaluating R&D and IP-conditioned tax incentives, and will place these in the context of the current OECD base erosion and profit shifting project. The third and final section will conclude and provide tax policy recommendations for tax policy makers globally.

5.2 The History of European Commission Guidance to EU Member States

Due to the diversity of R&D tax incentives across Member States, the European Commission announced in 2005, in its 'Communications on the contribution of taxation and customs policy to the Lisbon Strategy and on a common approach for research and innovation', its intention to promote a more consistent and favourable tax environment for R&D, whilst at the same time recognizing and respecting Member State competence over national tax policy (European Commission 2005a, b). This led in 2006 to the publication of the Communication 'Towards a more effective use of R&D tax incentives in favor of R&D', and the accompanying 'Commission Staff Working Document' which are intended to provide guidance to help Member States improve their R&D tax treatment (European Commission 2006a, b).

5.2.1 EU Member State National Sovereignty and Competence

In principle, EU Member States maintain national sovereignty and competence over national tax policy, including the setting of tax rates and the determination of tax base thresholds. However, the European Commission has consistently pursued a strategy of trying to coordinate R&D tax policy throughout the EU. To this end, the Commission provided guidance to assist Member States in improving their R&D tax treatment and to clarify the legal conditions arising under EU law, most notably the relevant European Court of Justice (ECJ) jurisprudence on the EU fundamental freedoms, and the EU rules concerning State aid which stem from the Treaty on the Functioning of the European Union (TFEU).

5.2.2 EU Law Constraints on Territorial Restrictions

In short, the European Commission guidance derived from EU law considers both explicit and implicit territorial restrictions to be incompatible with TFEU freedoms. Examples of explicit restrictions include legal provisions restricting the benefit of an R&D tax incentive to activities performed domestically, or provisions restricting the benefit of an R&D wage tax incentive to personnel working in a given EU Member State. Such territorial restrictions infringe upon the principle of 'freedom of establishment', by preventing companies from conducting or outsourcing their R&D elsewhere in the EU.[3]

[3]European Court of Justice, Judgment of 10 March 2005, Case C-39/04.

5.2.3 EU Law Constraints on State Aid

In principle, rules concerning EU State aid, derived from the TFEU, apply regardless of the form of the aid. Therefore, R&D tax incentives could be viewed to constitute EU State aid if the relevant criteria under Article 107 (1) TFEU are fulfilled. Practically, this means that any tax incentive should be evaluated in accordance to the regular EU State aid criteria, i.e. whether a selective advantage exists, state resources are involved, Community trade and competition is affected, and whether or not the measure is justified by the nature of the general taxation system. A comprehensive assessment of these conditions is provided in the 1998 European Commission 'Notice on the application of EU State aid rules to measures relating to direct business taxation', which also provides specific guidance (European Commission 1998). When considering an R&D tax incentive from a State aid perspective, the main criterion is the potential selectivity of the incentive. According to this notion, an R&D tax incentive can be considered as a general measure (not selective) if its potential beneficiaries are not restricted by way of size, location, sector or any other relevant factor.

In this context, the European Commission has provided additional guidance in the 'Research & Development & Innovation State aid Framework', which covered specific State aid aspects of Research & Development & Innovation (R&D&I) promotion by EU Member States (European Commission 2006c, 2014). The Framework sets out a series of guidelines concerning specific types of State aid, including assistance for R&D projects, aid to young innovative enterprises, and aid to innovation clusters, that all encourage additional R&D&I investments by private companies to stimulate growth and employment, and to improve Europe's competitiveness. The EU policy is based and focused on the viewpoint that R&D is an important objective of common interest and, therefore, State aid can be considered compatible in order to encourage private companies to invest in R&D&I.

Although EU legal guidance applies only to EU Member States, the guidance does deserve wider recognition in other jurisdictions outside the EU. The EU legal guidance seems to indicate that any form of restriction would be detrimental to a proper functioning of the EU internal market. This means that all design options for R&D tax incentives should be applied as generically and as widely as possible to cover most or all economic operators. Furthermore, EU guidance from 2006 onwards also includes the principles of good design for R&D tax incentives, which to this day can be considered valuable for tax policy makers everywhere, and which will be reflected on further in Sect. 5.4 of this chapter.

The granting of IP-conditioned tax incentives has been a relatively recent development across EU Member States. Therefore, the European Commission has not, to date, been able to develop well-balanced coordination initiatives in this respect. Section 5.3.2.2 focuses in more detail on very recent global (OECD) developments that may serve as a starting point for the generation of EU guidance concerning IP-conditioned tax incentives.

5.3 The Different Types and Impact of R&D and IP-Conditioned Tax Incentives in the EU

5.3.1 Countries with R&D Tax Incentives

A recently published European Commission taxation paper that investigated R&D tax incentives concluded that R&D tax incentive schemes are widely adopted in advanced economies, including perceived leaders of innovation such as the U.S. and Japan (European Commission 2015). Within the EU, only Germany and Estonia were found not to have a taxation policy aimed directly at stimulating innovation. The paper notes that R&D tax incentives diverge widely in terms of scope, application, procedures, and rates of tax applied across the 33 countries surveyed. It appears that R&D tax credits are the most popular type of incentive (present in 21 countries), followed by 'super deductions' (16 countries) and accelerated depreciation (13 countries):

- R&D tax credits are available in Austria, Belgium, Bulgaria, Czech Republic, Denmark, France, Ireland, Italy, Malta, the Netherlands, Poland, Portugal, Slovak Republic, Spain, Sweden and the UK.
- R&D 'super deduction' allowances are available in Croatia, Cyprus, Czech Republic, Denmark, Finland, Greece, Hungary, Latvia, Lithuania, the Netherlands, Poland, Romania, Slovenia, and the UK.
- R&D accelerated depreciation techniques are available in Belgium, Bulgaria, Denmark, Finland, Italy, Lithuania, Romania, Slovenia and the UK.
- R&D wage tax and social contribution incentives are available in Austria, Belgium, France, Finland, Hungary, Luxembourg and the Netherlands.

5.3.1.1 The Scope and Application of R&D Tax Incentives Across the EU

The wide variety of methods to treat R&D expenditure for tax purposes in EU Member States can be summarized based on some of the key elements of the R&D tax incentives. Almost all EU Member States have general corporate income tax provisions that allow for the deduction of R&D costs, if considered revenue expenditure; and allow amortization, if considered capital expenditure. Many Member States also offer the taxpayer the option to either deduct or amortize the R&D expenditure. The acquisition cost of any fixed assets used in R&D activities will usually have to be amortized.

The most common approach in Member States is to allow for the deduction of R&D costs in the year that they were incurred or alternatively, amortized in equal amounts over a period of several years. These costs include direct labor expenses, the cost of materials and energy, related interest expenses, depreciation in respect of fixed assets used for the purposes of R&D and subcontracted research. Furthermore, if the expenses are incurred for the development of an asset (tangible or intangible), then the asset will have to be depreciated over its useful economic life. Most commonly, only use of the straight-line method of depreciation is allowed.[4] Furthermore, other capital expenditure in respect of intangible assets, e.g. the acquisition cost of know-how, patents, copyrights, designs or models, trademarks and similar rights and goodwill, may usually be depreciated over several years using the straight-line method. Fixed assets such as buildings and industrial equipment used in the context of R&D, are also depreciated under the straight-line method. Some Member States allow for the accelerated depreciation of capital R&D expenditures. Qualifying capital expenditure includes expenditure incurred on facilities used for carrying out R&D work, including buildings and plant or machinery forming part of a building. The accelerated tax depreciation of the eligible costs is allowed up to 100 % of the expenditure.

Many Member States have also introduced specific R&D measures that provide for corporate tax allowances in the form of tax deductions of more than 100 % of the actual R&D expenditure ('super deductions'), tax credits as a percentage of R&D costs, and specific incentives under wage tax legislation (as available in Belgium, France and the Netherlands). In this context, R&D activities are usually defined as activities to further the research and development of new products, new processes and innovative technologies that do not negatively affect the environment or that restrict negative effects on the environment. Furthermore, it usually includes the construction, development and testing of a prototype, including the development of software. The corporate income tax provisions under the legislation of most Member States provide tax deductions for 'research' and 'development', and define these terms to include basic or fundamental research, applied research and 'experimental or ordinary research and development'.[5]

Some Member States offer R&D tax credits to encourage companies to undertake R&D activities. For example, the UK offers a system of tax credits of up to 25 % of the value of the qualifying R&D expenditure. The UK system also provides for a payable tax credit (cash refund) in a situation where an SME is making a

[4]The accounting method for calculating depreciation takes an equal amount (or percentage) of the asset's cost as an expense for each year of the asset's useful life.

[5]'Basic or fundamental research' is the experimental or theoretical work undertaken primarily to acquire new knowledge without any particular view to a specific practical application of that knowledge.

'Applied research' concerns the original investigation undertaken in order to acquire new knowledge that is, however, directed primarily towards a specific practical goal. In other words, this research is carried out in order to acquire new knowledge for the purpose of applying it in practice.

'Experimental or ordinary research and development' is systematic work, drawing on the knowledge gained from research and practical experience, that is directed to producing new materials, products and devices, or to installing new processes, systems and services, or to substantially improving those already produced or installed. The aim of this form of R&D is to apply scientific or technical knowledge to develop new or significantly improved materials, products, processes, systems or services.

loss. France offers an R&D tax credit system that is based on the volume of expenses incurred by a company in respect of its R&D activities. This volume-based tax credit consists of the actual R&D expenses made in the current year, with the related credit amounting to 30 % of these expenses.

In addition to corporate tax incentives, certain Member States, for example the Netherlands, Belgium, France and Spain, have also introduced incentives in the form of wage tax legislation. In the Netherlands for example, reductions in wage tax and social security premiums are available for entrepreneurs whose employees are directly engaged in carrying out R&D activities. In addition, this incentive is available to institutions, which although not conducting their own entrepreneurial activities, do perform R&D activities for Dutch companies. The reduction amounts to a percentage of the total salaries of such employees, and capped with a maximum annual reduction per employer. For the determination of the relevant R&D wage, the employer may choose between the actual R&D wage method, under which the reduction is based on the actual wage, or the simplified method under which the R&D wage is calculated by dividing the hours spent on R&D activities by the total number of hours actually worked in a given year, multiplied by the annual employment income.

5.3.1.2 The Evaluation of R&D Tax Incentives in the EU

Despite requests from the European Commission for further and more coordinated evaluations of R&D tax incentives, to date few Member States have undertaken detailed analyses of the performance and effects of the tax incentives that they offer. A European Commission taxation paper (European Commission 2014) has found that:

> the vast majority of studies surveyed concludes that R&D tax credits spur investment in R&D. The estimates of the size of this effect are widely diverging and not always comparable across methodologies. The wide range of results probably reflects differences in methodology as well as differences between countries and policies, but is difficult to disentangle those effects. Studies that are more rigorous econometrically and yield more precise estimates find that one euro of foregone tax revenue on R&D tax credits raises expenditure on R&D by less than one euro (Lokshin and Mohnen 2012; Mulkay and Mairesse 2013). The impact of R&D tax credits on R&D expenditure is informative on the effectiveness of R&D tax credits, but this is only a part of the puzzle. A second piece of the puzzle is the answer to the question whether R&D tax credits make firms more innovative and productive. The impact of R&D tax incentives on innovation and productivity by firms receiving those benefits, however, is less studied. R&D tax incentives appear to have a positive impact on innovation, although none of the studies has used exogenous variation to verify the causality of the relation.

These findings are consistent with previous studies that have concluded that R&D tax incentives positively influence the total amount of R&D undertaken, and that the additional R&D expenditure increases over time and more than compensates for the amount of tax expenditure (Klassen et al. 2004; Bloom et al. 2002).

To date, only a few EU Member States, including the UK and Ireland, have undertaken and published evaluations on R&D corporate tax credits. The UK system provides tax credits of up to 25 % of the qualifying R&D expenditure, and also provides an additional 25 % R&D tax credit for small and medium-sized enterprises (SMEs). SMEs can therefore deduct up to 150 % of the qualifying R&D expenditure when calculating their profit for tax purposes. The UK system also provides for a payable tax credit (cash refund) in the situation where an SME is actually making a loss. Ireland also offers two forms of tax credits that are related to R&D expenditure. Firstly, a non-incremental tax credit is available over a four-year period where capital expenditure is incurred on the construction or refurbishment of buildings. Secondly, an incremental tax credit is available for qualifying R&D expenditure that is not related to buildings. The incremental tax credit is set at 20 % of the qualifying expenditure on R&D. The tax credit can be offset against a company's corporation tax liability for the current year, and any unused available balance can be carried-forward indefinitely against any future corporation tax liabilities of the company.

The UK recently published its evaluation of R&D tax credits, which summarized the application and impact of the UK R&D tax credit system on R&D investment (United Kingdom 2015). The evaluation suggests that for every £1 of tax foregone by the tax authorities, between £1.53 and £2.35 of R&D expenditure is stimulated. Ireland also published its evaluation of the Irish R&D tax credit regime and came to the conclusion that Ireland had significantly increased its Business Expenditure on Research and Development (BERD) from 0.78 % of GDP in 2003, the year before the tax credit system was introduced, to 1.17 % of GDP in 2013 (Ireland Department of Finance 2013).

In addition to corporate tax incentives, certain Member States have also introduced R&D wage tax and social contribution reductions. These countries include Austria, Belgium, Finland, France, Hungary, Luxembourg and the Netherlands (European Commission 2014). The Netherlands offers a reduction in wage tax and social security contributions for companies whose employees are directly engaged in R&D activities. The reduction amounts to a percentage of the total salaries of concerned employees, capped with a maximum annual reduction per employer. The Netherlands has evaluated this regime and has concluded that the R&D wage tax incentive has reduced R&D labor costs. Companies are encouraged to use the R&D production incentive more intensively. Without the incentive, it is estimated that approximately 45 % of R&D conducted within the Netherlands would not have taken place in the country. Further qualitative analysis indicated that companies which took more risks, were encouraged to cooperate and actually carried out more R&D themselves rather than contracting it out (The Netherlands, EIM 2012).

5.3.2 *Member States with IP-Conditioned Tax Incentives*

An important aim of the tax policies of Member States is to promote R&D and the generation of IP, in order to create a knowledge-based economy to stimulate economic growth. From 2008 onwards, a significant number of EU Member States have introduced IP-conditioned corporate tax incentives which all result in a lower effective rate of corporate tax being applied to income derived from the licensing and/or the direct use of intangible assets, particularly patents, and on any capital gains made on the sale of IP. Currently, Belgium, Cyprus, France, Greece, Hungary, Luxembourg, Malta, the Netherlands, Portugal, Spain and the UK all offer IP-conditioned tax incentives, whereas other countries, including Italy, Ireland, Switzerland and Israel, are in the process of introducing IP-conditioned tax incentives. It is important to note that these tax incentives differ widely in terms of structure, scope of application, the effective rate of corporate tax to be applied, and the tax base.

The introduction of IP-conditioned tax incentives has been linked to an increase in competition between Member States in order to attract foreign direct investment (FDI), where IP-conditioned tax incentives play an important role in promoting the establishment of new operations in the respective Member States. The European Commission has referred to a large body of literature that has identified that multinational companies engage in profit-shifting activities in order to decrease their overall tax liability by using IP-conditioned tax incentives (European Commission 2014). It is reported that these tax incentives can result in a significant budgetary impact for governments, such as the loss of tax revenue. In the Netherlands, for example, the government has published tax revenue data concerning the Dutch IP-conditioned tax incentive, which demonstrates a budgetary impact of EUR 345 million for 2010, EUR 601 million for 2011, and EUR 852 million for 2012 (The Netherlands Ministry of Finance 2015).[6]

5.3.2.1 The Scope and Application of IP-Conditioned Tax Incentives in the EU

There is currently a wide variety of IP-conditioned tax incentives operating across the EU Member States.[7] A common denominator of the majority of IP-conditioned tax incentives is that they cover patents that have been generated by R&D. Some Member States go further and allow intangible IP, such as know-how, designs, business processes and models used for the production of goods or the provision of

[6]For more budgetary impact analyses see World Tax Journal 2015/1—Innovation through R&D Tax Incentives: Some Ideas for a Fair and Transparent Tax Policy by Paolo Arginelli.

[7]IP-conditioned tax incentives operate under different names in the EU member states such as patent boxes, IP-boxes, license boxes, innovation boxes and knowledge development boxes.

services, to be included in the scope of tax incentives. Some countries may even include other forms of IP, such as brands and trademarks, software, business secrets and secret formulas.

The effective rate of corporate tax levied is highly variable and can range from 0 % in Malta to 15.5 % in France. Some Member States allow only self-developed IP within the scope of the incentive, whereas other Member States extend the scope to IP that has been acquired. Eligible IP-income usually includes royalties and license fees, and also capital gains made from the sale of any qualifying IP. Furthermore, some Member States include income derived through the use of patented inventions in providing services, or used in their business processes. Turning to the treatment of R&D expenses, most Member States require such expenses to be allocated to IP income. As a result, these expenses are deducted at the lower IP-conditioned tax incentive rate. In this context, some noteworthy examples are provided below, which highlight the variety in design of the IP-conditioned tax incentives in operation.

Spain offers an IP-conditioned tax incentive which has been explicitly approved by the European Commission, and which applies a 50 % reduction on the revenue from certain intangible assets.[8] Eligible income includes the remuneration from the transfer of the right to use or exploit any patent, design and model, plan, secret formula or process. This includes the revenue from the right to use information concerning industrial, commercial, or scientific experience. However, revenue derived from, for example, the transfer of the right to use or exploit trademarks, literary, artistic or scientific works, including cinematograph films, and transferable personal rights such as image rights, does not qualify for the tax incentive.

The Netherlands IP-conditioned tax incentive offers an effective tax rate of 5 %, which compares favorably to the normal corporate tax rate of 25 %, and is applied to net income generated by a qualifying intangible to the extent that the net income from the intangible exceeds the related R&D expenses. Qualifying intangibles include those for which a Netherlands or foreign patent is granted to the taxpayer, and intangibles that originate from activities for which an R&D certificate is granted to the taxpayer by the Ministry of Economic Affairs. This certificate can be obtained for certain qualifying activities. As a result, the scheme can also be utilized by companies that do not intend to apply for patents following their R&D efforts, or that develop products that are not patentable, such as software-related intangibles. It is essential that the IP is developed by the Netherlands corporate taxpayer itself, who will carry all associated risks, benefit from any rewards, and be responsible for legal ownership of the IP. Furthermore, the taxpayer should be the registered and beneficial owner of the patents and the beneficial owner of the related intangible assets. Capital gains derived from a transfer of the qualifying intangible assets are

[8] EU State aid decision (N480/2007). Spain has specifically requested for EU Commission State aid approval. Other EU Member States have decided not to request for this specific approval based on their own analysis that their IP-conditioned tax incentive cannot be considered contrary to EU law.

also subject to the 5 % rate. Similar to the UK and Luxembourg, the Netherlands also applies its IP box regime to the royalties embedded in sales of products or services.

Belgium adopted its 'patent box' regime in 2008 that allows for a deduction of 80 % of the qualifying gross income derived from patents, and results in a maximum tax rate of 6.8 % being applied to eligible qualifying IP income. Under Belgium's 'patent box' regime, patents and other assets for which a supplementary protection certificate has been obtained are considered to be qualifying IP.

The IP-conditioned tax incentive operating in Luxembourg also allows for an 80 % exemption of income derived from certain IP rights, as well as capital gains realized upon a sale of these IP rights, resulting in a maximum effective tax rate of 5.84 %. Qualifying IP includes patents, software copyrights, trademarks, service marks, designs, models, and domain names. Patents also include utility models and supplementary protection certificates. Finally, Luxembourg also applies its IP 'patent box' regime to the embedded royalties from the sales of products or services.

In April 2013, the UK phased in an IP-conditioned tax incentive, which allows for a lower rate of corporate tax on income derived from patents. Eligible income includes profits derived from patented products, processes, services and several other innovations. The income includes royalties and income derived from patented services or sales of products. Qualifying companies include IP-owners and licensees who have been given the exclusive right to develop and exploit the IP in question. Qualifying IP includes patents granted by the UK Intellectual Property Office (UKIPO) or by the European Patent Office (EPO). The incentive includes a 'qualifying development' criterion that requires the creation, or a substantial contribution to the creation of the patented invention, or the performance of a significant amount of activity to develop the patented invention, any product incorporating the patented invention, or any process incorporating the patented invention.

Ireland is also considering the introduction of an IP-conditioned tax incentive. In the 'Road Map for Ireland's Tax Competitiveness', which was published as part of Budget 2015, the Minister for Finance announced the intention to introduce a competitive income-based tax regime for IP, in what will be known as the 'Knowledge Development Box' (Ireland Department of Finance 2015). One of the policy considerations for Ireland has been that as growth in the OECD economies is increasingly driven by investment in intangible assets, putting in place a competitive offering for knowledge-based investment that is related to R&D and innovation is considered key for Ireland's continued success in attracting foreign direct investment. To further substantiate this claim Ireland refers to international organizations that have identified that investment in R&D and innovation is good for growth in the global economy (OECD 2013a, b).

5.3.2.2 The Evaluation of IP-Conditioned Tax Regimes

To date, the effectiveness of most of the IP-conditioned tax incentives that have been introduced over the last 10 years has not been properly and consistently evaluated. More research into their budgetary impact, their effectiveness in stimulating R&D or in determining the location where R&D is conducted, and in generating patents, is required. In June 2015, the European Commission issued an important taxation paper concerning IP-conditioned tax incentives and also concluded that to date there has been little empirical evidence to demonstrate the impact of ‘patent boxes’ on R&D and the location of patent generation (European Commission 2015).

European Commission Research

The European Commission’s paper summarized the more general research findings concerning the negative relationship between the level of the corporate income tax rate and the number of intangible assets and patents held by a company (Dischinger and Riedel 2011; Ernst and Spengel 2011; Karkinsky and Riedel 2012; Ernst et al. 2014; Griffith et al. 2014). The paper suggests that a lower rate of tax does result in the generation of patents with a high earning potential, in particular. However, the European Commission does acknowledge that the underlying research has used older historical data that does not cover the introduction of the many recent ‘patent boxes’ referred to above, and focused mainly on analyzing the effect of the corporate income tax rate on directing the choice of patent location.

The European Commission’s paper also evaluated IP-conditioned tax incentives for the period between 2000 and 2011 for the top 2000 corporate R&D investors worldwide. The Commission concluded that IP-conditioned tax incentives have a strong effect in attracting patent generation, in large part due to their favorable tax treatment. In this aspect, some of the earlier research has confirmed that intangible assets constitute a major input and value-driver for multinational companies (Evers et al. 2014). This study seems to indicate that the related IP does not often have a clear geographical location and companies use this flexibility to relocate IP, and the associated income derived from it, to low-tax countries in order to reduce their overall tax liability. The study also shows that IP-conditioned tax incentives in Europe broadly fall into two categories. One category, which includes Belgium, Luxembourg, the Netherlands, and the UK, has elements that are better targeted at incentivizing R&D investment and innovation as they focus on patent generation and do not apply to any IP that is acquired. The second category, which includes Cyprus, Hungary, Malta, and the Swiss Canton of Nidwalden, focuses on attracting mobile IP income, and in particular do not require any real R&D activity to be conducted by the corporate taxpayer. Furthermore, the study demonstrated that IP-conditioned tax incentives produce substantial reductions in the effective tax burden of profitable investment projects. A key finding is that the treatment of expenses relating to IP income is generally more decisive for the effective tax burden than the nominal 'IP box' corporate tax rate.

OECD Concerns Relating to IP-Conditioned Tax Incentives

Irrespective of the lack of proper impact assessments of IP-conditioned tax incentives, serious international concerns have emerged in light of the current global debate about aggressive international tax planning, artificial base erosion and profit shifting by multinational companies. In 2013, with the support of the G-20, the OECD launched the 'Base Erosion and Profit Shifting (BEPS) Action Plan' to better coordinate global taxation and in order to fight tax base erosion and artificial profit shifting by multinational companies (OECD 2013a, b).

The OECD BEPS action points are due to be adopted by the G-20 at the end of 2015. One of the 15 action points includes countering harmful tax practices more effectively, taking into account transparency and substance. In this context, the OECD has come to the preliminary conclusion that the 'race to the bottom' concerning the mobile tax base has not lost its relevance (OECD 2014, 2015). The OECD has identified IP-conditioned tax incentives as preferential regimes that could be used for harmful tax base erosion and profit shifting. The IP-conditioned tax incentives are criticized for offering additional tax advantages to income that is already profiting from IP protection, and for having only a potentially small effect on driving and stimulating the level of R&D activity. The development of these incentives has raised concerns over the fact that they could have a significant effect on patent location without any real change in research activity, and could therefore constitute aggressive tax planning. The European Commission has also supported OECD concerns by publicly referring to the more recent econometric evidence that shows the importance of profit shifting through the strategic location of IP in the 2015 European Commission 'Action Plan for Fair and Efficient Corporate Taxation in the EU' (European Commission 2015a, b). In the accompanying Staff Working Document, the European Commission refers to several informative studies in order to substantiate its concerns. In particular, one study found that an increase of 1 % to the corporate tax rate reduced the number of patent holdings by approximately 3.5 % (Karkinsky and Riedel 2012). The estimates provided by another study indicate that the probability of patent relocation to a tax haven increases with the value of the patent and that controlled foreign company (CFC) legislation may be effective in reducing this form of profit shifting. A further study has found that mandatory documentation requirements are effective in reducing profit shifting by transfer pricing, however this is not the case for those subsidiaries with large intangible assets (Beer and Loeprick 2014). Finally, the Joint Research Center of DG Taxud European Commission has found that the presence of IP-conditioned tax incentives have a 'strong and significant' effect on patent applications (European Commission 2015a, b).

In order to address the concerns over IP-conditioned tax incentives, the OECD has suggested that these incentives should include substantial activity requirements (meaning that significant functions, activities and risks are involved), in order to target real R&D activity and to prevent the harmful effect of tax base erosion. The concept of 'substantial activity' is built upon the previous work carried out by the OECD in its 1998 report on harmful tax practices (OECD 1998). In order to design a 'substantial activity' requirement, the OECD has recommended a so-called 'modified nexus approach' that links IP-conditioned tax benefits to the amount of R&D expenditure incurred by companies in actually developing the IP (OECD 2014, 2015). The suggested approach will include a fraction where the eligible IP income for the IP-conditioned tax incentive is the sum of (qualifying expenditure incurred to develop the IP asset divided by the overall expenditure incurred to develop the IP asset) multiplied by the overall income generated from the IP asset concerned.

This approach effectively reduces the amount of eligible IP income under many of the IP-conditioned tax incentives currently in operation. Using this approach, qualifying expenditure specifically excludes all expenditure for activities undertaken by related parties (including third party R&D outsourcing), and expenditure in relation to acquired IP (Germany and UK 2014). The OECD also suggests the possibility of including a 'rebuttable presumption' that would allow a taxpayer to prove that more income should benefit from the IP-conditioned tax incentive by demonstrating a direct link between that income and the qualifying expenditures. According to the OECD, only patents and other intangible assets 'functionally equivalent to patents' should qualify as assets to benefit from the incentive. In practice, this would mean that marketing intangibles such as trademarks would not qualify for the benefits of IP-conditioned tax incentives. This focus on expenditure aligns with the underlying purpose of IP-conditioned tax incentives by ensuring that the incentives that are intended to encourage R&D activity are only available and provide benefit to taxpayers that do in fact engage in such activity. It is anticipated that such a focus will result in a strengthened requirement for companies to demonstrate real substance and development activity in specific Member States in order to be able to qualify for the respective tax incentives in these jurisdictions.

Following the publication of the OECD recommendations in 2014, the UK and Germany have cooperated in developing a joint proposal (the 'UK-DE Proposal') for consideration by the G-20 and OECD Member States. The aim of the UK-DE Proposal is to resolve the concerns that certain countries have expressed in relation to some of the features of the modified nexus approach. The UK-DE Proposal was published on 11 November 2014 and suggested that related third party outsourcing and acquisition costs may be considered to qualify, up to a ceiling of 30 % of the other qualifying expenditures. At present, it seems that both the OECD and the EU Member States are willing to agree to this relaxation of the modified nexus approach. Furthermore, the UK-DE proposal suggests that existing beneficiaries of the current IP-conditioned tax incentives should be phased out by June 2021, leaving sufficient time for any possible restructuring. It is intended that the current IP-conditioned tax incentives should be closed to new entrants by June 2016. This would give both governments and companies sufficient time for transition to the new IP-conditioned tax incentives, including the modified nexus provision.

In November 2014, the EU Council of EU Member States widely supported the OECD modified nexus approach, including the UK-DE proposal, for IP-conditioned tax incentives (EU Council 2014). In light of the 'EU Action Plan for a Fair and Efficient Corporate Tax System in the European Union', it seems likely that the EU is following the path of the OECD in suggesting that going forward a modified nexus approach could be the new European standard for IP-conditioned tax regimes. In 2015 the European Commission publicly announced that: "*the Commission will continue to provide guidance to Member States on how to implement patent box regimes in line with the new approach so as to ensure that they are not harmful, and will carefully monitor this implementation. If, within 12 months, the Commission finds that Member States are not applying this new approach consistently, it will prepare binding legislative measures to ensure its proper implementation.*"

Similarly, but rather less explicitly, in its 2015 working paper on IP-conditioned tax incentives the European Commission suggested that the link between the advantages of 'patent boxes' to the requirement for real research activity in the Member State concerning the patent could potentially decrease the dominant tax effect of 'patent boxes' on patent location, and raise the level of local inventorship. The OECD's 'modified nexus' approach could offer some potential to mitigate the role of 'patent boxes' as new tax competition tools. The European Commission paper adds: "*the possibility to grant the 'patent box' tax regime to patents that have been acquired, were pre-existing, or contain embedded royalties, seems to make patent location even more sensitive to the tax advantages offered by 'patent boxes.' The same can be said for 'patent boxes' broadening their scope to other rights such as trademarks, design and models, copyrights, or domain names.*"

These developments most likely mean that probably all of the IP-conditioned tax incentives being operated by EU Member States, and other OECD Member States, will have to be amended following G-20 and OECD agreement on the BEPS project by the end of 2015.

5.4 Conclusions and Recommendations

Following a comprehensive review of the current landscape of R&D tax incentives and IP-conditioned tax incentives, it remains clear that more research and empirical evidence is required to fine-tune the tax policies of EU Member States, and that further fine-tuning and modifications are to be expected concerning the current IP-conditioned tax incentives based on the ongoing international debate over aggressive tax planning.

5.4.1 EU Design Recommendations for R&D Tax Incentives

In 2006, the European Commission launched guidance concerning the design of features of R&D tax incentives as as part of the EU package of legal guidance. In the European guidance, reference was made to the Committee for Scientific and Technical Research (CREST 2006), which serves as a scientific advisory committee to the European Council and the European Commission and which provided for an expert report with an overview and analysis of the various R&D tax incentives in Member States and other relevant countries. The report highlighted the variety and design characteristics of the various types of tax incentives, the extent of which reflects the diversity of situations in the countries concerned. These include, for example, general taxation policy, industrial structure, R&D performance of the private sector, and many other factors. The European Commission summarized a number of the guiding principles that can be defined regarding the main design options, features and relevant contingency factors, in the European Commission Staff Working Document that is annexed to the Communication on R&D tax incentives (European Commission 2006a, b). These principles were updated in the 2015 European Commission taxation paper on R&D tax incentives (European Commission 2015).

These guidelines particularly focus on generic design and implementation principles, the different types of regimes and relief available, and the eligible R&D expenditure. Furthermore, the guidance focuses on the systematic and consistent evaluation of the impact, both at the individual company level and on the economy at large, which is crucial for a more effective use of R&D tax incentives. Therefore, Member States implementing such measures are invited to adopt a systematic and consistent approach for their evaluation along the lines defined in the accompanying Commission Staff Working Document. The main messages of the European Commission include:

- ensuring that tax incentives are easily accessible for a broad range of R&D companies;
- including elements of simplicity as well as low administrative and compliance costs;
- principles for evaluation of tax incentives;
- the need for delivery to be timely, efficient and predictable.

For multinational companies that engage in R&D activities, the starting point will always be a long-term strategy where comprehensive, complex, and often expensive feasibility studies are undertaken across many jurisdictions and covering staffing, legal, tax, outsourcing and consideration of many other elements of the R&D equation. In this context, a timeframe of between 5 and 10 years will usually be the minimum period that calculations and predictions will be based upon. However, in many EU Member States, it is not uncommon for tax legislation to change rapidly, depending on various political changes or budgetary fluctuations. In the context of R&D and IP-conditioned tax incentives, several Member States have continuously amended their regimes by first widening the scope and eligibility criteria, only to subsequently reduce the scope and limit the budgetary impact a few years later. These frequent tax law amendments lead to significant tax uncertainty for companies engaged in long-term R&D strategies. Therefore, the implementation of the European Commission recommendations will not only lead to a better tax policy for all concerned Member States, but should also lead to more tax certainty for multinational companies.

Following the European Commission's guidance from 2006, the Commission's taxation paper published in 2015, which reviewed more than 80 R&D tax incentives in 31 countries, established 20 principles of best practice, that include the scope of the tax incentive instrument, the targeting of the incentive, and organizational best practice. The paper found that volume-based R&D tax credits are preferred over incremental credits since incremental incentives can make it more attractive for companies to gradually increase their R&D investment, rather than making a substantial single large R&D investment. Furthermore, incremental schemes often result in higher administrative and associated compliance costs. Yet another of the proposed good practice principles is that tax incentives should only be aimed at R&D activities that are likely to contribute to the worldwide stock of knowledge (the 'novelty' requirement), rather than supporting activities limited to the advancement of a company's own state of expertise. According to the European Commission, the impact of a tax incentive on innovation will depend on how strictly this 'novelty' requirement will be applied.

The paper further suggests that as R&D expenditure may precede by several years any revenue generated from the innovation, it is good practice to provide a carry-over facility and an option to receive the benefit in the situation where a company is not profitable (cash refunds). Such a feature would offer companies more flexibility and certainty in order for them to better make their investment decisions. This is especially relevant for young, entrepreneurial start-up companies that are typically not profitable during in their first few years of operations.

With respect to how a tax incentive is to be organized and administered, the paper suggests that it is good practice to have a one-stop, online application procedure. In addition, the time it takes for the relevant tax authorities to make a decision on eligible expenses should be as short as possible, and in any event should not exceed one year. Several countries have already introduced an option for smaller companies to receive an immediate refund, as these companies typically experience more constrained liquidity.

Finally, the paper reiterates that high-quality company-level data is indispensable for a rigorous quantitative evaluation and should be collected according to international standards. For 17 countries no evaluation studies have been identified. Currently, only a few countries, including the Netherlands and France, have frequent recurring evaluations. In general, the quality of the identified evaluation studies is reported to be mixed, and in many cases do not meet the standards of peer-reviewed academic journals.

Based on best practice guidance and the tax incentives reported, the European Commission has created a ranking or index of these incentives. The incentives were scored against the twenty best practice principles and the scores were then used to compute an overall index. The instrument that has the highest overall benchmarking score is the French tax credit system, for young innovative enterprises (Jeunes Entreprises Innovantes). This French incentive provides generous support to young SMEs for which R&D expenditure represents at least 15 % of total costs. The novelty requirement of the R&D is set according to best practice ('new to the world'). The immediate refund option and short response time means that companies can obtain faster funding and reimbursement. The Norwegian SkatteFUNN tax credit system also received a high score and came second in the Commission's index. This largely generic Norwegian scheme only offers a preferential rate to SMEs. The application procedure for the R&D tax credit is relatively straightforward with companies being able to apply online for the credit. A one-stop agency is available and several guidance documents have also been published. The introduction of the policy followed a public consultation and following implementation it has been subsequently evaluated on various occasions. Finally, coming third in the Commission's index is Denmark's Accelerated Amortization system that scored well for good organizational practice and does not target specific groups of companies.

5.4.2 *Recommendations for IP-Conditioned Tax Incentives*

To date, the European Commission has not explicitly published any official recent guidance on IP-conditioned tax incentives. The OECD BEPS developments are leading to a coordinated 'modified nexus' that to a certain extent will result in a streamlining of most IP-conditioned tax incentives. This approach has been endorsed and adopted by all EU Member States during the course of 2015. However, it should be noted that these guidance notes concerning the design of incentives were mainly agreed upon in order to try and combat aggressive international tax planning and base erosion through the use of IP-conditioned tax incentives. The modified nexus approach will result in IP-conditioned tax incentives not being used in the future to merely change the IP-location without adding any significant local R&D activities. However, this guidance does not provide any details about the effectiveness and efficiency of the design of tax incentives, and the application and evaluation of IP-conditioned tax incentives, including how any additional R&D activity is to be measured.

The European Commission guidance provided to all Member States relating to the R&D tax incentives described in Sect. 5.4.1, remains accurate and current. Moreover, this guidance is not only to be applied to R&D tax incentives, but should also be considered as the guiding principles for IP-conditioned tax incentives. It appears that not all of the Member States have paid due attention to the guidance provided to them by the Commission from 2006 onwards.

Learning from the experiences of designing and implementing R&D tax incentives, when designing or revising IP-conditioned tax incentives, Member

States should ensure that these incentives are transparent and easily accessible to a wide range of companies. In principle, general measures are best used to reach more companies whilst at the same time remaining within the parameters of relevant EU law and treaties such as the TFEU and relevant provisions concerning State aid and fundamental freedoms. On the other hand, targeted measures are best used to reinforce technological leadership or to build critical mass, but these must be carefully designed to avoid distortion of the market. Furthermore, the nature and basis of tax incentives should not change too frequently. Certainly, from a business perspective, elements of simplicity, low administrative and compliance costs, reliability and stability are extremely important considerations for companies engaged in innovation.

In order to provide a reliable and stable framework, incentives should be fixed for a relatively long period of time, and an effective and simple application procedure should be put in place. Auditing rules and procedures should be kept as straightforward as possible for the benefit of companies and the taxation authorities. Furthermore, certainty should be maintained regarding the amount of tax relief available in situations where the level of a company's profit may vary over time in order to encourage and assist the company with the early planning of its investments. The basis and scope of tax incentives should also not change too frequently in order to enhance the predictability of eligible R&D activities and expenditure. In addition, the clear identification of the beneficiaries and the objectives of the incentive help to facilitate the post-implementation evaluation of the effectiveness of the incentive.

In relation to the evaluation of IP-conditioned tax incentives, the EU guidance from 2006 remains in place. Certainly, the aims and objectives of IP-conditioned tax incentives should be very clearly defined, and the evaluation should focus on identifying how much additional R&D activity is to be attributed to the IP-conditioned tax incentive. The evaluation should also include verifying whether the IP-conditioned tax incentives have met their specific objectives and whether the application and administrative procedures were efficient. Therefore, when an EU Member State, or any other country, is considering the revision of an existing tax incentives or the introduction of a new incentive to the R&D policy toolbox of instruments to support R&D, which may also include direct grants or subsidies, guarantee mechanisms and risk capital support measures, a thorough analysis of all the available European guidance should be an important part of the policy decision process.

Given the continued and indeed increased focus on innovation and economic growth in many jurisdictions in the world, R&D tax incentives and IP-conditioned tax incentives are high on tax policy makers' shortlist of incentive measures. It is most likely that this trend will continue as Member States try to compete with one another to keep, develop and attract the best and most innovative companies and highly trained people to their countries, ensuring the path to a truly knowledge-based economy. In doing so, tax policy makers should take note of the significant body of work that has already been undertaken by many administrations, researchers and international organizations, including the detailed guidance on the principles of good design. EU Member States are also to be encouraged to further comprehensively evaluate the potential and impact of IP-conditioned tax incentives on driving and increasing R&D activity and the subsequent generation of valuable innovation.

References

Bloom N, Griffith R, Van Reenen J (2002) Do R&D tax credits work? Evidence from a panel of countries 1979–1997. J Public Econ 85(1):1–31

CPB (2015) Study on R&D tax incentives. Taxation Papers, 52

Dischinger M, Riedel N (2011) Corporate taxes and the location of intangible assets within multinational firms. J Public Econ 95:691–707

Ernst C, Spengel C (2011) Taxation, R&D tax incentives and patent application in Europe. ZEW Discussion Paper No 11-024

Ernst C, Richter K, Riedel N (2014) Corporate taxation and the quality of research and development. Int Tax Public Finance, pp 1–26

Evers L, Miller H, Spengel C (2014) Intellectual property box regimes: effective tax rates and tax policy considerations. Int Tax Public Finance, pp 1–29

Griffith G, Miller H, O'Connell M (2014) Ownership of intellectual property and corporate taxation. J Public Econ 112:12–23

Karkinsky T, Riedel N (2012) Corporate taxation and the location of patents within multinational firms. J Int Econ 88(1):176–185

Klassen KJ, Pittman JA, Reed MP, Fortin STEV (2004) A cross-national comparison of R&D expenditure decisions: tax incentives and financial constraints. Contemp Acc Res 21(3):639–680

Lokshin B, Mohnen P (2012) How effective are level-based R&D tax credits? Maastricht Economic and Social Research Institute on Innovation and Technology (MERIT), working paper 040

Mulkay B, Mairesse J (2013) The R&D tax credit in France: assessment and ex-ante evaluation of the 2008 reform. Oxford Econ Papers 65(3):746–766

Westmore B (2013) R&D, patenting and growth: the role of public policy. OECD Economics Department Working Papers 1047

EU, OECD and country-specific documents

CREST Expert Group Report (2006) Evaluation and design of R&D tax incentives, 17 March 2006. Available from http://ec.europa.eu/invest-in-research/pdf/download_en/280206_handbook.pdf

European Commission (1998) Notice on the application of the state aid rules to measures relating to direct business taxation. OJ C 384, 10.12.1998, p. 3

European Commission COM (2003) 226, Investing in research: an action plan for Europe

European Commission COM (2005a) 488, Implementing the community lisbon programme: more research and innovation—investing for growth and employment: a common approach

European Commission COM (2005b) 532, Implementation of the community lisbon programme: the contribution of taxation and customs policies to the lisbon strategy

European Commission COM (2006a) 728, Towards a more effective use of tax incentives in favour of R&D

European Commission SEC (2006b) 1515, Commission staff working document annex to the communication towards a more effective use of tax incentives in favour of R&D
European Commission COM (2010) 2020, A European strategy for smart, sustainable and inclusive growth
European Commission taxation paper N.52-2014, a study on R&D tax incentives (CPB in consortium with: CAPP, CASE, CEPII, ETLA, IFO, IFS, HIS)
European Commission COM (2015a) 302, A fair and efficient corporate tax system in the European Union: 5 key areas for action
European Commission SWD (2015b) 121, Staff working document, Corporate Income Taxation in the European Union
European Commission taxation paper N.57–2015, Patent boxes design, patent location and local R&D
European Community Framework for State aid for R&D&I (2006/C 323/01) and updated in 2014 C (2014) 3282
European Union Council Conclusions (2014) (Council 16603/14)
European Union Presidency Conclusions: Lisbon European (2000) (Council 23 and 24 March 2000)
Germany and United Kingdom (2014) https://www.gov.uk/government/publications/proposals-for-new-rules-for-preferential-ip-regimes-germany-uk-joint-statement 11 November 2014
Ireland Department of Finance (2013) Review or Ireland's R&D tax credit 2013
Ireland Department of Finance (2015) Public consultation paper: the knowledge development box, January 2015
OECD report (1998) Harmful Tax Competition—an emerging global issue
OECD (2013a) New sources of growth: Knowledge-based capital report from October 2013
OECD Base erosion and profit shifting (BEPS) (2013b). Available from http://www.oecd-ilibrary.org/taxation/action-plan-on-base-erosion-and-profit-shifting_9789264202719-en
OECD Base erosion and profit shifting (BEPS) (2014). Available from www.oecd.org/tax/beps-2014-deliverables.htm
OECD Base erosion and profit shifting (BEPS), action point 5 deliverable: Countering harmful tax practices more effectively, taking into account transparency and substance, 2014 and 2015. Available at http://www.oecd.org/ctp/countering-harmful-tax-practices-more-effectively-taking-into-account-transparency-and-substance-9789264218970-en.htm, http://www.oecd.org/ctp/beps-action-5-agreement-on-modified-nexus-approach-for-ip-regimes.pdf, http://www.oecd.org/ctp/explanatory-paper-beps-action-5-agreement-on-modified-nexus-approach-for-ip-regimes.pdf
OECD Base erosion and profit shifting (BEPS) (2015). Available from http://www.oecd.org/ctp/beps-2015-final-reports.htm
The Netherlands, EIM (2012) Evaluatie WBSO 2006–2010: Effecten, doelgroepbereik en uitvoering Zoetermeer, February 2012
The Netherlands, Ministry of Finance (2015) AFP/1117/U—AFP/1031 U, Gebruik innovatiebox 2010–2012, 13 Jan 2015
United Kingdom HM Revenue and Customs (2015) Evaluation of research and development tax credit, March 2015

Chapter 6
Incentives for Chinese Inventors: A Proposal for a New Inventor Remuneration Scheme with German Elements

Oliver Lutze

Abstract China has stated its intention to more efficiently improve its capability to innovate by reforming its reward and remuneration system for employed inventors. Recently, a new draft Service Invention Regulation (SIR) has been published and is intended to significantly increase the amount of remuneration available to employed inventors in order to increase the level of innovation. The draft SIR follows a system and methodology similar in some aspects to Germany's principles of defining statutory remuneration rewards. The simplification of the procedure together with fewer possibilities to make deductions will, in effect, lead to employed inventors receiving especially high remuneration. As a result, the SIR may conflict with the interests of existing research-based companies with sizable R&D activities in China. These companies will undoubtedly attempt to legally define and affirm their own remuneration schemes, but potentially face uncertainty concerning the validity of their schemes, and regular disputes with employed inventors could follow. The unpredictability of the requirements for remuneration could become a negative factor for companies contemplating R&D investments in China. It also remains to be seen whether China's proposed rewards and remuneration incentives will have the desired effect of stimulating innovation by individual employed inventors working outside of the large well established research companies.

Keywords Inventor remuneration law · China · Germany · Draft service invention regulation · Rewards and remuneration · Comparative analysis · Statutory amounts for remuneration · Incentives for inventors

---

Oliver Lutze is Chief Representative, Spruson & Ferguson (Asia), Shanghai, China.

O. Lutze (✉)
Spruson & Ferguson (Asia) PTE LTD, 1045 Huai Hai Road (M), 42/F 4203A, Shanghai 200031, China
e-mail: Oliver.Lutze@spruson.com

D. Prud'homme and H. Song (eds.), *Economic Impacts of Intellectual Property-Conditioned Government Incentives*, DOI 10.1007/978-981-10-1119-1_6

6.1 Introduction

China has stated its intention to develop into an innovative country by 2020, according to the officially published 2006 policies (Hu 2011). In this regard, incentives have been found to be a critical point in fostering the desired development, and they need to motivate creative people working in R&D. An important element of an effective incentive regime is a remuneration system for employed inventors and other creators of innovative work (Fu and Mu 2014; Fu 2015). Therefore, the Chinese government is developing laws and regulations in order to incentivize individuals and encourage innovation.

China's latest draft Service Invention Regulation (SIR) aims to encourage the inventive activity of individual employed inventors. The State Intellectual Property Office (SIPO) is the leading government authority in the legislative process concerning this draft regulation. The first draft was published and made available to stakeholders in August 2012. A further draft was published in August 2014, and the most recent draft was submitted to the Legislative Affairs Office of the State Council for final discussion in April 2015. (Also, a revised version of China's Law on Promoting the Transformation of Science and Technology Achievements, which is directed at encouraging individuals to contribute to the development and commercialization of innovation, took effect on October 1, 2015. Although this law is not further discussed in this chapter, its effects are similar to those of the SIR regulation described below.)

It is therefore important to consider the potential effects of this new regulation. The latest draft of the SIR is the result of two rounds of public discussion, and is considered to be in a mature format shortly before being issued. This chapter analyses the potential outcome of the introduction of the regulation into the Chinese legal system for companies carrying out R&D.

In order to analyze the potential effects of the new regulation we have made a comparative analysis of the latest version of China's SIR and German invention remuneration practice, including its historical developments. It is the first comparison of its kind, and it is hoped that it will be instructive and helpful in predicting the economic effects of the SIR on innovation in China.

The chapter will also consider relevant cases decided by Chinese courts, and the public comments made by IP court judges in deciding remuneration disputes. By providing an update on recent developments, this study aims to evaluate the full economic impact of the regulation.

The following section explains the concept behind the new draft SIR. It includes a review of literature relevant to the analysis of incentive elements for employed inventors in state-mandated systems and proposes alternatives. Section 6.3 sets out the basic framework for assessing the economic effects of the Chinese laws and regulation, while Sect. 6.4 defines the methodology used in this chapter to come to the conclusions. The main analysis is presented in Sect. 6.5, which also identifies and discusses the opportunities and risks that may result from the planned Chinese law reform. The last section (Sect. 6.6), includes a few modest recommendations by the author as a long-term practitioner in China, that may be useful to consider in further amendments of the law in order to achieve the intended effect of encouraging and stimulating innovation without over burdening research-based companies.

6.2 The Concept of Stimulating Innovation Through State-Mandated Inventor Incentives

The intention of the new SIR is to create a revised and more detailed incentive system for employed inventors and creators in China. In this regard, it defines what employers have to pay to fulfill the requirement of 'reasonable rewards and remuneration', in compliance with Article 16 of the Patent Law. It defines how employers have to provide further incentives to employed inventors and creators. A new system is detailed by the SIR that affects the service inventions/creations of all employed inventors, which can be protected as intellectual property rights (IPRs). The SIR details the statutory amounts of rewards and remuneration that employers have to pay to their inventors, if they have not individually agreed with the inventors on such additional compensation or have a company policy in place that regulates remuneration.

However, the new SIR will increase the incentives paid to Chinese inventors significantly by providing revised rights to obtain rewards and remuneration. The remuneration provisions follow, if not exceed, countries with very high statutory incentives.

6.2.1 China's Motivation for the New SIR

The remodeled system for incentives can be viewed as the outcome of internal research conducted by SIPO that was referred to during a recent Inventor Remuneration Rules Workshop on July 17, 2015 at Renmin University in Beijing, co-organized with IP Key, an EU-China platform co-funded by the European Union and the Office for Harmonization in the Internal Market (OHIM, now EUIPO), relating to the SIR (Lutze 2015). The SIPO research found that Chinese inventors employed by small and mid-size enterprises (SMEs) are often suppressed by their managers, resulting in insufficient awards and remuneration being offered to innovative personnel. According to the research, there are cases where inventors have not been named, in favor of the general managers or company owners. Therefore, the SIR has a strong focus on increasing the rights of inventors and the enforceability of such rights in cases of negligence by the employers. Obviously, the SIR intends to reflect the China-specific environment and foster innovation through high state-mandated incentives and increased rights for employed inventors.

This is also evident when looking at the official explanations provided together with the first draft of the SIR. There it is clearly stated that in order to prevent a deprivation or suppression of the legitimate rights of the inventor by the employer, companies are required to adhere to certain standards in the treatment of their inventors. Clearly, this is an indication that the high mandatory payment standards of the draft regulation shall not be replaced with significantly lower standards by company practices, without justification and approval of the inventors. According to the explanation, the SIR should encourage the reporting and commercial exploitation of more inventions by ensuring that inventors can benefit by receiving monetary incentives. This is based on the assumption that by removing part of the suppression experienced by inventors by giving them more rights, China's innovation capabilities will increase.

6.2.2 *Reward and Remuneration in China's New Draft SIR*

According to Chinese patent law, there are two statutory types of incentives for employees. Firstly, rewards are payable as an acknowledgement of a successful inventive effort that leads to an invention which is protected by a patent right. Secondly, remuneration is to be paid if an invention protected by an IP right is commercialized. The SIR sets new standards for rewards and remuneration that will be compared to actual and historical practice below.

6.2.2.1 Rewards

The monetary value of rewards is increased in the new SIR. For example, the payable amount of the reward upon the grant of an invention patent is currently still set at a minimum amount of at least 3000 RMB (approximately USD 475) according to Rule 77 of the Implementing Regulations of the Patent Law. These rewards will be increased according to Article 20 of the SIR to an amount equating to at least 200 % of the average monthly wage of an employee in the company. In the case of a research-based company, this can be a significant increase (for example, the average wage for a scientific researcher, according to the China Labor Bulletin of June 10, 2013, is 6000 RMB and so 200 % would be equivalent to 12,000 RMB.

Although Article 20 of the SIR provides that these statutory terms only apply in the absence of an individual agreement with the inventor or a legally established company remuneration policy, they are still important. This is because Article 18 of the SIR renders all individual agreements and company policies potentially invalid if they eliminate the rights of the inventor that he is entitled to in accordance with the other articles of the SIR. Therefore, it is unclear whether the courts will require companies to pay at least the statutory amounts based on Article 18 of SIR if a monetary payment is made.

6.2.2.2 Remuneration

The standards for remuneration have been increased for patented service inventions that are commercially exploited. Currently, the patent law, according to Rule 78 of the Implementing Regulations of the Patent Law, states that at least 2 % of profits should be paid to the inventors when exploiting service inventions covered by an invention or utility model patent. The SIR will raise this statutory monetary amount to at least 5 % of the profits for invention patents. It will additionally include plant variety protection (PVP) rights at the same percentage as invention patents. In the case of other inventions or creations protectable as IPRs, such as designs, utility models and integrated circuit layout designs, the employees are entitled to obtain at least 3 % of the profits. Alternatively, 0.5 % of the sales revenue (or 0.3 % respectively for IPRs other than invention patents and PVP rights) can be paid. Further multiples of the annual average salary of the employer's entity can be paid.

Also, in the case of the licensing and sale of patents covering service inventions to third parties, the statutory amount of remuneration is increased from at least 10 % of the revenue to at least 20 % of the revenue, and therefore has been effectively doubled.

The intention to provide higher amounts to inventors is clearly reflected in this change to the law. However, in the same way as for rewards, Article 21 of the SIR allows companies to enter into individual agreements with inventors concerning remuneration, or the enacting of company remuneration policies. Article 18 of the draft regulation will not allow much flexibility to deviate from such statutory standards by rendering all 'unreasonable' agreements and company policies invalid.

6.2.3 Do State-Mandated Service Inventor Regulations Encourage Innovation?

Generally, policymakers in China had the option to choose a system like the system operating in the Netherlands, U.S. or UK (with the exception of very rare cases where it has been found by the courts that outstanding benefits were obtained by the patent), where usually no additional incentive is provided by law in addition to salary, because scientists in these countries are considered to be 'hired to invent'. Chinese policymakers could also have chosen to provide extensive rights to their employees. This would follow the approach of other countries including Germany, Japan, Korea, Finland, Sweden and France that have introduced provisions in their laws and/or court supported practices that allow employees to claim significant remuneration amounts in addition to their salaries.

As demonstrated by the SIR, China will further increase reward and remuneration amounts that are required to be paid to employed inventors, according to the proposed revisions and addition of statutory laws and regulations. What does such an approach to increased state-mandated regulations mean? Certainly, the literature is divided when it comes to evaluating the effects on fostering innovation and the resulting economic benefits.

Some of the strongly incentivizing state-mandated systems, especially the German system, have been criticized for providing too high an additional compensation without justification, demonstrated by provocative article titles such as 'Money (f)or Nothing' (Meier et al. 2005). The German industry as a whole was against the new law. A study of the opinions of the German Industry Association (BDI) and the German Employers' Association (BDA) on the Act of Employee Inventions was published (BDI/BDA 1998), and expresses a concern that the law leads to competitive disadvantages for German industry in international competition. This study identified a high bureaucratic burden and a significant number of disputes, combined with a lack of freedom for employers to decide on IP strategies, as being a major disadvantage for German industry.

The Japanese state-mandated system has been observed as consisting of ambiguous regulations that lead to various disputes with inventors that impede innovation by directing resources away from new innovation projects (Kappos and Nagasawa 2014). Scientific studies of the Japanese system using surveys of inventor behavior also confirm that interest in solving challenging technical problems is not driven by monetary incentives, and that the high payments under the Japanese system guide researchers to safer and less disruptive technology projects (Owan and Nagaoka 2011). This evidently leads to a slowdown in break-through innovation.

However, there are findings to the contrary. A study has found that a system without state-mandated remuneration loses innovation strength over time. For the U.S, it has even been suggested that a reversed patent ownership in favor of inventors be introduced, to allow them to financially benefit from their innovations (Kamprath 2012) in order to foster innovation capabilities.

6.2.4 Are State-Mandated Service Invention Regulations Necessary to Stimulate Innovation?

Throughout the literature it becomes obvious that there are important alternatives to state-mandated systems for remuneration.

It has been found that formal management structure and training intensity play a more important role in commercializing innovation in high technology sectors than financial incentive systems (Cosh et al. 2007). Empirical evidence shows that non-executive stock options granted to employees engaged in research have a positive effect on corporate innovation, especially if they have a long average expiration period and they are more broadly distributed among research personnel (Chang et al. 2015).

A further study of the Japanese system could not find evidence to demonstrate that the prospect of greater monetary compensation from the state-mandated system affects the quantity or quality of patents, or the likelihood that they will be commercialized (Onishi and Owan 2010). A later survey of Japanese companies by the same author indicated that state-mandated monetary incentives based on revenue generated by the invention appear to increase patent quality, but are most effective in small companies (Onishi 2013). Other researchers in Japan now consider monetary awards as being less effective and to even have a negative impact on the development of new products and services and technological superiority, especially in bigger companies (Kanama and Nishikawa 2015). Furthermore, other articles have commented on the importance of avoidance of salary dispersion in R&D groups, and also advocate a more even distribution (Yanadori and Cui 2013). In summary, the intended positive effects of state-mandated systems appear to be limited, and are more pronounced and effective for small companies.

Other studies have found that long-term incentives are to be preferred in order to achieve positive effects in corporate R&D (Lerner and Wulf 2007). Non-monetary awards such as training opportunities and career development can also be effective incentive tools.

However, a survey of German inventors' behavior has found that monetary awards are most significant in effecting behavior (Leptien 1995). Further surveys confirm the importance of the amount of monetary remuneration to the performance of German inventors, but also suggest dysfunctional negative effects (Harhoff and Hoisl 2007). The two surveys of inventors demonstrate a motivational effect on the individual researchers based on state-mandated remuneration. A review of the law and economics of employee inventions has even found that the very detailed German legal system is flawed as a model for state-mandated remuneration (Merges 1999), because it creates conflicts in R&D teams and results in high administrative costs in dealing with the calculation of remuneration and disputes.

Therefore, there are often different views on the existing state-mandated systems and on which effects on innovation are created in certain sections of the economy. It is especially difficult to estimate the economic effect of any provided individual incentive compared with the additional costs incurred by companies. Instead, it appears that state-mandated remuneration systems are not necessary for countries in order to improve high innovation strength. The Global Innovation Index 2014 (GII), co-published by Cornell University, the European Institute of Business Administration (INSEAD), and the World Intellectual Property Organization (WIPO), does not indicate that individual rewards and remuneration have an effect on the innovation capabilities of any country, even though human factors were the main focus of this study (Global Innovation Index 2014). Some of the 'hire to invent' countries with no state-mandatory remuneration are ranked higher [UK (2), the Netherlands (5), US (6)] than the countries with established and practiced remuneration systems [Germany (13), France (21) and Japan (22)]. These rankings may suggest that non-monetary factors, that are mentioned in this study, such as career development, international exchange and career opportunities, are still very important in driving the innovation capability of a country's economy. State-mandated remuneration is obviously not necessary to achieve a high ranking.

6.3 Basic Framework for Assessing Optimal Conditions of China's SIR

State-mandated remuneration systems can have a profound influence on the innovation environment of a country. The Japanese employee remuneration system changed from a state-mandated system that was rarely acknowledged by companies, to one that attained high attention following changes in court practice. After the Tokyo District Court awarded an employee-inventor more than USD 180 million in the case of Nakamura v. Nichia, and further changes were made in practice (Schnapf 2004), it became clear that inventors need to be remunerated by providing them with a very significant share of the revenue of the commercial use of their invention by the employer. The issues of a potentially non-optimal policy became evident as summarized in other papers (Kappos and Nagasawa 2014). For example, overly high remuneration awards according to a complex regulation, led to the loss of funds that would otherwise have been available for fostering innovation. Companies spent time and money on costly disputes with their employed inventors (litigation costs) and maintain an office administration to calculate remuneration in such way as to avoid such disputes (transaction costs).

Clearly, the money spent on high levels of remuneration for individual inventors' awards, reduces the ability to invest in further research. In this way, remuneration could have a negative effect on employment creation in R&D. The negative influences experienced due to a government regulation can only be accepted if positive effects counterbalance them. Therefore, a state-mandated policy should be evaluated according to accepted standards with a view on its assumed effects.

A sub-optimal regulation can certainly be irrelevant if it is not complied with. For example, the Japanese law was widely non-practiced until the early 2000s. However, it is evident that it is not the intention of policymakers that a regulation is to be considered irrelevant, because it would be superfluous and only add unnecessary costs to the parties addressed by such policies.

This demonstrates that a policy, such as the new SIR, needs to be evaluated according to well-established standards in order to measure the effectiveness of the new regulation. In the following sections of this chapter, China's draft SIR is evaluated in accordance with the previously established OECD standards for regulation quality (OECD General Distribution 1995) that have been further developed into checklists (Argy and Johnson 2003). This chapter will look at selected criteria. The criteria chosen relate to clauses in the SIR that are most influenced by following concepts which appear to be modeled from German provisions and concepts.

Specifically, we ask the following questions when comparing China's SIR to the inventor regulations in the other countries mentioned: (1) Is the regulation clear, consistent, comprehensive, and accessible to users (OECD (1995), question 8)? (2) What is the appropriate level of government involvement (OECD (1995) question 5) to encourage innovation? (3) Do the benefits of the regulation justify the costs (OECD (1995), question 6)? and (4) how will compliance be achieved (OECD (1995), question 10)? The analysis provided in the discussion section is a modest attempt to address these questions.

Other factors will not be considered, although it may be apparent that there are further general issues that will also need the attention of Chinese policymakers. One of those is the inconsistency with governing laws, including for example the patent law. The patent law has not been amended and provides different statutory requirements for remuneration at a lower level to the new SIR regulation. In the following discussion it is assumed that those inconsistencies will be resolved by policy and legislators. However, they may create significant uncertainties and negative economic effects if not resolved.

6.4 Methodology

The research question posed in this chapter was explored using several research methods. Firstly, the legal provisions of the German service invention practice and history were compared to those in the latest version of China's SIR. The German law was chosen for comparison given that it is widely acknowledged by officials at SIPO and elsewhere in the Chinese government and among Chinese academics, that China's SIR is heavily modeled on the German system. The analysis is especially based on the experiences of similar provisions in the German system, created by the Act on Employee's Inventions in the German law ('AIE') promulgated in 1957, and the corresponding Guidelines for Remuneration for Employees' Inventions in Private Practice ('GL') issued by the Ministry of Labour and Social Works in 1959, especially looking at their history and proposed reforms of the law.

Secondly, recent case law in China, Germany, and Japan (another country with service invention rules on which, as acknowledged by Chinese policymakers, China's SIR has also been modeled upon) was reviewed. Thirdly, a literature review was conducted on the positive and negative economic effects recorded concerning service invention remuneration systems in China, Japan, and elsewhere in jurisdictions with such systems. Fourthly, the author draws on extensive personal experience as a practitioner managing intellectual property, including helping to set up and apply service invention policies in companies, mostly multinational companies, and subsequently providing advice on such remuneration matters to clients in China.

The results of this research, and experience in the field, are used to analyze the overarching research question of this paper by working within the OECD framework questions as mentioned in Sect. 6.3.

6.5 Discussion

6.5.1 Is the Regulation Clear, Consistent, Comprehensive, and Accessible to Users?

As mentioned in Sect. 6.2.2.1, the SIR stipulates very significant amounts of rewards. Employers can deviate from these by entering into individual agreements with inventors or setting legally enacted company remuneration laws. This was already foreseen by the existing statutory terms for rewards of the current patent law, and has always created uncertainty among employers and their employed inventors. This will be again an issue with the new SIR.

Under the current patent law, there is already an uncertainty as to whether the statutory terms of Rule 77 of the Implementing Regulations of the Patent Law are mandatory if individual agreements or company policies deviate. The same uncertainty will apply with the increased standards of the SIR.

In order to clarify this specific problem and other uncertainties, members of the IP Tribunal of the Shanghai High People's Court already took the initiative to draft the Guidance on Hearing on Rewards or Remunerations Disputes of Service Invention Made by an Employee-Inventor or Designer' (the 'Guidance'), following a workshop at the East China University of Political Sciences and Law in June 2013. The opinion of this group of judges of the Shanghai High Court was considered of high importance as they, at that time before the establishment of a specialized IP court, finally came to a conclusion concerning all remuneration disputes in Shanghai. The judges concluded that agreements on remuneration between employer and employee could be lawfully entered into in accordance with industrial research features, the purpose of corresponding patent applications, or the type of patent exploitation. The courts would object only to 'extremely low and unreasonable' conditions. However, this published guidance subsequently disappeared from official publications and seems to not be fully supported by all stakeholders in China. However, English language publications can still be found (Newsletter Beijing East IP Ltd. 2013).

A recent decision of the Shanghai IP Court appears to indicate that the Guidance mentioned above has at least not changed (Newsletter Beijing Sanyou IP Agency 2015). The court decision found that a valid agreement prevailed over the statutory terms, even if it allowed rewarding the inventor with lower monetary amounts than the statutory terms, and by defining remuneration according to certain ranges that were applied at the company's discretion. However, there is still uncertainty whether the statutory terms of the SIR remain as mandatory minimum amounts, as this is an isolated decision of a court in Shanghai.

To some industry sectors the new increased mandatory amounts are threatening, because these sectors file hundreds of patent applications every year, many of which will be granted. For example, given the highly cumulative nature of knowledge in the industry, the number of telecom inventions is especially high. The top Patent Cooperation Treaty (PCT) applicants, including Chinese companies

Huawei and ZTE, file more than 2000 published patent applications every year (WIPO 2015). Certainly, a huge number of these filings are due to the efforts of employed inventors at Chinese R&D centers, and to which the new law would be applicable. Therefore, the uncertainty in the SIR is of high concern to these innovative companies in China, as well as to other companies whose Chinese R&D centers file many patent applications.

However, this uncertainty is of concern not only to companies with China-based R&D operations that file a high volume of patent applications, but also to those companies producing innovations of high commercial worth and potential. This is because the state-mandated rules for incentives provide for the sharing of benefits from the commercial sales of patented products. Therefore, the remuneration payable to inventors in respect of such high-value inventions can become very significant indeed.

The remuneration relating to commercial use of patented inventions (see Sect. 6.2.2.2) is also determined by statutory terms or can be governed by individual agreements and company rules. There is the same uncertainty as to whether companies are permitted to deviate from the statutory terms. If deviations are allowed, companies still do not understand the extent of allowable deviations before such deviations would be considered 'unreasonable', according to Article 18 of the SIR.

The Guidance on Hearing on Rewards or Remunerations Disputes of Service Invention Made by an Employee-Inventor or Designer (the 'Guidance') of the Shanghai High Court mentioned above, also makes statements on this issue. Employers should have almost full flexibility to agree on the terms of remuneration based on their industry sector. The Guidance also states that the "the amount can be either more *or less* than the statutory standard (emphasis added)". Nevertheless, as previously mentioned, this Guidance was never intended to be binding and can no longer be found in any official publication. It has to be assumed that a court could potentially find that a strong deviation from the statutory terms leads to invalidity of the agreements or policies, in accordance with Article 18 of the SIR. This is even more likely when considering the intention of the legislators (see Sect. 6.1) to encourage companies to provide more incentives.

However, if courts deviate from the Guidance of the Shanghai courts, it would mean that courts have to impose, by their own initiative, higher standards on the parties after finding a deviation from the statutory terms invalid. In Japan, such standards imposed by the courts have been criticized for not finding a proper balance because the employer's contribution to an invention is often not adequately recognized (Yasaki and Goto 2006).

Inventors themselves will also lack clarity concerning their rights. Disputes concerning company policies or agreements will probably become frequent. This could lead to a slowdown in R&D investment in China, as has been observed in Japan (Kappos and Nagasawa 2014).

This uncertainty means that many research-based companies in China are resistant towards the new regulation. Companies need predictability of financial terms in order to be able to make decisions. If no, or only uncertain, deviations are permitted for all industry sectors from the state-mandated terms of the new regulation, there will probably be a general resistance against the new law.

6.5.2 *What Is the Appropriate Level of Government Involvement to Encourage Innovation?*

In view of the uncertainty as to whether companies can establish non-state-mandated systems, the statutory amounts for reward and remuneration according to Article 20 and 21 of the SIR will have to be considered core provisions of the draft law. Accordingly, the rewards will be increased significantly and the payment of very high remuneration amounts (for example, 5 % of profits) that depend on net sales/profits may be mandatory. The German system is a long established example of such statutory required payments and will serve as a reference in the following discussion.

6.5.3 *Comparative Analysis of Different Statutory Elements of the SIR*

6.5.3.1 Rewards

The German system does not currently present any requirements for rewards at the time of patent grant. However, a historical review shows that there was a law reform discussion around the year 2000 to introduce similar fixed sum statutory payments. Those law-mandated remuneration amounts would have to be paid by employers to inventors at an early stage of obtaining patent rights.

The law reform was triggered by a study (BDI/BDA 1998) of BDI and BDA concerning the Act of Employee Inventions, discussed in Sect. 6.2.3. The study was highly negative of the existing law. The law reform discussions resulted in a fully drafted new law that was ready for submission to parliament and which was made publicly available (Deutscher Bundestag 2001). Similar to the SIR, it included a fixed remuneration amount to be paid by employers for every service invention. A sum of 750 EUR would have to be paid after the transfer of ownership of an employee's invention to the employer. This was an initial compromise between all stakeholders including companies, unions, patent attorneys and law school academics. When the German unions later suddenly objected to the 750 EUR amount, the Ministry of Law suggested increasing the amount to 1200 EUR, but the consent of the German industry overall was lost (Franke 2004). An especially high number of German industrial patent filers blocked the draft law with its increased fixed amount of remuneration.

This indicates that the same hurdles may be experienced in China when considering the implementation of the SIR, because large innovative Chinese companies are likely to strongly oppose the increased amounts of remuneration. If a company has a high average employee salary base, the payments may be higher than those that led to criticism and failure of the German law reform. This may indicate that the chosen level of remuneration is not appropriate and may be set too high.

6.5.3.2 Remuneration

The statutory terms for the remuneration in the SIR appear to mirror the principles of the German Act of Employee Inventions and the corresponding Guidelines for Remuneration for Employees' Inventions in Private Practice (GL), as they are dependent on net sales or related profits. According to the GL, the remuneration can be calculated according to German practice by different methods, but the predominant method of 'license analogy' applies the following formula (6.1):

$$V = A \times (L \times B) \tag{6.1}$$

wherein V represents the remuneration; A is the inventor's share factor; L is a license rate factor and B is the reference value (usually the net sales turnover value of the patented product).

The share factor A is calculated from several assumptions concerning the inventor and the creation of the invention, but usually is between 10 and 20 % for an R&D scientist. Typical license factors for technical inventions are published and are technology dependent (Trimborn 2009), and vary widely. For example, they may range from 0.1–0.6 % for chemical mass products, to 8–10 % for medicines. B is a net value deducting certain operational costs and employee benefits as deductions (Trimborn 2009). Moreover, higher sales figures are 'scaled down' by a factor of up to 80 % using a suitable reduction method according to Sect. 11 of the GL.

The statutory terms of the SIR would follow the same principle. However, they allow much less opportunity to adjust the amounts by making deductions. The calculated amount according to the Chinese SIR would be identical to the GL, if one assumes that no reductions are made on B, the margin of the product is 10 % and the license rate B is always 3.3 % (at an average Share factor A of 15 %), and no further deductions (especially no 'down scaling' of high net sales) are allowable. Therefore, the statutory terms of the SIR could be considered to be a generalization of the German method with restrictive limitations for employers. It is immediately evident that this will be of concern to industries where a license factor of 3.33 % is not suitable, for example in the production of commodities in high volume, and for industries where turnovers are extremely high, for example in the pharmaceutical industry. Therefore, the minimum statutory terms calculated on profits or turnover must allow deviations in the future to avoid payment at a non-appropriate level.

Especially in the event of high turnovers and profits, and due to the 'scaling down' of sales/profits not being available, some individuals could obtain extremely high remuneration awards, even when compared to the awards of the German system. Certainly, the literature does not favor dispersion of incentives (see Sect. 6.2.4) to achieve positive behavioral changes among researchers, as it creates behavior that is focused on achieving remuneration at low risk rather than taking more risky approaches to innovation.

The same observation of very high state-mandated remuneration holds true for the statutory terms related to the licensing or sale of patent rights. In the German system the revenue from licensing is multiplied routinely with a so-called 'conversion factor' of 30 % (licensing) or 40 % (sales) to estimate the inventor's share of the revenue (Trimborn 2009). The SIR defines 20 % as the minimum remuneration of the revenue, which appears to be a similar 'conversion factor'. However, the German system further allows for know-how deductions from the revenue, considering that every licensing or patent sale also includes know-how transfer. This deduction can be very significant (approximately up to 50 %). Other cost deductions are also allowable, for example the cost of patent filings. Furthermore, the inventor share factor A has to be considered and as mentioned above, can be assumed to be 15 % on average. Compared with the 20 % of the SIR, only 2.2–3.0 % of the licensing or patent sale revenue would be paid to inventors in Germany. The SIR terms exceed the remuneration under the German system by giving inventors more than six-fold the remuneration provided under German law, because share factors and deductions are not considered. Therefore, the Chinese system provides much higher remuneration for employee inventors than the German system, which internationally is considered as being generous, as also demonstrated by the fact that some inventors earn as much remuneration from their inventions every year as their gross annual salary (Harhoff and Hoisl 2007).

In order to avoid the uneven distribution of the German system observed by Harhoff and Hoisl, companies in many Chinese industries will likely try to set up their own remuneration schemes based on company policies or individual standard agreements with inventors. Even now, Chinese advisors recommend that companies pay lump sums rather than monetary benefits dependent upon sales revenue (Shen and Dang 2014). This appeared to be permitted in view of the comments provided in the non-binding Guidance of the Shanghai High Court (see above), where this is explicitly supported. Such lump sums would prevent excessive high claims and uneven distribution of remunerations in companies with very high commercial revenues from patented products. It further avoids the high administrative burdens associated with complex formulas with numerous variables that have to be calculated by IP and accounting professionals, and which are often disputed.

Interestingly, the practical application in China would then take the same approach that was also suggested in the German draft law of 2001 (Deutscher Bundestag 2001). Here, a mandatory lump sum system for all industries was included in the law according to Table 6.1.

Table 6.1 Lump sums considered in the German reform law draft (Deutscher Bundestag 2001)

Sales amount/revenue from the invention (euros)	Lump sum remuneration (euros)
>5 million/>125,000	5000
>10 million/>250,000	10,000
>20 million/>500,000	15,000
>50 million/>1.25 million	20,000
>100 million/>2.5 million	25,000
>200 million/>5.0 million	30,000
>500 million/>12.5 million	60,000

This lump sum scheme was well accepted by all stakeholders in Germany at the time (Franke 2004). This scheme could be a model for drafting China remuneration concepts for companies as it includes a scaling down provision for higher sales amounts.

However, it is important to note that China appears to intend to reward Chinese inventors with very significant financial amounts to foster innovation by individuals. Therefore, it is unclear whether the courts in China would allow companies to follow such schemes.

Meanwhile, the first disputes with employee inventors concerning remuneration have been decided by the courts. Such decisions, especially those involving company remuneration schemes (for example, Shanghai High People's Court, 2nd instance civil judgment of Zhang Weifeng vs. 3M, April 22, 2015), are highly anticipated and followed by research-based companies and industries. Although in the 3M case, the inventor was awarded a high level of remuneration based on statutory remuneration and not the company remuneration scheme, the comment of the first instance court that the employer's remuneration scheme included 'unreasonable' provisions may be of future relevance and concern to employers that have set remuneration policies.

Furthermore, the clarifications made by the court are relevant as they broaden remuneration claims. For example, it was decided that the statutory remuneration claim should be calculated from global turnover figures and shall extend to the whole group of affiliated companies of the employer.

After such clarifications, the state-mandated terms in China may be the highest state-mandated standard globally. Currently, many employers in the newly established research-based companies and R&D centers of global status in China are concerned about the potential claims that inventors may make against their employer under the SIR. They often make reference to historical development in Japan, where changes to the remuneration practice led to concerns about the negative effect on the capability to innovate when the Tokyo District Court rendered its decision in Nakamura v. Nichia. This may deter investment into China's new R&D centers.

6.5.3.3 Do the Benefits of the Regulation Justify the Costs?

As discussed above, state-mandated remuneration will significantly increase employers' costs. This not only relates to the direct cost of remuneration payments, but also to the costs of related transactions costs, for example costs associated with efforts to mitigate risks by setting company policy, the establishment of administrative units to deal with such matters, and litigation costs for disputes.

China intends to use high statutory remuneration to foster the maximum level of motivation. This will lead to industry resistance, as observed in Germany and Japan. The resulting high dispersion of the income among scientists may not lead to the creation of more innovation, as indicated by the literature.

China's new draft law will only be efficient if it addresses the small and mid-size companies where inventors are often suppressed. Therefore, the state-mandated remuneration system should mainly be focused on smaller or mid-size entities. This was the initial concept of the legislator at the outset of drafting the policy.

However, this requires that larger research-based companies be allowed more flexibility to deviate from the high state-mandated amounts of remuneration. The uncertainties concerning whether companies can deviate, as discussed above, will potentially be a crucial point. Only if advanced research companies with numerous patent filings can be excluded from the state-mandated system, can the draft policy address the target set by the government and justify the costs.

If the SIR with its statutory terms is intended to be important for small and mid-sized Chinese companies, its effectiveness in this sector needs to be discussed and evaluated. These companies have little or no experience in IP management. Therefore, it is an important question as to whether these companies will comply with the regulation and whether the new policy can indeed support the inventors' important role in innovation in such entities.

6.5.3.4 How Will Compliance Be Achieved?

As discussed above, compliance by smaller or mid-size Chinese companies will be important to achieve positive effects from the statutory terms. However, this would require that inventors know about the law. There are doubts as to whether enough inventors have sufficient knowledge. Germany has had a remuneration law in effect since 1957, but in the main three industries (mechanical engineering, electrical and chemical) where 80 % of employed inventors work (Leptien 1995) a high number of inventors did not have good knowledge of the law (Harhoff and Hoisl 2007). In view of the fact that those three industries all have well-established remuneration systems, it can be validly assumed that in other companies in Germany the knowledge of the law is even lower. For China, this means that inventors outside of the big companies will likely have little knowledge of their rights. In practice, it will not make a difference that enforcement rights to ensure compliance with the law are strengthened (Article 32 of the SIR), because inventors are unlikely to exercise their rights. Therefore, compliance by small and mid-size companies is expected to be generally poor. This would not achieve the desired effect of the law in this sector.

The new law will have a greater effect in sectors with larger companies. These companies will definitely opt for circumventing the statutory section of draft law by introducing their own regulations or will offer individual agreements to inventors. However, in light of the first court decisions against their peers, such as the 3M case mentioned above, and the perceived threat, there is a higher chance of compliance. Nevertheless, the quick and efficient establishment of remuneration programs is currently hindered by the uncertainty of what is allowable, as discussed above. Even if companies intend to comply, they are currently waiting for further developments. Strong judicial enforcement of the statutory rights of inventors could have a very detrimental effect on innovation investment as it will create resistance, since the terms of the statutory incentives are not acceptable to many industry sectors.

6.6 Conclusions and Policy Recommendations

The following conclusions can be drawn from the present discussion. High and excessive amounts of state-mandated remuneration may lead to the occurrence of disputes and non-acceptance of the law. They are harmful to the development of large innovative companies in various industries, as discussed above with reference to Germany and Japan. Experience with the German system gives some indication of how to avoid excessive remuneration claims. The 'scaling down' of very high sales in calculating remuneration according to a formula, as present in the German system, would be able to resolve such issues. Scaling down also takes into consideration the contributions made by the employer in successfully commercializing the invention.

Policy Recommendation 1: Avoid excessive remuneration claims by not allowing high turnovers to be used for blockbuster inventions, for example by using the 'scaling down' method used in Germany.

Based on the evaluation of employer company contributions in different industries, companies seem to need more guidance on the available flexibility to set up their own schemes for lump-sum remuneration. The existing uncertainty identified in this study could be overcome by amending the SIR.

Policy Recommendation 2: Reword Article 18 of the SIR to give companies certainty that self-established remuneration systems can be only rendered invalid in exceptional circumstances, but can otherwise significantly deviate from state-mandated terms.

The suggestion from German industry discussed above in Sect. 6.2 and Table 6.1, could be a model system for many industry sectors in China. But would it be found to be in compliance with the SIR? In this regard, it will be crucial that excessive amounts of remuneration do not return to the system following the decisions of the courts adjudicating remuneration disputes. It would be harmful if the courts could easily and regularly overrule reasonably drafted company remuneration policies. If there is uncertainty in the law it is crucial that the courts provide guidance quickly in order to avoid negative regulatory effects. Clear Supreme Court guidance is desirable as soon possible after the SIR becomes effective. This is especially needed for larger, research-based companies.

Policy Recommendation 3: The Supreme Court to provide guidance to the lower courts on how to test the 'invalidity of company policies or agreements' under Article 18 of the SIR.

As previously discussed, compliance in smaller and mid-size companies may be difficult to achieve due to inventors lacking knowledge of the new law. It is doubtful whether more rights for inventors and higher statutory remuneration will resolve this problem. For this target group, it may be beneficial to not solely focus on monetary benefits for inventors as a driver for innovation. The inventor may be motivated by many other means, including promotions, exposure to collaboration with foreign peers or recognition in the organization or scientific community, as shown to be effective by the Global Innovation Index study referred to above. Much of this additional support can be provided by R&D and executive managers of the employees. Their development may be more relevant than providing maximum monetary benefits. School, university and government programs could aim to teach a different culture of innovation and people management in order to more effectively stimulate innovation.

Policy Recommendation 4: Examine and evaluate other Chinese policies to create an innovation and good management culture outside of monetary benefits.

Acknowledgements The author wishes to thank the Office for Harmonization in the Internal Market (OHIM) (now EUIPO), for permission to use materials collected for a 'Workshop and reports on inventor remuneration rules' at the Renmin University co-organized with IP Key in Beijing on July 17, 2015, and a related report for this paper. Spruson & Ferguson (Asia) are also thanked for allowing the author the time to conduct research for this chapter during working hours.

References

Argy F, Johnson M (2003) Mechanisms for improving the quality of regulations: Australia in an international context. Productivity Commission Staff Working Chapter, July

BDI/BDA (1998) Studie zu den Auswirkungen des Arbeitnehmererfindungsgesetz in der Praxis, Berlin, Germany

Bundestag D (2001) Drucksache 14/..., 14. Wahlperiode, Gesetzentwurf der Bundesregierung, Entwurf eines Gesetzes zur Änderung des Gesetzes über Arbeitnehmererfindungen. Downloaded on 8 Sept 2015 from http://www.gesmat.bundesgerichtshof.de/gesetzesmaterialien/15_wp/ArbEG/ArbEG-index.htm

Chang X, Fu K, Low A, Zhang W (2015) Non-executive employee stock options and corporate innovation. J Financ Econ 115(1):168–188

Cosh A, Fu X, Hughes A (2007) Management characteristics, managerial ownership and innovative efficiency in high-technology industry. Oxford University. SLPTMD Working Paper Series No. 007

Franke E (2004) VPP (publisher) Rundbrief 02/2004

Fu X (2015) China's path to innovation. Cambridge University Press, Cambridge

Fu X, Mu R (2014) Enhancing China's innovation performance: the policy choices. China World Econ 22:42–60

Global innovation index (2014) The global innovation index: human factor in innovation. Downloaded 2 Sept 2015 from http://www.wipo.int/edocs/pubdocs/en/economics/gii/gii_2014.pdf

Harhoff D, Hoisl K (2007) Institutionalized incentives for ingenuity—patent value and the German Employees' Inventions Act. Res Policy 36:1143–1162

Hu A (2011) China in 2020: a new type of superpower. The Brookings Institution, Washington

Kamprath R (2012) Patent reversion: an employee-inventor's second bite at the apple. 11 Chicago-Kent J Intel Prop 186

Kanama D, Nishikawa K (2015) Does an extrinsic reward for R&D employees enhance innovation outcomes? Evidence from a Japanese innovation survey. R&D Management, online pre-publication, 6 Oct, Wiley Online Library. doi:10.1111/radm.12165

Kappos D, Nagasawa K (2014) Japan's article 35: are employee-inventor monetary award laws impeding Japanese innovation? Jpn AIPPA J 39–46

Leptien C (1995) Incentives for employed inventors: an empirical analysis with special emphasis on the German Law for employee's inventions. R&D Manag 25(2):213–225

Lerner J, Wulf J (2007) Innovation and incentives: evidence from corporate R&D. Rev Econ Stat 89:634–644

Lutze O (2015) Comparison on employee invention laws and regulations—Germany vs. China. Report for IP Key (publ.). Workshop on inventor remuneration rules at Renmin University. Downloaded 11 Dec 2015 from http://www.ipkey.org/en/activities/upcoming-activities/item/3326-inventor-remuneration-rules-workshop

Meier J, Schubert T, Jaenichen H (2005) Employees' invention remuneration—money (f)or nothing? Biotechnol Law Report 24:168–175

Merges R (1999) The law and economics of employee inventions. Harvard J Law Technol 13:1–54

Newsletter Beijing East IP Ltd. (2013) Shanghai High People's Court issued guidance on hearing rewards or remunerations disputes of service invention made by an employee-inventor or designer. Downloaded 7 Sept 2015 from http://www.beijingeastip.com/en/NewsShow.aspx?p=3&id=857dd04f-b11f-4631-a3e0-056f0e98b210&nid=4d67f8af-9dc9-42cd-a63d-2d67ef7d6a33

Newsletter Beijing Sanyou IP Agency Ltd. (2015) From Shanghai Intellectual Property Court on the case of Mr. Liang vs. Shanghai Zhongji Company, Newsletter 201507. Downloaded 14 Sept 2015 from http://www.san-you.com/en/news/NewsZWInfo.asp?NewsID=127&subNewsID=268&mtypeID=8

Onishi K (2013) The effects of compensation plans for employee inventions on R&D productivity: new evidence from Japanese panel data. Res Policy 42:367–378

Onishi K, Owan H (2010) Incentive pay or windfalls: remuneration for employee inventions in Japan. RIETI Discussion Paper Series 10-E-049

Owan H, Nagaoka S (2011) Intrinsic and extrinsic motivations of inventors. RIETI Discussion Paper Series 11-E-022

Schnapf D (2004) Japanese statute: bane of employers, special to The National Law Journal. The National Law Journal of Oct 11, 2004. Downloaded 15 Mar 2016 from http://www.nationallawjournal.com/id=900005416288/Japanese-statute-bane-of-employers

Shen L, Dang X (2014) How to reward and remunerate your inventors in China. Managing IP online article 3323120. Downloaded 12 Sept 2015 from http://www.managingip.com/Article/3323120/How-to-reward-and-remunerate-your-inventors-in-China.html

Trimborn (2009) Employees' inventions in Germany. Carl Heymanns Verlag, Cologne, Germany

WIPO (2015) Telecoms firms lead WIPO international patent filings. WIPO Press Release PR/2015/774. Downloaded 9 Sept 2015 from http://www.wipo.int/export/sites/www/pressroom/en/documents/pr_2015_774_annexes.pdf#page=1

Yanadori Y, Cui V (2013) Creating incentives for innovation? The relationship between pay dispersion in R&D groups and firm innovation performance. Strateg Manag J 34(12):1502–1511

Yasaki Y, Goto A (2006) Contribution-proportional remuneration rule for employee inventions and its effects on effort and investment incentives. Econ Innov New Technol 15(7):665–678

Part II
Studies of China

Chapter 7
The Upsurge of Domestic Patent Applications in China: Is R&D Expenditure or Patent Subsidy Policy Responsible?

Hefa Song, Li Zhenxing and Xu Dawei

Abstract This chapter studies the impact of Chinese government policies on the upsurge of domestic patent applications in China. We find that the explosion in the number of patent applications in China is significantly correlated with increased expenditure on R&D by companies, universities and other entities. However, based on regression modeling, we also find that provincial government subsidy programs have played a crucial role in the upsurge in domestic applications since 2010. Disconcertingly, patent quality is diminished by these subsidy programs due to the distorted incentive structure that they create for filing patent applications. The Chinese experience has important policy implications for other countries.

Keywords Patent applications · Subsidies · Government incentives · Policy

7.1 Introduction

In recent years, China has experienced rapid growth in the patenting of inventions. Statistics from China's State Intellectual Property Office (SIPO) indicate a steady growth in the number of domestic patent applications from 1999 to 2013. In 2011, China was ranked in top place globally for the number of filed domestic patent applications, according to SIPO statistics. Furthermore, in 2011 China was ranked

H. Song (✉)
Center for IPR Research and Training, Institute of Policy and Management, Chinese Academy of Sciences, Beijing, China
e-mail: hfsong@casipm.ac.cn

L. Zhenxing
Chinese Academy of Sciences Institute of Policy and Management, Beijing, China

L. Zhenxing · X. Dawei
Sino-Danish Center for Education and Research, Beijing, China

X. Dawei
School of Management, University of Chinese Academy of Sciences, Beijing, China

D. Prud'homme and H. Song (eds.), *Economic Impacts of Intellectual Property-Conditioned Government Incentives*, DOI 10.1007/978-981-10-1119-1_7

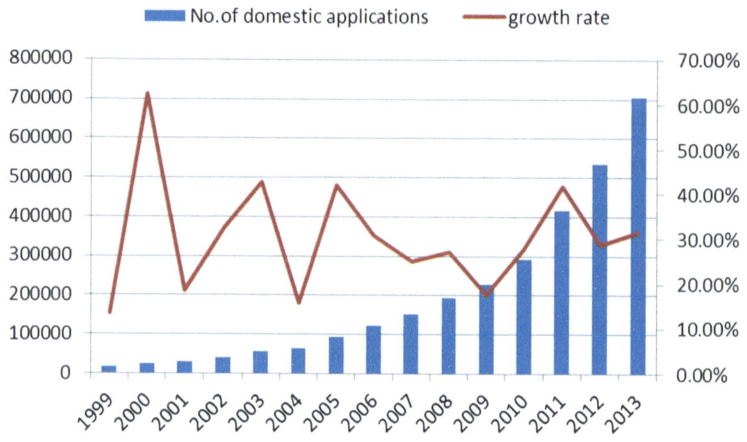

Fig. 7.1 Number of domestic applications received by SIPO and growth rate

in fourth place globally according to the number of filed Patent Cooperation Treaty (PCT) applications (Fig. 7.1).

There are many potential reasons for the upsurge in patenting activity, one of which is the steady growth in national expenditure on R&D, especially as a percentage of GDP. The growth in R&D expenditure is considered to be striking, and based on the rising R&D expenditure, the year 2013 witnessed a milestone when overall R&D expenditure by both government agencies and private entities exceeded two percent of GDP. Patents are often considered as a good representation of efforts in technological development and innovation (Griliches 1990), and the rapid increase in R&D expenditure is an important factor that leads to an upsurge in patenting activity (Hu and Jefferson 2009) (Fig. 7.2).

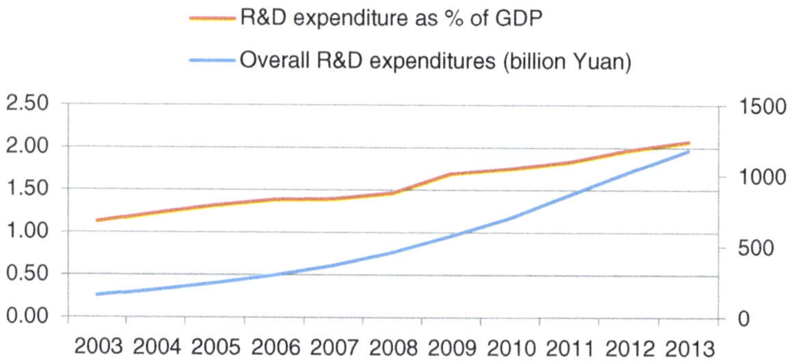

Fig. 7.2 Overall R&D expenditure and its percentage of GDP

Government subsidy programs supporting patent applications are also regarded as an important factor behind such a rapid increase in patent applications. Several studies have identified a significant effect of these programs on the upsurge in patent applications in certain Chinese provinces (Yang et al. 2012; Zhang and Luo 2009). One study found that the number of government subsidy policies and the upsurge in patenting activity was significantly correlated between 1999 and 2007. However, the research to date has only shown that subsidy programs have had a significant effect on the growth in the number of applications, but they have not provided insight into how different types of subsidies (for example, the value of subsidies offered) given at different points in time, influence patenting activity. For example, one study used a dummy variable that indicated whether or not a region had launched its patent subsidy program, but did not consider the amount of subsidy for each application/grant and its effect on encouraging patenting activity. Furthermore, existing research appears only examine the effect of older patent subsidy policies, rather than focusing on recent patent subsidy policies in China.

Mindful of this gap in the literature, this chapter seeks to contribute to the literature in three ways. Firstly, it analyzes the effects of the amount of China's provincial patent subsidies on the upsurge in patenting inventions in China. Secondly, it assesses the impact of new (as recent as 2013) Chinese patent subsidy policies on the growth of patenting inventions in China. Thirdly, the implications from this research for policymakers are discussed.

This chapter makes these contributions while attempting to answer the following overarching questions:

- What is the exact effect of the different factors that have led to the upsurge in the filing of domestic patents in China in recent years?
- What are the implications of these factors for patent quality?
- What may other countries learn from the Chinese policy experience that is directed at building a more IP-intensive economy?

The chapter uses a comprehensive approach that analyzes the economic, legal factors and institutional changes in an attempt to answer these questions.

7.2 Institutional Changes and China's Upsurge in Patenting Activity

7.2.1 Institutional Changes and the Patent System

From the perspective of government initiatives, between 2001 and 2013 there were several dividing milestones in the evolution of China's patent system and innovation system that are worthy of highlighting. Firstly, in 2001, China joined the World Trade Organization (WTO) and became a member of Agreement On

Trade-related Aspects of Intellectual Property Rights (TRIPs), which signaled that the legal and intellectual property (IP) protection environment in China would be improved. The integration of China into the global trading system has drastically changed the business environment of domestic companies, who were forced to make patenting a more important part of their business strategy.

Secondly, with Chinese companies encountering an increased number of IP-related lawsuits in international competition, the central government found it more urgent to strengthen national innovation capacity. In 2006, China issued the Outlook of National Medium to Long Term Science and Technology Development Plan (2006–2020). In order to implement the plan, many supplementary policies were issued to promote R&D and patenting activities, including tax reductions and financial policies. The central government also set the goal that the share of R&D expenditure should reach 2.2 % of China's total GDP by 2015.

The third key milestone came in 2008, when the government promulgated the National Intellectual Property Strategy (2008–2020), which stated the aim of China becoming an advanced country in terms of the creation, utilization, protection and management of IP. As the first national IP strategy, it significantly improved and increased the attention of the public on IP, and was regarded as a fundamental step towards turning China into an innovative country. On the national level, an inter-ministerial joint committee was also established to ensure that implementation of the IP strategy would be supported by every stake-holding ministry. As such, many IP-incentive policies became organizationally feasible.

The last critical point came between 2010 and 2011 in the form of important central-level policies that established the first clear nationwide quantitative patent targets. To implement the National IP Strategy, in 2010 SIPO issued the National Patent Development Strategy (2011–2020), in which the government stated that the total number of invention patents, utility model and industrial design applications would reach two million in 2015. In 2011, the Chinese central government issued the Twelfth Five-Year Plan for National Economic and Social Development. The plan set the target that from 2011 to 2015 the number of invention patents owned, expressed as ownership per 10,000 residents, would be increased from 1.7 in 2010 to 3.3 in 2015.

The period between 2010 and 2011 was the first time that China established clear national targets for the number of patents, and these targets for the first time became a performance indicator of provincial governors assessed by the central government. To meet these targets, and to ensure positive performance evaluations, both the central and provincial/local governments issued a series of policies, including subsidy programs, an appraisal system focusing more on patents, and more intensified enforcement of IP protection. Based upon the author's own experience of working closely with multiple provincial and county IP bureaus/offices in China, these offices were informed of these quantitative patent targets in advance, and so many offices started creating incentive policies as early as 2010 to meet the targets.

7.2.2 Factors Leading to the Upsurge in Patenting Activity

There are many factors that may influence patenting decisions. Regions with larger GDP tend to produce more applications, because a larger GDP is indicative of more active economic activity. Furthermore, in such regions the competition also tends to be more intensified, which makes it more imperative for inventors to patent their innovations. Meanwhile, legislation that provides for stronger IP protection and better enforcement of IP under the law is also favorable and supportive of an increased number of patent applications.

Institutional factors have also been studied in terms of their impact on patenting propensity. For example, the legislative changes in the U.S. in the 1980s led to the so called 'patent portfolio race' in the semiconductor industry, and resulted in more applications during that period (Hall and Ziedonis 2001). Another study also found that foreign direct investment (FDI) is positively correlated with more patent applications (Hu and Jefferson 2009). The reason is that with the economy becoming more open, multinational corporations are able to demonstrate to local stakeholders the critical value of patents in keeping a competitive advantage. Multinationals, despite concerns about IP appropriability in China, also file more applications in China to increase their freedom-to-operate potential (Keupp et al. 2012).

Existing research also extensively debates the factors that led to the upsurge in patenting activity in China in particular. The actual effects of various government incentive policies intended to stimulate IP are rather controversial. Domestic and foreign scholars often criticize these policies for creating a huge quantity of patents while patent quality worsens. One author pointed out that China's IP policies will hamper the country's innovation progress, since the quantitative targets set by the government are overly simplistic, and fail to adequately emphasize commercialization, and may therefore lead to decreases in patent quality. It was also argued by the same study that problematic rules and procedures for patent applications, examinations and enforcement of patent rights would undermine patent quality in China (Prud'homme 2012). It has been suggested that Chinese government policies are more concerned with promoting patent quantity while ignoring patent quality and the technological development of the country is asymmetrical to the number of patent applications (Giacopello 2012).

Inside China, provincial governments are usually held responsible for the upsurge in patenting activity, since they are under pressure from the central government to achieve quantitative patent targets (Prud'homme 2012; Lei et al. 2012). Some empirical research has also found that provincial subsidy programs were responsible for the upsurge (Yang et al. 2012). Some authors also pointed out that patent quality declined under such subsidy programs (Dang and Motohashi 2015), while others argued that the upsurge in patenting activity does not necessarily lead to a decline in quality if the quality of the patent examination process remains stable. On the other hand, other researchers wondered why such a dramatic upsurge in patenting activity could happen in the first place, since IP protection in China continues to be weak (Hu and Jefferson 2009). For example, they argued that if the applicant cannot capture value from the patenting and protection of their IP rights, why would they file an application? Our research provides further evidence on how such an upsurge became possible with the impact of government patent subsidy programs.

This chapter mainly considers two factors in support of the upsurge in patenting activity, and analyzes to what extent these factors have contributed to the exploding number of applications from selected provinces during the extended period from 2002 to 2013. The following two major factors are considered.

7.2.2.1 'Whole Society R&D Expenditure'

R&D is one of the most important factors for generating patentable inventions (Liu 2012). Empirical studies have shown that eliminating patent protection would reduce R&D incentives (Eaton and Kortum 1999). It is reasonable to regard R&D expenditure as a critical factor driving the growth in patenting activity. Therefore, in order to gain protection of their IP, the inventive outcomes of R&D efforts are likely to be patented. However, historical research has tended to consider the implications of R&D expenditure by large and medium-sized enterprises, while ignoring the R&D expenditure by universities and research institutes. Hence, the concept of 'whole society R&D expenditure' is used in our paper. This indicator considers R&D investment from both the public and private sectors, and therefore provides a more complete picture of China's R&D endeavors. By using R&D as an explanatory variable, it was found to be not necessary to include other variables, such as GDP and/or the number of R&D personnel, since R&D expenditure in a province actually reflects the economic strength and R&D effort of a region. However, considering the time delay between R&D investments, the generation of patentable inventions, and the application for patents, we assume that patent applications in a certain year could be the result of prior R&D expenditure made both one year and two years previously. A previous study also considered only one-year and two-year lags in order to simplify the discussion.

7.2.2.2 Provincial Government Subsidies

As previously mentioned, R&D expenditure by itself does not convincingly explain the patenting fluctuations observed in recent years in China. Government incentive policy is likely another crucial factor that influences applicants to apply for more patents. In order to measure the extent to which the subsidy programs of provincial governments affect the incentive, the subsidy policies were collected and used as another major explanatory variable. Although it varies from province to province, subsidy policies share many common features. The total amount of subsidy an applicant may obtain for each patent/patent application depends on both the application subsidy, and the rewards for patent grants. Application subsidies are the kind of subsidies that applicants will unconditionally obtain after filing patent application documents to SIPO, while rewards for patent grants will be given only when the invention is finally granted a patent right. Since it also takes time for policies to diffuse and be communicated to applicants, there is also a delay before the effect of subsidy policies can be observed on the behavior of applicants.

7.3 Research Methods

7.3.1 Data Collection

The data concerning R&D expenditure was obtained through publicly available statistic yearbooks compiled by China's central government agencies, including the National Bureau of Statistics and the Ministry of Science and Technology. The data concerning domestic patent applications were retrieved from SIPO's website. This chapter also collects information from 2002 to 2013 concerning the subsidy policies of each provincial government through the official websites of provincial IP offices.

In total, we gathered 65 policy documents that either issued a subsidy program or revised a former subsidy policy between 2002 and 2013. These subsidies cover the costs of official fees associated with patenting, but sometimes other costs, such as patent attorney fees, are also covered. One study identified that subsidy programs in China started in 1999, but our data collection does not include policies that commenced before 2002 for two reasons. Firstly, many policies in the early years did not clearly state the amount of subsidy obtainable. Secondly, government funding pool before 2002 was set at a relatively low amount. For example, Beijing initiated a subsidy program in 2000, and the total funding available was limited to only 1 million RMB. If we assume that all the available funding was used for invention patents, each application would only have received less than 300 RMB. However, since 2002 the Beijing IP office has paid subsidies according to the amount of SIPO charges, and further provides an additional 1000 RMB to pay patent attorney fees. Therefore, this chapter only considers policies issued after 2002. A summary of the policies collected is shown in Table 7.1.

Table 7.1 Summary of the provincial subsidy policies (2002–2013)

Item	No.
No. of provinces that have issued subsidy policies from 2002 to 2013	31
No. of provinces that cannot identify the issued year of subsidy policies	3
No. of provinces whose amount of subsidy cannot be identified	8
No. of provinces to be analyzed in the regression model	20
No. of subsidy policies retrieved	65
No. of policies of which the subsidy amount cannot be identified	14
No. of subsidy policies to be analyzed in the regression model	51

Table 7.2 Number of subsidy policies for each province (2002–2013)

	Province	No. of subsidy policies
1	Anhui	2
2	Beijing	3
3	Fujian	4
4	Guizhou	3
5	Hainan	3
6	Hebei	3
7	Heilongjiang	2
8	Henan	2
9	Hubei	2
10	Hunan	4
11	Inner Mongolia	2
12	Jiangsu	2
13	Jiangxi	2
14	Liaoning	2
15	Shandong	3
16	Shanghai	4
17	Shanxi	2
18	Shan'anxi	2
19	Sichuan	2
20	Zhejiang	2
	Total	**51**

Source websites of provincial IP offices

It can be seen from Table 7.1 that all of the provincial governments in China (31 in total) have issued subsidy programs. Three provinces were eliminated because the year of policy issuance could not be identified, and a further eight provinces were eliminated because the amount of subsidy could not be identified. This left 20 provinces for our study to focus on. In total, 51 subsidy policies clearly indicated both the year of issue and the amount of subsidy. In summary, our study is based on 51 subsidy policies of 20 provincial governments (see Table 7.2).

7.3.2 Descriptive Analysis

In terms of the distribution of the subsidy polices, it can be seen from Fig. 7.3 that there are three vertices that occurred in 2003, 2006, and 2010, respectively. In January 2003, the Ministry of Science and Technology started to implement a 'talent, patent, and technology standard' strategy with the aim of improving science and technology competitiveness.[1] Many provincial governments issued subsidy

[1] http://www.most.gov.cn/ztzl/qgkjgzhy/2003/mtbdzl/200605/t20060509_32046.htm.

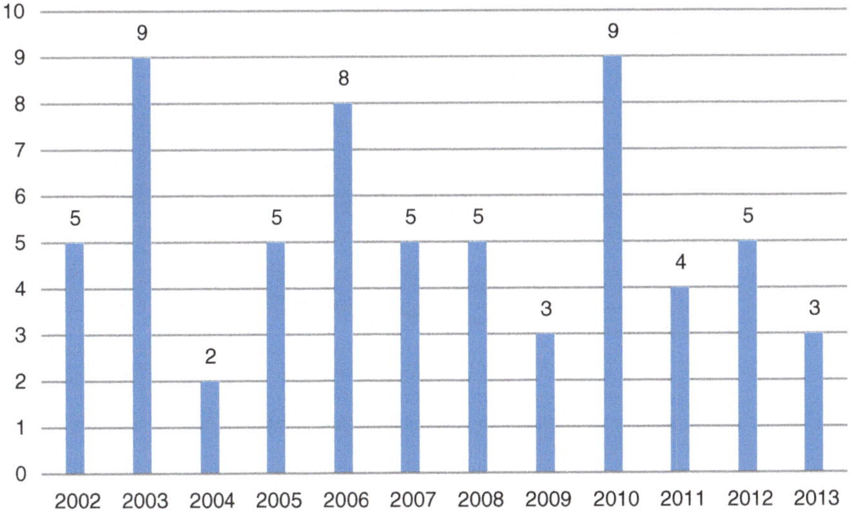

Fig. 7.3 Number of provincial subsidy policies: time distribution

programs to implement the strategy, and hence the number of policies peaked in 2003. The vertex in 2006 is probably due to the provincial response to the Outlook of National Medium to Long Term Science and Technology Development Plan (2006–2020), promulgated in 2006. This policy document was anticipated by provinces even before its official promulgation, and set out goals to build an innovation-driven country. The vertex in 2010 is probably explained by provincial offices anticipating, and quickly reacting to, the quantitative patent targets set out in the National Patent Development Strategy published in 2010, and the 12th Five Year Plan. Furthermore, as mentioned in Sect. 7.2.1, based upon our experience working directly with provincial IP offices, these offices were often informed in 2010 of the forthcoming patent targets and started preparing to meet them by creating and drafting patent subsidy policies even before the plans were officially published.

Figure 7.4 shows the relationship between three important variables. It can be seen that R&D investments, the number of applications, and the accumulated number of subsidy policies have all seen a steady growth during a period of more than ten years. In particular, the number of invention patent applications increased much more rapidly after 2010, while at the same time R&D investment also increased at an accelerated pace. In terms of growth rate, the growth in invention patenting reached a peak in 2011. However, the R&D growth rate either one or two years prior did not witness such a dramatic change. Figure 7.5 clearly indicates that the accelerated patent growth since 2010 could be driven by factors other than R&D growth, which we hypothesize is primarily driven by provincial patent subsidy policies.

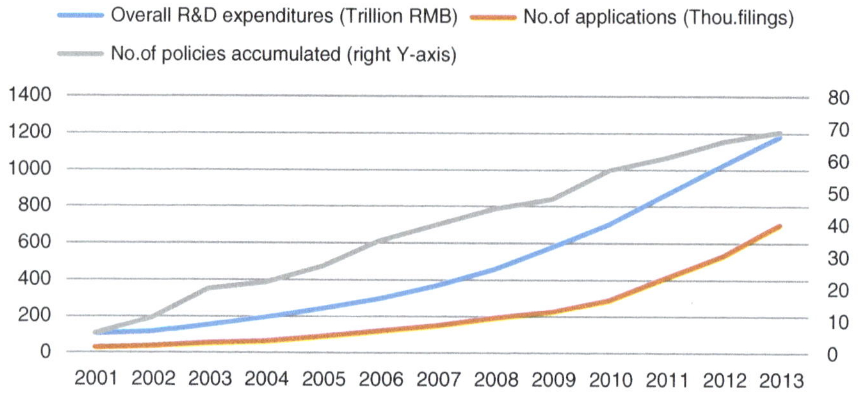

Fig. 7.4 R&D, the number of applications and accumulated number of subsidy policies

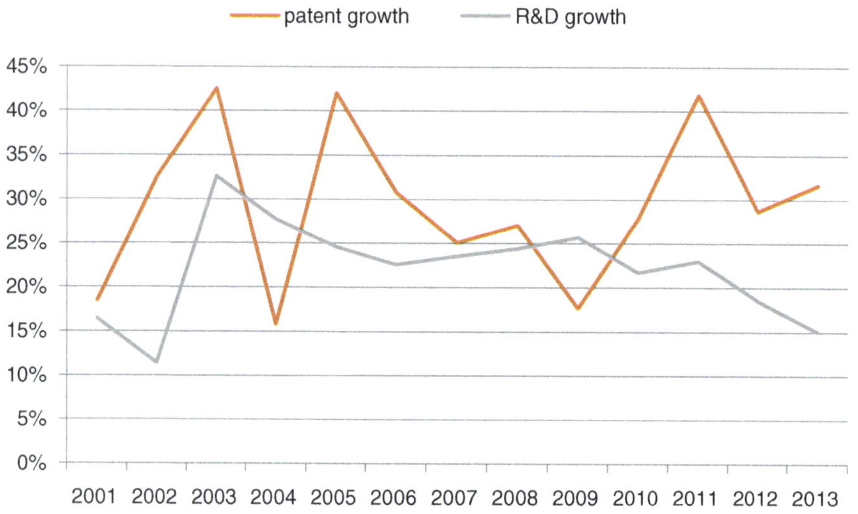

Fig. 7.5 Invention patent growth rate and R&D growth rate

7.3.3 Quantitative Model

7.3.3.1 Regression Model Analysis of the Number of Patent Applications

We contend that the sharp upsurge in invention patent applications in 2011 is directly related to institutional changes in China before 2011. As mentioned in Sect. 7.2 of this chapter, the National Patent Development Strategy (2011–2020), promulgated in 2010, and the 12th Five Year Plan, which followed soon thereafter, set the first nationwide quantitative targets. Furthermore, as mentioned, provincial IP offices were often informed in 2010 of the forthcoming patent targets and started preparing to meet them by creating patent subsidy policies even before the plans themselves were officially published for public consumption.

According to our experience working directly with provincial IP offices, in order to ensure positive annual performance evaluations by the central government, which were now tied to meeting quantitative patent targets, it was perceived to be necessary for provincial governments to more quickly institute, and make more ambitious, patent subsidy policies than they were used to. Therefore, we argue that subsidy policies launched during and after 2010 are more sizeable and are more rapidly instituted and diffused than those in prior years, which were not directed at meeting specific quantitative patent targets *set by the central government* or tied to performance evaluations of government officials.

Conventionally, from our experience, it usually takes two years for patent subsidy policies to take effect after being enacted, since the process of understanding the policies, receiving notice of acceptance of the policies from SIPO, and to obtain confirmation that the proposed subsidy policy had passed government examination, is quite lengthy. In this chapter, considering that the policy delay effect between 2002 to 2009 and 2010 to 2013 is likely to be different, this chapter uses a regression model analysis that considers such a difference between the two periods. To simplify the discussion, we assume a one-year lag for the effect of policies following their introduction for the period from 2010 to 2013, in contrast to a two-year lag effect for 2002–2009. Since the stated variable in this paper is the number of invention patent applications $(\mathrm{PAT}_{it})^2$ of a provincial unit, the regression model the paper uses are:

$$\begin{aligned}\log \mathrm{PAT}_{it} = {} & \beta_{1i} + \beta_2 \cdot \log \mathrm{RND}_{it-1} + \beta_3 \cdot \log \mathrm{RND}_{it-2} + \beta_4 \cdot \mathrm{ES}_{it-2} \cdot \mathrm{DVF}_t \\ & + \beta_5 \cdot \mathrm{ES}_{it-1} \cdot \mathrm{DVS} + u_{it} \\ & (\mathrm{t} = 2004,\ 2003\ldots 2013;\ \ \mathrm{i} = 1, 2, 3\ldots 20)\end{aligned} \tag{7.1}$$

β_{1i} varies according to the specific provincial units analyzed $(\mathrm{i} = 1, 2, 3\ldots 20)$, hence some important provincial fixed effects are considered in the current regression model. The explanatory variable includes R&D (RND in the equation), and expected subsidy (ES), which are described in Sect. 7.3.3.2 below. R&D expenditure as an explanatory variable could be delayed for one or even two years, depending on the R&D cycle. For example, the delay effect means that the number of applications from 2005 may be explained by R&D expenditure in 2003 and 2004. In the equation above, $\log \mathrm{RND}_{it-1}$ and $\log \mathrm{RND}_{it-2}$ reflects R&D output that are one year delayed and two years delayed, respectively. The time starts from 2004, because there is a two-year delay for the period from 2002 to 2009.

[2]Our model only addresses the impact of subsidy policy on invention patent growth, though other forms of patents may also experience an upsurge due to incentivizing policies.

There are two dummy variables in the Eq. (7.1). The first is in order to control for the first stage (2004–2009), ES is two-year delayed (DVF in the equation). The second is in order to control for the second stage (2010–2013), ES is delayed for only one year (DVS in the equation). They are defined as:

$$DVF_t = \begin{cases} 1, t = 2004, 2005\ldots2009 \\ 0, t = 2010, 2011\ldots2013 \end{cases} \quad DVS_t = \begin{cases} 1, t = 2004, 2005\ldots2009 \\ 0, t = 2010, 2011\ldots2013 \end{cases} \tag{7.2}$$

Therefore, for the first period of 2004–2009, the ES is considered as being two-year delayed. While for the second period, starting in 2010 and ending in 2013, the ES is considered as being one-year delayed. Therefore, Eq. (7.1) thus takes into account the difference of such policy delay effects at different stages.

7.3.3.2 Equation for Expected Subsidy

ES is the Expected Subsidy for invention patent applications, which basically includes fees for application, document printing, examination, and maintenance during the application stage. For reference, the typical fees charged by SIPO in respect of invention patents, are listed below.

Based upon a review of the provincial subsidy measures of all 20 provinces analyzed for this chapter, the typical patent subsidy amount offered to a successful subsidy applicant was identified for each province. In practice, the provincial government subsidies consist of two parts: the application subsidy (AS_{it}) and the granted rewards (GR_{it}). Annex A provides a list of the AS and GR provided by each of the 20 provinces analyzed in this chapter, according to the years analyzed. The AS is given to any applicant who files an application document accepted by SIPO, while GR is only given to applicants that succeed in obtaining a patent right.

The AS and GR per province cover some, or all, of the patent fee costs mentioned in Table.[3] Upon review of the patent subsidies collected, it is apparent that some provincial governments do not subsidize patent applications, but instead only give rewards after patents have been granted. In this situation, the AS value for these provinces is set as zero (see Annex A for a list).

Furthermore, it also has to be considered that not all invention patent applications can be granted, and therefore subsidies for grants should consider the possibility of passing the substantive examination by the local IP office. Hence, we create the parameter of PGR_i which stands for the average possibility (in terms of time) of passing the substantive examination for a province. Next, the ES (expected subsidy) in this chapter is calculated as:

[3] In some instances, some provincial governments in China provide subsidies related to patents that cover other costs related to patenting.

$$ES_{it} = AS_{it} + PGR_i \times GR_{it} \quad (t = 1999, 2000...2013;\ i = 1, 2, 3...20) \quad (7.3)$$

The equation expresses the Expected Subsidy for applicants in the regions consisting of application subsidy (AS_{ii}) and granted rewards (GR_{it}). For PGR_i, this chapter finds that the average time span from filing an application to obtaining a patent right is approximately two years. This chapter calculates the *PGR* based on the Eq. (7.4):

$$PGR_{it} = GPAT/APAT_{it-2} \quad (t = 2004, 2003...2013;\ i = 1, 2, 3...20) \quad (7.4)$$

In Eq. (7.4), $GPAT_{it}$ is the number of patents granted in the year *t*. $APAT_{it-2}$ s the number of applications in the year $t-$ 2. It should be noted that the indicator *PGR*, in effect, allows the model to distinguish the effect of the possibility of an application from a province in year *t* to get their patents granted, which further affects their expected amount of subsidies based on Eq. (7.3).

7.3.3.3 Correlation Analysis of Variables

Before conducting the regression, we first conducted a correlation analysis. If the variables were not statistically correlated, regression analysis may have limited value. Table 7.4 shows that all the variables are correlated at the 0.01 level. Therefore, we can continue the regression model in the next section.

Table 7.3 Invention patent fees during the application stage (RMB)

Fee for application	900
Fee for document printing	50
Fee for examination	2500
Fee for maintenance (during the application)[a]	300
In total	3750

[a]During the examination stage, if the patent has not been granted by the second year, a maintenance fee should be paid to ensure that the application is still valid from the third year until the grant

Table 7.4 Correlation matrix of the variables

		ES	PAT	RND
ES	Pearson correlation	1	0.267**	0.314**
	n	240	240	240
PAT	Pearson correlation	0.267**	1	0.925**
	n	240	240	240
RND	Pearson correlation	0.314**	0.925**	1
	n	240	240	240

**$p < 1\ \%$

7.3.3.4 Limitations of the Method

Although we have taken a number of steps to ensure the rigor of our modeling, it should be noted that we may have omitted some yearly fixed effects from our estimations. As such, our findings should be treated with caution as to representing intensively tested correlations, let alone causality. Ideally, future research could strengthen our modeling approach.

7.4 Results and Discussion

7.4.1 Results

Considering the heterogeneity of each province, this chapter uses the fixed effects least squares dummy variable model (LSDV) to estimate the coefficient in Eqs. (7.1) and (7.2). The results are shown in the following tables.

Therefore, the regression model for application number is formulated as:

$$\begin{aligned}\log PAT_{it} =& 3.66 + 0.58 \cdot \log RND_{it-1} + 0.46 \cdot \log RND_{it-2} + 7.73 \times 10^{-6} \cdot ES_{it-2} \cdot DVF \\ &+ 10.2 \times 10^{-5} \cdot ES_{it-1} \cdot DVS_t + u \\ &(\mathrm{t} = 2004, 2003\ldots 2013;\quad \mathrm{i} = 1, 2, 3\ldots 20)\end{aligned}$$

It is shown in Table 7.5 that both RND values, which are one-year delayed and two-year delayed, are significantly correlated with the number of patent applications, indicating that R&D investment made one year and two years previously, contributes greatly to the upsurge of patent applications in the recent years. In terms of government subsidies, our model has identified that during 2004–2009, subsidy policies (ES) do not exert a significant effect on generating more applications. This result appears to indicate that the upsurge of applications from 2004 to 2009 is highly correlated with more R&D investment and growing patenting awareness, while policy incentives may have played a much lesser role and is not measureable in the regression model formulated by this research.[4] In contrast, during the period from 2010 to 2013, it is found that subsidy policies (ES) are shown to have a significant effect on the number of applications, with the confidence level at 0.01 (See Table 7.5).

[4]Two reasons our findings differ from in this regard may be because we examined the value of subsidies rather than the number of subsidy policies, and also used a different time frame of analysis (2004–2009 instead of 2001–2007).

Table 7.5 Regression results for Eq. 7.1

Variables	Coefficient (and standard error)	t-statistic
Constant	3.661244 (0.193939)**	18.87836
LOG(RND(-1))	0.577326 (0.225308)*	2.562385
LOG(RND(-2))	0.457221 (0.228200)*	2.003594
ES(-2)*DVF	7.73E-06 (3.65E-05)	0.211691
ES(-1)*DVS	0.000102 (3.83E-05)**	2.671194
R^2	0.964	
Adjusted R^2	0.959	
F-statistic	205.704	
Number of observations	200	

*$p < 5$ %; **$p < 1$ %

7.4.2 Discussion

Our results indicate that R&D investment is an important driver for patenting growth in China. However, patent subsidy policies from 2010 to 2013 also increased the propensity of invention patenting activity in China. It is argued that one of the reasons for this is that since 2010, provincial governors may have taken more effective measures to implement these subsidy policies, since for the first time their performance assessments are tied to meeting specific quantitative patent targets set by the central level government. In practice, most of the application subsidies need to be approved by the local/provincial government, therefore the efficiency of the approval process would influence the expectation of obtaining the promised subsidies greatly. Our experience working with local officials also convince us that local IP offices have sped up the approval process to accelerate the policy stimulation. Further, other authors have commented that using patent targets as an evaluation indicator in the assessment of local officials induced more patent applications (Prud'homme 2012; Lei et al. 2012). The results in this chapter also provide evidence for this argument.

Perhaps another reason for the significant policy incentive is that after years of interaction between government and industry, Chinese companies became better aware and more familiar with government policies, and have employed them faster in recent years. The widely adopted use of information technology has also facilitated the dissemination of government policies and so the impact is greater.

However, it should be noted that the coefficient during this period of time (2010–2013) is still quite small. An important reason is that the independent variable used in this paper is ES (average subsidy on each application), while the dependent variable is the total number of applications in a region. The coefficient is smaller, which indicates that the elasticity of total applications to cost of patenting is relatively small. Secondly, this chapter only addresses the impact of subsidy policies on the growth of invention patents, and the results indicate that the incentive effect of subsidy policies on the upsurge in invention patents is not as great as expected.

Thirdly, another reason for the limited effect, as measured by the current study, is that this chapter does not consider the subsidy programs launched by local (i.e. sub-provincial) governments, instead only those at the provincial level are considered. In the Chinese institutional system, pressure for filing more applications at the provincial level would be transferred to the local level. To fulfill the objective, local governments also launched many subsidy programs between 2010 and 2013. In many cases, applicants to these programs are required to use the application fee receipt from SIPO as certification in order to be able to apply for patent subsidies from local governments. However, we have not found an effective approach for collecting information concerning all the subsidy programs at the local level, as, depending on the definition used, there are hundreds or thousands of local (e.g. counties, other units) governments in China.

Although the intention of our study was not to measure the quality of China's domestic patent applications, the results, however, do provide implications concerning patent quality. The charge for filing an application for an invention patent with SIPO is 3750 RMB (refer to Table 7.3). Considering that 60 % of applications enjoyed a 70 % fee waiver applied by SIPO, which is a usual practice in China, the real cost of each application is only 2175 RMB ($3750 \times 0.6 \times 0.3 + 3750 \times 0.4$). As many applicants received further subsidies from provincial/municipal level governments, the real cost for filing a patent application is far less. Furthermore, according to our investigation, due to the level of subsidies in some cases applicants may even make money simply by filing patent applications.

It has been argued that patent quality is probably hampered by the application incentives provided by the subsidy policies. As has previously been pointed out, a fundamental problem with the present patent system is that it discourages 'good' patent behavior, and creates more incentive for applying for low quality patents (Wagner 2009). Patent quality will not be improved until applicants have strong and unequivocal incentives to obtain high quality patents. Based on a questionnaire survey of more than 300 patent examiners and attorneys, Liu et al. (2012) found that the incentives for patenting exert greater influence on the decision to apply for patents than considerations of the IP protection environment, or the capability of patent office examinations to determine patent quality. In this respect, we contend that patent quality in China may be negatively affected by the significant lowering of patenting fees due to government subsidies. Before the subsidy policies were introduced, applicants may not have sought to patent some of their lower quality inventions due to the high application fees and relatively low benefit it returns. However, with the support of government subsidies, the cost of patenting inventions is much lowered and the incentive for applying for lower quality patents is somewhat increased.

7.5 Conclusions and Policy Implications

This chapter discusses the factors behind the recent upsurge in Chinese domestic patent applications. We have identified that the explosion in the number of patent applications in China is highly correlated with increasing R&D investment from both government and enterprises, while patent subsidies also played an important role from 2010 to 2013. This being said, the limitations of the method we used to reach this conclusion, as explained in the methodology section, should be considered. The Chinese experience of mass patenting subsidies has many future policy implications.

Firstly, since most subsidy programs do not differentiate between the types of applicant, such mass unconditioned subsidy programs are unsustainable. With the growing number of patent applications and grants, provincial governments find it increasingly difficult to have adequate budget to provide such subsidies. An appropriately designed subsidy should only support smaller companies or other economically disadvantaged entities. For large (and perhaps some medium-sized enterprises), or high-tech firms recognized by the Ministry of Science and Technology, the need to subsidize their patenting activity is highly questionable, since they either already have adequate financial resources or receive other forms of support (Long et al. 2013). Government programs should support entities that can proportionally benefit the most from such support, instead of subsidizing all companies overwhelmingly, regardless of the applicant type.

Secondly, in the design of these subsidy programs, it is important to clarify their primary objectives. The purpose of the Chinese central government including a patent indicator in the national 12th Five Year Plan was to improve patenting awareness and enhance the innovation capability of Chinese industries. However, considering the complexity of innovation capability, most subsidy policies lose sight of the primary goal, and instead focus only on quantity. This is another rationale to explain why patent quality will decline with the implementation of such policies with goals deviating from those originally intended. Since 2013, concerns over patent quality have exerted great pressure on the continuation of subsidy programs. Furthermore, in December 2013 SIPO issued a policy calling for an improvement in the quality of patent applications. As a consequence, most provinces then started to revise their subsidy programs.

Thirdly, subsidies should be properly structured in order to truly encourage innovation or the commercialization of new inventions. Through only subsidizing patent applications or rewarding patent grants, the mere target seems to simply encourage more patenting, regardless of quality. However, innovation is not just the introduction of inventions into the social system, rather it requires ensuring that inventions actually have economic effects and value (Schumpeter 1942). Therefore, there is still a great gap to bridge between producing more patents and enhancing national innovation capacity. From this perspective, subsidies targeting only patent applications and grants, at least at China's current stage of technological development, are likely to be a waste of public resources. This chapter proposes that government subsidies should instead be moved down the innovation value chain to provide monetary support to patent commercialization and entrepreneurial activities, rather than just for filing patent applications.

Fourthly, on the technical level, governments should make sure that applicants properly obtain subsidies, which often presents a significant challenge. In Chinese practice, most of the subsidies consist of application subsidies and grant reward subsidies. To obtain application subsidies, the applicant usually needs only to hand in a certification that SIPO has already accepted the patent application. However, in many cases the applicant may withdraw the application after obtaining the subsidy. Such moral hazards create further misuse of public resources. It is observed that subsidies given on condition of the patent being finally granted provides a stronger incentive for applicants to file applications of better quality.

Finally, the workings of patent subsidy programs in China raise questions over the appropriateness of governance of China's IP regime. With these subsidy programs, SIPO received a large amount of patent fees and employed more examiners to deal with the surge in the number of applications. As part of this process, many provincial governments' fiscal resources were transferred to a department of the central government, and ultimately, the surplus of patent fees was given to the central government. It is debatable whether it is appropriate that provincial governments, who were tasked with meeting patent targets set by the central level, in turn are also required to 'subsidize' the central government in this way.

Appendix A: Subsidy amounts for each province

Province	Period	Application subsidy	Grant reward
Zhejiang	2002	3000	0
Zhejiang	2003	3000	0
Zhejiang	2004	3000	0
Zhejiang	2005	3000	0
Zhejiang	2006	0	4000
Zhejiang	2007	0	4000
Zhejiang	2008	0	4000
Zhejiang	2009	0	4000
Zhejiang	2010	0	4000
Zhejiang	2011	0	4000
Zhejiang	2012	0	4000
Zhejiang	2013	0	4000
Shanghai	2002	0	0
Shanghai	2003	3450	0
Shanghai	2004	3450	0
Shanghai	2005	3450	0

(continued)

(continued)

Province	Period	Application subsidy	Grant reward
Shanghai	2006	3450	0
Shanghai	2007	3450	0
Shanghai	2008	3450	0
Shanghai	2009	3450	0
Shanghai	2010	3450	0
Shanghai	2011	3450	0
Shanghai	2012	3260	0
Shanghai	2013	3260	0
Shandong	2002	0	0
Shandong	2003	0	0
Shandong	2004	0	0
Shandong	2005	0	0
Shandong	2006	1500	1500
Shandong	2007	1500	1500
Shandong	2008	1500	1500
Shandong	2009	0	4000
Shandong	2010	0	4000
Shandong	2011	0	4000
Shandong	2012	0	4000
Shandong	2013	0	4000
Sichuan	2002	1000	0
Sichuan	2003	1000	0
Sichuan	2004	1000	0
Sichuan	2005	1000	0
Sichuan	2006	1000	0
Sichuan	2007	1000	0
Sichuan	2008	1200	0
Sichuan	2009	1200	0
Sichuan	2010	2415	0
Sichuan	2011	2415	0
Sichuan	2012	2415	0
Sichuan	2013	2415	0
Shan'anxi	2002	0	0
Shan'anxi	2003	3500	0
Shan'anxi	2004	3500	0
Shan'anxi	2005	3500	0
Shan'anxi	2006	3500	0
Shan'anxi	2007	3500	0
Shan'anxi	2008	3500	0
Shan'anxi	2009	1000	0

(continued)

(continued)

Province	Period	Application subsidy	Grant reward
Shan'anxi	2010	1000	0
Shan'anxi	2011	1000	0
Shan'anxi	2012	1000	0
Shan'anxi	2013	1000	0
Shanxi	2002	0	0
Shanxi	2003	1200	0
Shanxi	2004	1200	0
Shanxi	2005	1200	0
Shanxi	2006	1200	0
Shanxi	2007	1200	0
Shanxi	2008	1200	0
Shanxi	2009	1200	0
Shanxi	2010	1200	0
Shanxi	2011	1200	0
Shanxi	2012	1200	0
Shanxi	2013	1200	0
Inner mongolia	2002	3450	0
Inner mongolia	2003	3450	0
Inner mongolia	2004	3450	0
Inner mongolia	2005	3450	0
Inner mongolia	2006	3450	0
Inner mongolia	2007	3450	0
Inner mongolia	2008	3450	0
Inner mongolia	2009	3450	0
Inner mongolia	2010	3450	0
Inner mongolia	2011	3450	0
Inner mongolia	2012	3450	0
Inner mongolia	2013	3450	0
Liaoning	2002	0	0
Liaoning	2003	0	0
Liaoning	2004	0	0
Liaoning	2005	3450	0
Liaoning	2006	3450	0
Liaoning	2007	3450	0
Liaoning	2008	3450	0
Liaoning	2009	3450	0
Liaoning	2010	3450	0
Liaoning	2011	3450	0
Liaoning	2012	3450	0
Liaoning	2013	3450	0

(continued)

(continued)

Province	Period	Application subsidy	Grant reward
Jiangxi	2002	2070	0
Jiangxi	2003	2070	0
Jiangxi	2004	2070	0
Jiangxi	2005	2070	0
Jiangxi	2006	500	2500
Jiangxi	2007	500	2500
Jiangxi	2008	500	2500
Jiangxi	2009	500	2500
Jiangxi	2010	500	2500
Jiangxi	2011	500	2500
Jiangxi	2012	500	2500
Jiangxi	2013	500	2500
Jiangxi	2002	2000	0
Jiangxi	2003	2000	0
Jiangxi	2004	2000	0
Jiangxi	2005	2000	0
Jiangxi	2006	3450	0
Jiangxi	2007	3450	0
Jiangxi	2008	3450	0
Jiangxi	2009	3450	0
Jiangxi	2010	3450	0
Jiangxi	2011	1000	3000
Jiangxi	2012	1000	3000
Jiangxi	2013	1000	3000
Hunan	2002	0	0
Hunan	2003	0	0
Hunan	2004	0	2000
Hunan	2005	0	2000
Hunan	2006	0	2000
Hunan	2007	0	2000
Hunan	2008	0	2000
Hunan	2009	0	2000
Hunan	2010	0	2000
Hunan	2011	0	3000
Hunan	2012	0	3000
Hunan	2013	0	3000
Heilongjiang	2002	0	0
Heilongjiang	2003	0	0
Heilongjiang	2004	0	0
Heilongjiang	2005	0	0

(continued)

(continued)

Province	Period	Application subsidy	Grant reward
Heilongjiang	2006	0	0
Heilongjiang	2007	0	0
Heilongjiang	2008	0	0
Heilongjiang	2009	0	0
Heilongjiang	2010	3450	1000
Heilongjiang	2011	3450	1000
Heilongjiang	2012	3450	1000
Heilongjiang	2013	3450	1000
Henan	2002	475	0
Henan	2003	475	0
Henan	2004	475	0
Henan	2005	475	0
Henan	2006	475	0
Henan	2007	475	0
Henan	2008	475	0
Henan	2009	475	0
Henan	2010	1500	0
Henan	2011	1500	0
Henan	2012	1500	0
Henan	2013	1500	0
Hebei	2002	0	0
Hebei	2003	0	0
Hebei	2004	0	0
Hebei	2005	800	1000
Hebei	2006	800	1000
Hebei	2007	800	1000
Hebei	2008	1000	1500
Hebei	2009	600	1500
Hebei	2010	600	1500
Hebei	2011	600	1500
Hebei	2012	600	1500
Hebei	2013	1000	2000
Hainan	2002	475	0
Hainan	2003	475	0
Hainan	2004	475	0
Hainan	2005	1000	0
Hainan	2006	1000	0
Hainan	2007	1000	0
Hainan	2008	0	3000
Hainan	2009	0	3000

(continued)

(continued)

Province	Period	Application subsidy	Grant reward
Hainan	2010	0	4000
Hainan	2011	0	4000
Hainan	2012	0	4000
Hainan	2013	0	4000
Guizhou	2002	0	0
Guizhou	2003	0	0
Guizhou	2004	0	0
Guizhou	2005	0	0
Guizhou	2006	0	2400
Guizhou	2007	0	2400
Guizhou	2008	0	2400
Guizhou	2009	0	2400
Guizhou	2010	0	2400
Guizhou	2011	0	2400
Guizhou	2012	0	2600
Guizhou	2013	0	2600
Jiangsu	2002	2000	0
Jiangsu	2003	2000	0
Jiangsu	2004	2000	0
Jiangsu	2005	2000	0
Jiangsu	2006	3450	0
Jiangsu	2007	3450	0
Jiangsu	2008	3450	0
Jiangsu	2009	3450	0
Jiangsu	2010	3450	0
Jiangsu	2011	1000	3000
Jiangsu	2012	1000	3000
Jiangsu	2013	1000	3000
Fujian	2002	3450	0
Fujian	2003	3450	0
Fujian	2004	3450	0
Fujian	2005	3450	0
Fujian	2006	3450	0
Fujian	2007	3450	0
Fujian	2008	3450	0
Fujian	2009	3450	0
Fujian	2010	3450	0
Fujian	2011	3450	0
Fujian	2012	0	5000
Fujian	2013	0	5000

(continued)

(continued)

Province	Period	Application subsidy	Grant reward
Beijing	2002	1000	0
Beijing	2003	1000	0
Beijing	2004	1000	0
Beijing	2005	1000	0
Beijing	2006	2150	0
Beijing	2007	2150	0
Beijing	2008	2150	0
Beijing	2009	2150	0
Beijing	2010	2150	0
Beijing	2011	2150	0
Beijing	2012	2150	0
Beijing	2013	2150	0
Anhui	2002	0	0
Anhui	2003	0	3000
Anhui	2004	0	3000
Anhui	2005	0	3000
Anhui	2006	0	3000
Anhui	2007	0	3000
Anhui	2008	0	3000
Anhui	2009	0	3000
Anhui	2010	0	5000
Anhui	2011	0	5000
Anhui	2012	0	5000
Anhui	2013	0	5000

References

Dang J, Motohashi K (2015) Patent statistics: A good indicator for innovation in China? Patent subsidy program impacts on patent quality. China Econ. Rev 35:137–155

Eaton J, Kortum S (1999) International technology diffusion: Theory and measurement. Int. Econ. Rev 40:537–570

Giacopello F (2012). Rise in quantity, fall in quality: assessing China's patent filings. Intellect Property Mag. Available from http://www.hfgip.com/downloads/201212001.pdf

Griliches Z (1990) Patent statistics as economic indicators: A survey. J. of Econ. Lit 28:1661–1707

Guo J-H, Yang X-Y (2010) Research on measurement and improving strategy of patent grant policy, taking example of Shanghai. Stud. in Sci. of Sci 1:17–25

Hall BH, Ziedonis RH (2001) The patent paradox revisited: An empirical study of patenting in the US semiconductor industry, 1979-1995. RAND J. of Econ 32:101–128

Hu AG, Jefferson GH (2009) A great wall of patents: What is behind China's recent patent explosion? J Dev Econ 90:57–68

Keupp MM, Friesike S, Von Zedtwitz M (2012) How do foreign firms patent in emerging economies with weak appropriability regimes? Archetypes and motives. Res Policy 41:1422–1439

Lei Z, Sun Z, Wright B (2012) Are Chinese patent applications politically driven? OECD. Available from http://www.oecd.org/site/stipatents/4–3-Lei-Sun-Wright.pdf

Liu Y, Wen K, Guo J (2012) The determinants of Chinese patent quality based on the process management. Sci. Res. Manag 12:104–109

Long T, Yun L, Fangjuan Y (2013) Subsidy policy that supports coordinated development of patent quality and application quantity. Sci. & Technol. Prog. and Policy 30:99–104

Prud'homme D (2012) Dulling the cutting edge: How patent-related policies and practices hamper innovation in China. European Chamber, Beijing; University Library of Munich, Germany

Schumpeter JA (1942) Socialism, capitalism and democracy. Harper and Brothers, New York

Wagner RP (2009) Understanding patent quality mechanisms. Soc. Sci. Electron. Publishing 157:2135–2173

Yang F-J, Liu Y, Tan L (2012) Empirical analysis on the Impact of regional patent subsidy policy. Chinese J. of Manage. Sci 20:733–739

Zhang Q-H, Luo J-W (2009) Analysis on the influence of the patent funding policy of Shanghai for the figure of patent application. Stud. in Sci. of Sci 5:682–685

Chapter 8
The Evolving Environment for Intellectual Property Tax Management in China

Alan Garcia, Josephine Jiang, Conrad Turley and Mimi Wang

Abstract This chapter provides an overview of existing Chinese tax law provisions having an impact on the conduct of R&D and the use of IP in China, including the licensing of IP by foreign multinational enterprises to their Chinese operating subsidiaries. The tax challenges for companies, and consequent issues for the attention of policymakers, are organized according to a three-part framework for evaluating IP tax management. Policy recommendations are then set out, highlighting the likely future trends in Chinese and international tax policy.

Keywords China · Intellectual property · Know-how · Multinational enterprises · R&D super deduction · High and new technology enterprise (HNTE) · Base erosion and profit shifting (BEPS) · Tax management · Transfer pricing · Value added tax · Corporate income tax · Tax treaty · Withholding tax

---

Alan Garcia (corresponding author) is a tax partner in the Shanghai office of KPMG China and Leader of the KPMG China Centre of Excellence for R&D Incentives. He is also Asia Pacific Regional R&D Leader within KPMG.

Josephine Jiang is a tax partner in the Beijing office of KPMG China focused on R&D tax matters as well as M&A and International Tax.

Conrad Turley is a tax senior manager in the Beijing office of KPMG China focused on International Tax and M&A. He previously worked for the EU Commission Tax Directorate in Brussels.

Mimi Wang is a tax director in the Shanghai office of KPMG China focused on transfer pricing.

A. Garcia (✉)
KPMG China Centre of Excellence for R&D Incentives, Beijing, China
e-mail: alan.garcia@kpmg.com

J. Jiang · C. Turley · M. Wang
KPMG China, 8th Floor, KPMG Tower, Oriental Plaza, 1 East Chang An Avenue, Beijing 100738, China
e-mail: conrad.turley@kpmg.com

D. Prud'homme and H. Song (eds.), *Economic Impacts of Intellectual Property-Conditioned Government Incentives*, DOI 10.1007/978-981-10-1119-1_8

8.1 Introduction

In a global economy that is increasingly knowledge-based, the contribution of intellectual property (IP) is often of great importance to business success. IP, such as local know-how, patented cutting-edge technology, or a well-known brand names associated with high standards of quality, brings enhanced value to businesses. Levels of revenue, business sustainability, and growth can all be closely related to IP.

In a Chinese context, foreign Multinational Enterprises (MNEs) producing or selling their products in China or developing their IP in China, as well as Chinese MNEs that are expanding into overseas markets, need to be aware of the tax implications of different approaches to IP management. Numerous Chinese and global tax matters may need to be taken into account, and key trade-offs invariably must be made when balancing commercial, contractual, and financial opportunities. Moreover, some existing IP management structures may now be outdated as a consequence of the G20/OECD Base Erosion and Profit Shifting (BEPS) global tax reform initiative.

As it stands, there is a gap in the existing Chinese tax literature regarding a holistic overview of the tax considerations for IP management in a China context, covering all significant tax issues. Furthermore, the pace of recent change means that the existing literature on IP tax management, dealing as it does with individual topics such as Transfer Pricing (TP), Value Added Tax (VAT), or tax treaty relief, is in many cases out of date.

This chapter seeks to address this gap in the literature by explaining current key tax factors pertinent to IP tax management in China and seeking to draw out the lessons for policymakers. While most of the recent relevant new Chinese tax measures have been directed at limiting the use of certain tax planning techniques (including those in relation to IP management), it is important that tax policy also facilitate the flow of technology across borders, the cross-pollination of technology across countries, and the proper functioning and recognition of MNE global value chains.

This paper is divided into five sections. The next Sect. 8.2 introduces a framework for IP tax management in China. Section 8.3 discusses the methodology. Section 8.4, Discussion, considers the three key fields of IP tax management in China. Section 8.5, Conclusions and Policy Recommendations, sets out views and suggestions that draw on the preceding substantive analysis.

8.2 The Objectives of IP Tax Management in China

At a policy level, governments have an incentive to create a domestic business environment that fosters and supports innovation and the development and application of new technologies. Technologically advanced domestic enterprises can produce innovative products and services that are competitive in global markets, thus supporting domestic employment and investment. To the extent that MNE global economic activity is now channeled through world-spanning global value chains (GVCs),[1] governments may hope to attract innovative activities, which occur at various points within MNE value chains, and locate them within their own domestic jurisdictions (UNCTAD 2014; OECD et al. 2013).

Policies to attract innovative economic activity may yield technology import advantages such as creating high-quality/highly paid jobs locally and generating cluster and spin-off/spillover effects,[2] and may instigate a trickle-down spread[3] of technology across other sectors of the domestic economy. While such policies may initially bear costs in terms of subsidy provision and reduced tax revenue, the theory is that innovation incentives may ultimately drive an increase in local tax revenue via employment taxes, profits tax, etc. (Arginelli 2015).

As a result of the perceived economic benefits of "local" innovative activity, governments increasingly attempt to lower barriers to entry and/or encourage new and ongoing innovation by making efforts to lower the immediate effective tax burden on such enterprises. Chinese tax policymakers, by their inclusion of relevant innovation incentives in Chinese tax law (as discussed below), clearly evidence their policy intent to harness the benefits of technology import and spin-off effects for the Chinese economy. Innovative, eligible companies may be entitled to a reduced effective tax rate by accessing such tax incentives. MNEs may harness the benefits of such tax incentive policies for innovative activity through their IP tax management strategies. At the same time as leveraging government incentives, effective IP tax management by MNEs will aim to mitigate the tax disadvantages

[1]The global value chain concept is used to analyze how commercial activities are coordinated across geographies to bring a product from conception through its design, its sourced raw materials and intermediate inputs, its marketing, its distribution, and its support, to the final consumer.

[2]Cluster and spin-off/spillover effects concern the value-adding linkages created by foreign MNEs with the local economy. Real value for a country's domestic economy is created where the foreign MNEs do not exist as an island separate from the local economy but rather use local suppliers and service providers extensively. This allows the latter to learn from the MNEs and build their capacities, and can ultimately create an ecosystem of companies and infrastructure that increases the attractiveness of the country as a location for more of such MNEs (e.g. mobile phone manufacturing, development, and software design in the Pearl River Delta). The extent of potential cluster and spin-off effects will vary depending on the nature of the industry, as well as the stage of the MNE "value chain" being attracted into the country (e.g. whether it is just distribution/procurement or also top management, engineering, and product development functions), and can also be influenced by whether the company produces solely for export or also sells in the local market, and whether the acquisition was by way of M&A or a new greenfield investment (OECD, WTO, UNCTAD 2013).

[3]The term "trickle down" is allied with the idea of spin-off/spillover effects and considers the mechanisms by which high-technology manufacturing or research activity, conducted by a small number of enterprises, may, through engagement with other local enterprises, allow the latter to embrace and use the technology of the leading firms and enhance their productivity, leading to benefits for the entire economy.

that can arise from unintended[4] by-products of other government tax policies (e.g. customs and indirect tax management). Going further, some MNEs may look to manage the spread of their operations across different tax jurisdictions to reduce their overall effective tax burden.

These elements of IP tax management may be categorized as:

(1) Topic Area 1: Benefitting from Chinese innovation tax incentives;
(2) Topic Area 2: Mitigating cross-border tax "friction"; and
(3) Topic Area 3: Leveraging available tax opportunities from the distribution of operations across jurisdictions.

This tiered approach to assessing IP tax management strategy is advocated in tax practice and tax academia (see, for example, Macovei and Rasch 2011). The three elements need to be balanced against each other and ultimately must also serve the underlying commercial purpose of an MNE's transactions and business dealings.

Foreign MNEs seeking to benefit from Chinese national tax incentives may need to arrange their operations so that the local Chinese entity is developing know-how that benefits that local entity. The foreign MNE may also need to acknowledge that the local Chinese entity is developing know-how and/or formal IP that may benefit its broader MNE global network. This acknowledgement may have knock-on implications for other aspects of the MNE's tax management (notably transfer pricing, as discussed below). The extent to which such innovative activity occurs and such incentives are used in China may be dependent on the degree to which an MNE is comfortable with the legal protection for IP available in China, and the extent to which the further development of the IP in China, as opposed to elsewhere, is acceptable from commercial and corporate strategy viewpoints.

Particularly in cases in which it is preferred that substantive rights over the IP be maintained outside China, but also more generally in cases in which any cross-border transactions are necessary in the exploitation of the IP, the use of the IP in China may give rise to the above-mentioned tax friction, which needs to be managed. At the same time, maintenance of IP outside China has sometimes been viewed as commercially advantageous and potentially beneficial from a tax perspective. This being said, an increasingly negative view is being taken, by both governments and the public, of variants of some legacy IP structures (i.e. structures put in place at a time when tax rules were different and when the attitudes of the public and policymakers towards certain forms of tax planning were different). It is increasingly apparent that the optimal balance in IP tax planning may have shifted to the use of simpler structures and, where commercially acceptable, to potential "on-shoring" and acknowledgment of MNE IP and know-how in China.

---

[4] Government tax policy does not, typically, deliberately set out to stymie economic activity. However, the number and variety of different tax provisions (each logical and coherent within itself) lead to interactions/frictions among the different taxes, in practice, which can be particularly difficult for enterprises to navigate and can discourage enterprises from conducting otherwise economically optimal economic transactions.

8.3 Methodology

In this chapter we draw on our experience as professional tax advisors, as well as on literature from leading tax journals, to highlight how IP tax planning in China can best be reconciled with fundamental commercial considerations. The three-part structure mentioned in Sect. 8.2 of this paper is adopted for the analysis, looking at how MNEs (1) benefit from Chinese innovation tax incentives, (2) mitigate cross-border tax "friction," and (3) leverage available tax opportunities from the distribution of operations across jurisdictions.

The difficulties for firms in implementing each of the above elements of IP tax management, and additional policy considerations regarding the type of tax behavior that governments seek to foster, inform the subsequent policy recommendations. In conducting our analysis, we reference key Chinese legislation and tax authority guidance, as well as relevant statistical data, including data drawn from reports of the Chinese Academy of Science and Technology for Development.

8.4 Discussion

8.4.1 Focus Area 1: Benefitting from Chinese Innovation Tax Incentives

8.4.1.1 The Changing Context of National Law Tax Incentives

To the extent that a Chinese foreign invested enterprise (FIE) within an MNE group, be it a Wholly Foreign Owned Enterprise (WFOE) or a joint venture with a Chinese partner, derives substantial income from China, the use of Chinese innovation-linked tax incentives can contribute significantly to the bottom line. The importance of these incentives is growing, and will continue to grow in future, in consequence of the ongoing shifts in TP practice, mapped out further below.

Prior to the introduction of the new Corporate Income Tax (CIT) law in 2008, Chinese tax incentive policy had been highly geared towards encouraging foreign investment in China, particularly in the manufacturing sector. This was intended to bring capital, foreign expertise and technology into China and foster the export sector as the leading driver of economic growth. From 2008 onwards, tax incentive policy no longer discriminated between foreign and domestic investors, and focused more on encouraging certain innovative or socially beneficial activities (e.g. R&D, environmental protection) and on supporting certain identified high-value-added industries (e.g. software and integrated circuits) that were regarded as drivers of innovation, rather than supporting manufacturing activity indiscriminately.

The importance of these incentives for foreign MNEs is now accentuated in particular by developments in Chinese TP[5] practice. Historically, MNEs with significant manufacturing operations in China were less concerned about booking[6] income in their Chinese entities, given the tax holidays[7] and lower tax rates available for FIEs. When these incentives were removed post-2008, many groups shifted to toll manufacturing arrangements (and equivalents),[8] under which the Chinese manufacturing entity would operate on a "limited risk" basis. A "limited risk" arrangement for a Chinese entity means that the MNE's offshore principal entity would bear all inventory and product risk and would hold the IP rights to product and process technology and brands, and pay the Chinese entity a fee, reflecting the simple functions conducted and the lack of risks borne. Equivalent "limited risk distributor" arrangements could be used for sales to Chinese customers, and limited risk contract research and development (R&D) arrangements could be used for outsourced development work. The locations of the "principal" entities, dealing within the Chinese entities within the MNE group, could be chosen according to business requirements, and also to manage the effective tax rate for the MNE principal (Bates et al. 2008).

However, a significant shift in Chinese TP regulation has been gathering steam over the last five years. Chinese tax authorities may now insist that greater profits must be booked to Chinese manufacturing, distribution, and R&D service entities. Authorities have argued this on the basis that a "market premium" accrues to distributors from China's expanding consumer base; this results from the fact that

---

[5]Transfer Pricing (TP) is the setting of prices for goods and services sold between controlled/related legal entities within an MNE. TP has increasingly become a focus for tax authorities—driven by the fact that an increasing number of cross-border transactions occurring within global value chains are becoming internal to MNEs (OECD et al. 2013). Global value chains (GVCs) are typically coordinated by MNEs, with cross-border trade of inputs and outputs taking place within their networks of affiliates, contractual partners, and arm's-length suppliers. MNE-coordinated GVCs are estimated to account for some 80 % of global trade.

[6]In line with MNE group accounting policy, and having respect for individual countries' TP rules, income generated within an MNE's global value chain may be "booked" to, or recognized in, different legal entities constituting the MNE. In cases in which tax rates in various jurisdictions in which an MNE operates are very high, particular care will be taken that group accounting policies, including revenue recognition policies and cross-entity expense allocations, do not inadvertently result in "overbooking" of income in higher-tax jurisdictions.

[7]A tax holiday is a period, typically several years, during which the enterprise is not subject to tax, i.e. has a "holiday" from tax impositions.

[8]Toll manufacturing, also referred to as contract processing/consignment arrangements, is characterized by the foreign principal supplying raw materials/components to the Chinese manufacturer for processing and by the goods remaining legally in the possession of the foreign principal throughout the process. Contract manufacturing/import processing/buy-sell arrangements are distinguished by the raw materials passing into the legal ownership of the Chinese manufacturer during processing and then being sold back to the foreign party subsequently. Despite this distinction, from an economic (and therefore TP) perspective, the arrangements can be approximated by arranging for contractual risks relating to the materials, goods, and processes to be borne by the foreign entity.

the rise of the Chinese middle class and its demand for high-status foreign brands has allowed foreign companies to earn sales margins above those generated from sales of the same products in mature markets. Tax authorities have also argued that "cost savings" can be realized by MNEs' manufacturing and contract R&D operations due to the use of China's supplier network clusters and pool of low-wage, technically educated workers. "Market premium" and "cost savings" are collectively referred to as Location-Specific Advantages (LSAs).[9] Furthermore, tax officials may assert that, through the experience of making goods and/or building market share, the local Chinese subsidiaries of MNEs are creating new intangible assets (both production and marketing intangibles),[10] or are contributing to the value of the intangible property registered by the MNE overseas. Thus Chinese tax officials may demand that more MNE profits be allocated to China, regardless of whether such entities are claiming any R&D or other incentives.

Not only may it be required by Chinese tax authorities, on the basis of the above, that more revenue be booked to the China entities, but payments by the latter to related overseas parties for services and royalties may be viewed with skepticism and potentially denied tax deductions. The approach taken by some Chinese tax authorities is to ask why, if the Chinese entity has developed and possesses its own local IP, it should be making payments abroad related to access to intellectual property held offshore, given the duplication of payment implied (Jiang 2015). A stricter approach to the deduction of such payments has resulted, and is detailed further below under Topic Area 3.

Faced with the possibility of more profit being "trapped" in China on the basis of the new TP rules (forming a larger tax base to which CIT can be applied), Chinese innovation-linked local tax incentives are becoming increasingly important in reducing the effective tax burden on the expanded tax base. A further new factor likely to be of particular significance in driving this trend forward is the change to the Chinese "permanent establishment" (PE) tax threshold, which is set to be implemented as a consequence of the G20/OECD BEPS initiative,[11] in which China is a leading participant.

[9]The LSA concept was first formally set out by the Chinese State Administration of Taxation (SAT) in its 2012 contribution to a United Nations guide on TP for developing countries. See U.N. Practical Manual on Transfer Pricing for Developing Countries, paragraphs 10.3.4.1 to 10.3.4.3.

[10]Marketing intangibles include brand and customer relationships/goodwill. Chinese tax authorities may assert that simply modifying the product presentation/packaging to reach a Chinese customer base (e.g. a brand name written in Chinese characters), extensive local advertising spend, or the experience of selling to Chinese customers gives rise to local marketing intangibles (not recognized on the balance sheet, and perhaps not having any "legal existence") whose "possession" by the local Chinese entity diminishes or negates the value and benefit to the Chinese entity of any brand IP licensed from an MNE entity overseas.

[11]See OECD, May 2015, Discussion draft "BEPS Action 7: Preventing the Artificial Avoidance of PE Status"; see also KPMG China, June 2015, China Tax Alert: China tax planning to be impacted by BEPS Action 7 permanent establishment proposals, http://www.kpmg.com/CN/en/IssuesAndInsights/ArticlesPublications/Newsletters/ChinaAlerts/Documents/China-tax-alert-1506-12-China-tax-impacted-by-BEPS-Action-7.pdf.

PE is the threshold, set according to China's tax treaties with other countries, that determines when a foreign company has sufficient "tax presence" in China for that company to be taxed directly on its profits arising from economic activities conducted in China. That is, the application of the PE concept determines whether a foreign enterprise is to be treated as having a "tax branch" in China, in addition to and separate from whatever subsidiaries the MNE might already have in China.

Briefly stated, many of the distribution arrangements (e.g. Singapore/Ireland/HK sales hubs) used at present by MNEs to sell to Chinese customers avoid the necessity of having a local China-based buy-sell distributor, thus reducing China tax payments. These may involve local Chinese related-party "marketing support" companies that facilitate sales from the offshore sales hub to Chinese customers, but do not trigger PE.

In the future, this may no longer be tenable, as a China PE may well be deemed by tax authorities to arise under new Chinese BEPS-influenced PE rules currently under development (OECD 2015a, b). A general move to local buy-sell distributors is consequently anticipated. Due to the TP trends mentioned above (i.e. LSAs, local market intangibles), as well as the BEPS-influenced TP focus on functions rather than risks in attributing profits, MNEs may not be able to restrict the profits attributed to these local buy-sell distributors by asserting that a "limited risk" arrangement is being used. Consequently, as a result of both the PE changes as well as the TP changes, MNEs may be more reliant than ever on national-law "innovation tax incentives" to limit the effective tax rate in China.

8.4.1.2 Varieties of National Law Tax Incentives

Chinese national-level innovation-related tax incentives, whose underlying policy intent is technology import and the generation of innovation spin-off and cluster effects, are generally directed either at (i) innovation activities or (ii) industries regarded as innovation drivers. These typically take the form of "CIT holidays," lower CIT rates, VAT refunds, and more liberal or bonus tax deductions. Provincial- and municipal-level governments can also offer tax incentives for innovation activities financed out of the local allocation of tax revenues, though the Chinese central government has more recently been clamping down on the granting by local governments of tax incentives not aligned with national policies.[12]

[12]Guofa (2014) No. 62, "Notice of the State Council on putting in order tax incentive policies," issued in 2014, requires the State Council to sign off on new incentives, and required that all provincial governments abolish all reliefs inconsistent with national law by 2015. However, the pace of change is proving somewhat too rapid for orderly transition, the measure was temporarily suspended by SAT Circular 25, issued May 2015, though it could be restarted in future.

As an example of industry-specific innovation incentives, approved software production companies and integrated circuit (IC) design companies can access tax holidays (two-year exemption, three-year half CIT rate) or, alternatively, lower CIT rates of 10 %. VAT refunds (refunds on self-produced software are not subject to CIT if invested back into R&D) and relaxed rules on tax deductions also apply[13] to such software and IC design companies.

In addition to the tax holidays mentioned above for software/IC design companies, equivalent or longer tax holidays are also available for IC production enterprises, and for energy conservation and emission reduction projects employing new technological innovations. Enterprises operating in key innovation industries (including the pharmaceutical and IT industries, and transport, telecom, electronics, and instruments manufacturing) can benefit, under SAT Circular 75 (2014), from accelerated depreciation allowances (60 % of standard timeframes) and can directly expense purchases of R&D-related equipment.

Aside from the above incentives directed at "innovative industries," national-level tax incentives geared towards general "innovative activity" include the High and New Technology Enterprise (HNTE) incentive, Advanced New Technology Enterprise (ATSE), the R&D super deduction, and the exemptions for gains on transfers of patented technology up to a value of 5 million RMB (with a 50 % CIT rate applying to transfers with a value above 5 million RMB).

HNTE

The HNTE program offers a 15 % CIT rate (as opposed to the usual 25 % CIT rate), and also raises the ceiling for deduction of employee training expenses to 8 % of employee compensation. This has been popular with both MNEs and local enterprises. In order to qualify, the enterprise must:

- be registered at least one year at the time of the application;
- own the intellectual property (IP) rights of key technologies which show core support to the enterprises' main products or services;
- fall within one of eight specified industrial fields;[14]
- have sufficient science and technology personnel involved in R&D activities;
- perform R&D and incur sufficient R&D expenses;

[13]Employee training expenses may be deducted without limit, whereas normally a ceiling of 2.5 % of total employee remuneration deductions applies.

[14]Guokefahuo (2016) No. 32—Administrative Measures on Accreditation of High-technology enterprises directs that investment must be in the "High-New-Technology Areas with Key State Support," namely electronic information technology, bioengineering and new medical technology, aeronautical and space technology, new material technology, high-tech service, new energy and energy saving technology, resource and environment technology, and advanced manufacturing and automation.

- generate sufficient profits from High-New-Technology products;
- pass the "innovation ability assessment" test[15]; and
- not have experienced significant safety and quality incidents or environmental violations

In practice, a number of challenges have been observed in terms of obtaining and retaining HNTE relief.

- A recent HNTE regulatory change, Guokefahuo (2016) No. 32, now means that it is not sufficient for the Chinese entity to obtain a five-year worldwide exclusive license to IP. It should also be noted that patentable IP is required (know-how alone is insufficient). In some cases, companies may register early-stage work with the Chinese patent authorities to satisfy the requirements —whether this suffices is judged by and agreed with the local tax authorities on a case-by-case basis, as is the rather nebulous matter of what precisely qualifies as key technologies which show core support to the enterprises' main products or services. In this regard, it should be noted that it is the local tax authorities who are responsible for administering the HNTE program, even though the program was originally promulgated at the central State Administration of Taxation (SAT) level.
- Ongoing product innovations may mean that the key technologies/core IP in which the HNTE enterprise has an interest may need to be reassessed on a yearly basis. If it has been contractually arranged that an overseas MNE group enterprise possesses the rights to new IP connected with the products sold (whether this IP enhancement has been generated in China or elsewhere), then the HNTE enterprise may need to "renew" its interest in the key technologies/core IP. Such renewal might need to be pursued through outright acquisition of the new core IP from the overseas MNE entity possessing it.
- If sales of the HNTE enterprise's products have been rising, the HNTE enterprise may, due to an insufficiently commensurate rise in the level of R&D expenditures, cease to satisfy the ratio of R&D-expenses-to-turnover requirement.[16]
- In practice, it has been found that HNTE reapplications have been declining in recent years in some jurisdictions. This may in part be due to (1) the balance that

[15]According to Guokefahuo (2016) No. 32—Administrative Measures on Accreditation of High-technology enterprises, the specific assessment standard has not yet been announced. The previous HNTE accreditation rules specified four assessment criteria on a merit-point basis (i.e. Core IP Sufficiency [max 30 points], Capability to Convert R&D Findings into Products and Services [max 30 points], Ability to Execute and Manage R&D Activities [max 20 points], Growth of Revenue and Total Assets [max 20 points]), and points are awarded based on this evaluation. A company needs 71 points or more to qualify for HNTE.

[16]The ratio of R&D expenses to turnover (over the most recent three years or the enterprise's operating history, whichever is shorter) must exceed the following ratios on a sliding scale: 5 % if revenue is below 50 million RMB; 4 % if revenue is between 50 million and 200 million RMB; and 3 % if revenue is above 200 million RMB. At least 60 % of an HNTE's R&D expenses must be incurred inside the PRC.

MNEs have had to strike between accessing HNTE status for their FIEs and maintaining MNE group-wide TP policies (this is discussed further under Topic Area 2 below); and (2) an increasingly vigilant audit approach taken by the Ministry of Finance and some local tax authorities when assessing HNTE eligibility.

In some cases, MNEs have characterized their China subsidiaries as limited-risk distributors/manufacturers/R&D services providers, engaged in "routine" activities. However, as detailed above, FIEs that have obtained HNTE qualification are expected to perform value-adding functions, conduct substantial R&D activities, and use key technology, resulting in the creation of IP of which they can claim legal ownership. In this case, the tax authorities may raise a query regarding the "limited risk" allocation for TP purposes and HNTE status. It is entirely possible that an entity may be limited risk and still qualify for the HNTE program, but documentation should be maintained to reflect this scenario.

It is also important to note that HNTE status and royalty payments to offshore parents are *not, technically, mutually exclusive.* It is entirely possible that an entity in China may both own and generate local core IP *and simultaneously* pay royalties for other IP that it uses during the course of any given year.

- However, faced with potential revocation of HNTE status if they do not fulfill these requirements and upward TP adjustments if they do, some MNEs have refrained from obtaining HNTE status at all. Insofar as the Chinese tax authorities are now actively disregarding the contractual niceties of limited-risk arrangements (regardless of whether such entities have HNTE status or not), and using the LSA and local intangibles concepts to attribute increased taxable profits to MNE FIEs in any case, it may instead be logical for some companies to pursue HNTE status.

HNTE recognition is the responsibility of a committee comprised of the science and technology bureau, tax authority, and finance authority at the provincial and/or city level, prior to being granted by the science and technology bureau. Pursuant to the old HNTE regulations, HNTE status was valid for three years before an enterprise needed to apply for reassessment. Between 2010 and 2013, auditing and tightened standards led to some companies not passing reassessment.[17] This may be a reflection of the looser standards that were applied in earlier years and the impact of SAT efforts to inject more rigor into previously permissive local tax authority practices. The tougher enforcement approach, as well as the TP considerations mentioned above, may in part be behind this trend of fewer companies passing reassessment, as illustrated in Fig. 8.1.

However, an extensive 2014 HNTE audit program conducted by the authorities in eight provinces across China revealed that 97 % of companies *retained* their HNTE status. This recent high level of compliance seems to suggest that companies

[17]Companies are also being audited between reassessments.

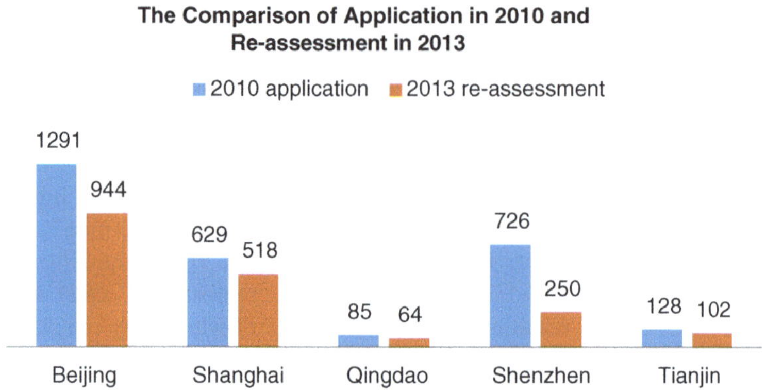

Fig. 8.1 Decline in HNTEs passing reassessment may bear out tougher enforcement approach. *Source data* HNTE list released by science and technology bureaus of each city

are now reviewing HNTE status much more carefully as a consequence of the lessons learned from the 2013 audit experience.

Following a review of the HNTE program conducted by US and Chinese experts in July 2014, which became a key input into the agreements reached at the December 2014 US-China Joint Commission on Commerce and Trade (JCCT),[18] a report was published by the US-China Business Council[19] that highlighted a number of HNTE policy improvements, including:

- more consistent interpretation of the HNTE criteria by relevant authorities;
- enhanced and more detailed regulations and guidelines regarding HNTE criteria;
- implementation of the legal principle of estoppel to safeguard prior HNTE approvals and limit retrospective penalties in cases in which relevant authorities have previously approved status; and
- removal of the requirement that the core IP be owned by the Chinese entity.

The release of the Guokefahuo (2016) No. 32, referred to earlier, shows that the government will continue to encourage and support HNTE. While the in-charge authorities have relaxed the HNTE recognition requirements in some respects, the release of No. 32 increases HNTE audit protocols and documentary evidence thresholds. As such, companies seeking HNTE status will need to actively plan and prepare in advance to manage the tightened audit procedures and certification/documentation requirements. In particular, companies are advised to consider the below points:

[18]U.S. FACT SHEET: 25th U.S.-China Joint Commission on Commerce and Trade; https://ustr.gov/about-us/policy-offices/press-office/fact-sheets/2014/december/us-fact-sheet-25th-us-china-joint.

[19]The US-China Business Council 2014 US-China Joint Commission on Commerce and Trade (JCCT) Recommendations, 2014.

- the changes in respect of the IP requirements, and application documentation, suggest that in-charge authorities may place more emphasis on (1) technology advancement, and (2) the connection between IP and R&D activities, core technology and the main products (services) of the applicant.
- the HNTE application documents are now more specific and rigid in respect of issues such as "certification approval and relevant qualification" and, when this is combined with tighter regulatory supervision of the HNTE program, it is apparent that companies must focus on contemporaneous record keeping and systematic management of R&D activities.

If, as discussed, the trend in TP practice progressively compels MNEs to make greater use of the HNTE incentive, then such companies should engage in comprehensive preparation and plan in detail to ensure that the status can be secured and maintained. The full extent of the challenge with TP trends is further detailed below, under Topic Area 2.

ATSE

Another tax incentive program in China is the Advanced Technology Service Enterprise incentive,[20] which may apply until the end of 2018. This program applies to providers of:

- Information Technology Outsourcing (ITO);
- Business Process Outsourcing (BPO); and
- Knowledge Process Outsourcing (KPO) services

in relation to IT and software-related services, data processing and management, R&D, and business process design. Such providers must be located in one of the 21 pilot cities.[21] This provides the same 15 % CIT rate as the HNTE incentive and an increased ceiling for deduction of staff education expenses, and also adds a VAT exemption for income derived from offshore outsourcing services. Compared to HNTE, the qualification thresholds regarding IP ownership and R&D investment may be less relevant (especially in relation to ITO and BPO), though there are requirements concerning the education level of staff and the proportion of income from "offshore advanced technology services" (≥ 35 % of annual income).

[20]Clarification on CIT incentives for Advanced Technology Service Enterprise Cai Shui (2014b) No. 59, jointly issued by the MOF, SAT, MOC, MOST and NDRC on 8 October 2014 (Circular 59).

[21]These include Beijing, Tianjin, Shanghai, Chongqing, Dalian, Shenzhen, Guangzhou, Wuhan, Harbin, Chengdu, Nanjing, Xian, Jinan, Hangzhou, Hefei, Nanchang, Changsha, Daqing, Suzhou, Wuxi and Xiamen.

R&D Super Deduction

The R&D super deduction (150 % of the expense incurred)[22] is likely for many enterprises to be more easily accessed than HNTE status. This is because the former does not focus on R&D expenses as a percentage of turnover, or on the percentage of revenue derived from hi-tech products. The incentive also does not require that core IP be registered and owned by the Chinese entity. Rather, it focuses on the expenditure incurred being relevant to the development of new knowledge and innovation, which involves improved products and/or processes.

The application of new knowledge of science and technology or substantial improvements to existing technologies, processes, or products requires these R&D activities to lead to tangible improvements.[23] Importantly, this may include the customization and localization in China of products and processes that result in technical improvements to know-how that may originally have been based offshore (e.g. manufacturing a modified product using locally improved equipment). To the extent that, as noted above, in future more MNE profit is likely to have to be booked to China due to the TP trends, the R&D super deduction may also receive a fresh look from MNEs looking to control their overall effective tax rates in the face of the TP changes.

The net saving for eligible R&D activities equates to 12.5 %[24] for every eligible expense incurred in the relevant year of income. R&D super deduction claims must be lodged annually as part of the income tax filing.

Securing and retaining the relief hinges on being able to identify and trace eligible R&D expenses to the relevant categories, and being able to document the technical aspects of product or process development in sufficient detail to substantiate that it occurred and met requisite standards of innovation. Tax and Science Bureau audits may probe the meeting of this standard by checking, inter alia, prototype specification challenges, manufacturing process improvement, product enhancement, engagement with outside specialists and the reconciliation of such activities with relevant expenses.

In practice we note that the science and local tax bureaus have generally taken a reasonable approach when assessing R&D Super Deduction entitlement. However, on rare occasions, it is possible that some tax officials may take a restrictive

[22]The deduction is claimed at the time of the booking of the expense to the income statement; this may be in the year in which the expense is incurred (for expenses booked directly to the income statement) or in a later year (in cases in which the relevant expense is "capitalized" to the balance sheet and later makes its way to the income statement by way of accounting depreciation or amortization).

[23]Notice on Policy Improvement of Research and Development Expenses Super Deduction Cai Shui (2015) No. 119.

[24]Assumes headline CIT rate applicable be 25 %. The net tax saving will be 7.5 % if a reduced CIT rate of 15 % (e.g., for HNTE) applies.

approach if eligible activities are booked, for example, to "cost of goods sold."[25] Tax regulations in China[26] also indicate that expenses "that have not formed intangible assets through current profit and loss" and "amortization of intangible assets" may be claimed under the R&D Super Deduction. But the regulations do not clearly state that "depreciation of tangible assets" can also be deducted at the accelerated R&D rate. In comparison to other R&D incentive programs globally, it makes sense to allow such depreciation deductions in China and not penalize companies for conducting R&D in respect to items that may ultimately be booked to the balance sheet as depreciable assets.

This occasional "tax accounting" driver of R&D eligibility in some tax provinces is unique to China and generally does not exist in other countries providing similar R&D incentive programs. This focus on the accounting treatment of expenses seems at odds with the policy intent behind the R&D Super Deduction program, and appears to be an unwarranted limitation on the application of the incentive in cases in which taxpayers are engaging in precisely the innovative activity that the Chinese government is looking to foster with the program.

The uptake and usage of the R&D Super Deduction is hindered by the above obstacles, thus blunting somewhat the effectiveness of the Chinese government's innovation policy. The issues could be remedied, and uptake of the incentive encouraged, by the following measures:

- increased consistency across different tax provinces in China regarding *application procedures*, including: consistent deadlines, documentation requirements, Science and Technology review protocols etc.;
- increased consistency regarding *interpretation* of the R&D Super Deductions rules, including a focus on the *activity* itself as a driver of eligibility rather than the tax accounting treatment, confirmation that tax depreciation of tangible assets is an allowable expense, confirmation that costs directly incurred in relation to proving the R&D objective can be claimed, and consistent interpretation of the criteria across different tax provinces etc.; and
- more detailed and considered public guidance materials to help tax payers understand the scope of eligible activities and expenses and increased reliance on transparent protocols.

---

[25]"Cost of goods sold" is an accounting classification for costs and expenses (e.g. material, labor, and allocated overhead) that are properly attributable to the sales of goods made during a particular accounting period. Costs of goods purchased and produced within an accounting period are added to the recorded value of the opening stock of the period, and then the cost of the goods sold is deducted from this value using any of a number of approaches—specific identification, first-in, first-out (FIFO), or average cost (leaving the value of closing inventories, as adjusted downwards for spoilage/value loss). The booking of otherwise-eligible R&D expenses (whether as material, labor or allocated overhead) to "cost of sales" for accounting purposes may complicate their tracing to R&D products/processes and cause certain tax authorities to conclude incorrectly that such expenses are not R&D-related.

[26]Notice of Ministry of Finance and State Administration of Taxation on trialling the R&D Super Deduction; issue date 01.012012; document number: Cai Shui (2013a) No. 13.

8.4.1.3 Topic Area 1 Conclusions: Challenges for MNEs and Issues for Policymakers

Looking ahead, MNEs are expected to have to book more of the income from their global value chains "onshore" into China. This is as a result of the development, current and anticipated, of Chinese rules on TP and PE. To a great extent, the changes being made in China are in line with international global tax reforms, though in some respects the application of TP concepts by China is novel and different from that of other countries (in particular the concepts of LSAs and local intangibles).

As a result of the potential increase in Chinese tax exposure arising from the TP and PE changes, MNEs are expected to be highly incentivized to secure Chinese "innovation incentives." These efforts would consist partly of arranging the conduct of global innovation activities so that a greater proportion of this is conducted in China, and partly of putting in place systems to track spending and activities to meet tax authority information requirements necessary to access the reliefs. To the extent that the TP and PE changes may push MNEs in the direction of making greater use of Chinese innovation tax incentives, this trend supports Chinese innovation policy and might be viewed by Chinese policymakers positively as contributing to their achievement of the original goals of these incentives.

However, certain administrative and procedural hurdles regarding the application of Chinese innovation tax incentives, as well as some substantive issues, currently frustrate the optimal use of these incentives by taxpayers. Structural and procedural design flaws in the current innovation system hinder the Chinese government's innovation policy goals. It would be beneficial both for taxpayers and for the Chinese government if policymakers remedied these flaws. Thoughts on such remedies are set out in the Conclusions section of this chapter.

8.4.2 Focus Area 2: Mitigating Tax "Friction"

It is clear from Topic Area 1 above on "Benefitting from Chinese innovation tax incentives" that:

- where IP assets can be transferred to China to support the HNTE incentive, or
- where R&D activities are actually conducted in China (including localization and customization of products or processes), or
- where the MNE operates in certain innovative industries,

an enterprise operating in China can reduce its effective CIT rate significantly, in addition to contributing to the achievement of its overall commercial objectives.

However, to the extent that the local FIE engages in IP-related transactions with the rest of the MNE group overseas (as it invariably will), a lack of attention to managing tax "friction" can lead to erosion of the tax position. In particular, in cases in which substantive IP rights are retained overseas and significant royalty payments are paid by the China entity, awareness of the CIT withholding tax (WHT), tax treaty, TP, VAT and customs implications is paramount. *Consistent* documentation that adequately reflects the underlying commercial substance, as well as TP and local Chinese incentive regulations, is critical.

Consideration in this section is given to the case in which the IP is licensed from the MNE "home country"/seat of principal operations, while the particular issues that arise when a special IP holding company in a preferred third-country tax jurisdiction is interposed are dealt with under Topic Area 3. This is because the use of a special IP holding company may give rise to other particular considerations.

8.4.2.1 CIT and Remittance Administration in Relation to Technology Agreements and Services Licensed Directly from the MNE

Payments by the Chinese entity to the offshore MNE regarding technology licenses (patents, know-how, etc.) are subject to WHT at 10 % (or a reduced treaty rate where applicable) on the grounds that, for tax purposes, they constitute royalties. Difficulties can arise if the Chinese WFOE has also entered into technical service agreements with foreign-related parties and the service provision by the foreign-related party for the Chinese WFOE is considered by the tax authorities to be related to the technology licenses (for example, to involve the transfer of know-how). In such cases, the tax authorities may deem that the service payment by the Chinese entity to the offshore provider constitutes a royalty, and require application of the 10 % WHT rate in relation to the technical service; in contrast, if the payment were treated as simply payment for a service, then, as long as the provision of the service does not constitute a PE in China, no CIT exposure should arise for the foreign company.

The authorities are understood to look, in particular, for transfers of know-how through services that are provided in parallel with the licensing of legally protected intellectual property[27] (e.g. copyrights, trademarks, and patents) or in parallel with the leasing of equipment. This is linked to the tax authorities' description[28] of know-how as "proprietary technologies," including (non-publicized) information or materials of a technical nature that are necessary for the manufacturing of products.

Consequently, taxpayers need to be careful when contracting for and delivering services related to training, machine installation, design or marketing services, trouble-shooting advice, etc. This is because written deliverables (e.g. formulae, designs, drawings, procedures, and methods) or evidence of accumulated skills and

[27]This is specifically provided for in SAT Circular 75 (2010).

[28]Guoshuihan (2009b) No. 507.

experience in the hands of a licensor firm's professional personnel could be viewed as know-how that helps the licensee of the legally protected intellectual property or the lessee of the equipment to use that property/equipment in manufacture/promotion/sale of goods. If this is the case, tax authorities may deem such services to constitute a payment for a technology license, and apply the 10 % WHT.

Services from related parties fall under particular suspicion. This is because staff from other MNE group entities who assist or train may be presumed by the authorities to possess experience with and knowledge of the wider MNE's unique technology and customized equipment and processes.

Getting such contracting right is very important, as disagreements with tax authorities on the matter of this treatment can lead to complications and delays in remitting service fees from China. Tax authorities can refuse to stamp the remittance tax recordal,[29] which must be presented to the bank to process payments, if they disagree with the taxpayer's tax characterization and consider that WHT should be applied to the payments as royalties. Banks in turn may decline to process service fee payments if these have been deemed by the tax authorities to constitute royalties for technology import, but no formal technology import registration[30] has been completed with the local department of commerce.

A further matter with which care needs to be taken is that engineers, technicians, or other staff sent to China in connection with service provision do not stay so long as to create a Service PE risk. China's tax treaties typically set the time limit at 183 days within a 12-month time period, with the presence of different staff members on connected projects being aggregated. Some older treaties provide for a six-month rule, which some authorities interpret as meaning as little as a presence of one day each month over the course of a six-month period.

In cases in which staff presence unavoidably exceeds the treaty-defined time limits, care needs to be taken that staff be formally seconded to the China WFOE. In such cases, detailed contracting and operating protocols should be put in place to avoid any PE risk for the overseas entity.[31]

[29]The tax recordal requirement is governed by Announcement (2013) No. 40 which applies to payments in excess of USD 50,000. The tax authorities may also be prompted to probe service arrangements with payments beneath this amount by the registration of cross-border service agreements with the tax authorities, required under Provisional Administrative Measures Governing Tax Collection on Contracted Projects and Provision of Services by Non-resident Enterprises (Decree No. 19), promulgated by the State Administration of Taxation on 20 January 2009.

[30]Technology transfer arrangements are required, under the amended Administrative Measures Governing the Registration of Technology Import and Export Contracts (2009), to be registered with the local Ministry of Commerce (MOFCOM) within 60 days of the contract taking effect.

[31]See KPMG China, June China 2013, PRC Non-Resident Enterprise Tax Series: Managing Chinese taxable presence exposures from secondment arrangements, https://www.kpmg.com/CN/en/IssuesAndInsights/ArticlesPublications/Documents/Chinese-taxable-presence-exposures-from-secondment-201306.pdf.

8.4.2.2 TP Considerations and IP Management

When managing TP risk, the general overriding principle in terms of IP tax management is that the royalty paid to the IP owner shall be commensurate with the contribution the IP makes to the economic value of the local operations. However, this simple statement conceals a world of complexity.

Several years ago, tax authorities were generally willing to accept TP reports that justified the pricing fees under related-party IP licensing arrangements with reference to third-party licensing arrangements observable in the marketplace (with little scrutiny applied by the authorities to how comparable the arrangements were). The authorities at that time would accept royalty rates as long as they did not exceed a rule-of-thumb rate (Chi et al. 2012).[32]

A more sophisticated and assertive approach in China first emerged in relation to loss-making FIEs, with Chinese tax authorities posing the question: Why would the Chinese operations license the IP in the first instance if they cannot realize any economic gain from licensing the IP? This campaign resulted in the unwinding of losses by many FIEs, or denial of their tax loss carry-forwards.[33] The campaign has subsequently moved beyond loss-making companies to challenge even profitable FIEs on their TP practices. The focus here is on FIEs that, while profitable, form part of an MNE value chain in which the profitability recorded in the China FIE appeared low against its contribution to the global value chain. The Chinese tax authorities, in seeking to make an upwards TP adjustment to the taxable profits of the FIE, are effectively making a claim on the profits of the MNE's overseas value chain and, as noted above, this is often being done on the basis of the LSAs and local market intangibles[34] that the Chinese tax authorities attribute to the local FIE.

---

[32]Generally speaking, local tax authorities at that time rarely questioned royalties that were less than or equal to a 5 % rate.

[33]Tax loss carry-forwards are the practice of taking a loss calculated for tax purposes in one year, and offsetting it against the taxable income of future years, thus reducing the tax payable calculated for those later years. The idea is that a company's total taxed income over time will thereby reflect its actual income, being the net sum of periodic gains and losses (though a five-year limitation on loss carry-forwards in China limits the achievement of this in practice). When making TP adjustments, tax authorities have the option of going back in time and requiring the taxpayer not to record the loss in the first place (by adjusting recorded revenue upwards or adjusting recorded expenses downwards), or looking to limit the tax loss carry-forward, offset against taxable profits, in a more recent year of tax assessment.

[34]The licensing of the trademark of Head & Shoulders to its Chinese operations is an oft-cited example of the use of the "local intangibles concept" by Chinese tax authorities to argue for allocating more of the profits in MNE global value-chains to China. Authorities have argued on numerous occasions that the original overseas-registered Head & Shoulders' trademark is not worth much to the company's Chinese operations. This is because Head & Shoulders' Chinese name (with which Chinese consumers are familiar) bears no resemblance to its English name, even if "Head & Shoulders" in English is also printed on the shampoo bottles. The argument is that the Chinese name of Head & Shoulders constitutes the relevant marketing intangible in a Chinese market context. As the Chinese FIE developed this and built up China market share on the basis of this Chinese name, the Chinese FIE thus owns the most valuable marketing intangible that the

China's new approach to TP for IP is drawing on the concept of DEMPE (development, enhancement, maintenance, protection, and exploitation) functions that has emerged from the OECD BEPS process. This plays down the role of financing IP development and emphasizes DEMPE functions in determining where the profits from developing and using IP are allocated. An important difference is that while developed countries may emphasize the place from which DEMPE functions are controlled, China may emphasize where they are performed, and if ongoing production and sales activity in China points to enhancement and exploitation of the IP in China, then Chinese authorities may demand greater profit allocation to China.

A central theme of the BEPS initiative is that profits should be taxed in accordance with value creation. Value creation is not a straightforward concept; indeed, many economists have not been able to agree on just what creates value. As traditional transfer pricing methods receive increased scrutiny and challenge, there will likely be a move towards more value-based analysis, i.e. assessing where value is created and allocating systemic profits along the value chain, particularly, for Chinese tax authorities, in the area of IP. Prudent taxpayers would do well to re-examine their IP arrangements now to ensure their internal documentation reflects a legacy position adequately. Alternatively, such companies may do well to consider modified TP structures more closely aligned to a post-BEPS world.

As mentioned, one particular approach used in some investigations has been for tax authorities to probe the potential tension between assertions made by a taxpayer in securing HNTE relief and parallel arrangements for licensing IP from an overseas MNE-related party. Chinese tax authorities are sometimes of the view that HNTE relief is appropriately granted only to Chinese taxpayers who are able to self-generate or own core IP, and hence they may be skeptical when these HNTE entities also license IP from the home country. In some cases, where the core IP of the Chinese operations is developed based on IP licensed from overseas MNE-related parties, the Chinese tax authorities' view can be that the value of the licensed IP may have diminished over time. As mentioned under Topic Area 1, it is nonetheless important to note that HNTE status and royalty payments to offshore parents are *not, technically, mutually exclusive.* It is entirely possible that an entity in China may both own and generate local core IP *and simultaneously* pay royalties for other IP that it uses during the course of any given year. This is ultimately a question of fact, and once again requires the Chinese taxpayer to give due attention

(Footnote 34 continued)

MNE possesses in relation to the China market. Consequently, excess profits arising from the China market in relation to the Head & Shoulders product should be booked to (and taxed in) the Chinese FIE. This viewpoint results in the conclusion that substantial payments by the Chinese FIE to the overseas parent for use of the original trademark would be unwarranted and should not be granted tax deduction, given that this would deplete the share of the MNE global value-chain profits derived from the Head & Shoulders product that are currently booked in the Chinese FIE.

to relevant documentation and internal policies from a global, local, commercial, and tax perspective.

Despite the possibility that MNEs may use offshore IP and simultaneously develop core IP locally, anecdotally it seems a fair number of taxpayers who qualify for the HNTE relief have ceased paying royalties to their offshore holding companies, while some taxpayers who may otherwise qualify for HNTE relief have not applied for it out of fear that it may compromise their group TP policy. We have also seen cases in which companies that previously possessed HNTE status have decided not to renew their HNTE certificates. It is possible that this outcome may be avoidable if companies maintain comprehensive internal documentation that reflects the substance of the arrangement, and contains specific details pertaining to the technologies and know-how developed, both locally and offshore.

8.4.2.3 Customs Duty

Beyond CIT, the use of foreign IP in Chinese operations can result in customs duty implications. Imports of materials, products, tools, and machinery for use in innovative industries in China will all be subject to customs duty (though exemptions[35] can be provided for the import of tools and machinery used in certain preferred innovative industries).

However, customs authorities may assert that the payment of royalties is linked to the import of goods and machinery, and insist on customs duty being levied on the value of the royalty payments as well. A clear example of this would be cases in which the importer cannot contractually purchase the imports without paying certain royalties. Beyond this, customs authorities have argued that technology paid for via royalties under a license agreement is in fact "embedded" in the imported goods or equipment. As such, customs authorities may take the position that a proper calculation of customs duties must include this royalty amount. Customs authorities have been known (in a similar fashion to tax authorities) to argue that service agreements involve the transfer of production or marketing intangibles/know-how, that these intangibles are embedded in the products/imported machinery (or were used in the overseas processes which led to their creation, and that, in consequence, customs duty should apply to these amounts, too).

Taxpayers have sought to deal with this linking by customs authorities of IP licenses to imports of customized equipment for the purpose of imposing customs duty on the former by showing that the payments under the license/service agreements related to technology/know-how that was used solely in domestic production/marketing processes carried on in China. Alternatively, they have sought to show that the same components/equipment may be sourced from third

[35]Notice of the State Council on the Adjustment of Tax Policies for Imported Equipment, Guo Fa (1997) Document No 37.

parties, and so the MNE proprietary technology/know-how licensed from related parties should not be automatically linked to such components/equipment.

Dealing with the use of foreign IP in China is indeed a highly complex matter, complicated by the inherent tension between TP and customs practices. In cases in which TP analysis supports putting a low value on imports used to generate China WFOE profits, this may satisfy tax authorities but be unacceptable to customs authorities, given the lost customs revenue. Striking a balance is a challenging task, achievable only by applying a rigorous methodology, preparing good quality supporting documentation, and maintaining good liaisons with tax and customs authorities.

8.4.2.4 VAT

Since 2011 China has progressively changed[36] its system for imposing indirect taxes on provision of services, with the Business Tax (BT) being replaced by the VAT. BT led to greater costs for businesses, as, unlike the system for VAT, there was no BT input credit granted to an enterprise on supplies incurred by the enterprise, against either output VAT or BT on sales. Consequently, BT led to a cascading series of tax charges.

The transition to VAT for license fee payments (as well as for any service payments that the tax authorities may choose to treat as payments for know-how and subject to WHT) substantially eliminates the indirect tax cost of licensing into China. This being said, cash-flow burdens can be created by the necessity of paying VAT sometime before an offsetting input credit can be claimed. To the extent that licenses/services are subjected to customs duty, the customs office may impose import VAT on the full value of the imported technology, while the tax authorities again impose VAT on each individual payment—a double VAT outcome. The input VAT credit should, one hopes, ultimately be claimable for these VAT impositions, but some enterprises have sought to work out arrangements with the tax authorities to avoid the second VAT imposition.

8.4.2.5 Topic Area 2 Conclusions: Challenges for MNEs and Issues for Policymakers

Foreign MNEs contribute to China's successful industrial upgrading by licensing technology into China. Chinese technology imports are set to grow as China's role in the global economic order and global value chains evolves.

Over the last 30 years, China has become an integral part of foreign MNEs' global value chains in its provision of manufacturing and processing services, and is

[36]By October 2015, the final industries to transition to VAT (financial services, construction and real estate, and entertainment) will have done so.

now on a steep ascent up the value chain, with increasingly high-value elements of foreign MNE value chains being located in China. As Chinese enterprises develop and shift simpler activities from their value chains overseas to Southeast Asia and Africa, the trend towards China occupying the higher value-added end of global value chains is now also mirrored in the value chains of Chinese MNEs.

Conduct of these higher-value-added activities often involves the import of more foreign technology as an input into Chinese high-tech exports, as the FIEs of foreign MNEs (as well as Chinese MNEs) combine foreign patents with their own homegrown technology. Facilitating the inflow of foreign know-how and expert services thus facilitates Chinese innovation and exports, and deserves the support and attention of Chinese policymakers.

MNEs, as noted above, can struggle to balance the challenges of managing WHT, TP, VAT, and customs in relation to IP license fee payments and expert service fee payments. The possibilities for Chinese policymakers to address these issues are set out in the Conclusions section below.

8.4.3 Topic Area 3: Tax Opportunities from the Distribution of Operations Across Jurisdictions

8.4.3.1 Use of IP Holding Structures

The existence of a cross-border dimension to an MNE's China IP management activity, in addition to creating "tax friction" that needs to be managed as outlined under Topic Area 2, also introduces opportunities to benefit from concentration of IP ownership in favorable tax jurisdictions or countries with preferential IP regimes. That said, it is of course crucial that efficient IP tax management practices reflect the underlying commercial substance of the arrangement.

Simply put, to the extent that it is commercially relevant, a China WFOE within an MNE may avail itself of an MNE's overseas-developed technology through cross-border service and license agreements and obtain a tax deduction at the 25 % standard PRC CIT rate, while the income from these service fees and royalties is potentially taxed through an overseas entity within the MNE group at a lower rate. Another chapter of this book, by Vinod Kalloe, has outlined the advantages of the leading EU regimes for IP management that might be used in this regard.

While the use of such arrangements has been given some additional support by the movement from BT to VAT (outlined above), which would help to eliminate the indirect tax leakages, the fact that CIT WHT is imposed on gross payments made to overseas entities means that, even considering the WHT alone, the tax deduction benefit for the WFOE may be largely clawed back[37] (dependent on levels of profit

[37]A royalty paid out of China by an FIE, if fully tax deductible, can produce a Chinese cash tax saving of 25 % of the amount of the payment made (15 % if the HNTE rate applies). So a royalty

margin). While the China-HK Double Taxation Agreement (DTA) offers a sizeable general royalty WHT reduction to 5 %,[38] most of China's other DTAs offer royalty WHT reductions only in relation to leases of equipment (i.e. the WHT rate for patents, brand IP, and know-how cannot be reduced below 10 %).

Moreover, recent changes in TP practice, as listed under Topic Area 1, increase the risk for outbound payments of royalties and service fees to "low-function"[39] foreign related-party entities. These Chinese tax law changes arise against a backdrop of the general tightening of international tax rules on cross-border tax planning across the world, in the context of the BEPS initiative. The impact of BEPS on the tax regimes of favored IP holding jurisdictions is clearly brought out in Vinod Kalloe's chapter, and it has been widely noted (Arginelli 2015) that IP regimes currently in use in various states will need to change as a consequence of the new BEPS global minimum standard[40] for offering IP tax incentives.

The relevant regulation tackling use of low function entities is SAT Announcement 16.[41] This announcement, released in March of 2015, may be read to imply that if the tax authorities find that a foreign company within the MNE group, to which a Chinese subsidiary pays royalties for intangibles licensing, only holds the legal rights to the intangibles and did not contribute (through research or other efforts) to the value of the intangibles, then the authorities may deny a tax deduction for the payment.

Such a situation could arise in cases in which, for example, ownership of the IP is registered with an overseas entity different from the one that "created" the IP. If Announcement 16 is applied overzealously by Chinese tax authorities, it may have

(Footnote 37 continued)

of 10 RMB would produce a Chinese cash tax saving of 2.5 RMB (this does not consider what tax would be imposed on the 10 RMB received in the country of the payee). However, a WHT rate of 10 % means that out of the 10 RMB royalty paid, one must be handed over by the payer to the Chinese tax authorities in WHT. This reduces the Chinese cash tax benefit from 2.5 RMB to 1.5 RMB. This is referred to as a "clawback" of the benefit of the tax deduction.

[38]It should be noted that "substance" and other requirements for treaty relief can have an impact on the use of IP holding companies in HK.

[39]"Low function" entities are those that do not have the capacity to perform functions, to undertake risks, or to carry out substantive operations. This is linked to the concept of "commercial substance," developed in Chinese tax law, which declares an entity to have insufficient substance in cases in which it has no or insignificant assets, operations, business premises, or local employees.

[40]The OECD has recommended a new "substantial activity" requirement for IP regimes using a "modified nexus approach" that links the IP-conditioned tax benefits to the amount of R&D expenditure incurred by companies in developing the IP. See OECD BEPS Action Point 5 2014 Deliverable: Countering Harmful Tax Practices More Effectively, Taking into Account Transparency and Substance (16 September 2014) http://www.oecd.org/ctp/countering-harmful-tax-practices-more-effectively-taking-into-account-transparency-and-substance-9789264218970-en.htm.

[41]Gonggao (2015) No. 16, SAT Announcement Regarding CIT Matters on Outbound Payments to Overseas Related Parties (Announcement 16[2015]).

an impact on many sub-licensing arrangements in which the IP is licensed via a sub-licensor.[42] These would be cases in which the sub-licensor may not have contributed to the development of the IP, but simply manages the IP licensing arrangements on behalf of the ultimate licensor. Deductions may be lost in China even in instances in which the royalty is ultimately taxed at the licensor level.

At the same time, Announcement 16 also lays out a range of circumstances in which payments by a Chinese subsidiary to a foreign company within the MNE group for services from that foreign company are to be denied tax deductions. The circumstances set out reflect the positions taken by the SAT in a letter to the UN in 2014 and in subsequent speeches by senior SAT officials. Broadly, if the foreign company rendering the services does not appear to have much in the way of substance, or if the services are deemed not to be needed by the subsidiary (either because the subsidiary does the relevant tasks itself already or because the value of the services to its business is questionable), then no tax deduction is allowed. Announcement 16 allows for tax adjustments to go back 10 years, and could have significant retrospective impact on existing MNE operations.

Since its introduction, Announcement 16 has been used in some instances by different divisions within tax bodies to advance other agendas, such as deterring outbound remittances altogether. These applications of Announcement 16 have not only exacerbated MNEs' tax burdens but have also negatively affected their cash flow positions. This is despite the fact that Announcement 16 was originally intended as a tool to manage MNEs' transfer pricing arrangements.

There are also many aspects of Announcement 16 that are unclear. For example, the retrospective application rule may potentially be used to adjust the pricing of a transaction that had complied with the transfer pricing rules before the BEPS initiative but is considered no longer fit for purpose in the post-BEPS world.

It is evident that the use of IP holding companies in connection with Chinese IP tax management is facing strong headwinds. In the future, as the channels for cross-border IP tax planning are restricted, recourse to Chinese domestic tax incentives may increase, to the extent commercially feasible and reconcilable with concerns that MNEs may have in relation to the protection of their IP in cases in which it is owned by Chinese group entities.

This is a two-way development, having an impact not just on China-inbound investing foreign MNEs but also on China-outbound investing Chinese MNEs. A progressive tightening by the Chinese tax authorities of "outbound" tax rules regarding Chinese MNEs—some of which have considered transferring the IP rights relevant to their growing international operations to offshore jurisdictions—has seen the application of China's Controlled Foreign Company rules. These rules, on the books since 2008 but applied for the first time only in late 2014, will influence how Chinese MNEs conduct their IP planning. This relates in particular to

[42]It is not clear what activities would constitute "substantive" activities and, in particular, whether sub-licensing would be considered substantive in the context of Announcement 16.

a focus on the "substance" of the IP development and management activity in any offshore hubs that such MNEs choose to use.

8.4.3.2 Topic Area 3 Conclusions: Challenges for MNEs and Issues for Policymakers

Chinese tax policy measures to restrict the ability of MNEs to take advantage of competing tax systems are in line with the global trend, and are inevitable. MNEs, driven by measures like Announcement 16 and equivalents in other countries, are already in the course of simplifying/consolidating their global IP structures in cases in which the substance of their IP holding companies was deemed insufficient. Progressively, MNEs are taking a more holistic view of the use of IP management companies, limiting their use to cases in which a substantial entity, staffed by legal and technology experts coordinating and conducting IP for the group from the IP holding company's jurisdiction, is indispensable to the MNE's broader commercial plans.

As intangible assets grow relentlessly in importance as the real driver of MNEs' global value, MNEs may seek to establish such substantive entities on a much more frequent basis. Chinese policymakers need to be aware that both Chinese MNEs as well as foreign MNEs will make greater use of such substantive global IP development and coordination centers in future, and relevant recommendations are set out in the Conclusions section below.

8.5 Conclusions and Policy Recommendations

IP is increasingly difficult to manage from a commercial and tax perspective in China. Policymakers in China have the ability to enhance innovative activity and technology transfer in a number of key areas. The key to successful policy development, as in any jurisdiction, is for the relevant in-country authorities (sometimes with differing agendas and/or revenue targets) to understand tax triggers and work together to manage competing priorities in a cohesive and holistic fashion. As noted previously, we draw on the MNE issues and policy considerations above to set out a number of recommendations below.

- Topic Area 1 noted that due to the greater China tax exposure potential arising from forthcoming TP and PE changes, MNEs are expected to be more incentivized to secure Chinese "innovation incentives." It has been noted that this trend supports Chinese innovation policy, and might be viewed positively by Chinese policymakers as contributing to the achievement of the original goals of the Chinese tax innovation incentives.

However, certain administrative and procedural hurdles regarding the application of Chinese innovation tax incentives, as well as some substantive issues, currently frustrate the optimal use of these incentives by taxpayers. Structural and procedural design flaws in the current innovation system hinder the Chinese government's innovation policy goals. It would be beneficial both for taxpayers and for the Chinese government if policymakers remedied these flaws.
It thus makes sense for Chinese policymakers to clarify the qualifying criteria for HNTE and the R&D Super Deduction (as outlined in detail above), and ensure consistent and transparent interpretation of the rules so that these incentives can have the maximum impact in raising Chinese innovation and investment. Clarity, consistency, and transparency across Chinese tax districts and across different government departments would lead to enhanced overall tax compliance and help the innovation tax policies to contribute to the generation of broader long-term innovation spill-over benefits for the Chinese economy.

- As discussed under Topic Area 2, conduct of progressively higher-value-added activities in China by foreign MNEs and by Chinese MNEs requires the import of more foreign technology as an input into Chinese high-tech exports. Facilitating the inflow of foreign know-how and expert services facilitates Chinese innovation and Chinese exports and deserves the support and attention of Chinese policymakers.
  MNEs, as noted above, can struggle to balance the challenges of managing WHT, TP, VAT, and customs in relation to the payments of IP license fees and expert service fees. There is sometimes a lack of clarity in the rules regarding when WHT should apply to services and when Service PEs may exist, and when license fees and service fees should be included in the calculation of customs. Policymakers might therefore consider how better guidance can be established and how greater consistency of approach among local tax authorities can be ensured.
  In the TP space, the rapid evolution of global TP guidance in relation to IP makes it essential that the SAT set out firm guidance and ensure consistency of application, as this will limit "tax friction." The SAT is scheduled to issue TP guidance in the first half of 2016, following on from the issuing of the OECD's global TP reform guidance in October 2015. Given the two-sided nature of TP, with increased profit in one country needing to be mirrored by decreased profit in another to limit double taxation, the SAT would also ideally focus on developing mutual agreement procedures with other countries, and potentially mutually binding arbitration mechanisms as well, to deal with the inevitable differences in inter-country TP outcomes that will occur.

- Chinese tax policy measures to restrict the ability of MNEs to take advantage of competing tax systems are in line with the global trend, and are inevitable. Even so, as intangible assets increase relentlessly in importance as the real driver of MNEs' global value, Chinese policymakers need to be aware that both Chinese MNEs as well as foreign MNEs will make greater use of substantive global IP development and coordination centers in future.

China should appreciate that IP holding regimes that comply with the new OECD Action 5 substance standards have been recognized by the global community as an acceptable and useful way for globe-spanning MNEs to manage IP effectively. Therefore, Chinese policies such as Announcement 16 should be nuanced to permit the MNE global ecosystem to sustain IP management entities. What is more, the SAT should ensure that anti-avoidance rules are applied consistently by local authorities and are not used in contexts outside of the original SAT policy intention.

References

Literature References

Arginelli P (2015) Innovation through R&D tax incentives: some ideas for a fair and transparent tax policy. World Tax J 7(1):3–71

Bates S, Kung P, Perryman Z, Tao A (2008) Chinese contract manufacturing structures: Navigating the new landscape. J Int Taxation 19(8):23–39

Chi C, Leung HY, Wang M (2012) Licensing intellectual property to China—transfer pricing challenges. Asia-Pac J Taxation 16(2):44–57

Garcia A, Yang B, Jiang J, Zhang W (2014) Created in China: the fast pace of innovation, R&D incentives and economic development. Int Tax Rev. Downloaded 6 Sept 2015 from http://www.internationaltaxreview.com/Article/3406622/Created-in-China-The-fast-pace-of-innovation-R-D-incentives-and-economic-development.html

Jiang Y (2015) Value creation theory of the BEPS report and China's reasonable share in global value allocation. Int Transf Pricing J 4:223–229

KPMG China (2013) PRC non-resident enterprise tax series: managing chinese taxable presence exposures from secondment arrangements. Available from https://www.kpmg.com/CN/en/IssuesAndInsights/ArticlesPublications/Documents/Chinese-taxable-presence-exposures-from-secondment-201306.pdf

KPMG China (2015) China tax alert: China tax planning to be impacted by BEPS action 7. Available from https://www.kpmg.com/CN/en/IssuesAndInsights/ArticlesPublications/Newsletters/ChinaAlerts/Documents/China-tax-alert-1506-12-China-tax-impacted-by-BEPS-Action-7.pdf

Macovei A, Rasch M (2011) Tax and strategic management of intangibles. Intellect Asset Manag. Downloaded 6 Sept 2015 from http://www.iam-media.com/Magazine/Issue/46/Features/Tax-and-the-strategic-management-of-intangibles

OECD (2015a) Preventing the artificial avoidance of permanent establishment status, action 7—2015 final report, OECD/G20 base erosion and profit shifting project. OECD Publishing, Paris. Available from http://dx.doi.org/10.1787/9789264241220-en

OECD (2015b) Countering harmful tax practices more effectively, taking into account transparency and substance, action 5—2015 final report, OECD/G20 base erosion and profit

shifting project. OECD Publishing, Paris. Available from http://dx.doi.org/10.1787/9789264241190-en
OECD, WTO, UNCTAD (2013) Implications of global value chains for trade, investment, development and jobs. Available from http://www.oecd.org/trade/G20-Global-Value-Chains-2013.pdf
UN (2013) Practical manual on transfer pricing for developing countries. Available from http://www.un.org/esa/ffd/documents/UN_Manual_TransferPricing.pdf
UN Conference on Trade and Development (UNCTAD) (2014) Investing in the SDGs: an action plan. World investment report. Available from http://unctad.org/en/PublicationsLibrary/wir2014_en.pdf
US China Business Council (2014) 2014 US-China joint commission on commerce and trade (JCCT) recommendations. Available from https://www.uschina.org/sites/default/files/2014.03.20%20%20USCBC%20JCCT%20Recommendations%20Final.pdf

References to Laws and Regulations

Cai Shui (2013a) No. 13, "Notice of Ministry of Finance and State Administration of Taxation on trialling the R&D Super Deduction" (Circular 13 [2013])
Cai Shui (2013b) No. 70, "Ministry of Finance and SAT Circular on Policy Issues Relevant to the Pre-Tax Super Deduction of Research and Development Expenses" (Circular 70 [2013])
Cai Shui (2014a) No. 75, "Circular of the Ministry of Finance and the State Administration of Taxation on Accelerated Depreciation" (Circular 75 [2014])
Cai Shui (2014b) No. 59, "Clarification on CIT incentives for Advanced Technology Service Enterprise jointly issued by the MOF, SAT, MOC, MOST and NDRC" (Circular 59 [2014])
Gonggao (2013) No. 40, "Announcement of the State Administration of Foreign Exchange and State Administration of Taxation on Issues relating to Tax Recordal Filing for Payments to Foreign Parties under Service Trade, etc." (Announcement 40 [2013])
Gonggao (2015) No. 16, "SAT Announcement Regarding CIT Matters on Outbound Payments to Overseas Related Parties" (Announcement 16 [2015])
Guo F (1997) No. 37, "Notice of the State Council on the Adjustment of Tax Policies for Imported Equipment" (Circular 37 [1997])
Guofa (2014) No. 62, "Notice of the State Council on putting in order tax incentive policies" (Circular 62 [2014])
Guofa (2015) No. 25, "Notice of the State Council on Preferential Policies for Taxation and Other Aspects" (Circular 25 [2015])
Guokefahuo (2008a) No. 172, "Administrative Measures on Accreditation of High-technology enterprises directs that investment must be in the 'High-New-Technology Areas with Key State Support'" (Circular 172 [2008])
Guokefahuo (2008b) No. 362, "Notice of the Ministry of Science and Technology, the Ministry of Finance and State Taxation Administration on Circulation and Implementation of Guidelines for Identification and Qualification of High-tech Enterprises" (Circular 362 [2008])
Guoshuifa (2008) No. 116, "Notice of the State Administration of Taxation on Administrative Measures for the Pre-tax Deduction of Enterprise Research and Development Expenses (for Trial Implementation)" (Circular 116 [2008])
Guoshuifa (2009) No. 19, "Measures Governing Tax Collection on Contracted Projects and Provision of Services by Non-resident Enterprises" (Circular 19 [2009])
Guoshuihan (2009a) No. 601, "Circular of the State Administration of Taxation on Interpretation and Determination of 'Beneficial Owners' under Double Taxation Agreements" (Circular 601 [2009])
Guoshuihan (2009b) No. 507, "Notice of State Administration of Taxation on Issues Relating to Implementation of Royalties Clauses under Double Taxation Agreements" (Circular 507 [2009])
Qiyesuodeshuifa (2008) Corporate Income Tax Law

Chapter 9
Evaluating Patent Promotion Policies in China: Consequences for Patent Quantity and Quality

Cheryl Xiaoning Long and Jun Wang

Abstract Using patent data at the provincial level from 1985 to 2010, we find that the average quality of Chinese patents has declined; thus, the dramatic rise in the number of patents most likely has not produced a proportionate increase in the country's total innovation capacity. In addition, we find evidence that the patent promotion policies (PPPs, namely preferential tax policies, subsidies, and subsidies for patent filing and maintenance fees) adopted by various government agencies in China can explain both the quantity increase and the quality fall in Chinese patents.

Keywords Patent quantity · Patent quality · Patent promotion policies · China

9.1 Introduction

Technological development is the key engine for a nation's sustained economic growth, and China has placed an increasingly greater focus on an innovation-driven economy. The numbers of patent applications and approvals are often used as measures for a country's inventiveness. China has seen dramatic improvement in the past three decades. In particular, the number of Chinese patent applications

---

Cheryl Long is a Cheung Kong Scholar Professor of Economics with WISE and School of Economics at Xiamen University (China), and a research associate at Colgate University (U.S.)

Jun Wang is an assistant professor with the Intellectual Property Research Institute at Xiamen University

---

C.X. Long (✉)
WISE and School of Economics, Xiamen University, Xiamen, China
e-mail: cxlong@xmu.edu.cn

C.X. Long
Colgate University, Hamilton, USA

J. Wang
Intellectual Property Research Institute, Xiamen University, Xiamen, China

D. Prud'homme and H. Song (eds.), *Economic Impacts of Intellectual Property-Conditioned Government Incentives*, DOI 10.1007/978-981-10-1119-1_9

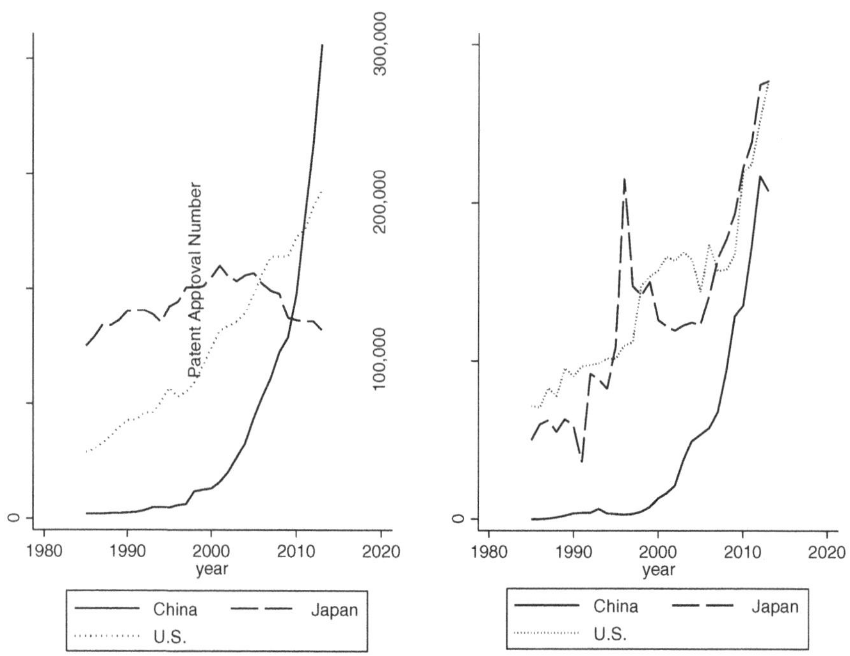

Fig. 9.1 Comparison of invention applications and approvals among China, Japan, and the U.S

surpassed those of the U.S. and Japan in 2011, making the country number 1 by this measure (see Fig. 9.1, left panel).

However, there are signs that the quality of Chinese patents has not been maintained during the same period. Figure 9.1 (right panel) shows that the number of approved patents in China is yet to catch up with those of the U.S. and Japan, the top two countries by this measure. In other words, the number of patent applications may have inflated the improvement in China's total innovation capacity.

To more carefully study the evolution of China's innovation capacity over time, we will construct panel data at the provincial level, based on China's Patent Database. In the study, we will explore both the quantity and the quality of Chinese patents. More importantly, we will argue that the government-sponsored PPPs (namely preferential tax policies and subsides linked to patent ownership, as well as subsidies for patent filing and maintenance fees) in China have not only led to a larger number of patents but also resulted in lower average patent quality. Specifically, we find higher per capita numbers of patent applications and approvals in province-years with PPPs, on one hand. On the other hand, the approval rate and the renewal rate for patents tend to be lower in these same province-years, while the withdrawal rate tends to be higher. The various regional PPPs can be put into two categories. One group of patent promotion policies links monetary incentives with patent ownership, by which tax deductibles, tax refunds, or R&D subsidies are offered to patent holders, whereas the other category of PPPs provides subsidies to patent holders to pay patent application fees or patent maintenance fees.

Compared with prior research on Chinese patents, we make contributions in several areas. First, we focus on the quality aspect of China's recent patent explosion and highlight the role of government policy in such development. Furthermore, equipped with patent-level data, we are able to aggregate information at different levels, which allows us to study how patent promotion policies impact different types of firms differently.

The rest of the chapter is structured as follows: Sect. 9.2 reviews related literature. Section 9.3 provides background information on PPPs and the patent application process in China and discusses measures for patent quality. Data sources used for estimation as well as preliminary patterns are described in Sect. 9.4. The main empirical results are presented in Sect. 9.5, while Sect. 9.6 provides some further discussions as well as concluding remarks.

9.2 Literature Review

Among the research papers that study patent promotion policies in China, Li (2012) provides evidence that the PPPs that help with application fees and maintenance fees have increased patent quantity but have not impacted patent quality. Lei et al. (2013) find that the number of domestic applications in China increases each December, suggesting pressure to meet patent quotas toward the end of the year. Dang and Motohashi (2013) claim to have found evidence showing a larger number of inferior patent applications and a higher rejection rate due to the patent promotion policies that help with application fees.

In response to the recent patent explosion in China, several theories have been proposed to explain why it has happened. Firstly, (Hu et al. 2005) and Cheung and Ping (2004), for example, make the argument that China's innovation capacity has been improving rapidly, resulting in the fast growth in the number of patents. Secondly, Hu and Jefferson (2009) and Yueh (2009) argue that the improvements in China's IP have provided an important guarantee for patent growth. In particular, Hu and Jefferson (2009) provide empirical evidence that the patent law revisions of 2000 are significantly correlated with the increase in the number of patent applications. Both views above, however, fail to address the concurrent decline in patent quality during the same period. They also neglect a big part of the government's role in China's patent explosion.

More generally, a large body of literature explores the effects and mechanisms of policies on patents and innovation. On one hand, Jaffe and Lerner (2001, for the U.S.), Czarnitzki and Hussinger (2004, for Germany), Ebersberger (2004, for Finland), Zhu and Xu (2003, for China), and Li (2012) find evidence that policy initiatives supporting innovation have positive effects. On the other hand, many studies, including Mansfield (1986, for the U.S.), Goolsbee (1998, for the U.S.), and Sakakibara and Branstetter (2001, for Japan), find little effect of the policies.

Prud'homme (2012), Zhang (2010), and Dang and Motohashi (2013), all for China, further argue that the patent promoting laws and policies may lead to a negative impact on patent quality. However, more detailed empirical studies still need to be done to evaluate how government policies affect patent development in China.

9.3 PPPs, the Patent Application Process, and Patent Quality Measures

9.3.1 Patent-Promoting Policies

In the current study, we will focus on PPPs at the provincial level in China because they are the largest in number among government policies impacting patents and provide regional variations in adoption time to facilitate analysis. More importantly, in contrast to laws that provide substantive or procedural protection for patents, PPPs incur direct fiscal costs. In other words, governments make the conscious decision to sacrifice fiscal revenue, at least in the short term, in return for improved innovative capacity. It is therefore essential that we evaluate the effectiveness of these policies.

The various regional PPPs can be put into two categories. One group of patent promotion policies links monetary incentives with patent ownership, by which tax deductibles, tax refunds, or R&D subsidies are offered to patent holders, whereas the other category of PPPs provides subsidies to patent holders to pay patent application fees or patent maintenance fees. These policies will either increase the benefit from or lower the cost of obtaining and maintaining patent applications, thus leading to a larger number of patents. However, their impacts may be different for the following reasons: The first type of PPPs provides more general monetary benefits, while the second type of PPPs only offers limited benefits by focusing on application fee and maintenance fee subsidies. Thus, the first type of promotion policies (referred to as PPP1 henceforth) may have a bigger impact on the quantity of patents than the second type of policies (referred to as PPP2 henceforth).

While studies have consistently found a positive impact of PPPs on patent quantity (Hu and Jefferson 2009; Zhang 2010; Li 2012), the implications for patent quality may not be as positive. Given that the approval process is not perfect, some innovations of inferior quality will inevitably be approved (see more details in Sect. 9.3.2). Because the implementation of the PPPs will attract more innovations into the patent application pool, many of which may be of lower quality, the percentage of such inferior innovations will likely increase, thus lowering the average quality of approved patents. In later sections, we will empirically study the impact of these patent promotion policies on patent quantity and quality.

9.3.2 *Overview of the Patent System and Measures of Patent Quality*

China established its modern patent system only in 1985, when the Patent Law was first passed, followed by revisions in 1992, 2000, and 2008. The patent law defines three types of patents: inventions, utility models, and designs, where invention applications must pass both a preliminary and substantive examination, while the other two require only the passage of a preliminary examination. To pass the preliminary examination, the application must be complete with all the required materials submitted. To pass the substantive examination, in contrast, the application must also satisfy the three criteria of novelty, creativity, and practicability, thus requiring a substantially higher quality of innovation. To begin any patent application, application materials must be prepared and submitted, which can be handled by either a patent agent or the applicant himself.[1] The procedures then differ depending on whether the application is for an invention or one of the other two types of patents.

For an application involving a utility model or an exterior design, a preliminary examination regarding formality is conducted, and the application is approved if no reason is found for rejection. In contrast, a much lengthier process ensues in an invention application. The patent office first goes through a preliminary examination, whose successful conclusion will be followed by the publication of the patent application within eighteen months of its filing, during which the publication of the patent application can also be accelerated at the request of the applicant. Within three years of the application, the patent office conducts the substantive examination of the application, if requested by the applicant. If the request for substantive examination is not made within the three-year period, the application is considered withdrawn. Only after the successful conclusion of the substantive examination is the patent application approved; otherwise, the application is rejected. Even after the approval, an invention or another patent could be invalidated by the patent re-examination committee if the validity of the patent is successfully challenged.

To continue with these stages in the patent application process, various fees must be paid. Within two months of the application's submission, the applicant must pay the application fee, the invention publication fee, and an additional application fee in the case of an invention application. To request the substantive examination, a corresponding fee of 2500 RMB is required. The applicant of an invention patent not approved two years after submission must also pay the application maintenance fee starting from the third year. If the applicant fails to pay in full and on time any of the fees listed above, the application will be considered withdrawn. Once approved, the protection duration for inventions is 20 years, while that for utility models and designs is ten years. The protection is not automatic, however. An annual fee must be paid to maintain the patent rights; the fee rises substantially at

[1]Foreign companies without a legal entity in China must use a Chinese patent agent to file patents in China.

three-year intervals, and failure to pay the annual fee will result in the termination of the patent rights, whether it is an invention patent, a patent for a utility model, or a patent for an exterior design.

Based on the description above, whether a patent application results in protectable patent rights or not is thus determined by both the patent examiner and the applicant. While the examiner may reject an application based on the patentability requirement, the applicant may also decide to terminate the application because it is too costly to continue the patent application process and the expected marketability or profit from the patent (if obtained) does not warrant the cost. In other words, patents with lower quality are less likely to be approved by the patent examiner, and they are also more likely to be withdrawn by the applicants themselves.

As a result, we will use both the *approval rate* and the *withdrawal rate* as measures of average patent quality (see Ye et al. 2012). Similarly, it is costly to maintain patent rights after they are obtained; thus, applicants with a lower valuation of expected marketability or profit from their patents are more likely to stop paying annual fees, resulting in the termination of the patent rights. Hence, we will also use the probability of patent renewal to measure patent quality (see, for example, Schankerman and Parkes 1986; Lanjouw et al. 1998; Bessen 2008; Zhang and Chen 2012). Among the three measures discussed thus far, the *approval rate* and *renewal rate* are positively correlated with patent quality, while the *withdrawal rate* is negatively correlated with patent quality. Note that the *approval rate* and the *withdrawal rate* measure the average quality of patent applications, whereas the *renewal rate* provides an average quality measure for approved patents.

9.4 Data Sources and Description

The data sources used in the study are discussed here, as well as the preliminary patterns observed in the data. The first set of data sources provides information on the patent promotion polices at the provincial level in China, which include preferential tax policies and subsides linked to patent ownership, as well as subsidies for patent filing and maintenance fees. To locate PPPs linking monetary rewards to patent ownership, we search for relevant provincial level legislation and regulations from Beida Fabao (http://www.pkulaw.cn), Beida Fayi (http://www.lawyee.net/), and the Compendium of Chinese Laws (maintained by the Chinese Court website) (http://www.chinacourt.org/law.shtml) using keywords including "patent," "award," "preferential tax treatment," and "subsidy." These three databases cover mostly the same materials but occasionally complement one another; thus, combined, they include practically all legislation, regulations, and executive orders by central and local governments throughout the history of modern China. We then read all legislation and regulations that pass the keyword selection to verify them for accuracy, i.e., to verify that the legislation or regulation indeed provides monetary incentives for patent holders. To collect information on PPPs providing application fee and maintenance fee subsidies, we resort to the Annals of Chinese

Intellectual Property Rights (2000–2008) and read the work reports of each province to decide whether and when the region has given a PPP such subsidies.

Based on the information collected, we construct two dummy variables to indicate whether a province has a certain type of PPP in place in a certain year as follows: If a type I PPP (or PPP1) was in effect in a province before January 1 in a certain year, then the dummy variable, PPP1, takes the value of 1 for that year; otherwise, the dummy takes the value of 0. A dummy variable indicating the effective date of patent fee subsidies, PPP2, is similarly constructed.

Tables 9.1, 9.2 and 9.3 list the various PPPs adopted by Chinese provinces, their adoption years, and the coverage of these policies. As shown in the table, up until 2011, nine provinces implemented 12 qualifying PPP1s, where both coastal regions and inland provinces are represented and the timing of the PPP1 does not seem to correlate with the level of regional per capita GDP. In terms of specific measures, all but one such policy involve a tax reduction. While the earlier policies target inventions and utility models, PPP1s implemented after 2000 apply to all kinds of patents. Twenty-nine provinces adopted policies focusing on patent fee incentives (PPP2s) by 2007. As there is less variation in PPP2s, especially in later years, our work will focus more on PPP1s, the policies that provide more general tax and subsidy incentives.

Table 9.1 Regional PPP adoptions over time (PPP1s.)

Panel A: PPP1s (policies involving more general incentives)						
Year	Province	Specific policy	Patent type coverage	Applicant type coverage	Specific amounts of support	Requirements
1995	Guangdong	Tax refund	Invention and utility	Firms	Unclear	Patent first applied
1997	Liaoning	Tax refund	Invention and utility	Firms	Return 50 % newly-added VAT	Invention and utility first applied
1998	Hubei	Tax refund	Invention and utility	Firms	Return 25 % newly-added VAT and income tax	Patent first applied
1999	Jilin	Tax refund	Invention and utility	Firms	Return 100 % newly-added VAT	Invention and utility first applied
2000	Shanghai	Subsidies	All patents	All applicants	Subsidies of importing patents	Patents first applied
2005	Beijing	Tax incentives	All patents	All applicants	Unclear	All patents
2005	Anhui	Tax deduction	All patents	All applicants	Unclear	All patents
2007	Chongqing	Tax incentives	All patents	Firms	Unclear	All patents
2009	Jiangxi	Tax incentives	All patents	All applicants	Unclear	All patents
2009	Jiangsu	Tax deduction	All patents	Firms	Unclear	All patents
2009	Qinghai	Tax deduction	All patents	Firms	Unclear	All patents
2011	Tianjin	Tax incentives	All patents	All applicants	Unclear	All patents

Table 9.2 Regional PPP adoptions over time (PPP2s)

Panel B: PPP2s (policies involving patent fee incentives)			
Year	Province	Specific policy	Patent type coverage
1999	Shanghai	Subsidies for application and maintenance fees	Cover all
2000	Beijing	Subsidies for application fees	Cover all
2000	Tianjin	Subsidies for application fees	Invention and utility
2000	Guangdong	Subsidies for application fees	Invention
2000	Jiangsu	Subsidies for application fees	Cover all
2000	Chongqing	Subsidies for application fees	Cover all
2001	Zhejiang	Subsidies for application fees	Invention
2001	Heilongjiang	Subsidies for application fees	Cover all
2001	Guangxi	Subsidies for application fees	Cover all
2001	Hainan	Subsidies for application fees	Invention
2001	Sichuan	Subsidies for application fees	Invention and utility
2001	Shanxi	Subsidies for application fees	Cover all
2002	Fujian	Subsidies for application fees	Cover all
2002	Jiangxi	Subsidies for application fees	Invention and utility
2002	Henan	Subsidies for application fees	Cover all
2002	Guizhou	Subsidies for application fees	Cover all
2002	Inner Mongolia	Subsidies for application fees	Invention
2002	Xingjiang	Subsidies for application fees	Cover all
2003	Shanxi	Subsidies for application fees	Cover all
2003	Anhui	Subsidies for application fees	Cover all
2003	Shandong	Subsidies for application fees	Invention
2003	Yunnan	Subsidies for application and maintenance fees	Cover all
2003	Tibet	Subsidies for application fees	Cover all
2004	Jilin	Subsidies for application fees	Invention
2004	Hunan	Subsidies for application and maintenance fees	Cover all
2005	Hebei	Subsidies for application fees	Invention
2005	Qinghai	Subsidies for application fees	Cover all
2006	Liaoning	Subsidies for application fees	Invention
2007	Hubei	Subsidies for application fees	Cover all

Notes All the PPP2s cover all applicant types

The second set of data sources covers patent data, which comes from the SIPO (State Intellectual Property Office) patent application database and includes information on 5.6 million patent applications filed between 1985 and 2010. We exclude patent applications from non-residents of China, as they do not have filing location information within China, resulting in a sample of close to 4.3 million patent applications. The database includes the patent application number, application date,

Table 9.3 Regional PPP adoptions over time

PPP1s (policies involving more general incentives)			
Year	Province	Specific amounts of subsidies	Requirements
1995	Guangdong	unclear	Patent first applied
1997	Liaoning	Return 50 % newly-added VAT	Invention and utility first applied
1998	Hubei	Return 25 % newly-added VAT and income tax	Patent first applied
1999	Jilin	Return 100 % newly-added VAT	Invention and utility first applied
2000	Shanghai	Subsidies of importing patents	Patents first applied
2005	Beijing	Unclear	All patents
2005	Anhui	Unclear	All patents
2007	Chongqing	Unclear	All patents
2009	Jiangxi	Unclear	All patents
2009	Jiangsu	Unclear	All patents
2009	Qinghai	Unclear	All patents
2011	Tianjin	Unclear	All patents

Notes All the PPP2s cover all applicant types

publication date, patent number if approved, current legal status, and applicant name and address. Based on such preliminary information, we further construct the following variables: patent type (invention, utility model, or design), location of applicant, type of applicant (individual versus firm, etc.), time of application withdrawal, time of approval, time of termination, per capita GDP, and per capita FDI. By aggregating the variables at the provincial level, we are also able to produce the provincial-level panel data for 1985–2010, including the number of patent applications, patent approvals, approval rate, withdrawal rate, and renewal rate.

As discussed in Sect. 9.3.2, we will use the approval rate, withdrawal rate, and renewal rate to measure patent quality in the empirical study. To compute the approval rate for a province in a year, we divide the number of patent applications filed in the year that are eventually approved by the total number of patent applications filed in that year. Similarly, we replace the numerator with the number of application withdrawals to compute the withdrawal rate. For the renewal rate, we compute separate rates for different lengths of duration and include in these calculations only patents that have terminated during our sample period. For example, to obtain the renewal rate after three years (or the three-year renewal rate) for a certain province for a given year, the number of patents filed for application in the year, are eventually approved, and are terminated before 2010, is assigned as the denominator. The number of patents among the above that are renewed after three years is assigned as the numerator. As a result, a higher approval rate or renewal rate and a lower withdrawal rate correspond to a higher average quality of patents.

Finally, we collect information on various provincial characteristics from various editions of China Statistical Yearbooks, including measures on population size, economic development, and human capital quality. Table 9.4 gives the descriptive statistics of the patent variables used in the empirical analysis. As shown in the table, after the PPP implementation, both the per capita patent applications and the per capita patent approvals increased significantly, which are consistent with the predicted impact of PPPs discussed above. In contrast, while the approval rate increased significantly, the withdrawal rate and renewal rate both decreased significantly. The changes in patent quantity and the change in renewal rate are

Table 9.4 Summary statistics

Variables	Whole sample (N = 792)		With policy (N = 255)		Without policy (N = 537)		t-statistic
	Mean	S.D.	Mean	S.D.	Mean	S.D.	
Applications (per 10,000 persons)	1.38	2.99	3.31	4.61	0.47	0.71	13.94***
Per capita firm application	0.53	1.49	1.42	2.37	0.10	0.17	12.79***
Per capita firm invention application	0.16	0.53	0.44	0.87	0.02	0.03	11.10***
Approvals (per 10,000 persons)	1.12	2.32	2.65	3.53	0.39	0.60	14.37***
Per capita firm patent approval	0.42	1.14	1.12	1.81	0.09	0.15	13.10***
Per capita firm invention approval	0.05	0.18	0.14	0.29	0.01	0.01	10.58***
Patent approval rate	0.81	0.09	0.83	0.08	0.81	0.09	3.69***
Firm patent approval rate	0.84	0.11	0.84	0.10	0.84	0.11	0.86
Firm invention approval rate	0.43	0.21	0.43	0.21	0.40	0.19	2.07**
Patent withdrawal rate	0.11	0.07	0.08	0.06	0.13	0.07	−8.43***
Firm patent withdrawal rate	0.09	0.09	0.07	0.07	0.10	0.09	−5.23***
Firm invention withdrawal rate	0.42	0.22	0.25	0.17	0.51	0.19	−17.59***
Patent renewal rate (over 3 years)	0.41	0.17	0.34	0.24	0.45	0.12	−8.04***
Firm patent renewal rate (over 3 years)	0.46	0.20	0.37	0.26	0.49	0.16	−7.69***
Firm invention renewal rate (over 3 years)	0.51	0.28	0.33	0.30	0.57	0.25	−10.20***
Patent renewal rate (over 4 years)	0.20	0.11	0.15	0.14	0.21	0.10	−7.43***
Firm patent renewal rate (over 4 years)	0.27	0.16	0.19	0.19	0.21	0.18	−8.67***
Firm invention renewal rate (over 4 years)	0.34	0.26	0.19	0.23	0.40	0.25	−9.45***
Patent renewal rate (over 5 years)	0.11	0.08	0.10	0.13	0.20	0.12	−11.20***
Firm patent renewal rate (over 5 years)	0.17	0.13	0.18	0.13	0.13	0.14	−10.40***
Firm invention renewal rate (over 5 years)	0.24	0.22	0.09	0.14	0.29	0.22	−11.18***

***Significant at 1 %. **Significant at 5 %. *Significant at 10 %

consistent with the predictions of PPP effects on patent quantity and quality made in Sect. 9.3.1, whereas the change in the withdrawal rate is the opposite to the prediction. These comparisons are, of course, inconclusive due to the existence of other affecting factors. We will explore these patterns in more detail in the sections below.

9.5 Results and Discussion

In this section, we will conduct a provincial-level analysis to study the various impacts of PPPs. Specifically, we explore the empirical implications of patent promotion policies at the provincial level by looking at how patent quantity and quality change after the introduction of the PPP. To measure quantity effects, we use per capita patent applications and per capita patent approvals, while patent quality is measured by the approval rate, withdrawal rate, and renewal rate. To take into account determining factors other than the PPP, we control for various provincial characteristics in the following two-way fixed-effect estimation:

$$Y_{i,t} = \alpha + \beta_1 PPP1_{i,t} + \beta_2 PPP2_{i,t} + \gamma \mathbf{X}_{i,t-1} + \eta_i + \mu_t + \varepsilon_{i,t}, \tag{9.1}$$

where $Y_{i,t}$ is the outcome measure for province i in year t, $PPP1_{i,t}$ and $PPP2_{i,t}$ are the corresponding PPP measures (=1 if the PPP1 was in place before January 1 in year t, =0 otherwise), and β_1 and β_2 give the effects of the PPP policies on the outcome variable. A set of control variables are captured in $X_{i,t-1}$, which is a vector of provincial characteristics in the previous year, including population, per capita GDP, and per capita FDI (all in logs), when we use the data for the period 1985–2010. Provincial fixed effects, η_i and year fixed effects μ_t are included to address other unobserved province and time variations, while $\varepsilon_{i,t}$ is the random error term. Note that two important explanatory variables for patent measures, per capita R&D expenditure (in logs) and the percentage of industrial employment in R&D personnel, are not available for the whole 1985–2010 period. However, we add them to the estimation for the more recent period of 1998–2010, when information becomes available, with the results included in the appendix.

9.5.1 *PPP Effects on Patent Quantity*

The results from estimation model 1, using patent quantity as the outcome variable, are shown in Table 9.5, where the first column presents the estimation results using the whole sample of patent applications. As shown in column 1, the implementation of both types of PPPs is correlated with a higher number of per capita patent applications, with the first type of PPPs (those with more general tax and subsidy benefits) having a larger impact (about three times) than the second type of PPPs,

Table 9.5 PPP effects on per capita patent applications

Variables	(1) Whole Sample	(2) Firms only	(3) Firm inventions	(4) Firm utility models	(5) Firm designs
PPP1	1.562***	0.880***	0.360***	0.199***	0.831***
	(0.280)	(0.151)	(0.0607)	(0.0572)	(0.0988)
PPP2	0.505*	0.269*	0.110*	−0.0193	0.141***
	(0.274)	(0.148)	(0.0595)	(0.0468)	(0.0514)
Ln (population)	21.66***	11.97***	4.173***	4.340***	2.810***
	(1.259)	(0.678)	(0.273)	(0.254)	(0.296)
Ln (percapit_gdp)	2.819***	0.957***	0.406***	0.167	0.482***
	(0.587)	(0.316)	(0.127)	(0.118)	(0.130)
Ln (percapita_FDI)	0.119	0.0647	0.000166	0.0349*	0.00729
	(0.0886)	(0.0478)	(0.0192)	(0.0180)	(0.0200)
Year FE	Yes	Yes	Yes	Yes	Yes
Province FE	Yes	Yes	Yes	Yes	Yes
Obs.	769	769	769	769	769
R^2	0.748	0.704	0.628	0.697	0.613

Notes Standard errors are in parentheses
***Significant at 1 %. **Significant at 5 %. *Significant at 10 %

which have a narrow focus on subsidizing patent application and renewal fees. This is consistent with our previous prediction, as the supply of patent applications is most likely more elastic with respect to the implementation of PPP1. The other empirical findings are also in line with expectations, where larger and richer provinces tend to have more patent applications per capita. The level of foreign direct investment, however, is not shown to correlate significantly with patent applications.

As all patent promotion policies cover firms that apply for and hold patents but are only sometimes available to other entities, we consider firm applicants the main beneficiaries of these policies. Thus, in columns 2–5, we focus on patent applications filed by firms only, with column 2 covering all firm patents, whereas columns 3–5 specifically investigate inventions, utility models, and exterior designs. The results in these columns all present the same pattern; i.e., both types of PPPs are associated with higher per capita patent applications, and the first type of promotion policies tends to have a larger impact.

The comparison of the impact size across the columns is informative. While firm applications constitute merely 37 % of the total number of patent applications, the size of the PPP's impact on firm patents is more than half of the PPP's impact on the whole patent sample, suggesting that the policies are indeed more effective in inducing firm patent applications, which is good news for policy makers. A less sanguine pattern is the following, however: The PPP's impact on firm design patents is substantially larger than those on inventions and utility models, although the three categories make up similar proportions in the total. This suggests that the

Table 9.6 PPP effects on per capita patent approvals

Variables	(1) Whole sample	(2) Firms only	(3) Firm inventions	(4) Firm utility models	(5) Firm designs
PPP1	1.097***	0.665***	0.141***	0.201***	0.832***
	(0.227)	(0.117)	(0.0219)	(0.0573)	(0.0989)
PPP2	0.430*	0.225*	0.0646***	−0.0190	0.141***
	(0.223)	(0.115)	(0.0215)	(0.0469)	(0.0515)
Ln (population)	15.46***	8.831***	1.015***	4.343***	2.827***
	(1.022)	(0.527)	(0.0985)	(0.255)	(0.296)
Ln (percapit_gdp)	2.564***	0.798***	0.246***	0.169	0.482***
	(0.477)	(0.246)	(0.0459)	(0.118)	(0.130)
Ln (percapita_FDI)	0.101	0.0601	−0.00465	0.0349*	0.00752
	(0.0720)	(0.0371)	(0.00694)	(0.0180)	(0.0200)
Year FE	Yes	Yes	Yes	Yes	Yes
Province FE	Yes	Yes	Yes	Yes	Yes
Obs.	769	769	769	769	769
R^2	0.723	0.698	0.561	0.696	0.612

Notes Standard errors are in parentheses
***Significant at 1 %. **Significant at 5 %. *Significant at 10 %

PPPs may have induced more patents with less innovation content, which is particularly true in the case of PPP1, the policies that promote patents through tax rebates or R&D subsidies.

Table 9.6 shows similar patterns when per capita patent approvals is used as the measure for patent quantity. The effect of PPPs on patent approval is large and significant, with the first type of PPPs having a large and more significant impact. Firms are still the main beneficiaries of the patent promotion policies, and again, the number of designs experiences a substantially larger increase than the other two types of patents.

It is worth noting that the effects on patent quantity found are not only statistically significant but also economically important. In particular, the number of patent applications increases by about 1.6 per 10,000 residents after the implementation of PPP1s, which is about 55 % of the standard deviation of per capita patent applications. Likewise, the number of patent approvals increases by 1.1 per 10,000 residents after the implementation of PPPs, which is 48 % of the standard deviation of per capita patent approvals. If we use 2000 as a baseline, introducing the PPP will increase China's per capita patent applications and per capita patent approvals by 265 and 165 %, respectively, which are equivalent to a rise of 340,000 patent applications and 210,000 patent approvals a year.

The above results, therefore, are supportive of the prediction that the implementation of PPPs helps improve patent quantity. The policy is thus effective in increasing patent quantity. However, as some of the findings in Tables 9.5 and 9.6 (columns 3–5 in each table) indicate, the increased patent quantity caused by the adoption of PPPs is likely to be accompanied by a reduction in patent quality. What does this imply for the total innovative capacity of Chinese regions? We turn to study this issue next.

9.5.2 The Effect of PPPs on Patent Quality

Since the ultimate goal of the PPPs is to improve a region's innovative capacity, it is thus essential that the aggregate innovation content increase at some point with the increase in innovation quantity. Hence, it is equally important to study the impact of PPPs on patent quality.

In line with the discussion in Sect. 9.3.2, we will use the approval rate, withdrawal rate, and renewal rate as the patent quality measures. While we expect the approval rate and renewal rate to be positively correlated with patent quality, we expect the withdrawal rate to be negatively correlated with patent quality. Table 9.7 presents the empirical findings regarding the average quality of patent applications, where columns 1–3 use the approval rate as the quality measure, while columns 4–6 use the withdrawal rate.

The results suggest the following patterns: Firstly, with the presence of a PPP of the first type, the approval rate for patents filed by firms significantly decreases (column 2) and the withdrawal rate for patents filed by firms significantly increases (column 4), while the approval rate and withdrawal rate for the whole sample of patent applications show similar but insignificant trends. Secondly, we do not observe the above correlations for patent promotion policies based on patent application fee and renewal fee subsidies. The first pattern above is consistent with firms being more impacted by the PPPs, which was envisioned by the policy makers to begin with, but with an unfortunate twist in its quality implication. The two patterns combined, in contrast, seem to suggest that the fee subsidy-based patent promotion policies may be more desirable, as they do not cause any significant decline in patent quality, to the extent that the approval rate and the withdrawal rate can accurately reflect patent quality. A plausible explanation is that the fee subsidy regime does not draw as many inferior innovations into the patent application pool.[2]

The quality implications of PPPs are further explored in Table 9.8, which presents estimation results using the renewal rate as the dependent variable. While the structure of the table largely follows that in Tables 9.5, 9.6, it includes three panels to correspond to the results for three-year, four-year, and five-year renewal rates, respectively. The results show that the presence of a PPP of the first type (PPP1) is negatively and significantly correlated with the renewal rates of patent applications

[2]It should, however be noted that patent fee subsidies are likely to somewhat reduce average withdrawal rates; given that the application fees are paid for the patentee, they are less likely to withdraw a patent out of realization that it might not be "worth their money" to examine. This effect may have masked the underlying negative impact on patent quality of patent fee subsidies.

Table 9.7 PPP effects on the patent approval rate and withdrawal rate

Variables	(1) Approval rate	(2) Approval rate (firms only)	(3) Approval rate (firm inventions)	(4) Withdrawal rate	(5) Withdrawal rate (firms only)	(6) Withdrawal rate (firm inventions)
PPP1	−0.00251	−0.0141*	0.000348	0.00209	0.0154*	−0.0189
	(0.00816)	(0.0069)	(0.0262)	(0.00947)	(0.00824)	(0.0323)
PPP2	−0.00180	−0.0137	0.0203	0.0128	0.0256	−0.0221
	(0.00800)	(0.0157)	(0.0259)	(0.0125)	(0.0166)	(0.0319)
Ln (population)	−0.155***	−0.151***	−0.147	0.0471	−0.0134	0.0102
	(0.0367)	(0.0529)	(0.119)	(0.0532)	(0.0629)	(0.180)
Ln (percapit_gdp)	0.0318*	−0.0116	−0.0160	−0.0218	0.00664	−0.0274
	(0.0171)	(0.0299)	(0.0551)	(0.0326)	(0.0421)	(0.0668)
Ln (percapita_FDI)	0.00493*	0.0116**	0.00564	−0.00102	−0.00528	−0.00196
	(0.00259)	(0.00517)	(0.00833)	(0.00307)	(0.00563)	(0.0180)
Year FE	Yes	Yes	Yes	Yes	Yes	Yes
Province FE	Yes	Yes	Yes	Yes	Yes	Yes
Obs.	769	766	758	769	766	758
R^2	0.661	0.483	0.453	0.635	0.445	0.574

Notes: Standard errors are in parentheses
***Significant at 1 %. **Significant at 5 %. *Significant at 10 %

Table 9.8 PPP effects on patent renewal rate

Variables	(1) Whole Sample	(2) Firms only	(3) Firm inventions	(4) Firm utility models	(5) Firm designs
Renewal over 3 years					
PPP1	−0.0529***	−0.0479**	−0.0498	−0.0282*	−0.146**
	(0.0105)	(0.0202)	(0.0477)	(0.0136)	(0.0576)
PPP2	−0.0183*	−0.0254	−0.00406	−0.0300	0.0455
	(0.00996)	(0.0191)	(0.0450)	(0.0184)	(0.0278)
Obs.	740	737	642	725	689
R^2	0.900	0.730	0.415	0.741	0.515
Renewal over 4 years					
PPP1	−0.0331***	−0.0490***	−0.00246	−0.0462**	−0.115**
	(0.00848)	(0.0169)	(0.0455)	(0.0194)	(0.0464)
PPP2	−0.00143	−0.0106	0.0417	−0.0142	0.0561**
	(0.00803)	(0.0160)	(0.0429)	(0.0158)	(0.0224)
Obs.	740	737	642	725	689
R^2	0.846	0.707	0.366	0.738	0.486
Renewal over 5 years					
PPP1	−0.0220***	−0.0299**	0.00392	−0.0286**	−0.0560**
	(0.00587)	(0.0144)	(0.0394)	(0.0135)	(0.0264)
PPP2	0.000233	−0.0120	−0.0337	−0.00542	0.0341**
	(0.00555)	(0.0136)	(0.0372)	(0.0157)	(0.0157)
Obs.	740	737	642	725	689
R^2	0.840	0.680	0.341	0.719	0.439

Notes ***Significant at 1 %. **Significant at 5 %. *Significant at 10 %
All models control for the logs of population, per capita GDP, per capita FDI, and year and province fixed effects. Standard errors are in parentheses

for the whole sample of approved patents and for all firm patent approvals (columns 1 and 2). In other words, the average quality of approved patents (as evidenced by the renewal rates) declines with the presence of the first type of PPPs (i.e., patent promotion policies involving monetary rewards for patent holders).

Additional patterns emerge when we segregate firm patents into different categories. While approved inventions filed by firms do not show a decline in the renewal rate (or quality), we observe a significant drop in renewal rates for both approved utility models and exterior designs filed by firms (columns 3–5). The different patterns between inventions and the other two types of patents may be explained by the fact that invention approvals need to go through substantive examinations, where applications of inferior quality are routinely rejected. Utility models and exterior designs, in contrast, only require preliminary examination before getting approved, thus increasing the likelihood of applications of lower quality getting through the approval process.

In contrast, the patent promotion policies that only rely on patent fee subsidies once again are generally not associated with a decline in patent renewal rates. In fact, the four-year and five-year renewal rates show a positive correlation with the implementation of PPP2s for exterior designs patents filed by firms. While this may imply the potential superiority of using this type of PPPs (PPP2s) regarding the influence on patent quality, the results may reflect the artificial boosting of renewal rates due to the coverage of renewal fees in the PPP2s.

To summarize the results from the provincial-level analyses above, we have observed an increase in quantity but a decline in the average quality of patent applications and approvals in response to the passage and implementation of patent promotion policies, especially those PPPs that extend general tax rebates and subsidies to patent holders (PPP1s). A possible explanation as to why the patent fee-related policies (PPP2s) do not have as significant a negative impact on patent quality as patent promotion policies linking monetary rewards to patent ownership (PPP1s), is the greater incentive provided by the latter type of policies, which usually offers monetary rewards much larger than patent application fees or renewal fees.[3] Compared to previous studies, ours is the first that focuses on PPP1s, with results that are generally consistent with those from Dang and Motohashi (2013). Our findings regarding PPP2s are similar to those of Li (2012) and Lei et al. (2013).

9.5.3 Robustness Checks

In addition to the empirical results presented above, we have also conducted the following robustness checks: First, we excluded data in the later years (2005–2010) from the sample to recalculate all the estimations in order to address the concern that many patent applications filed in recent years have not yet completed the application process, thus creating a data truncation problem. Second, we included additional control variables including per capita R&D expenditure and per capita science and technology personnel into the estimation, with the goal of taking into account more influencing factors. The cost of this approach, however, is that such data are only available after 1998, which explains our choice to exclude these variables in the main results. (Please refer to Tables 9.9 and 9.10 in the Appendix.)

All results from these robustness checks are largely similar to the findings presented above. Thus, they provide additional empirical support for the two arguments we make in this chapter: namely that the adoption of PPPs, especially those involving tax rebates and general subsidies, has led to increased patent quantity but also a decline in patent quality.

A potential concern with our empirical approach in this chapter is the issue of endogeneity. For at least two reasons, one may not be able to interpret our findings that link PPPs with patent quantity and quality as causal relationships. First, it is

[3]Please also see Prud'homme (2012) for an alternative explanation related to the requirement of the HNTE tax scheme, where firms with a certain number of patents obtain the high-tech firm designation and the ensuing corporate income tax rebates.

possible that provinces adopting PPPs may have higher per capita patent numbers to begin with, as these are the same regions that have an incentive to keep their advantages. Thus, the positive correlation we observe may be due to reverse causality. In addition, it could be that regions that choose PPPs are capable of doing so thanks to their higher income level and greater fiscal capacity, which simultaneously implies a higher innovation level. In other words, the observed patterns could be due to simultaneity rather than the cause-effect story we attempted to tell previously. In both cases above, the provinces choosing to adopt the PPPs may not be randomly assigned (with regard to the levels of patent quantity and quality), and our estimation findings may thus suffer from the problem of endogeneity.

We address this potential problem in two ways. In the first approach, we directly test whether lagged patent quantity can account for the adoption of PPPs by regressing the PPP1 and PPP2 dummy on per capita patent applications, per capita patent approvals, population size, per capita GDP, and per capita FDI, all lagged by one year, as well as province and year fixed effects. We find no significant impact of lagged patent quantity on the adoption of PPP1 or PPP2, which supports our belief that the adoption of patent promotion policies is largely exogenous to the regions' innovative capacity or economic development level.[4]

Our other approach is the counter-factual test, where we replace PPPs with their one-year leading values in the original estimations to see whether the significant correlations observed before could be duplicated. If our findings are due to reverse causality or simultaneity, we expect to see similar results even when the value of the PPP is replaced by its leading value. None of the significant results are preserved in the counter-factual test, however, giving us more confidence in the causal-effect argument.

9.6 Conclusion and Policy Recommendations

To summarize, we have made two main findings based on provincial panel data on Chinese patents and PPPs. On the one hand, such policies have led to more patent applications and patent approvals; on the other hand, they have also resulted in a decline in average quality for both patent applications and approved patents. While the first finding is both straightforward and in line with expectations, the second finding, although perhaps not surprising to economists, is certainly not desired by policy makers.

As we understand it, the key explanation for policy makers missing such a negative consequence, unknowingly or intentionally, is that insufficient consideration may have been given to how individuals respond to government policies. Indeed, they will respond to policies as intended by the policy maker, such as

[4]Adding R&D/capita S&T personnel/capita in the explanatory variables reduces our sample size but does not change the results.

applying for more patents when incentives are provided for doing so. However, they will also respond in ways that may not be desirable to the policy maker. In particular, they may make more applications for patents related to innovations of inferior quality.

To better design policies that promote innovation and patent filing without sacrificing quality, several lessons may be drawn from the findings obtained in this analysis. First, promotion policies should be offered to patent holders only when patent quality can be sufficiently guaranteed. Our finding that inventions protected by invention patents do not suffer from quality deterioration after PPP adoption provides support for this argument, as a substantive examination is required for granting invention patent applications in China and therefore their quality can be carefully evaluated. Furthermore, a more effective way to promote patents may be to subsidize the invention patent application process.[5] As the supply elasticity of patents will be small for these policies, their adoption will not lead to a flood of inferior innovations into the patent application pool, consistent with the finding that promotion policies subsidizing patent application fees do not lead to declined patent quality.

Although the early goal of China's patent-promoting policies was more likely meant to increase the public's IP awareness via more patent filings rather than to stimulate high-quality patents and innovation, the country's long-term objective will have to be increased competitiveness for Chinese firms if it is serious about moving from a manufacturing powerhouse to an innovative one. Given the evidence shown in this chapter and other studies linking PPPs with inferior patent quality, it is thus necessary that the government ensure that proposed PPPs encourage quality patents, even if this does not exactly match the timing of their initial strategy.[6]

Acknowledgements The authors appreciate the financial support from the National Natural Science Foundation (Grant No. 71273217) and the Fundamental Research Funds for the Central Universities (Grant No. 20720151001 and Grant No. 20720151287).

Appendix I: Additional Results from Robustness Tests

[5]One should be careful with renewal fee subsidy policies, however, as they may artificially increase the renewal rate without enhancing patent quality.

[6]See also Prud'homme (2015).

Table 9.9 PPP effects on per capita applications and approvals (1998–2010)

Variables	Per capita applications	Per capita applications (firms)	Per capita applications (others)	Per capita approvals	Per capita approvals (firms)	Per capita approvals (others)
PPP	1.846***	1.200***	0.133	0.768*	0.636***	0.0212
	(0.543)	(0.289)	(0.0875)	(0.449)	(0.230)	(0.0796)
Ln (population)	24.07***	12.92***	2.373***	16.82***	9.445***	1.511***
	(2.449)	(1.304)	(0.394)	(2.023)	(1.037)	(0.359)
Ln (percapit_gdp)	−0.443	0.0836	−0.0402	−0.889	−0.213	−0.0891
	(1.392)	(0.741)	(0.224)	(1.150)	(0.589)	(0.204)
Ln (percapit_FDI)	−0.690***	−0.466***	−0.0525	−0.376*	−0.266**	−0.0268
	(0.246)	(0.131)	(0.0396)	(0.203)	(0.104)	(0.0360)
Ln (percapit_R&D)	1.848***	0.600**	0.414***	1.959***	0.635***	0.425***
	(0.450)	(0.239)	(0.0724)	(0.371)	(0.190)	(0.0658)
Ln (percapit_S&T)	−0.382	−0.654*	0.0440	0.0730	−0.387	0.104
	(0.660)	(0.351)	(0.106)	(0.545)	(0.279)	(0.0966)
Year FE	Yes	Yes	Yes	Yes	Yes	Yes
Province FE	Yes	Yes	Yes	Yes	Yes	Yes
Obs.	390	390	390	390	390	390
R^2	0.853	0.839	0.818	0.831	0.826	0.779

Notes Standard errors are in parentheses
***Significant at 1 %. **Significant at 5 %. *Significant at 10 %

Table 9.10 PPP effects on firm withdrawal and renewal rate (1998–2010)

Variables	Withdrawal Rate	Withdrawal Rate (firms)	Withdrawal Rate (others)	Renewal Over 3 years	Renewal Over 3 years (firms)	Renewal Over 3 years (others)	Renewal Over 5 years	Renewal Over 5 years (firms)	Renewal Over 5 years (others)
PPP	0.00834	0.0277*	0.000346	−0.0330*	−0.0315	−0.0242	−0.0228**	−0.0437**	−0.0177**
	(0.0105)	(0.0159)	(0.00881)	(0.0184)	(0.0301)	(0.0182)	(0.00881)	(0.0213)	(0.00758)
Ln (population)	−0.0568	−0.158**	0.00642	−0.331***	−0.330**	−0.293***	−0.219***	−0.0395	−0.212***
	(0.0471)	(0.0717)	(0.0397)	(0.0907)	(0.148)	(0.0896)	(0.0434)	(0.105)	(0.0373)
Ln (percapit_gdp)	−0.000932	0.00730	−0.00637	−0.106**	−0.0828	−0.0900*	−0.0216	−0.00539	−0.0318
	(0.0268)	(0.0407)	(0.0226)	(0.0494)	(0.0807)	(0.0488)	(0.0236)	(0.0572)	(0.0203)
Ln (percapit_FDI)	−0.00319	−0.0151**	0.00594	−0.000976	−0.0225	0.00713	0.0128***	0.00355	0.0119***
	(0.00474)	(0.00720)	(0.00399)	(0.00840)	(0.0137)	(0.00830)	(0.00402)	(0.00972)	(0.00346)
Ln (percapit_R&D)	0.0139	0.0252*	0.00715	−0.00650	−0.0287	−0.00708	−0.00615	0.00492	−0.00628
	(0.00865)	(0.0132)	(0.00729)	(0.0152)	(0.0249)	(0.0151)	(0.00730)	(0.0176)	(0.00628)
Ln (percapit_S&T)	−0.0125	−0.0223	−0.0104	0.0556**	0.0659*	0.0428*	0.0289***	0.0634**	0.0131
	(0.0127)	(0.0193)	(0.0107)	(0.0225)	(0.0368)	(0.0222)	(0.0108)	(0.0260)	(0.00927)
Year FE	Yes	Yes	Yes	Yes	Yes	Yes	Yes	Yes	Yes
Province FE	Yes	Yes	Yes	Yes	Yes	Yes	Yes	Yes	Yes
Obs.	390	390	390	361	361	361	361	361	361
R^2	0.726	0.530	0.794	0.949	0.892	0.948	0.933	0.862	0.927

Notes Standard errors are in parentheses
***Significant at 1 %. **Significant at 5 %. *Significant at 10 %

References

Bessen J (2008) The value of U.S. patents by owner and patent characteristics. Research Policy 37:932–945

Cheung KY, Ping L (2004) Spillover effects of FDI on innovation in China: Evidence from the provincial data. China Economic Review 15:25–44

Cohen A, Einav L (2003) The effects of mandatory seat belt laws on driving behavior and traffic fatalities. Rev Econ Stat 85:828–843

Czarnitzki, D., & Katrin H. (2004). *The link between R&D subsidies, R&D spending and technological performance*. ZEW discussion papers, no. 04-56 (downloaded on 10 March 2014 from http://www.econstor.eu/bitstream/10419/24065/1/dp0456.pdf)

Dang, J., Motohashi, & Z. (2013). *Patent statistics: A good indicator for innovation in China? Patent subsidies program impacts on patent quality*. IAM discussion paper series #029 (downloaded on 20 November 2015 from http://pari.u-tokyo.ac.jp/unit/iam/outcomes/pdf/papers_131118.pdf)

DeLeire T (2000) The wage and employment effects of the Americans with Disabilities Act. Journal of Human Resources 35(4):693–715

Ebersberger, B. (2004). *Labor demand effect of public R&D funding*. VTT working papers (downloaded on 21 April 2014 from http://www.vtt.fi/inf/pdf/workingpapers/2004/W9.pdf)

Goolsbee A (1998) Does government R&D policy mainly benefit scientists and engineers? The American Econmic Review 88:298–302

Hu AG, Jefferson GH (2009) A great wall of patents: What is behind China's recent patent explosion? Journal of Development Economics 90:57–68

Hu AG, Jefferson GH, Qian JC (2005) R&D and technology transfer: Firm-level evidence from Chinese industry. Review of Economic Statistics 4:780–786

Jaffe AB, Lerner J (2001) Reinvention public R&D: Patent policy and the commercialization of national laboratory technologies. Rand Journal of Economics 32:167–198

Lanjouw JO, Pakes A, Putnam J (1998) How to count patents and value intellectual property: The uses of patent renewal and application data. Journal of Industrial Economics 46:405–432

Lei, Z., Sun, Z., & Wright, B. (2013). *Are Chinese patent applications politically driven? Evidence from China's domestic patent applications. OECD* (downloaded on 19 November 2015 from http://www.oecd.org/site/stipatents/4-3-Lei-Sun-Wright.pdf)

Li X (2012) Behind the recent surge of Chinese patenting: An institutional view. Research Policy 41:236–249

Long, C., & Wang, J. (2015). *Does copyright protection improve firm performance? A study of Dehua ceramic firms*. Manuscript

Mansfield E (1986) The R&D tax credit and other technology policy issues. *The* American Economic Review 76:190–194

Peltzman S (1975) The effects of automobile safety regulation. The Journal of Political Economy 83(4):677–725

Prud'homme D (2012) Dulling the cutting edge: How patent-related policies and practices hamper innovation in China. University Library of Munich (downloaded on 22 June 2014 from http://mpra.ub.uni-muenchen.de/43299/1/MPRA_paper_43299.pdf)

Prud'homme D (2015) China's shifting patent landscape and state-led patenting strategy. Journal of Intellectual Property Law & Practice 10:619–625

Sakakibara M, Branstetter L (2001) Do stronger patents induce more innovation? Evidence from the 1988 Japanese patent law reforms. RAND Journal of Economics 32:77–100

Schankerman M, Pakes A (1986) Estimates of the value of patent rights in European countries during the post-1950 period. Economic Journal 96:1052–1076

Ye JY, Li CL, Lei Z, Cao HP (2012) Patent apply of advanced publicity, patent quality and technical knowledge dissemination. World Economy 8:115–133 (In Chinese)

Yueh L (2009) Patent laws and innovation in China. International Review of Law and Economics 29:304–313

Zhang HY (2010) What is behind the recent surge in patenting in China? International Journal of Business and Management 5:83–91

Zhang GP, Chen XD (2012) The value of invention patents in China: Country origin and technology field differences. China Economic Review 23:357–370

Zhu PF, Xu WM (2003) On the impact of government's S&T incentive policy on the R&D input and its patent output of large and medium-sized industrial enterprises in Shanghai. China Economic Research 6:45–53 (In Chinese)

Chapter 10
University Patent Licensing and Its Contribution to China's National Innovation System

Yun Liu, Long Tan and Yi-jie Cheng

Abstract Patent licensing is one of the most important methods of technology transfer, and universities can be an important source of patent licensing within national innovation systems (NIS). In this chapter we examine how Chinese universities, including those supported by government programs aimed at developing science and technology, and patents, contribute to China's NIS through patent licensing. To do this, we develop a composite dataset from multiple information sources and use a combination of research methods such as text mining, scientometrics, and social network analysis, to analyze the structural features of patent licensing activities by Chinese universities. We find that universities that are part of Project 211, which is a government program to support technological development in certain Chinese universities, play an important role in patent licensing. We find that increased patent licensing between entities in lesser-developed regions and universities in relatively more developed regions—particularly those with more capabilities to develop patented technologies worth out-licensing—could be useful to better diffuse technology throughout China's NIS. Furthermore, this may be feasible since geographic distance itself does not appear to significantly inhibit patent licensing by universities in China. Considering these findings, we discuss ways in which the Project 211, and some other Chinese policies, could be improved in order to better contribute to technology transfer in China's NIS.

Yun Liu: Director of Research Center for Scientific Assessment and Innovation Management and Professor, School of Management and Economics, Beijing Institute of Technology, Beijing, China

Long Tan: School of Management and Economics, Beijing Institute of Technology, Beijing, China

Yi-jie Cheng: School of Management and Economics, Beijing Institute of Technology, Beijing, China

Y. Liu (✉) · L. Tan · Y. Cheng
School of Management and Economics, Beijing Institute of Technology, Zhongguancun South Road 5, Beijing, China
e-mail: liuyun@bit.edu.cn

D. Prud'homme and H. Song (eds.), *Economic Impacts of Intellectual Property-Conditioned Government Incentives*, DOI 10.1007/978-981-10-1119-1_10

Keywords Patent licensing · National innovation systems · Universities · China · Project 211

10.1 Introduction and Literature Review

According to the Triple Helix theory, universities are believed to be at the core of innovation systems (Leydesdorff and Etzkowitz 1996). Since the concept of national innovation systems (NIS) was proposed in the late 1980s, further approaches to study China's NIS from many different angles have endlessly emerged, and may even have come to completely different conclusions. Nevertheless, most scholars conclude that Chinese universities have been playing an increasingly significant role in China's NIS (Wu and Zhou 2012; Yang and Welch 2012). According to China's National Bureau of Statistics, in 2011 there were 2409 higher education institutes in China, collectively referred to in this chapter as universities. The universities employ approximately 600,000 research and development (R&D) personnel, who undertake 49 % of national R&D programs, and run over 70 % of national laboratories. Chinese universities have been regarded as some of the most important knowledge resources within the nation's progress in building its NIS and in increasing its competitive capacity since the 1978 reform and opening policy (Luan et al. 2010).

Statistics from the State Intellectual Property Office (SIPO) indicate that the share of university patent applications of the national total number of applications grew from 1.7 % in 2000 to 6.7 % in 2011 (Fig. 10.1). The growth in patent applications from Chinese universities is much faster than that of any other kind of institution. For example, the average annual growth rate of patent applications by Chinese universities from 1999 to 2010 was 42.3 %, while applications by enterprises and research institutions rose by only 29.5 and 38.7 % each year, respectively.

In addition to teaching students, universities have many social functions, of which the generation, diffusion, transfer, use, and exploitation of knowledge are essential (Molas-Gallart and Sinclair 1999; Wang et al. 2013). According to China's National Bureau of Statistics, in 2011 Chinese universities' share of the value of contract deals in domestic technical markets was 5.2 % (2.49 billion RMB). Patent licensing, academic enterprise startups, contract research, joint research agreements, and consulting are the main methods for the transfer and commercialization of university research (Li 2012; Mowery and Ziedonis 2002).

10.1.1 Government Policies for Stimulating Generation and Diffusion of Technology

Many governments have realized the need to improve policy measures in order to stimulate the generation of technology, patents, and technology transfer by universities, and have been exploring and introducing ways to do so. The Bayh-Dole

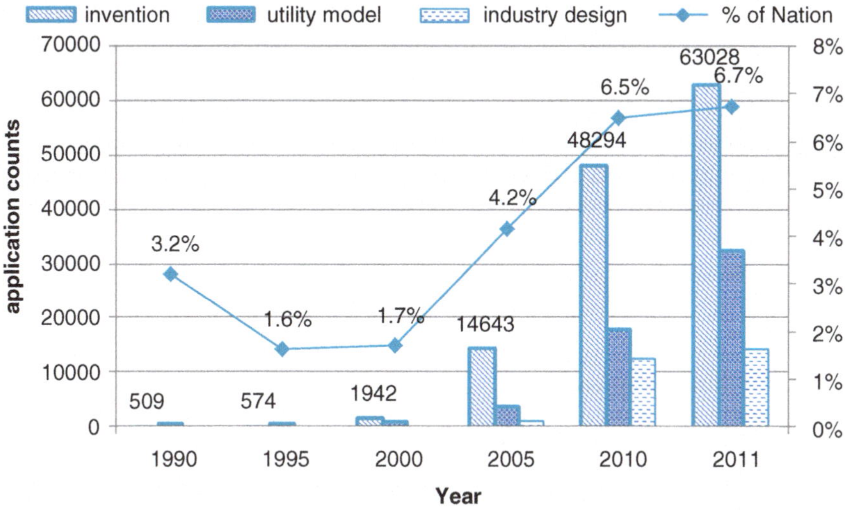

Fig. 10.1 Trends in Chinese university patent applications. *Source* SIPO

Act and the Stevenson-Wydler Act in the United States are the most famous examples, and have widely been studied, both by scholars and governments outside of the United States (Link et al. 2011; Tan et al. 2012).

There are many Chinese laws aimed at encouraging the commercialization of university inventions. For example, China's Law of Scientific and Technology Progress stipulates that the State shall establish and develop a technology market to promote the commercialization of scientific and technological achievements. The law, which is similar in several ways to the Bayh-Dole Act, provides several important provisions governing the ownership of intellectual property (IP) generated by public funding. China's Law on the Transformation of Scientific and Technological Achievements indicates that the State should encourage R&D research institutions, colleges and universities, and other institutions, to join efforts with manufacturers in order to transform and commercialize their scientific and technological achievements. Furthermore, as of 2015, several provisions intended to improve the commercialization of IP rights by universities have been introduced into the draft 4th revision of China's Patent Law. These include provisions aimed at creating a platform to improve technology transfer and the commercialization of research by China's universities and research institutions.

The Chinese government has introduced several important national programs to support knowledge generation. These include, for example, Project '211' (1991), the Engineering Program '985' (1998), and Program '2011' (2012), to enhance the research capacity of universities. The National Science and Technology programs such as Program '863' (1986) and Program '973' (1997), are mostly implemented by universities (Zhang et al. 2013).

Project 211 and Program 985 are worth briefly discussing in more detail in order to provide a better understanding of the composition of these programs. Universities within the top 100, in terms of patent applications and grants, account for 71.4 and 70.6 % of all applications and grants, respectively, and are mainly universities participating in the Project 211 and Program 985 (Science and Technology Development Center of MoE 2012). The aim of Program 985 is to accelerate the development of world first-class universities and to produce a group of world leading disciplines by 2020. Program 985 involves nearly 100 universities and key disciplines of the 21st century, and is conducted by the Chinese government. The aim of Project 211 is to cultivate high-level talent for national economic and social development strategies. Box 1 below provides further details of Project 211 in particular.

Box 1: China's Project 211

Project 211 is a constructive program of nearly 100 universities and disciplines in the 21st century conducted by the government of China. The program aims to cultivate high-level talent for national economic and social development strategies.

Brief history of the program

Project 211 is a program of the National Key Universities and Colleges initiated in 1995 by the Ministry of Education of the People's Republic of China. The intention was to raise the research standard of high-level universities, and to cultivate strategies for socio-economic development. During the first phase of the program from 1996 to 2000, approximately USD 2.2 billion was distributed (Li 2004).

Today, China has 116 institutions of higher education (about 6 %) designated as Project 211 institutions for having met certain scientific, technical, and human resources standards and for offering advanced degree programs. Project 211 universities take on the responsibility of training four-fifths of all doctoral students, two-thirds of all graduate students, and half of all students from abroad and one-third of overseas undergraduates. They offer 85 % of subjects designated as 'key' by the State, hold 96 % of the State's key laboratories, and consume 70 % of scientific research funding.[1]

How it works and general requirements

The Chinese government has spent billions of dollars in order to develop Project 211 universities.[2] As discussed further in Sect. 10.3 of this chapter, this research is sometimes protected by patents.

China's Project 211 requires great efforts in training and developing a large number of academic leaders and competent teachers who have high academic attainments and prestige, both at home and abroad. In particular, the

[1]"Over 10 billion RMB to be invested in 'Program 211'"—People's Daily Online.

[2]www.moe.edu.cn/.

training of young academic leaders should be accelerated, so as to maintain a stable teaching and administrative contingent with political integrity and academic quality, rational structure and professional competence.

Steps are to be taken to improve efficiency through moderate institutional expansion, enhance scientific research, and strive for the commercialization of research findings so as to accelerate the pace of transferring scientific achievements into productivity. While facilitating the reform of the administrative as well as the internal management system of universities, efforts will be made to strengthen international exchange and cooperation in higher education, and raise the international profile of Chinese higher education institutions.

Benefits provided to participants

After several years of effort, some 100 institutions of higher learning covering a group of key disciplinary areas, have greatly improved their quality of education, scientific research, management and institutional efficiency. In addition, these institutions have also made remarkable progress in reforming the management system, and have consequently become the foundation for training high-level professional manpower and in solving major problems for the country's economic construction and social development. As a result of these efforts, this group of institutions set up national standards in overall quality, with some of the key universities and disciplinary areas approaching or reaching the advanced international standards. The majority of these institutions have enhanced their facilities and staff competence, in addition to noticeable achievements in human resources training and scientific research. Adapting to regional and sectoral development needs, these institutions are expected to play a key and exemplary role in innovation in China.

10.1.2 Patent Licensing in China: The Focus of This Chapter

The external commercialization of patent technology, through trade or licensing, is an important feature of open innovation (Chesbrough 2006). The total value of global technology license receipts grew annually by 10.7 % from 1980 to 2004 (Granstrand 2004), which represents noteworthy growth of patent licensing around the world. In relation to inventions, most studies have focused on the licensing activities of enterprises (Gassmann et al. 2010; Lichtenthaler and Ernst 2007), and the determinants of invention (Gambardella et al. 2007). Other literature has examined the most visible aspects of technology transfer, licensing and co-patenting by universities, and especially to industry (Motohashi and Yun 2007; Wu and Zhou 2012). We have found that existing studies share the common feature that they examine patent licensing from a micro perspective. However, a macro view, including from a country and intra-country perspective, is needed to shed more light on the subject.

This chapter attempts to shed light on the structural features of patent licensing activities by Chinese universities from multiple perspectives. In particular, we want to answer the following questions:

- What is the contribution of universities as a technology source to the patent licensing system of the whole country, especially when compared with other innovators and licensors such as enterprises, research institutes and private enterprises in China's NIS?
- What kind of patents, and in what pattern, are mainly out-licensed by Chinese universities?
- Is there a significant gap between the licensing activities of different universities, for example between the high-level Project 211 universities and the relatively low-level non-Project 211 universities?
- Who are the main licensing targets, i.e. the licensees, of Chinese universities?; and
- What are the regional characteristics and regional correlation of Chinese universities' patent licensing when the province is considered both the technical source and the destination?

In order to answer these five questions, a composite dataset was established with multiple sources and a combination of research methods was applied, namely, text mining, scientometrics, and social network analysis (SNA). We consider all three types of patents available in China in our analysis, namely invention patents, utility model, and design patents.[3]

As far as we know, this chapter appears to be the first to use patent licensing data to quantitatively and empirically disclose the structural features of Chinese universities' patent licensing, and to help understand the role of universities in the NIS of China, as a technology source. Our analysis starts by considering IP strategy and relevant polices as motivating factors, and then analyzes the behavior of patent licensing Project 211 universities and non-Project 211 universities, in order to reflect the impact of China in promoting scientific achievement transformation

[3]Three types of patents, namely, invention, utility model and industrial design patents have been protected in the Chinese Mainland ever since the first patent law was enacted in 1984. Of these, invention patents are strictly examined and are believed to be of high quality under the international standards concerning novelty, creativity and utility. Regardless of the differences in the patent system across countries, which may lead to diversity of patent quality and value, invention patents or simply 'patents' are taken as the universal and basic measurement of innovation activity all across the world (Zuniga et al. 2009; van Zeebroeck et al. 2008). Utility model and industrial design patents are also important because inventors can make 'small inventions' by absorbing and improving complex inventions of high quality as quickly as possible, in order to adapt to the changing market and especially any lagging innovation competence. Some argue that incremental innovation is important for a developing country like China (Breznitz and Murphree 2010). For these reasons, in this chapter the three types of patents are discussed.

policy and Project 211 implementation on university patent licensing. In this regard, our analysis contributes albeit very broadly, to research into the strategy behind, and the effects of, IP-conditioned incentives, the theme of the book in which this chapter is published. However, future research is needed to look more deeply into the effects of these government programs and policies on the invention and patent licensing activities of universities.

The remaining part of this chapter proceeds as follows: Sect. 10.2 introduces the data, and technical design and measures used in the study. Section 10.3 provides a comprehensive analysis of Chinese university patent licensing, which examines structural features in relation to patent type, licensing patterns, licensor, licensee, and region. Using these empirical results, we also further explore the regional technology correlation of China's 29 provinces, municipalities and autonomous regions. The last section concludes and proposes some policy suggestions.

10.2 Methodology

10.2.1 Dataset Structure

According to the Regulations of the Patent Law of PRC, and the Provisions of Registration of Patent Licensing Contracts, a patent licensing contract should be registered at SIPO within three months from its effective date. SIPO publishes these registration data on its website (http://www.sipo.gov.cn/tjxx/badjxx/), with structured and detailed information concerning the patent name, patent number, licensing pattern, licensor(s) name(s), licensee(s) name(s) and registration date etc., which represents one part of the data shown in this chapter (solid-lined boxes in Fig. 10.2). A patent can be licensed in three ways: (1) a simple license, where the patent can be licensed to, and utilized by, more than one licensee; (2) a sole license, where a patent can be licensed to only one licensee, but both parties to the contract can utilize the patent; and (3) an exclusive license, where a patent can be licensed to, and be utilized by, only one licensee.

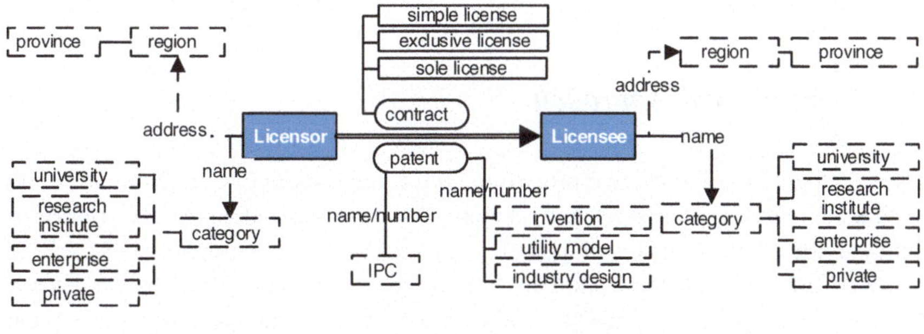

Fig. 10.2 Patent licensing and background information analysis

Various forms of patent licenses and patterns are possible. For example, one patent could be licensed to more than one licensee, and, on the other hand, one contract could involve more than one patent. In the following section, we apply the terms ‘patent count(s)’ and ‘contract(s)’, respectively, as the units of measurement. During the analysis, we noticed that there were a few co-owned patents, which means that there is more than one licensor in one contract for one patent. For these rare situations, only the first owner is considered. According to SIPO, the time span of the available published data is from 2008 to 2011, when the paper was finished, and in our paper we chose the data of 2011 as a dataset.

Furthermore, more information will be retrieved from various sources, as follows and shown by the dotted-line sections in Fig. 10.2:

(1) *Contractor category*. Based on the key terms listed in the name of licensor and licensee, the contractors are grouped into only four categories. These are universities, research institutes, enterprises and private individuals. A Visual Basic program in office excel is designed to help establish the categorization of the contractors.
(2) *Patent category*. As mentioned above, three types of patent are protected by China’s patent system. According to the coding regulation system of Chinese patent numbers, the fifth digit after year 2003 (or the third digit if before 2003) in the patent number represents the patent category, i.e. ‘1’ or ‘8’ for invention patents, ‘2’ for utility model patents and ‘3’ for industrial design patents.
(3) *IPC information*. According to the patent name and number, IPC (International Patent Classification) subgroups of all patents have been retrieved manually and individually, at the China and Global Patent Examination information Inquiry System (http://cpquery.sipo.gov.cn/index.jsp). Only the main IPC classification, or the first IPC classification, was recorded even though there may be more than one IPC classification assigned to a patent.
(4) *Regional classification*. Information concerning the contractors’ address is collected manually from the Ministry of Education of China (MOE), the State Administration for Industry and Commerce of China (SAIC), and other internet service channels. Each contractor is allocated only to one of the 31 domestic provinces, based on its address. Hong Kong, Macao and Taiwan are not considered here.

10.2.2 Analytical Approach

Based on the data collected and processed above, methodologies of quantitative and qualitative analysis, including general statistical methods and SNA, are applied to highlight the characteristics of patent licensing by Chinese universities, and in particular the regional correlation in technology in relation to the patent license (Streeter and Gillespie 1993). Following general statistical analysis, the characteristics of Chinese universities will be outlined in relation to patent types, licensing patterns, the contractor's profile, and regional distinctions.

Also, a regional (province level) relation matrix (non-symmetric matrix) is computed on the *direction* of one patent. We have defined this measure, which we call the 'regional licensing correlation,' as capturing the total number of contracts between any two regions. Fox example, if province X has licensed α contracts to province Y, and at the same time has been licensed β contracts from province Y, then, the regional licensing correlation between X and Y is $\alpha + \beta$. The direction of licensing is not important here when we only take correlation into consideration using Gephi software (Bastian et al. 2009).

Based upon this analysis, broad implications were drawn about the effectiveness of Project 211 (and very briefly, Program 985), and some other Chinese policies, to facilitate patent commercialization within China's NIS. Policy recommendations were then derived from these implications.

10.3 Results

10.3.1 University License Overview

In 2011, the total number of contracts was 21,664, which included 6024 contracts concerning invention patents (patent count 5557), 11,890 contracts concerning utility model patents (patent count 11,375), 3510 contracts concerning industrial design patents (patent count 3288) and 240 contracts concerning Patent Cooperation Treaty (PCT) patent applications (patent count 198). Up to 91.2 % of contracts are exclusively licensed. There were 5338 licensors in total, 58.7 % of which were private (non-service patent), and 32.4 % were from enterprises. There were only 224 universities, from which 1363 contracts were signed (see Table 10.1). However, we found that the average number of contracts by universities is much higher than that of other types of licensors (6.1). Then again, ranked according to the total number of contracts, there were no universities in the top 10 licensors, but there were eight enterprises, including three foreign-funded enterprises, one private individual, and one research institute.

Table 10.1 Statistics concerning the types of patent licensors in 2011

Licensor type	Number of licensors	Total contracts	Average number of contracts
University	224	1363	6.1
Research institute	246	835	3.4
Enterprise	1731	7452	4.3
Private	3132	12,009	3.8
Others	5	5	1.0
Total	5338	21,664	4.1

Taking university license contracts into consideration, 222 are domestic universities and the remaining two are foreign universities, namely the University of Rochester and Tokyo Institute of Technology. A total of four PCT patents (4 contracts) are licensed from these foreign universities to two multinational companies and the rest involving 1202 patents of invention and 130 utility model patents (1359 contracts in total) are licensed to domestic enterprises by the Chinese universities.

10.3.2 Structural Features of University Patent Licenses

10.3.2.1 Patent types and license patterns

Invention patents and exclusive licenses account for most of the contracts, focusing mainly on the fields of chemistry (organic chemistry, polymer chemistry) and physical methods and tools, the majority of which were newly granted patents. Out of the 1359 contracts (1332 patents), 1228 (1202 patents) were invention patents, 131 (130 patents) were utility model patents and there were no industrial design patents. Over 96 % of these patents were exclusively licensed (see Table 10.2).

According to the IPC Classification, the patents licensed by universities focused on three categories, namely section C (Chemistry, Metallurgy), section B (Performing Operations, Transporting) and section G (Physics), respectively accounting for 38, 18 and 13 % of the total contracts concluded in 2011 (see Fig. 10.2). A deeper analysis reveals that most of the contracts concerned the organic chemistry and high molecule (IPC Class: C08*), and physical measurement and testing (IPC Class: G01*) classifications (Fig. 10.3).

Figure 10.4 shows the temporal distribution of 1352 licensed patents based on the patent application number. The application date of invention patents was found to be mainly between 2006 and 2009 (accounting for 81.3 %). While the application date of utility model patents was found to be mainly between 2008 and 2010 (accounting for 80.2 %) and the proportion of patents applied for before 2004 was less than 10 %. Considering the average examination cycle of a patent application

Table 10.2 Statistics concerning the types and patterns of patent license of universities

Patent type	Contracts	Patent counts	License pattern	
Invention	1228	1202	Simple	31
			Exclusive	117
			Sole	17
Utility model	131	130	Simple	1
			Exclusive	128
			Sole	1
Industrial design	0	0	–	–

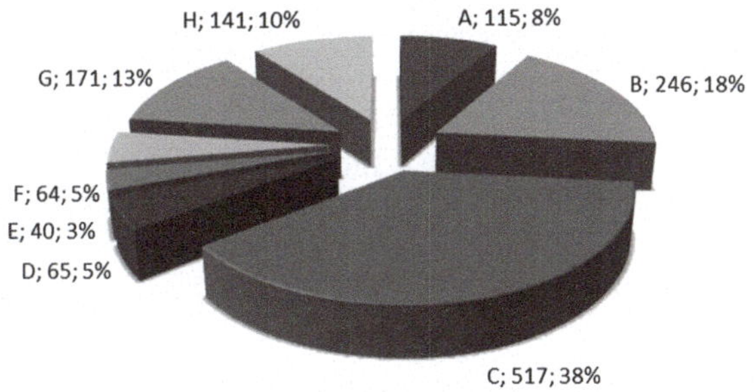

Fig. 10.3 IPC classification distribution of licensed patents by section

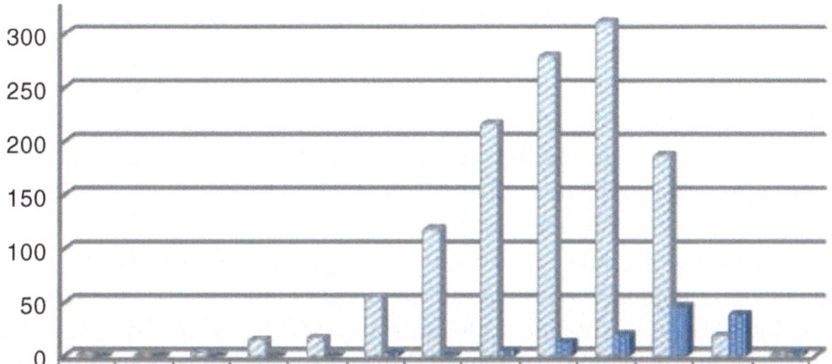

	1999	2000	2001	2002	2003	2004	2005	2006	2007	2008	2009	2010	2011
invention	1	0	3	15	17	55	118	216	279	311	187	19	1
utility model	0	0	0	0	0	3	1	5	13	20	46	39	3

Fig. 10.4 Time distribution of applications of licensed patents

(about 23 months for invention patents, and five months for utility model patents) and the period of patent protection (20 years for invention patents, and ten years for utility model patents), the vast majority of the patents licensed were newly granted patents.

10.3.2.2 Licensor Profile

Project 211 universities contribute most to the total number of patent licenses. Out of 222 domestic university licensors, 82 (or 37 %) are from Project 211 university projects. Table 10.3 shows that projects at Project 211 universities account for 63 % (or 857) of the total number of contracts. Each Project 211 university had 10.45 contracts on average, which is almost three times more than that of the non-Project 211 universities. The proportion of invention contracts from Project 211 universities (95 %) is significantly higher than that of non-Project 211

Table 10.3 Statistics concerning the licensors by type of university

Type of university		Project 211	Non-211	Total
Number of universities		82	140	222
Contract	Invention	813	415	1228
	Utility model	44	87	131
	Total	857	502	1359
Patent counts	Invention	808	414	1222
	Utility model	44	86	130
	Total	852	500	1352

universities (83 %). It was also found that more than 66 % of utility model contracts were from non-Project 211 universities. Therefore, we concluded that Project 211 universities are working significantly better than non-Project 211 universities when taking the total and/or average number of contracts, and patent quality (considering the ability to license a patent as an indicator of its economic value/quality) into consideration.

Universities having the most patent applications do not have the most patent licenses. We ranked the licensors by their licensed patent counts, and compared this with the number of patent applications. The results of the top 20 universities, ranked by licensed patent counts, are listed in Table 10.4. We found that in 2011, Zhejiang University, Tsinghua University and Southeast University are the top three applicants but they only rank 5th, 12th and 16th respectively, as licensors. South China University of Technology, Jiangnan University and Tianjin University are the top three licensors. Moreover, in the top 20 universities ranked by the number of patent licenses, there are 17 Project 211 universities and 10 Program 985 universities. We conclude that Program 211 universities have obvious advantages in terms of patent licensing.

Patent licenses are mainly concentrated in the developed eastern provinces. The distribution of addresses of licensors indicate that all of the Project 211 universities are located in 29 provinces, excluding Tibet and Ningxia. We also found that university licenses are mainly from the economically and technically developed eastern areas, where the economy, innovation and patent applications are more active (see Table 10.5). Jiangsu, Shanghai, Zhejiang, Guangdong and Beijing are the top five regions with the most contracts. In addition, these five regions also had the most patent applications in the same year (regional patent application data are from China Statistics Yearbook, 2012). Compared with the total number of universities, the involvement of universities in patent licensing is relatively low. For example, in total there are 153 universities in Jiangsu province, of which 25 had licensed their patents in 247 contracts in 2011.

Table 10.4 Statistics concerning patent contracts of the top 20 universities

Rank	University name	Licensed patent counts		Patent applications	
		Invention	Utility model	Invention	Utility model
1	South China Univ of Tech[b]	56	3	753	197
2	Jiangnan Univ[a]	55	1	350	66
3	Tianjin Univ[b]	50	5	763	50
4	Harbin Ins. Tech[b]	46	1	923	14
5	Zhejiang Univ[b]	45	0	1743	426
6	Xian Jiaotong Univ[b]	44	0	547	50
7	Donghua Univ[a]	31	5	416	95
8	Jiangsu Univ[a]	22	3	361	63
9	Zhejiang Univ of Tech	23	1	335	152
10	Sichuan Univ[a]	22	0	375	53
11	Shandong Univ[b]	20	2	565	161
12	Tsinghua Univ[b]	22	0	1100	79
13	Nanjing Univ of Tech	21	0	224	25
14	Nanjing Univ[b]	20	0	325	16
15	East China Univ of S&T[a]	19	0	279	11
16	Southeast Univ[a]	18	2	1012	332
17	Central South Univ[a]	19	0	376	35
18	HuazhongUniv of S&T[b]	18	0	434	62
19	Shanghai Jiaotong Univ[b]	17	0	932	78
20	Kunming Univ of S&T	11	6	286	120

[a]Project 211 university
[b]Program 985 university; patent application quantity was collected from the China Patent Inquiry System

Table 10.5 Statistics concerning patent contracts of the top 10 provinces

Rank	Regions	Contract	Number of universities as licensor	Total number of universities within the region	Patent	GDP per capita (RMB)
1	Jiangsu	247	25	153	348,381	61,022
2	Shanghai	132	14	66	80,215	82,560
3	Zhejiang	103	14	100	177,066	58,791
4	Guangdong	101	14	133	196,272	50,500
5	Beijing	84	16	114	77,955	80,394
6	Shannxi	84	11	100	32,227	33,197
7	Tianjin	77	8	59	38,489	86,496
8	Heilongjiang	69	11	82	23,432	32,637
9	Hubei	64	16	124	42,510	34,233
10	Sichuan	51	8	96	49,734	26,147

Table 10.6 Statistics concerning patent licensees

Type of licensee	Number of licensees	Contracts	Patent count
Research institute	1	1	1
University	2	2	2
Private	1	1	1
Enterprise	1057	1355	1348

10.3.2.3 Licensee Profile

The vast majority of the licensees are enterprises located mainly in eastern China. Broadly, cross-region licenses at the provincial level are characterized by significant regional differences. Table 10.6 shows the nature of licensees and indicates that over 99.7 % of the licensees are enterprises, and there are only two universities, one research institute and one individual. Most of the licensees are located in Jiangsu province (228 companies), Guangdong province (146 companies), Zhejiang province (102 companies) and other enterprise-dense and economically advanced eastern regions.

10.3.2.4 Regional Differences

A total of 1057 enterprise licensees were located in 29 provinces. A province can in-license or out-license patents. The outflow and inflow of the contracts of 29 provinces are summarized as follows. Jiangsu province holds a safe lead in

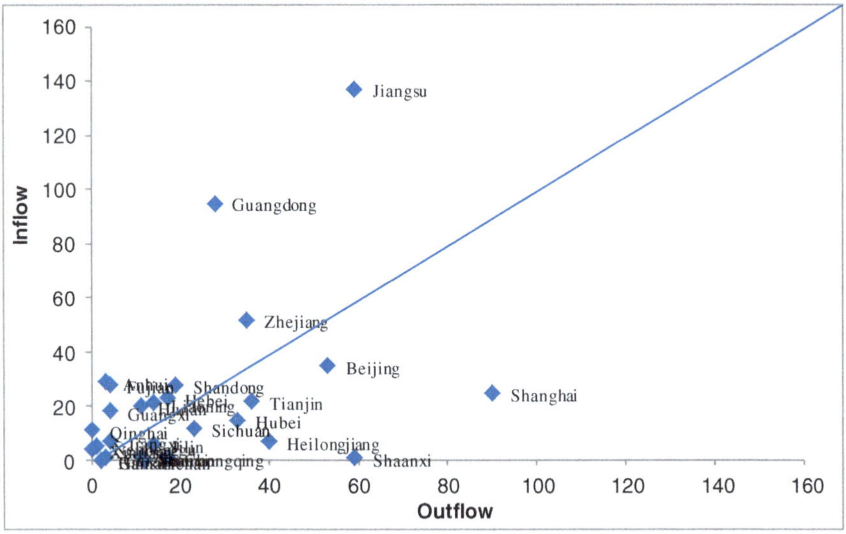

Fig. 10.5 Regional differences of patent licenses by inflow and outflow

acquiring technology, and at the same time is active in exporting technology. In contrast, Shanghai is most active in exporting patents and is relatively weak in acquisition. Guangdong also does well in making use of external science and technology sources, and Zhejiang and Beijing are more balanced in both directions. The five provinces mentioned above can be classified into one group, distinguished by demonstrating a high level of licensing activity. The other group consists of the remaining 24 provinces that are not so comparatively active. Figure 10.5 illustrates the numbers graphically.

10.3.3 Regional Licensing Correlation

As described in the methodology section, we have calculated the regional licensing correlation between the total number of contracts between pairs of regions in China. The results of this analysis are shown in Fig. 10.6. The graphical analysis shows

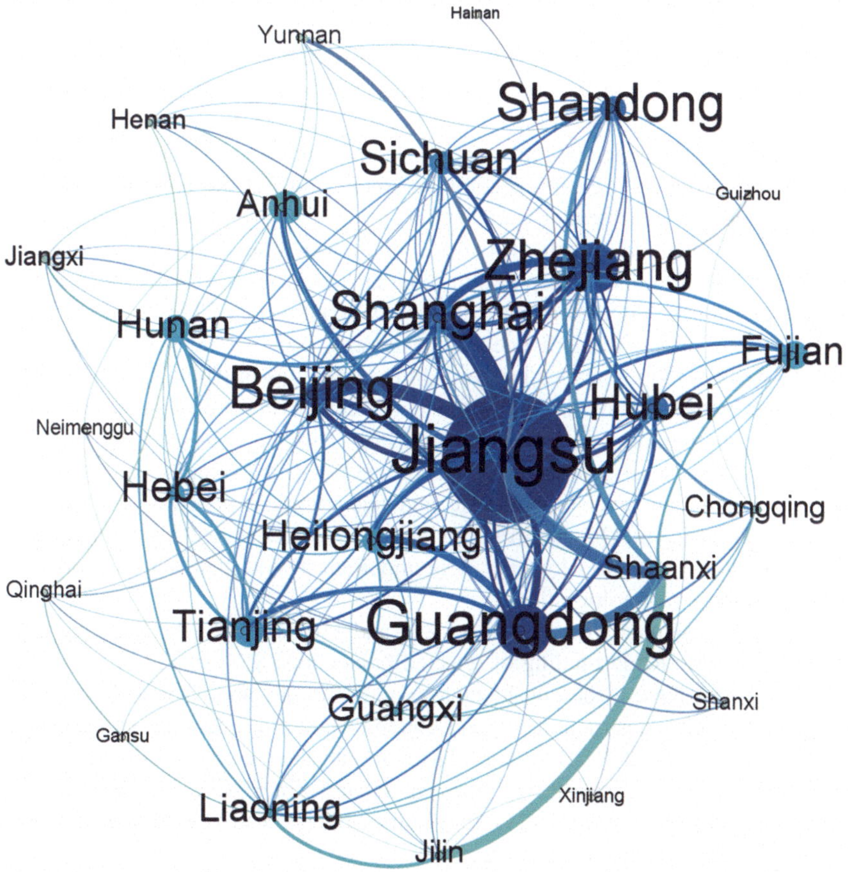

Fig. 10.6 Regional licensing correlation

that there are 29 nodes standing for 29 provinces and 238 edges on behalf of the correlation between any two nodes in the figure. The size of the node is weighted by the total number of contracts one province has licensed, and has acted as licensee, and the thickness of the edge is positively related to the regional licensing correlation.

Jiangsu is the most active province in the license network, with the strongest correlation with Shanghai, Beijing, Shaanxi, Anhui and Heilongjiang provinces. Shanghai-Zhejiang, Shanghai-Guangdong, Guangdong-Shaanxi, and Guangdong-Heilongjiang are also significantly active in licensing. Despite the geographical distance, the licensing correlation between Jilin and Shaanxi, Heilongjiang and Guangdong, Tianjin and Guangdong is still strong.

10.4 Discussion and Conclusions

Our analysis reveals several interesting findings. Firstly, universities only account for a small, although noteworthy, proportion of China's patent licenses, and most of the academic licenses are from Project 211 universities. Secondly, Chinese universities most often out-license their patents to domestic enterprises in China. Thirdly, invention patents and exclusive licenses account for most of these contracts. Fourthly, the developed regions in Eastern China bear most of the contracts, although cross-region licensing is common among most of the provinces.

These findings indicate that via patent licensing, Chinese universities have built up a national technical transfer network, within which academic knowledge and technology can flow into enterprises in different industries. From this perspective, the role of Chinese universities in technological spillover in China's NIS is noteworthy. Furthermore, through licensing networks, regional licensing correlation helps to weaken the imbalance between different regions in China's NIS. We also found that geographical distance does not preclude cross-province sharing of knowledge in the form of technology transfer. This suggests that geographical distance itself, at least, should not preclude entities (for example, enterprises) in regions with a low level of scientific and technological progress, for example Xinjiang, Yunnan, and Qinghai, from seeking to in-license patents from universities in other regions in China. However, it is important to note that other factors may complicate these technology flows.

Since the implementation of Project 211 and Program 985, the State has continued to increase R&D funding of selected universities. Project 211 and Program 985 universities have made considerable progress in developing innovation, team building, platform construction, support conditions, and in international exchanges and cooperation. Their R&D strength has markedly increased, and the number of published papers and patents has also significantly increased. Furthermore, our analysis indicates that Project 211 universities by far lead non-Project 211 universities in terms of patent licensing.

However, empirical results indicate that even for Project 211 universities, which represent high-level universities, 20 % do not license patents. As such, for these universities it could be argued that the contribution they make to the knowledge generation and sharing in China's NIS is not commensurate with the resources that they have been granted.

In fact, the problem of a low conversion of inventions into scientific products from Chinese universities has persisted for a long time. From our experience researching related issues on behalf of Chinese government agencies, one main reason to date for this has been that before the introduction of China's Law on Scientific and Technology Progress and the Transformation of Scientific and Technological Achievements, there was not an appropriate enough legal framework for transforming university inventions into innovations. The environment perpetuated unclearly defined property rights, including the right of use, the right of disposal and the right of revenue. Secondly, amidst the recent explosion in patent filings in China (Liu et al. 2013), the State appears to be more concerned with the output of scientific articles and patents, while paying less attention to the transformation and application of scientific and technological achievements. In this context, university teachers often apply for patents for the purpose of getting projects accepted, to receive certain titles or science and technology awards, and tend to lack enthusiasm for technology transfer and patent licensing.

At the same time, the absence of specialized technology transfer mechanisms in Chinese universities has also hindered the industrialization of scientific and technological achievements. Few Chinese universities have set up organizations similar to the U.S. Office of Technology Licensing (OTL). The positive benefits of such organizations can encourage Chinese universities to emphasize the importance of making quality patent applications, and establishing effective mechanisms to out-license them.

10.5 Policy Recommendations

In recent years in order to address these issues, the Chinese government has stressed the implementation of an innovation-driven development strategy and attaches great importance to scientific and technological achievements and their transformation and industrialization by universities and research institutes. In particular, China's Law on Transformation of Scientific and Technological Achievements, which was recently revised, reduced a series of university technology transfer barriers and increased the enthusiasm of Chinese researchers. Furthermore, China's draft 4th revision to the Patent Law has also given high priority to promoting patent transformation, implementation and application, including patent licensing by universities.

In order to better allow Project 211 and Program 985 universities to play a dominant role in enhancing China's basic research and in order to cultivate high-quality talent, these universities should be supported to play a more important function in knowledge creation, transfer and application, and in the transformation and upgrading of Chinese manufacturing and the development of emerging industries. This could be done by ensuring that government policies encourage researchers at these universities to not only develop patented technology, but to ensure it meets the needs of industry and can be out-licensed. It is important that strong Technology Transfer Offices (TTOs) be established, perhaps with government support, in universities around China. Staff in these offices need to be well trained in the legal and commercial aspects of patent licensing transactions so they can support universities in this process.

Regions with a low level of scientific and technological progress, such as Xinjiang, Yunnan, and Qinghai, for example, should be encouraged by the government to seek patent licenses, when useful, from universities across China. Geographical distance itself should not necessarily be viewed as a barrier to this technology transfer within China's NIS. For example, enterprises in the previously mentioned regions could be supported as they seek patent in-licensing from universities in Beijing, Shanxi, Shanghai, among other relatively developed regions.

Acknowledgments The paper was funded by the National Science Foundation of China (No. 71573017 and No. 71273030).

References

Bastian M, Heymann S, Jacomy M (2009) Gephi: an open-source software for exploring and manipulating networks. ICWSM 8:361–362

Breznitz D, Murphree M (2010) Run of the red queen. China Economic Quarterly, 21

Chesbrough HW (2006) Open innovation: the new imperative for creating and profiting from technology. Harvard Business Press, Cambridge

Gambardella A, Giuri P, Luzzi A (2007) The market for patents in Europe. Res Policy 36(8):1163–1183

Gassmann O, Enkel E, Chesbrough H (2010) The future of open innovation. R&D Manag 40 (3):213–221

Granstrand O (2004) The economics and management of technology trade: towards a pro-licensing era? Int J Technol Manage 27(2–3):209–240

Luan C, Zhou C, Liu A (2010) Patent strategy in chinese universities: a comparative perspective. Scientometrics, 84(1), 53–63

Leydesdorff L, Etzkowitz H (1996) Emergence of a triple helix of university-industry-government relations. Sci Public Policy 23(5):279–286

Li X (2012) Behind the recent surge of Chinese patenting: an institutional view. Res Policy 41 (1):236–249

Lichtenthaler U, Ernst H (2007) External technology commercialization in large firms: results of a quantitative benchmarking study. R&D Manag 37(5):383–397

Li L (2004) China's Higher Education Reform 1998–2003: A Summary (PDF). Asia-Pa Edu Rev V 1:14–22

Link AN, Siegel DS, Van Fleet DD (2011) Public science and public innovation: assessing the relationship between patenting at US National Laboratories and the Bayh-Dole Act. Res Policy 40(8):1094–1099

Liu Y, Tan L, Song SS (2013) Chinese patent explosion factors: an empirical analysis based on system and policy. In: Technology management in the IT-Driven services (PICMET), 2013 proceedings of PICMET '13, (pp. 1058–1069)
Molas-Gallart J, Sinclair T (1999) From technology generation to technology transfer: the concept and reality of the "Dual-Use Technology Centres". Technovation 19(11):661–671
Motohashi K, Yun X (2007) China's innovation system reform and growing industry and science linkages. Res Policy 36(8):1251–1260
Mowery DC, Ziedonis AA (2002) Academic patent quality and quantity before and after the Bayh-Dole Act in the United States. Res Policy 31(3):399–418
Science and Technology Development Center of MoE (2012) Intellectual property rights report of China's universities (2010). Tsinghua University Press, Beijing
Streeter CL, Gillespie DF (1993) Social network analysis. J Soc Serv Res 16(1–2):201–222
Tan L, Liu Y, Hou YY (2012) Analysis on rising of patent application of China's universities under Bayh-Dole Act System. Technol Econ 31(12):1–6
van Zeebroeck N, Stevnsborg N, De La Potterie BVP, Guellec D, Archontopoulos E (2008) Patent inflation in Europe. World Patent Inf 30(1):43–52
Wang Y, Huang J, Chen Y, Pan X, Chen J (2013) Have Chinese universities embraced their third mission? New insight from a business perspective. Scientometrics 97(2):207–222
Wu W, Zhou Y (2012) The third mission stalled? Universities in China's technological progress. J Technol Transf 37(6):812–827
Yang R, Welch A (2012) A world-class university in China? The case of Tsinghua. Higher Educ 63(5):645–666
Zhang H, Patton D, Kenney M (2013) Building global-class universities: assessing the impact of the 985 project. Res Policy 42(3):765–775
Zuniga P, Guellec D, Dernis H, Khan M, Okazaki T, Webb C (2009) OECD patent statistics manual

Chapter 11
A Study on the Effects of Intellectual Property Policies in China: Evidence from China's 'IP Demonstration City' Program

Yafeng Zhang, Haibo Liu and Zongzhen Jin

Abstract The impact of IP policies (IPPs) in China has attracted much attention, especially in the context of an upsurge in patent applications and grants. This chapter introduces and analyzes the IP Demonstration City (IPDC) Program in China. Following interviews with government officers from local IP offices in various IPDCs, we have identified the effects of the IPDC Program, which include an increase in IP creation, the growth of IP-related industries, the improvement of both companies' IP awareness and the governments' IP administrative system, and potentially an increase in the inflow of foreign direct investment. However, at the same time we have found that the effect of the program within many provinces appears to be relatively limited, although it may be stronger in less-developed provinces. Furthermore, the marginal economic return of the current IPDC Program decreases as more IPDCs are introduced, although in the long term a greater number

---

Zhang Yafeng (corresponding author), PhD candidate and researcher, Institute of Policy and Management, Chinese Academy of Sciences

Liu Haibo, Professor, Institute of Policy and Management, Chinese Academy of Sciences

Jin Zongzhen, Assistant Professor, China National Institute of Standardization

---

Y. Zhang (✉) · H. Liu
Center for IPR Research and Training, Institute of Policy and Management, Chinese Academy of Sciences, Room 409, No. 15 Zhongguancun Beiyitiao Alley, Haidian District, 100190 Beijing, People's Republic of China
e-mail: zhangyafenghello@163.com

H. Liu
e-mail: 13910310263@126.com

Z. Jin
China National Institute of Standardization, Beijing, China
e-mail: jinzongzhen@126.com

Z. Jin
Center for IPR Research and Training, Institute of Policy and Management, Chinese Academy of Sciences, Room 1021, No. 4 Zhichun Road, Haidian District, 100191 Beijing, People's Republic of China

D. Prud'homme and H. Song (eds.), *Economic Impacts of Intellectual Property-Conditioned Government Incentives*, DOI 10.1007/978-981-10-1119-1_11

of IPDCs may eventually generate more general nationwide economic returns. In order to understand how different localities implement and benefit from central-level IP-conditioned government programs in China, we have conducted a brief case study of the cities of Changji and Quanzhou and analyzed the policies implemented by local governments to achieve and maintain IPDC status.

Keywords IP · IPPs · IP demonstration cities

11.1 Introduction

The impact of intellectual property policies (IPPs) in China has recently attracted much attention and has generated a heated discussion, especially in the context of an upsurge in patent applications and grants. In China, several administrative departments are in charge of IP, including the State Intellectual Property Office (SIPO), the Trademark Office, the National Copyright Administration, and several other authorities. All of these ministries, together with the State Council and provincial and municipal governments, have proposed and implemented a great number of IPPs to develop and utilize IP.

IPPs have had a huge impact on the development of China, and in particular have contributed to a large upsurge in the number of patent applications and approvals, trademark registrations, as well as an increased emphasis and focus by companies on IP. China has witnessed an explosive growth in the number of domestic patents over the past two decades. In 2014, there were 928,000 filings for invention patents in China, 801,000 of which were domestic; and 233,000 invention patent filings were granted, of which 163,000 were domestic. In contrast, there were only 93,400 domestic patent filings in China in 2005. The phenomenon of fast growth in the number of patent filings is very surprising (Fig. 11.1).

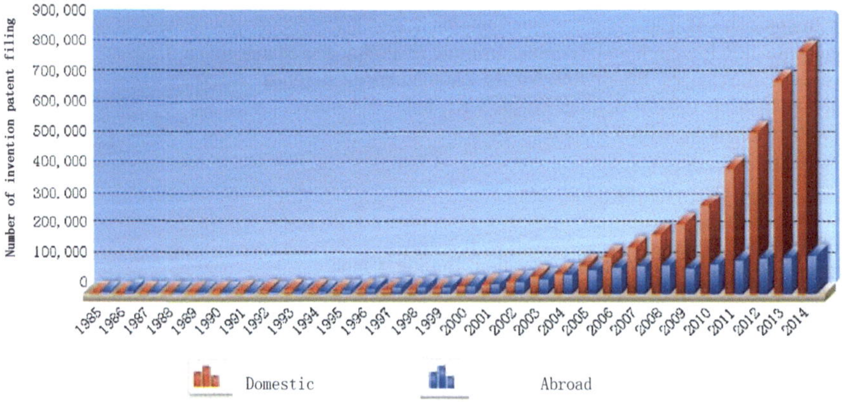

Fig. 11.1 Number of domestic and foreign filings for invention patents. *Source* SIPO

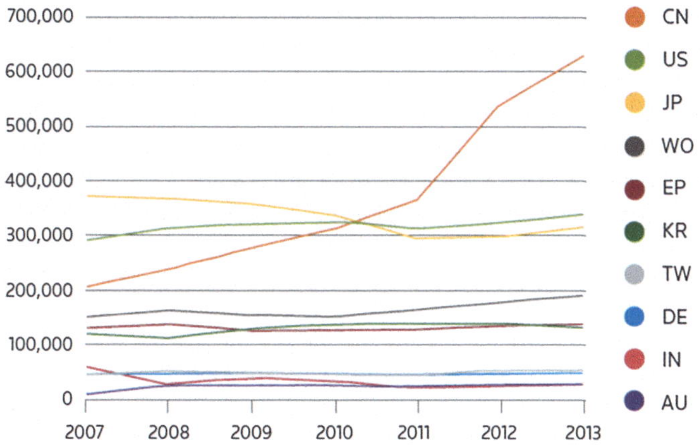

Fig. 11.2 Invention patent applications from 2007 to 2013. *Source* China's IQ (Innovation Quotient), Thomson Reuters (2015)

Figure 11.2 shows the volume of published invention applications (excluding utility models and designs) in China compared to other major countries from 2007 to 2013. It can be clearly seen that China has surpassed and dwarfed all of its competitors in terms of the number of patent filings. The factors responsible for China's rising patent activity include the intensification of research and development (R&D), the continuing inflow of foreign direct investment (FDI), the increase in the number of non-state enterprises, the shift in industrial structure and the improved legal system (Hu and Jefferson 2009; Li 2012; Zhan and Di 2013). However, the various IPPs implemented by the national or regional governments have played a more important role (Long and Wang 2015). Furthermore, the patent subsidy program implemented by provincial units has been a crucial factor (Warner 2015; Li and Xia 2011).

However, the role and effect of IPPs as an optimally efficient and effective IP system has yet to be established in China (Peng 2006). This may be due to a lack of coordination between the various ministries responsible for IP, and the conflicting nature of various IPPs implemented by different ministries potentially weakening the effects of the individual IPPs (Zhou and Liu 2010). Another study analyzed the impact of IPPs in China and found that the impact of administrative measures on technology innovation performance is very small (Sheng and Kong 2012). Furthermore, with the promotion of IPPs, some serious patent-related issues have emerged: the improvement of patent quality has lagged behind the increase in the number of patent applications, while the number of 'junk' patents and dormant patents has increased (Zhu and Zhang 2012). As a result, granted patents are not fully used (Mao 2015) and social resources are wasted (Ma 2009).

This chapter concerns one of the many IPPs operating in China, namely the IP Demonstration City (IPDC) Program, and is focused on the economic effects of the program. The predecessor of the IPDC Program began in 1999. The main purpose of this program is to promote the impact of IP in driving innovation and economic development across different regions of China by establishing a multi-level IP system across cities, science and technology (S&T) parks, companies and public institutions.[1] (Interestingly, since 2009 the Korean Intellectual Property Office (KIPO) has also designated a number of cities as model IP cities for the purpose of regional development. The designated local governments provide relevant information for strategic industries, promote technology transfer to vitalize the regional economy, and foster public awareness of IP. The designation of model IP cities is reported to enhance IP awareness and improve the competitiveness of SMEs (KIPO 2009).)

Compared with the existing research, the main contribution of this chapter lies in the following two points. Firstly, the topic of IPDCs (a type of IP-conditioned government incentive, according to the definition used throughout this book) has seldom been discussed, and this chapter provides much needed insights into the structure and workings of China's implementation of this program. Secondly, this study provides some preliminary insights into the economic impact of IPDCs, based on interviews, analysis of secondary sources, and several brief case studies.

The chapter is structured as follows: Sect. 11.2 reviews the IPPs and their impacts in China; Sect. 11.3 introduces the IPDC Program; Sect. 11.4 explains the methodology; Sect. 11.5 studies the effects of the program; and Sect. 11.6 provides conclusions and policy recommendations.

11.2 IPPs in China

In the 21st century, IP is playing an increasingly important economic role, and accordingly China has prioritized its development. In 2001, China joined the World Trade Organization (WTO), and promised to strengthen IP protection. In January 2004, the former vice-premier Wu Yi stated that the implementation of an effective IP strategy should be promoted. In 2006, the Medium and Long Term National S&T Development Plan for 2006–2020 was issued, and the objectives of national policies shifted to building an innovative economy. China has set a national target of becoming a leading innovative country by 2020, and the government issued the 2008–2020 National IP Strategy in 2008 and the 2014–2020 Action Plan on the Implementation of National Intellectual Property Strategy in 2014 to facilitate utilization, management, creation, and protection of IP.

[1]On a separate note, some recent studies have examined the strength of IP cultivation and protection in different regions of China. For example, one study calculated an index of the levels of IP in different areas of China since 2009 according to the output of IP, the level of IP market movement, comprehensive performance of IP (macroeconomic value, social progress performance, and enterprise development performance) and possibilities for IP creation (Wang 2014). Furthermore, in recent years, SIPO has conducted annual studies on 'patent strength' and IP development (SIPO 2012a, b, 2013).

As a key source of sustainable competitiveness, IP plays an important role in national and market competition. Yet institutions, especially IP-related laws and policies, are the foundation and guarantee of the use of IP (Wu 2001). The IP regime has greatly influenced technological innovation and economic growth, and the importance of IPPs has gained the attention of policymakers in many countries (Hall et al. 2013; Dong 2009a; Zhang 2001). A dynamic and adaptive IPP can have great impact on R&D, benefit to the consumer, industrial innovation ability, regional innovation ability and social welfare (Eichera and Garcia-Penalosa 2008). Indeed, properly implemented IPPs are helpful for a country in avoiding the 'growth trap' and in promoting the transformation of economic growth (Dong 2013). The creation and development of an effective IP strategy seems to be one final measure for countries to eliminate the issue of resource constraint (Dong 2009b).

In China, policies aimed at creating, utilizing, managing and protecting IP are an important part of national policy (Suttmeier and Yao 2011), and rapid economic development is greatly influenced by IPPs (Dutta et al. 2015). One article estimated the impact of the 1993 and 2001 patent laws in China and found that the amendment to the patent laws increased total factor productivity (TFP) growth (Fleisher and Zhou 2010). The various IP protection and subsidy policies put forward by governments create a favorable environment for IP creators (Dong 2009a). Both patent filing and trademark registrations have increased at a very fast rate in recent years, and the patent implementation rate (concerning licensing and otherwise using patents to create a product or improve a production process) of companies remains relatively high compared with foreign countries, and was found to be above 80 % during the period between 2005 and 2011 (WIPO 2014). It is interesting to note that the results of earlier studies that examined certain IP and R&D-related promotion policies in foreign countries, also suggested the positive effect of such policies (Jaffe and Lerner 2001; Czarnitzki and Hussinger 2004; Ebersberger 2004).

However, the emergence of a large number of patent applications in China due to the promotional incentives of IPPs raises some serious issues. One study has suggested that the framework of patent-related laws and policies in China may not have achieved its initial purpose, or may have even hampered innovation in China (Prud'homme 2012). Another study reviewed Chinese IPPs over a decade and argued that China had not chosen the optimal IP regime, and that the current IPPs are facing a serious crisis (Dong 2014).

The issue of patent quality in China is at the forefront of concerns. For example, using a validated patent quality measure, a recent report has shown that the average number of citations of inventions (in relation to patents from the field of data processing) published in 2008 is 1.17, far behind the corresponding average number of 6.72 citations in the U.S. (Thomson Reuters 2015). Furthermore, the very large number of patent applications can be viewed as the shadow of a huge'patent bubble'. Another issue is the accumulation of 'sleeping patents' (Gilbert and Newbery 1982; Tang and Sun 2006; Yuan 2009; Zhu and Zhang 2012), as although policies accelerate patent applications, the transformation and commercialization of patented technology does not have a good record in China (Wen and Wang 2013).

Therefore, sleeping patents are not only a waste of R&D resources, but also a waste of administrative resources. Furthermore, it is argued that government intervention may 'crowd out' healthy patent protection, and therefore have a negative impact on the motivation of companies to protect their IP (Wang and Gao 2015).

The evaluation of IPPs is of great importance in order to improve policies, and several studies have tried to measure or evaluate the performance of IPPs. For example, one study put forward a framework for the evaluation of the performance of regional IP strategies (Yi 2007). Another study established an index system from the three aspects of policy formulation, policy implementation and policy effect (Guo and Cao 2010). Another author used policy process theory to analyze the multi-dimensional effect of IPPs from the level of decision-making, time, space and innovation landscape (Yuan 2012). Another study established quantitative criteria for IPPs in terms of policy efforts, policy objectives and policy measures. The author found that policy efforts will restrict patent granting, and that the main administrative measures have only a small impact on technology innovation performance (Sheng and Kong 2012).

11.3 The IPDC Program

SIPO began to conduct official 'IP Pilot and Demonstration' work as early as 15 years ago. In 1999, SIPO issued the 'Guidelines on Promoting the Patent Pilot Work of Technological Innovation Cities', which was revised in 2002 after China joined the WTO in 2001.[2] In January 2004, SIPO issued the 'Guidance on the Work of IP Pilot and Demonstration', where cities, S&T parks, companies and institutions were brought into the area of the IP Pilot and Demonstration work, and detailed selection criteria and application procedures were formulated, so as to promote the popularization and development of IP through multi-level pilot and demonstration work.[3]

In 2008, the State Council issued the 'Outline of the National Intellectual Property Strategy (2008–2020)', which proposed to 'launch various kinds of pilot or demonstration projects for IP, and to improve the overall capacity to utilize IP and handle competition in IP'.[4] Thereafter, the work of the IP Pilot and Demonstration in China entered into a new period of executive arrangement. In November 2011, SIPO issued the 'Evaluation Method on the State Intellectual Property Pilot and Demonstration Cities (Districts)'[5] and the 'Notification on Strengthening the Classification Guidance Work of IP Demonstration Cities',[6] in

[2]See http://www.sipo.gov.cn/zcfg/flfg/zl/bmgfxwj/200804/t20080403_369030.html.

[3]See http://www.sipo.gov.cn/xtgls/bmgz/200901/t20090106_437127.html.

[4]See http://www.gov.cn/zwgk/2008-06/10/content_1012269.htm.

[5]See http://www.sipo.gov.cn/ztzl/ywzt/zscqsfszl/zcwj/201304/t20130412_791078.html.

[6]See http://www.sipo.gov.cn/ztzl/ywzt/zscqsfszl/zcwj/201311/t20131104_874717.html.

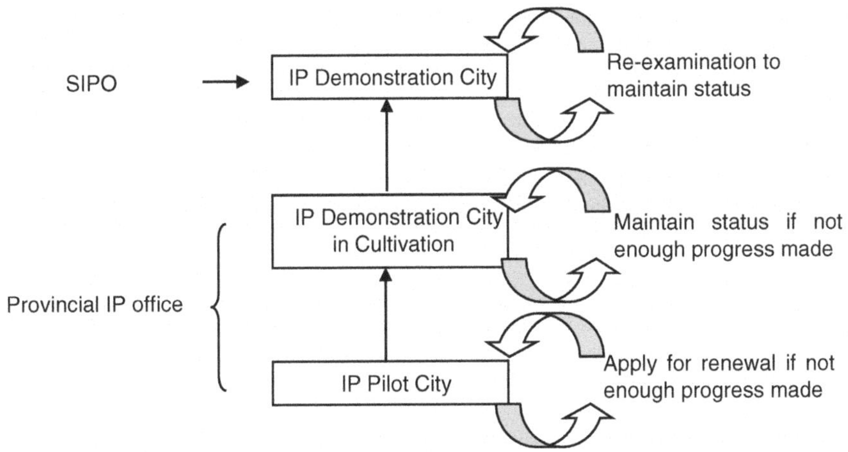

Fig. 11.3 Relationship between the different demonstration city programs

order to guide the pilot and demonstration cities according to their classification. In February 2013, SIPO added county-level cities into the remit of application of the IPDCs.[7] In June 2014, SIPO issued the most recent 'Evaluation and Management Method on the State Intellectual Property Pilot and Demonstration Cities (Districts)'[8] based on previous work, which confirmed the details of the findings of the pilot and demonstration cities.

At the end of 2015 there were 64 state IP demonstration cities in total, and another 80 cities had the qualification to apply for the title. The first, second, third, and fourth batches of 23, 18, 12, and 11 IPDCs were identified on 27 April 2012, 23 July 2013, 30 October 2014, and 6 November 2015, respectively (see Appendix B).

The program comprises several different categories of cities, namely the (1) IP Pilot City, (2) the IPDC 'in Cultivation' and the (3) IPDC. The IP Pilot City is the lowest city level while the IPDC is the highest city level. The relationship between them is shown in Fig. 11.3. The evaluation procedure of the IP Pilot Cities is divided into three steps: the first step concerns the application when the local government submits written materials to the provincial IP office. The second step concerns the evaluation and recommendation of cities and the provincial IP office will evaluate the cities and recommend those which satisfy the standard according to SIPO. The third step concerns the application submitted to SIPO by provincial IP offices, and SIPO will evaluate the cities and announce the evaluation result.

IP Pilot Cities have a term of three years. Every year the provincial IP office will check the IP pilot work, and those cities who obtain a score of less than 60 % (full score is 100 %) will be deprived of the title and are forbidden to apply for a further two years. For those pilot cities which cannot pass the evaluation after the expiration

[7]See http://www.sipo.gov.cn/ztzl/ywzt/zscqsfszl/zcwj/201311/t20131104_874718.html.

[8]See http://www.sipo.gov.cn/ztzl/ywzt/zscqsfszl/zcwj/201406/t20140613_965308.html.

Table 11.1 Evaluation index for IP pilot and demonstration cities

1st class	2nd class	Full score
Objective indicators	Creation (15), utilization (20), protection (20), management (30), service (15)	100
Institution establishment	Establishment of an IP administrative system (35), establishment of IP culture and talent (12), establishment of IP awareness and ability in companies (20), law enforcement work and assertion of IP rights (17), work on special themes (11), other work (5)	100
Special work	Special measures (5), excellent achievements (5)	10

Note The number in parenthesis in the middle column shows the score of a certain indicator
Source Evaluation and management method on the state intellectual property pilot and demonstration cities (districts)

of the pilot period (three years), they can apply for the title of IP Pilot City again and experience another 'pilot term' of three years. Those cities that satisfy the evaluation requirements in the term will experience a period of 'demonstration in cultivation' for a cycle of three years, on condition that the city governments create schedules for the period; those which do not submit these schedules will also be deprived of the qualification and are forbidden to apply for a further three years.

After undergoing a period termed the 'demonstration in cultivation' for at least one year,[9] the cities can apply for recognition as a state IPDC; the evaluation index is shown in Table 11.1. For those cities that do not reach the standard to apply for IPDC recognition after three years of 'demonstration in cultivation' period, they can directly enter into another round of such a period.

The evaluation procedure for IPDCs is divided into three steps, the first step is the release of the notification from SIPO each year; the second step involves the application submitted by municipal governments to provincial IP offices; and the third step involves the evaluation and recommendation from the provincial IP offices. SIPO will then evaluate the recommended cities and determine and finalize the list of IPDCs. After a city obtains the title of IPDC, it will be re-examined by SIPO every three years. Only those cities which satisfy the standard can keep the title, and those which do not pass the re-examination will have the IPDC title removed and are unable to re-apply for a further two years.

The main indicators of the evaluation index of IPDCs are shown in Table 11.1, with further details given in Appendix A. The emphasis of the index system lie in 'objective indicators' and institution establishment. The objective indicators mainly reflect the status of IP in companies, and include aspects such as the creation, utilization, protection, management and service of IP. Of these, 30 % of the score is attributed to management, representing the largest proportion of the total score.

The 'institution establishment' reflects the condition of the local government's IP work, and includes the following indicators: establishment of an IP administrative

[9]This means that those cities with high performances do not have to wait until the third year of the term of 'cultivation in demonstration' to apply for the IPDC title.

system, the establishment of IP culture and talent, the establishment of companies' IP awareness and ability, IP enforcement, and special themes. Of these, 35 % of the score is attributed to the establishment of IP administrative system, which represents the largest proportion of the total score.

Once cities obtain the title of IP Pilot City, IPDC in Cultivation, or IPDC, their governments undertake key initiatives to further strengthen their IP environments. As mentioned, these initiatives are part of an attempt to implement the larger National Intellectual Property Strategy.

The main initiatives to be undertaken by IP Pilot Cities and IPDCs in Cultivation include:

- establishing a multi-level IP work system comprising cities, S&T parks, and companies;
- establishing an IP-focused work system with special features;
- establishing an index system of work performance;
- promoting IP to drive economic and social development, and progress in technology; and
- mobilizing IP work in regions through the 'demonstration effect' in other regions.

For IPDCs, the main initiatives to be undertaken include:

- establishing IP administrative offices in charge of patents, trademarks, and copyright;
- constructing local IP policy and a regulatory system;
- improving local IP awareness;
- encouraging the creation of IP;
- enhancing the protection of IP in cities; and
- promoting the utilization of IP.

Provincial IP offices are in charge of IP Pilot Cities and IPDCs in Cultivation. The provincial IP offices should arrange for a special fund to support the work during the two periods and for special officers to undertake the respective work. Furthermore, the IP offices of the local cities which apply for the title of IPDC should also establish a fund for IP Pilot Cities, and they are required to provide favorable policies for county-level pilot cites. That is to say, the funds for IP Pilot Cities come from the provincial and local government, and are at the disposal of the IP offices only. The funds can be used to organize working conferences or training, or to launch activities to improve the ability to analyze and use patent information, improve the quality of patent filing, promote the implementation of an IP standard, and to improve design-based competitiveness, etc.

The Patent Affairs Administration Department of SIPO is in charge of the IPDCs and undertakes the work of granting the title of IPDC and subsequently re-examining the IPDCs. The Patent Affairs Administration Department is required to arrange for a special fund for IPDCs and to appoint special officers to undertake the respective work. Furthermore, the corresponding provincial IP offices should also establish a fund to support IPDCs, and they are also required to provide favorable policies for IPDCs. The purpose of SIPO and provincial level funds for IPDCs is the same as the use of the funds for IP Pilot Cities. In summary, the IPDC Program can be viewed as a package of IP policies that includes many kinds of policy tools concerning the creation of IP, the utilization of patents, the training of talented individuals, the enhancement of IP enforcement, and the improvement of IP management.

11.4 Methodology

This chapter uses the interview method to analyze the effects of the IPDC Program on those cities which obtain the title. Compared with other kinds of investigation methods, the interview method can access more abundant materials and capture more in depth information, thus enabling deep research on certain issues (Yan et al. 2008). In the present study there were 10 interviewees, all of which were government officials undertaking IPDC Program work in the IP offices of those cities which had obtained the title of IPDC. The interviews were conducted by phone, and each interview lasted for up to about 30 min and the interview transcript was recorded in writing while we conducted the interview.

We used semi-structured interviews centered on the effects of the IPDC Program on local economic development. The main specific questions included: "What effects do you think participating as an IPDC can have on the development of the local economy?"; "What effects do you think obtaining the title of IPDC can have on the development of the local economy?"; and "What disadvantages do you think the IPDC policy can have?". Based on the answers to these three main questions, we asked follow-up questions according to each specific interview. Additionally, we identified and collected more material and information from the internet to support the main findings of the interviews. This included patent data from the SIPO database, statistics data from the city or provincial statistics offices, local government work reports, and local Statistical Bulletins for National Economic and Social Development from local government websites. Based on the information obtained from interviews and the internet, we were able to summarize the impact of the IPDC Program on local economic development.

Additionally, in order to better understand how different localities implement and benefit from central-level IP-conditioned government programs in China, we conducted brief case studies of the cities of Changji and Quanzhou by analyzing the policies implemented by the local governments to fulfill and maintain their IPDC statuses and their achievements. Changji is one of the second batch of IPDCs, and this case study focuses on the government's preparatory work to fulfill the requirements to obtain IPDC status, and we highlight aspects of the process by which the city became an IPDC. Quanzhou is one of the first batch of IPDCs, and this case study focuses on the work that the local government undertook to maintain its status after obtaining the title of IPDC, and we summarize the main achievements of Quanzhou in implementing the program. The two cases are complementary as they demonstrate and highlight what needs to be done to obtain the title and then maintain the status.

It should be noted that there may be some tendency for government interviewees to have a positive view of policies because the effectiveness of the policies reflects on their performance. However, our interviewee feedback appears to be relatively objective, and is one of the most useful sources of information we could draw upon in performing the research for this chapter.

These research methods are only intended to provide preliminary insights into the workings of the IPDC Program in China. They should be supplemented with more detailed research in the future.

11.5 Effects of the IPDC Program

11.5.1 Change in the Number of Patent Applications

Although there are various types of IP, in this chapter we focus only on patents. This is because patents are supposed to be highly related to technology (Intarakumnerd and Charoenporn 2015), innovation (Li 2015; Long and Wang 2015; Sleuwaegen and Boiardi 2014; Buesa et al. 2010; Li 2009) and economic growth (Idris 2003). Here we choose the first batch of 23 IPDCs as a sample to analyze the change in the number of patent applications being made before and after IPDC status was obtained. The reason why only these 23 cities were chosen is because they all became IPDCs during 2012 and so the data is comparable. Furthermore, they are the first IPDCs to have been established in China, and so the effect of becoming IPDCs is more easily observed and identified than for the IPDCs that were established at a later date. Also, due to their earlier establishment, the data after they became IPDCs is more detailed and therefore useful for our analysis.

As can be concluded from Table 11.2, the number of invention patent applications and the total number of patent applications (invention, utility and design are three different types of patent under the Patent Law of China) in the first batch of IPDCs increased dramatically from 2009 to 2014. For most of the IPDCs, both the number of invention applications and the total number of patent applications doubled during this period. In the cities of Suzhou, Qingdao, Quanzhou and Wuhu, the number of applications increased between five to eight times. This change reflects the increase in patent applications made by the national IPDCs in China. However, it is as yet unclear whether this change in the number of patent applications was induced by the IPDC Program. Therefore, we conducted interviews to learn more about the effects of the IPDC Program.

Table 11.2 Number of patent application (2009–2014) for the first batch of IPDCs

	Year	2009	2010	2011	2012	2013	2014
Wuhan	Invention	6157	7048	9199	11,537	11,805	10,664
	Total	12,934	14,978	18,573	23,374	22,706	23,893
Guangzhou	Invention	7844	9700	11,940	13,850	14,648	12,852
	Total	17,705	22,060	28,972	34,555	36,388	39,737
Shenzhen	Invention	33,289	33,573	35,978	37,756	33,512	19,539
	Total	53,005	55,766	66,627	74,801	72,670	62,779
Changsha	Invention	3588	4887	7201	8478	7909	6881
	Total	6614	9310	14,026	16,466	15,678	15,817
Chengdu	Invention	6445	7509	10,469	14,623	16,933	16,665
	Total	22,285	24,266	32,934	45,375	45,705	49,445
Suzhou	Invention	4920	10,083	23,550	35,179	44,066	33,561
	total	13,110	31,625	95,150	134,491	105,951	82,280
Hangzhou	invention	10,375	11,755	13,938	17,329	17,619	13,541
	Total	25,302	29,975	40,233	54,293	49,800	43,366
Jinan	Invention	4102	4793	6785	10,394	11,911	10,944
	Total	10,735	13,042	17,663	21,719	20,281	20,262
Qingdao	Invention	2922	3865	5478	13,239	27,761	20,201
	Total	7168	9306	15,436	23,431	38,516	31,954
Zhengzhou	Invention	1843	2716	3585	4600	5154	4363
	Total	4709	6867	9939	13,436	15,041	15,800
Harbin	Invention	3991	4795	5327	7772	9972	7769
	Total	6036	7188	11,665	16,259	17,056	15,168
Nanjing	Invention	9352	11,108	15,128	20,082	22,427	18,904
	Total	15,081	18,592	26,571	35,326	37,352	37,318
Nantong	Invention	1736	5483	7979	8479	8524	7388
	Total	5798	18,326	33,082	40,898	26,310	21,522
Zhenjiang	Invention	1477	2255	3825	6839	9945	6556
	Total	4797	6047	11,267	17,171	20,244	20,684
Fuzhou	Invention	2148	2901	3412	4176	4220	3925
	Total	4546	6225	7579	9254	9082	9611
Dongying	Invention	642	538	522	593	779	634
	Total	2318	2062	2523	3156	3410	3430
Dalian	Invention	3377	4677	7424	9561	11,695	3790
	Total	8477	10,036	14,232	15,402	16,974	8606
Yantai	Invention	1235	1707	2164	3525	3724	2538
	Total	3348	4375	6102	7691	6971	6333
Luoyang	Invention	1144	1493	2717	3051	3551	3962
	Total	2632	3602	6262	6925	7231	8629
Quanzhou	Invention	301	640	1150	1605	1940	1907
	Total	1556	2801	6630	10,889	12,805	15,042

(continued)

Table 11.2 (continued)

	Year	2009	2010	2011	2012	2013	2014
Wenzhou	Invention	844	1119	1749	2322	2812	3074
	Total	4306	6329	9870	18,566	21,864	22,643
Xi'an	Invention	7056	9479	13,209	17,522	22,273	11,549
	Total	12,221	15,666	20,926	29,427	34,633	28,009
Wuhu	Invention	1427	1666	2669	4270	6294	8556
	Total	3832	6956	9515	14,395	13,767	14,692

Source The system of patent search and analysis of SIPO: http://www.pss-system.gov.cn/sipopublicsearch/enportal/index.shtml
Notes (As a searching method, we used a structured search of Chinese patent documents, and we searched the parameters 'application date' and 'address of the applicant'. For example, we entered the 'application date' = '2009', and the 'address of the applicant' = 'Wuhan', to obtain all of the patent applications made in Wuhan in 2009. We could then separate these into invention, utility model and design applications by using the filtering function of the system) The data concerning 'invention' means the number of invention patent applications; the data concerning 'total' means the total number of invention, utility and design patent applications

11.5.2 Effects of the Program

This section discusses several positive economic impacts of the IPDC Program, as reported by our interviewees. We also examine the other main economic impacts discussed in our interviews.

11.5.2.1 Increase in IP Creation

The increase in the creation of IP is a most obvious effect of the IPDC Program. This is a point mentioned by all the interviewees, and they are familiar with this change because they are directly involved in the day-to-day administration and monitoring of local IPPs and IP programs and their impact on the local IP environment. The increase in IP creation is mainly reflected in the increased number of patent applications, as shown in Table 11.2, and granted patents, and in the increased number of trademark and copyright registrations. This change can be attributed to several factors. Firstly, inventors' IP awareness has improved greatly following the training and publicity provided by the local government. Secondly, the local government established a special fund to support IP creation, especially in relation to patents. Thirdly, the IP service industry has greatly developed with the support of the local government, thus creating a favorable market atmosphere for the creation of IP.

11.5.2.2 Growth of IP-Related Industries

The utilization of IP is fundamental if the full economic effect is to be realized. The manufacture and sales of products using patented technology has dramatically increased, and more high-technology firms have been created and are applying for patents as a result of successful R&D achievements. As a result, more IP service firms have been established to provide legal services, information analysis, and consulting services. Seen from the perspective of the local economy, the development of IP-intensive industries is a direct way to consider and measure the role of IP in economic growth. The interviewee from Shenzhen commented that IP contributes to the increase and quality of local GDP. IP-intensive industries have become a new engine for driving economic growth in Shenzhen, with emerging industries reaching 1.88 trillion RMB in production value in 2014, contributing a great proportion of the local GDP.[10] Our interviews identified that the development of the IP service industry is supported and promoted in all IPDCs, and this includes IP agencies, and companies providing IP information searching, analyzing or consulting services.

11.5.2.3 Raising Companies' IP Awareness

As to be expected, alongside the development of IP-related industries and companies, implementation of the IPDC Program more generally raises the IP awareness of companies, for example manufacturing companies and trading companies. Using Wenzhou, in Zhejiang province as an example, Wenzhou is considered to be a relatively developed city in China, and the private economy makes up a great proportion of the local economy. However, most of the private companies were created without any IP assets. Furthermore, the IP management in many companies is weak, as demonstrated by the 'CR' case,[11] when the cigarette lighter industry in Wenzhou encountered many problems as a direct result of inadequate IP management.

However, the interviewee from Wenzhou told us that in the process of implementing the IPDC Program, the local government established an IP platform, enhanced IP protection and trained talented IP individuals, thereby benefiting the local companies and raising their awareness of IP. Furthermore, the interviewee from Zhengzhou, in Henan province also stressed the fact that local companies' awareness of IP has been greatly raised. The personal experience of the interviewee provides us with direct evidence, as he told us that when he and his colleagues went to visit a local company several years ago they were rejected because the manager

[10]See Economic Daily, available at: http://paper.ce.cn/jjrb/html/2015-03/23/content_235022.htm.

[11]The cigarette lighter industry used to be a main pillar industry of Wenzhou in the 1980s and 1990s, and the output represented 95 % of the Chinese market at its peak. Export volume reached 80 % of the total sales in China, and the export volume of lighters with a metal shell made up to 70 % of the world market. In 1994, the U.S. passed the Child Resistance Law ('CR'), which required lighters sold under USD 2 to be installed with a child resistance device. Although the technology is not complex, the patent is owned by foreign companies. Therefore, companies have to pay high licensing fees if they want to export to those countries where the CR has been passed. However, with the payment of such fees, the lighter manufacturers in China lost their cost advantage and were squeezed out of the international market. The main lesson of this case is that many companies in China, to their detriment do not own patents, or even do not know what IP is, let alone how to use IP.

of the firm did not know from which government office they were and what IP was. However, the situation is completely different now, and officers from the IP office are welcomed by companies in Zhengzhou.

11.5.2.4 Improvement of the IP Administrative System

One of the requirements of the IPDC Program is for local governments to establish work teams or IP offices under the leadership of the mayor. This can lead to IP development and protection being taken more seriously, from the top local government institutions downwards. Most of the interviewees reported that the IP administrative system had improved significantly, including structural organization, and personnel allocation, etc. At the same time, the attitude of local government officers towards IP has changed considerably, and they are now paying more attention to the importance of IP. Several years ago, officers working outside of IP administrations knew little about IP. In contrast, at present different administrations are cooperating with each other to promote the effect of IP in driving economic development. For example, authorities in charge of tax and IP work together to promote the creation of IP (for example, patent applications or trademark registrations) and the use of patented technology in manufacturing.

11.5.2.5 Increase in FDI Inflow

In the era of knowledge-based economies, the effect of IP in international economic and technological cooperation becomes more significant. The granting of the title of IPDC signifies the central government's approval of the work of the local government. With this title, the local government can be more active with publicity work and this can be important for attracting external investment, especially FDI. As foreign companies attach great importance to the IP environment of the cities where they are investing, cities that have been granted the title of IPDC are regarded as superior in protecting IP.

Table 11.3 shows the change in FDI in the IPDCs. As data for some cities is unavailable, only the data from part of the first batch of IPDCs was collected. However, the data is sufficient to demonstrate that FDI has greatly increased in most of the IPDCs. Although it is beyond the scope of this chapter to provide a detailed quantitative analysis of the possible correlations between IPDC status and FDI inflow, let alone a detailed discussion of causality, our interviewees did indicate that receiving the title of 'IPDC' was likely to have been important in encouraging FDI into IPDCs.

11.5.2.6 Demonstration Effect

Generally speaking, the interviewees confirmed the work and efforts of SIPO, and reported that they are satisfied with the policy incentives of the IPDC Program. However, most interviewees did not identify the 'demonstration effect' of the

Table 11.3 FDI from 2009 to 2014 concerning the first batch of IPDCs (10,000s US$)

Year	2009	2010	2011	2012	2013	2014
Wuhan	217,331	245,031	275,400	342,174	410,081	484,305
Guangzhou	378,401	497,384	674,734	680,188	711,428	803,975
Shenzhen	416,001	429,724	459,921	522,944	546,789	580,689
Changsha	203,260	223,757	260,116	297,666	340,043	297,666
Suzhou	822,653	853,511	891,222	916,490	869,805	811,978
Hangzhou	401,370	435,627	472,230	496,061	527,633	633,460
Harbin	62,202	70,010	79,404	190,001	226,242	271,490
Nanjing	239,199	281,601	356,440	413,031	403,262	329,074
Zhenjiang	144,081	161,462	180,759	221,410	309,678	130,374
Fuzhou	122,969	167,297	176,966	205,643	205,700	146,368
Dongying	16,506	20,975	14,035	16,232	19,335	22,003
Quanzhou	9591	16,108	198,154	120,592	132,803	154,609
Xi'an	121,872	156,653	200,522	247,800	312,994	370,310
Wuhu	64,229	78,103	104,111	131,655	160,548	200,340

program as being particularly strong. The concept of a 'demonstration effect' in modern China is sometimes linked back to Deng Xiaoping's idea that regions and their people should first develop in order to provide an example for other regions and people to aspire to (Deng 1983). It has also been used to describe the positive effect an economic policy or program in one region in China can create in other regions, whereby those latter regions seek to follow the example set by the former region (Fan et al. 2011). One author named this effect the 'overflow effect' of policy, because it is similar to the spillover of technology (Song et al. 2012).

Among all the interviewees, only the officer from Zhengzhou mentioned the 'demonstration effect' of Zhengzhou on other areas in Henan province. This is explained by the fact that the average level of IP is very low in Henan province, so that an outstanding city for IP, such as Zhengzhou, becomes a role model for the whole province. Most of the other interviewees only talked about the conditions of their local city, and said that the 'demonstration effect' is merely a form of intra-city encouragement for those cities.

Furthermore, it is clear that many cities situated in richer and more IP-intensive provinces such as Jiangsu, have attained IPDC status at different stages over the last few years, as shown in Appendix B. This may indicate that a 'demonstration effect' per se is not as important a factor for encouraging cities in such provinces to improve their scores across the IPDC indicators. Instead, although these cities have always been pursuing IPDC status, these cities may simply have started from a position from which it was easier to achieve higher scores in order for them to qualify for IPDC status. However, more research is needed to more clearly disentangle the effects in these situations.

At the same time, it is clear that over time more cities across different regions in China have reached the level where they can be granted IPDCs status. Specifically, 23, 18, 12, and 11 cities reached this level by 2012, 2013, 2014, and 2015, respectively. It is noteworthy that many of these cities are in different provinces (see Appendix B). This may indicate that there may at least be some positive inter-provincial effects of the IPDC policy, whereby awarding an IPDC in one province may create an incentive for cities in other provinces to improve their scores against the IP indicators assessed as part of the IPDC qualification program. It is also possible that the development of IPDCs is largely attributed to the publicity given to the policy by the central-level government and SIPO. More research is needed to more clearly disentangle the effects in these situations.

11.5.2.7 Marginal Economic Returns

The marginal economic returns of the programs established by current IPDCs decrease as more IPDCs are introduced. Furthermore, some cities may also be required to undertake the work of other types of demonstration programs, as required by different ministries of the central government, for example the Trademark Demonstration Program implemented by the State Administration for Industry and Commerce (SAIC), the Copyright Demonstration Program implemented by the National Copyright Administration (NCAC), and the Quality Demonstration Program implemented by the General Administration of Quality Supervision, Inspection and Quarantine (AQSIQ). Of these, the demonstration programs concerning IP, trademark and copyright share significant overlaps, especially in the requirement aspects. For example, all of the programs require the city governments to establish special offices and arrange for special officials to conduct publicity work, to promote the output, and to enhance the protection of certain types of IP. Furthermore, the indicators of trademark and copyright are also included in the evaluation of the IPDC Program. This kind of 'policy imitation' between ministries in China is significant, and it weakens the effect of the policy to some degree.

Despite these weaknesses, if better coordinated, more IPDCs may generate more general nationwide economic returns in the long term. This is for the simple reason that they may help improve IP development protection across China as a whole.

11.5.3 Case Study: Changji

In September 2013, Changji Prefecture in Xinjiang Autonomous Region was named as one of the second batch of IPDCs. Figure 11.4 depicts the procedure by which Changji obtained the title.

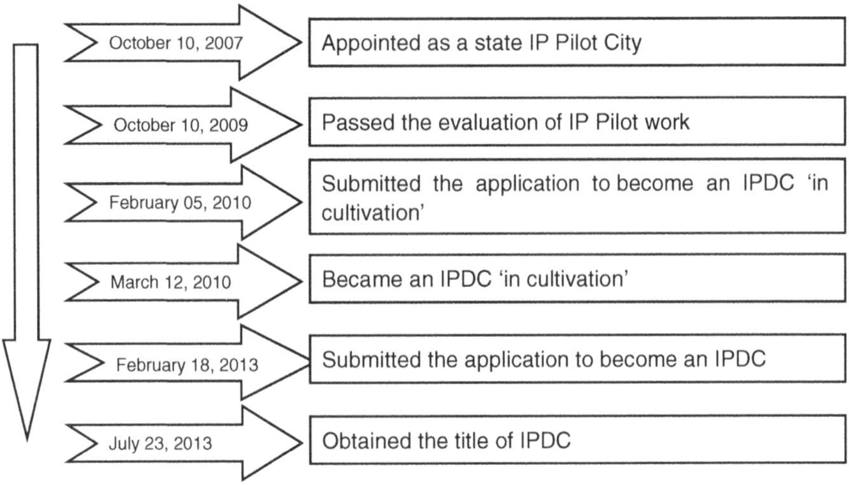

Fig. 11.4 The procedure by which Changji obtained the title of IPDC

Before obtaining the title of IPDC in 2013, the government in Changji completed the following initiatives, according to SIPO's requirements to become an IPDC. Firstly, the local government established a coordinated IP work system by setting up an IP work group led by the prefecture leader, and introduced the number of patent applications filed into the work performance evaluation criteria of lower level government officials. Secondly, a specific work mechanism was established, a special fund was set up to support the development of patented technology, and a series of patent-related documents were published on issues including the patent application process, patent management, patent prize, and patent enforcement, etc. Thirdly, the local government supported and promoted local companies to utilize their IP by arranging for IP specialists to help companies establish IP management offices and develop an IP strategy. Fourthly, the local government organized various activities to strengthen the awareness of IP by the public, government officers, and company staff, by holding lectures, broadcasting information films and providing training.

Through these activities and work, the IP administrative system and the capability to create IP in Changji, improved considerably. Furthermore, IP enforcement was also strengthened.[12]

[12]Xinjiang Intellectual Property Office. Available at: http://www.xjipo.gov.cn/Article/ShowArticle.aspx?ArticleID=14385.

11.5.4 Case Study: Quanzhou

In April, 2012, the city Quanzhou in Fujian Province was granted the title of state IPDC, and became one of 23 cities named IPDCs in the first batch. During the first three years (2012–2014), the government in Quanzhou completed the following work and activities, which were to a significant extent encouraged by the fact that the city was granted IPDC status in 2012 and wanted to maintain this status to enjoy the benefits mentioned in Sect. 11.5.2.

Firstly, Quanzhou invested a large amount of money into a special IP fund, and this amount increased from 3.8 million RMB (approximately 603,000 USD) in 2012 to 9 million RMB (approximately 1,449,000 USD) in 2014, representing a growth rate of 136.84 %. During this period, the total expenditure on IP at the municipal and county levels of Quanzhou was 118.95 million RMB.[13] These funds were predominantly spent on subsidies and awards concerning patents, and the organization of special activities (e.g. publicity and IP training).

Secondly, the government in Quanzhou improved the regional IP system to promote the creation and commercialization of patents. The documents issued include the 'Regulations on the evaluation of patent award in Quanzhou', the 'Medium and long development plan for the patent work in Quanzhou (2013–2020)', the 'Measures on promoting patent utilization in Quanzhou', the 'Opinions on improving the intellectual property work of strategic emerging industries', the 'Opinions on improving the work of trademark and brands', the 'Opinions on the work of implementing technology standard strategy', and the 'Opinions on the establishment of working mechanism of intellectual property complaints', etc.

Thirdly, the municipal IP administration established a working group and team to support experts to visit companies regularly and to provide a 'one-to-one' advisory service on IP issues. They provide advice on, for example, whether a company should establish an IP management department and how to realize this objective should it be required, and how a company can avoid infringing IP and protect its own IP.

Fourthly, the Quanzhou government took measures to enhance IP enforcement and protection. In 2013, the patent administrative enforcement unit was established to settle patent infringement disputes and to investigate patent counterfeiting. In 2014, 11 counties or districts in Quanzhou had established S&T or IP offices. Furthermore, the IP office in Quanzhou took measures to protect IP in exhibitions, including establishing a service platform and publishing brochures.

[13]Source: Fujian Intellectual Property Office. Available at: http://www.fjipo.gov.cn/html/12/25/6628_20151231958.html.

Table 11.4 The number of patent application and approvals in Quanzhou 2012–2015

	Invention		Utility		Design		Total	
	Applications	Granted	Applications	Granted	Applications	Granted	Applications	Granted
2012	1322	337	7254	5601	4943	3806	13,519	9744
2013	1830	399	9282	5302	7336	5302	18,488	13,267
2014	2140	541	8107	4941	8291	4941	18,538	11,456
2015[a]	3533[a]	896[a]	16,199[a]	8958[a]	7541[a]	8958[a]	27,273[a]	21,524[a]

Source The People's Government of Fujian Province
Note[a] The data for 2015 is the data collected in the first 11 months of the year, and as such, the figures for the full 12 months will inevitably be higher. Furthermore, the data in this table was provided by the local government, and there is a small difference between this data and data in Table 11.2, because different searching and statistical methods were used

Fifthly, under the guidance and support of the government in Quanzhou, a series of public IP service platforms were established, including the 'Quanzhou intellectual property information website', the '12330 hotline', the 'Exhibition and transaction platform for patented technology in Quanzhou', and a special patent document database in the areas of bathroom plumbing, and textiles.

Based on the above mentioned work, Quanzhou has made great progress in its approach to IP. During the first three years of demonstration, the number of patent applications and granted patents in Quanzhou was 50,505 and 34,467, respectively, and the respective growth rate was 17.10 and 8.43 % as can be seen in Table 11.4. Of these, the number of applications and approvals for invention patents was 5292 and 1277, respectively, and the respective growth rate was 27.2 and 26.7 %. Up until November 2015, the total number of applications and approvals in Quanzhou was 120,882 and 87,031, respectively, and there were nearly 200,000 valid trademarks. There were 144 well-known trademarks, and 756 trademark registrations under the Madrid Protocol. In addition to the volume of patents and trademarks, pledged financing reached 1.8 billion RMB (about 290 million USD), and the administrative enforcement departments investigated 4559 patent infringement and counterfeit cases.[14]

11.6 Conclusions and Policy Recommendations

Following an introduction to the IPDC Program in China, and by using the method of interview, this chapter has analyzed the effects of the IPDC Program. Our research indicates that the implementation of the IPDC Program has increased the

[14]Source: Fujian Intellectual Property Office. Available at: http://www.fjipo.gov.cn/html/12/25/6628_20151231958.html.

level of IP in the corresponding cities, including the number of patent applications and granted patents, and trademark and copyright registrations, etc. The awareness of IP by the public, companies and the government has increased. Furthermore, IP-related industries developed considerably, with more new products using patented technology being produced, and more companies applying for patents and trademarks. More IP service firms were also established. The IP administrative system of these cities is also improved, and the city image is improved with the title of IPDC.

However, at the same time, we found that the intra-provincial 'demonstration effect' of the program appears to be relatively limited in many provinces, although it may be stronger in less developed provinces. There may be some positive inter-provincial effects of the IPDC program, although the full extent of these are unclear. And the marginal economic returns of the current IPDC Program decrease as more IPDCs are introduced, although in the long-term more IPDCs may generate more general nationwide economic returns.

At present, China is implementing a national strategy with the aim of becoming an 'intellectual property power country'. In this context and considering the findings of this study, the following policy recommendations are put forward. Firstly, SIPO can require local governments where IPDCs are situated to introduce IP (for example, instances of properly addressing IP infringements) as an independent part of the local government work report, thus improving the importance of IP in the local governments' annual work. This is because IP is usually reflected as an aspect of S&T statistics in the annual government work report, and making it an independent part can improve its perceived importance. However, at the same time, it is important not to overemphasize simplistic measures of government work performance related to IP.

Secondly, the many different ministries in charge of IP in China should enhance cooperation between each other, especially when implementing similar policies. In relation to the IPDC Program, SIPO should communicate and cooperate with the Trademark Office and the National Copyright Administration to improve the efficiency of the program. Furthermore, *separate* programs for trademark demonstration cities and copyright demonstration cities may even be unnecessary. Thirdly, SIPO should provide more guidance, capital and training for IP Pilot Cities in areas where the level of IP is considered to be relatively weak.

Acknowledgements The authors wish to thank Dan Prud'homme from IP Key for his constructive suggestions for revising this paper. We also thank Song Hefa and Li Zhenxing from the Institute of Policy and Management and Liu Jie from SIPO for their help. We also want to express our thanks to the officers from the IP offices of Guangzhou, Shenzhen, Chengdu, Changsha, Zhengzhou, Wenzhou, and Harbin.

Appendices

Appendix A: Evaluation Index for IP Demonstration Cities

Objective indicators

1st class indicator	No.	2nd class indicator	Score (100)
Creation (15)	1	Number of valid invention patents per 10,000 people	4
	2	Number of granted invention patents per 1 billion RMB of regional GDP	3
	3	Rate of invention patents granted	4
	4	Rate of utility patents deemed to be waived	2
	5	Rate of designs deemed to be waived	2
Utilization (20)	6	Number of registered patent license contracts per 100 industrial companies above the designated size	4
	7	Rate of invention patents whose life ≤ 3 years	5
	8	Rate of utility patents whose life ≤ 3 years	4
	9	Rate of designs whose life ≤ 3 years	3
	10	Number of companies who reach the national IP management standard per 100 industrial companies above the designated size	4
Protection (20)	11	Number of cases of patent infringement disputes per 100 industrial companies above the designated size	10
	12	Number of settled patent forgery cases per 100 industrial companies above the designated size	5
	13	Number of professional law enforcement officers per 100 industrial companies above the designated size	5
Management (30)	14	Special fund for IP per 100 industrial companies above the designated size per 100 Chinese invention patent applications	4
	15	Rate of special expenditure for IP	6
	16	IP management ability	10
	17	Number of full-time administrative staff per 100 industrial companies above the designated size	10
Service (15)	18	Rate of invention patent applications via agencies	3
	19	Rate of utility patent applications via agencies	2
	20	Rate of design applications via agencies	2
	21	Number of local patent agencies per 100 Chinese invention patent applications	4
	22	Number of services for IP	4

Institution establishment indicators

1st class indicator	2nd class indicator	No.	3rd class indicator	Score (100)
Establishment of an IP administrative system (35)	Government's emphasis (7)	1	Government's regular research and plan concerning IP work	2
		2	City leaders' collective learning on the topic of IP	2
		3	IP work is included in the government's annual evaluation index system	1
		4	IP coordination mechanism	2
	Regulation construction (5)	5	IP regulation construction	5
	Working system (13)	6	Public administration and law enforcement ability	8
		7	Condition of directly controlled organs	2
		8	Condition of IP management institute at county level	3
	Expenditure Investment (10)	9	Rate of IP expenditure on general budget expenditure	5
		10	Amount of government IP expenditure	2
		11	Structure of government IP expenditure	3
Establishment of IP culture and talent (12)	Publicity work (6)	12	Job condition for publicity and government information	0.5
		13	Large scale promotional activities	1.5
		14	Number of news reports	1.5
		15	Condition of website construction	1.5
		16	Annual expenditure on publicity	1
	Talent work (6)	17	Condition of IP education and training	2
		18	Cultivation, introduction, policy and activity for IP talents	2
		19	Number of IP talents	1
		20	Annual expenditure on talent work	1

(continued)

(continued)

1st class indicator	2nd class indicator	No.	3rd class indicator	Score (100)
Establishment of IP awareness and ability in companies (20)	Policy document (3)	21	Condition of policies for supporting companies	3
	Work on pilot and demonstration, or superior firms (7)	22	Number of national firms and superior companies	1
		23	Number of provincial pilot/demonstration companies and superior companies	1
		24	Number of local pilot/demonstration companies and superior companies	1
		25	Measures or activities of pilot/demonstration companies and superior companies	2
		26	Annual expenditure of pilot/demonstration companies and superior companies	2
	Standard implementation work (6)	27	Number of companies which reaches the national standard	1
		28	Number of companies which participate in implementing the national standard	1
		29	Measures or activities for implementing the national standard	2
		30	Annual expenditure for implementing the national standard	2
	Trusteeship work (4)	31	Number of companies participating in trusteeship	1
		32	Measures or activities about trusteeship	2
		33	Annual expenditure on trusteeship work	1

(continued)

(continued)

1st class indicator	2nd class indicator	No.	3rd class indicator	Score (100)
Law enforcement work and assertion of IP rights (17)	Administrative enforcement (10)	34	Work condition of patent administrative enforcement	8
		35	Annual expenditure on patent administrative enforcement	2
	Right assertion and reported complaints (7)	36	Condition of capacity for assisting with rights assertion	2
		37	Condition of work for assistance with rights assertion	2
		38	Condition of reported complaints	1
		39	Annual expenditure for right assertion assistance and reported complaints	2
Work on special themes (11)	Theme 1: improve the patent quality (11)	40	Issued policies and evaluation index	3
		41	Measures or activities for promoting work	5
		42	Annual expenditure	3
	Theme 2: patent information analysis (11)	40	Condition of issued policies	3
		41	Measures or activities for promoting work	5
		42	Annual expenditure	3
Work on special themes (11)	Theme 3: design industry (11)	40	Condition of issued policies	3
		41	Measures or activities for promoting work	5
		42	Annual expenditure	3
	Theme 4: IP service industry (11)	40	Condition of issued policies	3
		41	Measures or activities for promoting work	5
		42	Annual expenditure	3
	Theme 5: patent navigation industry (11)	40	Condition of issued policies	3
		41	Measures or activities for promoting work	5
		42	Annual expenditure	3
	Theme 6: IP financing service (11)	40	Condition of issued policies	3
		41	Measures or activities for promoting work	5
		42	Annual expenditure	3

(continued)

(continued)

1st class indicator	2nd class indicator	No.	3rd class indicator	Score (100)
Work on special themes (11)	Theme 7: Industrialization of patented technology (11)	40	Condition of issued policies	3
		41	Measures or activities for promoting work	5
		42	Annual expenditure	3
Other work (5)	All except the above	43	Condition of issued policies	
		44	Measures or activities for promoting work	
		45	Annual expenditure	

Special work indicators

1st class indicator	2nd class indicator	No.	3rd class indicator	Score (10)
Special work (10)	Special measures and excellent achievements	1	Special measures	5
		2	Excellent achievements	5

Appendix B: List of IPDCs

City level	No.	1st Batch	2nd Batch	3rd Batch	4th Batch
Vice provincial city	1	Wuhan, Hubei	Xiamen, Fujian		
	2	Guangzhou, Guangdong	Ningbo, Zhejiang		
	3	Shenzhen, Guangdong	Changchun, Jilin		
	4	Chengdu, Sichuan			
	5	Hangzhou, Zhejiang			
	6	Jinan, Shandong			
	7	Qingdao, Shandong			
	8	Harbin, Heilongjiang			
	9	Nanjing, Jiangsu			
	10	Dalian, Liaoning			
	11	Xi'an, Shanxi			

(continued)

(continued)

City level	No.	1st Batch	2nd Batch	3rd Batch	4th Batch
Prefectural city	1	Chansha, Hunan	Dongguan, Guangdong	Foshan, Guangdong	Haidian, Beijing
	2	Suzhou, Jiangsu	Wuxi, Jiangsu	Changzhou, Jiangsu	Mianyang, Sichuan
	3	Nantong, Jiangsu	Zhuzhou, Hunan	Yichang, Hubei	Minxing, Shanghai
	4	Zhenjiang, Jiangsu	Taizhou, Jiangsu	Anyang, Henan	Huizhou, Guangdong
	5	Zhengzhou, Henan	Weifang, Shandong	Zhongshan, Guangdong	Xiqing, Tianjin
	6	Luoyang, Henan	Zibo, Shandong	Chaoyang, Beijing	Deyang, Sichuan
	7	Dongying, Shandong	Hefei, Anhui	Xiangtan, Hunan	Jiangbei, Chongqing
	8	Yantai, Shandong	Jiaxing, Zhejiang	Panzhihua, Sichuan	
	9	Fuzhou, Fujian	Nanyang, Henan	Nanchang, Jiangxi	
	10	Quanzhou, Fujian	Huzhou, Zhejiang		
	11	Wenzhou, Zhejiang	Changji, Xinjiang		
	12	Wuhu, Anhui	Xinxiang, Henan		
	13		Guiyang, Guizhou		
County level city	1		Changshu, Jiangsu	Jiangyin, Jiangsu	Jimo, Shandong
	2		Kunshan, Jiangsu	Danyang, Jiangsu	Haimen, Jiangsu
	3			Zhangjiagang, Jiangsu	Ningguo, Anhui
	4				Yiwu, Zhejiang

The vice provincial city, prefectural city and county-level city are different kinds of administrative areas in China.
In China, the administrative areas can be divided into several levels, the first level is the provincial level, and includes provinces, autonomous regions and municipalities; the second level is the prefecture level, and mainly includes the prefectural cities; the third level is the county level, and includes districts under the jurisdiction of cities, county-level cities, counties and autonomous counties; the forth level is the townships level, and includes towns and street communities.
The vice provincial cities are a type of special prefectural cities, and they belong to the provincial level. However, they receive special attention by the central government, for example the mayor of a vice provincial city is appointed and dismissed by the central government, and the administrative level of the mayor is a vice governor.
The county level city is part of the county level regions, which belong to prefectural cities.

References

Buesa M, Heijs J, Baumert T (2010) The determinants of regional innovation in Europe: a combined factorial and regression knowledge production function approach. Res Policy 39:722–735

Crarnitzki D, Hussinger K (2004) The link between R&D subsidies, R&D spending and technological performance. ZEW-Centre for European Economic Research Discussion Paper No. 04-056 (downloaded on 10 October 2015 from http://papers.ssrn.com/sol3/papers.cfm?abstract_id)

Deng XP (1983) Jiefang sixiang, shishi qiushi, tuanjie yizhi xiangqiankan (Liberate ideas, be practical, united toward the future). In: Deng Xiaoping Wenxuan (1975–1982) (Selected works of Deng Xiaoping [1975–1982]). People's Publishing House, Beijing

Dong T (2009a) What policy tools are right for prospering IPR creation? Concurrently discussing the social responsibility of creator of IPR. Kexuexue Yanjiu (Stud Sci Sci) 3:321–327

Dong T (2009b) On the relationship between the NIPS and Chinese economic development. Kexuexue Yanjiu (Stud Sci Sci) 5:641–652

Dong T (2013) The theoretical framework of IPR with Chinese characteristics. Zhishichanquan (Intellect Property) 5:7–18

Dong T (2014) Rethinking on the Chinese intellectual property policies. Zhishichanquan (Intellect Property) 3:57–60

Dutta S, Lanvin B, Wunsch-Vincent S (2015) The global innovation index 2015—effective innovation policies for development. (Downloaded on 15 Aug 2015 from http://www.wipo.int/publications/en/details.jsp?id=3978)

Ebersberger B (2004) Labor demand effect of public R&D funding. VTT working paper 9. Available at http://www.vtt.fi/inf/pdf/workingpapers/2004/W9.pdf

Eichera T, Garcia-Penalosa C (2008) Endogenous strength of intellectual property rights: implications for economic development and growth. Eur Econ Rev 52:237–258

Fan S, Kanbur R, Zhang X (2011) China's regional disparities: experience and policy. Rev Dev Finan 1(1):47–56

Fleisher BM, Zhou M (2010) Are patent laws harmful to developing countries? Evidence from China. Working Paper No. 09-07. Available at http://econ.ohio-state.edu/Fleisher/working_papers/PatentPaper_01_07_10.pdf

Gilbert RJ, Newbery DM (1982) Preemptive patenting and the persistence of monopoly power. Am Econ Rev 72(3):512–26

Guo J, Cao Z (2010) Construction and promotion tactics of evaluation system for intellectual property. Kexuexue yu Kexuejishu Guanli (Sci Sci Manag S&T) 3:31–38

Hall BH, Helmers C, von Graevenitz G et al (2013) A study of patent thickets. UK-IPO, South Wales. Available at https://www.gov.uk/government/uploads/system/uploads/attachment_data/file/311234/ipresearch-thickets.pdf

Hu AG, Jefferson GH (2009) A great wall of patents: what is behind China's recent patent explosion? J Dev Econ 90:57–68

Idris K (2003) Intellectual property: a power took of economic growth. WIPO Publication No. 888.1. Available at http://www.wipo.int/edocs/pubdocs/en/intproperty/888/wipo_pub_888_1.pdf

Intarakumnerd P, Charoenporn P (2015) Impact of stronger patent regimes on technology transfer: the case study of Thai automotive industry. Res Policy 44:1314–1326

Jaffe AB, Lerner J (2001) Reinvention public R&D: patent policy and the commercialization of national laboratory technologies. Rand J Econ 32:167–198

KIPO (2009) Annual report 2009. Korean Intellectual Property Office, Korean (downloaded on 5 July 2015 from http://www.kipo.go.kr/kpo/user.tdf?a=user.english.html.HtmlApp&c=60110&catmenu=ek07_01_01_10)

Li X (2009) China's regional innovation capacity in transition: an empirical approach. Res Policy 38:338–357

Li X (2012) Behind the recent surge of Chinese patent: an institutional view. Res Policy 41:236–249

Li X (2015) Specialization, institutions and innovation within China's regional innovation systems. Technol Forecast Soc Chang 100:130–139

Li W, Xia X (2011) The influence of patent promotion policy on regional patent growth: evidence from Ningbo. Kexuexue Yanjiu (Stud Sci Sci) 8:1176–1183

Long X, Wang J (2015) Motivation and quality effects of the patent upsurge in China. Shijie Jingji (World Econ) 6:115–142

Ma Z (2009) Rethinking on the objectives of intellectual property regime, the nature of patent and its institutional mission. Zhishichanquan (Intellect Property) 19(114):3–9

Mao H (2015) Theory and policy research on the patent implementation and industrialization. Yanjiu yu Fazhan Guanli (R&D Manag) 27(4):100–109

Peng M (2006) Establishment of the public policy system of intellectual property in China. Zhishichanquan (Intellect Property) 5:32–37

Prud'homme D (2012) Dulling the cutting edge: how patent-related policies and practices hamper innovation in China. European Chamber, MPRA paper No. 43299 (downloaded on 12 December 2014 from https://mpra.ub.uni-muenchen.de/43299/)

Sheng Y, Kong S (2012) An empirical study on the influences of intellectual property policy on technology innovation performance. Kexuexue Yanjiu (Stud Sci Sci) 11:1735–1740

SIPO (2012a) Nian quanguo zhuanli shili zhuangkuang baogao (Annual national patent strength status report). SIPO. Available from http://www.sipo.gov.cn/yw/2013/P020130426447058176596.pdf

SIPO (2012b) Nian quanguo zhishi chanquan fazhan zhuangkuang baogao (Annual national intellectual property development report). SIPO. Available from http://www.sipo.gov.cn/ztzl/ywzt/zlwzn/2012qgzscqfzzkbg.pdf

SIPO (2013) Nian quanguo zhuanli shili zhuangkuang baogao (Annual national patent strength status report). SIPO. Available from http://www.sipo.gov.cn/zscqgz/2014/201404/P020140429345620110367.pdf

Sleuwaegen L, Boiardi P (2014) Creativity and regional innovation: evidence from EU regions. Res Policy 43:1508–1522

Song W, Xu F et al (2012) Research on regional performance improvement of intellectual property policy from perspective of policy overflow: based on empirical analysis of China's 29 provinces. Kexuexue yu Kexuejishu Guanli (Sci Sci Manag S&T) 7:77–83

Suttmeier RP, Yao X (2011) China's IP transition: rethinking intellectual property rights in a rising China. The National Bureau of Asian Research, Special Report 29, Seattle and Washington, D. C. (downloaded on 14 Nov 2015 from http://www.nbr.org/publications/element.aspx?id=520)

Tang Y, Sun L (2006) Analysis of "sleeping patent" in patent conversion and its solution. Zhongguo Ruankexue (China Soft Sci) 8:73–78

Thomson Reuters (2015) China's IQ (innovation quotient), trends in patenting and the globalization of Chinese innovation. (Downloaded on 17 Oct 2015 from http://ip.thomsonreuters.com/sites/default/files/chinas-innovation-quotient.pdf)

Wang Z (2014) The 2014 China intellectual property index report (downloaded on 7 Dec 2015 from http://www.wipo.int/wipolex/en/details.jsp?id=15371)

Wang Q, Gao S (2015) Strategic motives of patent application-empirical evidence and policy implications. Yanjiu yu Fazhan Guanli (R&D Manag) 4:110–121

Warner E (2015) Patenting and innovation in China: Incentives, policy and outcomes. Pardee RAND Graduate School (downloaded on 3 May 2015 from http://www.rand.org/pubs/rgs_dissertations/RGSD347.html)

Wen X, Wang Y (2013) How to ward off the ache of "patent sleeping." People's daily overseas edition. Available from http://paper.people.com.cn/rmrbhwb/html/2013-01/05/content_1180558.htm

WIPO (2014) Summary of the study on patent's role in business strategies: research on Chinese companies' patenting motives, patent implementation and patent industrialization. CDIP/INF/8. Available from http://www.wipo.int/meetings/en/details.jsp?meeting_id=32087

Wu H (2001) Intellectual property law in the process of harmonious development of science and technology, economy and law. Faxue Yanjiu (Chin J Law) 6:128–148
Yan S, Yan S, Zhang M (2008) Forms of gender discrimination in firm's human resource development. Guanli Shijie (Manag World) 11:110–118
Yi Y (2007) Thinking on the establishment of the index system on evaluating intellectual property strategy. Zhishichanquan (Intellect Property) 1:32–36
Yuan X (2009) The causation of sleeping patents and its prevention. Kexue Yanjiu Guanli (Sci Res Manag) 4:168–174
Yuan Y (2012) Multi-dimensional effects of intellectual property policy—a new paradigm of policy process. University of Science and Technology of China, Hefei
Zhan A, Di Q (2013) A study on the driving forces and innovative capabilities behind China's patent explosion. Kexuexue Yanjiu (Stud Sci Sci) 10:1504–1511
Zhang H (2001) New characteristics of intellectual property protection in the process of economic globalization. Comp Econ Soc Syst 6:79–82
Zhou Y, Liu H (2010) Study on the synergetic operation model of IP public policy. Kexuexue Yanjiu (Stud Sci Sci) 3:351–356
Zhu X, Zhang C (2012) Patent subsidy policy: predicaments and outline for reform. J Zhejiang University (Humanit Soc Sci) 5:90–98

Chapter 12
Invention Patents Are Not for Everyone: Developing Less Industrialized Regions in China with 'Light' Intellectual Property

Zongzhen Jin and Haibo Liu

Abstract Intellectual property (IP) can be a main driver of regional technology innovation and economic development, but the IP needs of different regions vary. Invention patents have a significant influence on industrialized regions, especially new product and technological development in heavier industries. However, the cultivation of 'light IP' (designs, trademarks, copyrights, geographical indications, trade secrets, utility models, and new plant varieties) may be preferred over invention patents in regions rich in environmental resources and traditional culture, and where there is a desire to protect natural resources. Taking the green economic development of Lishui Prefecture in Zhejiang Province as a case study, the authors analyze how policies to encourage development and utilization of light IP enable the regional protection of the environment as well as economic growth. The approach of Lishui Prefecture is shown as an alternative development strategy to simply following central government-level advice to stimulate invention patents, and one that is useful for regions in China that are less industrialized but have rich natural resources.

Jin Zongzhen, Assistant Professor, China National Institute of Standardization; Ph.D. candidate, Chinese Academy of Sciences Institute of Policy and Management

Liu Haibo, Professor, Institute of Policy and Management, Chinese Academy of Sciences

---

Z. Jin
China National Institute of Standardization, Room 1021, No.4 Zhichun Road, Haidian District, Beijing 100191, China

Z. Jin (✉) · H. Liu (✉)
Center for IPR Research and Training, Institute of Policy and Management, Chinese Academy of Sciences, Room 419, No. 15 Zhongguancun Beiyitiao Alley, Haidian District, Beijing 100190, China
e-mail: jinzongzhen@126.com

H. Liu
e-mail: 13910310263@126.com

D. Prud'homme and H. Song (eds.), *Economic Impacts of Intellectual Property-Conditioned Government Incentives*, DOI 10.1007/978-981-10-1119-1_12

Keywords Patent · Light IP · Regional economic development · Development path · Green economy · Lishui Prefecture

12.1 Introduction

IP is an important tool to support, drive and facilitate the progression of technology and industrial development, and can have a direct positive effect on the market competitiveness of enterprises. However, IP is not the only type of property asset with value that is created from knowledge, as process innovation, and market behavior among other assets need to be considered. According to the concept and categorization defined by the World Intellectual Property Office (WIPO), IP refers to creations of the mind, and includes inventions, literary and artistic works, designs, symbols, names and images used in commerce, which all enable individuals to earn recognition or financial benefit from what they have invented or created.

Many scholars have studied the role of invention patents in relation to technological innovation and enterprise development, and generally conclude that invention patents are the most important indicator of regional science and technology capacity, and in driving industrial economic development (Liu and Buck 2007; Tsai et al. 2009; Malo 2009; Jin et al. 2012). However, comparatively far fewer papers have elaborated on the effects of non-invention patents and other forms of IP, such as trademarks, copyright, designs, geographical indications, and utility model patents, on market value, industrial innovation and economic development.

How does a patent, other than an invention patent, affect regional economic development? Is it more helpful to facilitate agricultural, forestry, tourism and leisure, and small-scale processing industries than an invention patent? Should localities with comparative advantages in light industry blindly follow central Chinese government policy advice by facilitating and promoting invention patents while ignoring the reality of their specific regional situation? Considering these questions, the key issue that we will consider and address in this chapter is how the appropriate form of IP may drive light industry development.

The objective of this chapter is to provide a better understanding of how regional governments use the various forms of IP to accelerate industrial development while taking into account their local conditions. Considering the fact that different regions have different modes of industrialized development, we have proposed a new development path, which is suitable for regions that are less industrialized and rich in natural resources. We construct and propose the theoretical concept of light IP, and analyze whether light IP is driving regional green economic development in Lishui Prefecture of Zhejiang Province. After studying the operational strategy concerning the light IP required by regions rich in natural resources and agricultural enterprises, we present our strategic thinking that light IP can drive regional green economic development, and can help address the contradictions between economic development and environmental degradation.

The chapter is organized as follows: Sect. 12.2 presents the different forms of IP required by different industries; Sect. 12.3 discusses the concept and connotation of light IP; Sect. 12.4 describes the economic decentralization and the government's IP-conditioned incentives in China; Sect. 12.5 details the research methodology; Sect. 12.6 focuses on the case study of light IP driving green growth in Lishui Prefecture; and Sect. 12.7 concludes and offers policy recommendations.

12.2 Different Types of IP for Different Industries

12.2.1 Invention Patents Promoting Economic Development

Following information retrieval and a technical review by the State Intellectual Property Office (SIPO), any invention for which an invention patent right in China is granted benefits from a 20-year period of protection, and must possess novelty, inventiveness and be capable of practical application. During the period of protection, the owner has the exclusive right to transfer, license, authorize, or abandon the patent. Additionally, the patentee is required to pay an annual fee for maintaining the patent protection. In China, utility models and registered designs are also considered to be patents, and their importance to the concept of light IPR is discussed in the next section.

Invention patents are closely related to the development of industrial and technical enterprises. Furthermore, invention patents have acted as the key performance indicator of regional science and technology capacity, and indicate the potential development and market competitiveness of a particular enterprise (Tsai et al. 2009; Malo 2009; Jin et al. 2012). One study concluded that invention patents are an imperfect measure of the total level of innovation in a given district (Furman et al. 2002). However, another study concluded that the number of patents can also be taken as an indicator of research productivity, despite the wide skepticism (Rassenfosse and Potterie 2009). The number of inventions owned can be used as an indicator of industrial innovation and technology advancement. Based on a review of the relevant literature, invention patents have been found to promote regional economic development as indicated by technology transfer, knowledge accumulation and legal protection.

Invention patents play a crucial role in the rapid development of certain industries, and especially in the chemical and pharmaceutical industries and sophisticated machinery industry.[1] One study found that invention patents and trade

[1]Invention patents are also heavily utilized in the ICT industry, although scholars have suggested that such usage creates patent thickets, which actually may discourage innovation and economic development (Cecere et al. 2014; Rentocchini 2011).

secrets were used by large chemical companies to protect new chemical products, and capture the market in the 19th century (Arora 1997). For the pharmaceutical industry, invention patents are essential. Without patent protection for a newly developed drug it would be impossible to recoup the significant investment necessary to bring the new drug to market (Luthi and Brice 2015). Invention patents are also important for industries concerned with the development of sophisticated machinery (Karvonen et al. 2016; Petroni and Panciroli 2002).

An increasing number of invention patents and regional knowledge accumulation and technology transfer will accelerate growth in industrialized regions and enhance companies' competitiveness. When analyzing the relationship between the number of invention patents held and the knowledge variance and performance of a company, one study found that the number of invention patents can indicate a company's degree of innovation, and can assist companies in creating new products and for new markets. This can be termed 'combinatorial innovation' (Li et al. 2014a). From the above, it can be seen that knowledge of an invention has a positive consequence on a company's performance.

The commercial activities of regional technological companies are effectively supported by the invention patent granted (Johnson and Liu 2011). In order to protect an inventor's property, the government provides a legal institution for protecting inventions and provides measures for law enforcement. The patentee has the exclusive right to manufacture, sell and use the invention patent, which facilitates the commercialization of scientific and technological achievements. This explicit invention patent right and enforcement protection helps researchers to utilize their invention patent, contributing to technology innovation, transfer and industrialization.

Although inventive activity has a significant effect on regional technological and economic development in developed regions, it has only a limited influence in developing regions. A study exploring the different effects of technology innovation capacity on regional economic growth found that the number of invention patent applications has a weaker impact on regional GDP growth than utility model and design applications, and the same effect is observed when considering industrial added value (Zhu and Zhang 2005).

As further discussed in the next section, there may be two main reasons why invention patents play different roles in improving the economy in developing and developed regions. Firstly, developed regions have an important advantage over developing regions as they are more capable of absorbing patent information, resulting in a greater accumulation of knowledge and technology. Secondly, invention patents are preferred by companies in developed regions compared with companies in developing regions. Due to a lower level of IP protection and enforcement in developing regions, the practice of copying and counterfeiting will discourage investment in technological development, leading to less technological achievement and commercial innovation.

12.2.2 Regional Development Through Specialization, and Utilization of Other Types of IP

Different types of IP have different economic impacts on different industries. Various forms of IP, other than invention patents, can enable sustainable economic development and social well-being in some developing regions. These regions may have a strong comparative advantage in the areas of agriculture, forestry, tourism and leisure, art and handicrafts, and small-scale processing industries distinct from the chemical and pharmaceutical industries. They may particularly benefit from IP outside invention patents, such as utility models and design patents, trademarks, geographical indications, and copyrights.

Other forms of IP have two prominent advantages over invention patents in developing regions. Firstly, they are cheaper and take less time to obtain and require a lower threshold of knowledge. Secondly, because the technical content is low, it is easier to identify and establish whether IP has been counterfeited or infringed. As mentioned below, these other forms of IP can have a close relationship with natural resources and traditional culture, both of which share particular geographical properties. Therefore, these other forms of IP can have geographical characteristics but little technical content to be identified and understood. As a result, these other forms of IP appear to be more suited than invention patents in terms of the lower degree of knowledge innovation required, and their ability to provide legal protection.

Different forms of IP have distinct effects on regional economic development.[2] In one study the correlation between technology innovation and economic growth was examined, using panel data from 31 provinces from 1985 to 2004 (Huang and Yu 2007). Some interesting results were found: utility model patents have the greatest impact on regional economic growth, with design patents coming second and invention patents having the least impact. In the context of a lack of investment into independent R&D and innovation capability, the findings of another study also show that utility model and design patents are more advantageous in encouraging technological progress (Xia et al. 2012).

Geographical indications have a prominent role in both the macro and micro aspects of modern agriculture. From the macro perspective, by constructing a regression model using data from the second national geographical indication research project, it was found that geographical indications contribute to agricultural economic development, specialization and scaled production (Li et al. 2014b). From the micro perspective, using a case study of Guanxi's pomelo industry in Pinghe, Fujian Province, the deep impact of geographical indications on the

[2]The same findings are found to be particularly prominent in relation to small and medium enterprises (Sui et al. 2005; Yuan and Liu 2014; Sukarmijan and Sapong 2014); (SCT). It is clear from the previously mentioned studies that what small- and medium-sized enterprises need the most in order to produce new products and expand their markets, are utility model and design patents, and copyright protection.

county's economy was emphasized, which demonstrates that they are essential in conserving the local ecological system, the regional historical tradition, and cultural psychology (Sun 2012). Additionally, trademarks and copyright also have a promotional effect on the food and beverage economy and the development of enterprises.

Traditional knowledge, trademarks, and copyrights are important in driving relevant industries forward in developing countries. Therefore, developing countries should seek to protect these forms of IP. Several authors believe that with the help of IP protection, traditional culture and art and handicrafts, are powerful factors in promoting regional economic development (Zhou and Wang 2011). Other authors state that trademark and geographical indications play a crucial role in transferring resource advantages into market advantages (Li and Dong 2009). A further study illustrates that the culture and art of the She ethnic minority is an important and crucial asset in attracting tourists and in selling their unique art works all over the world, thereby driving regional economic development, which in turn will help to protect and preserve traditional culture and knowledge (Wu et al. 2003).

In conclusion, we find that various forms of IP, other than invention patents, can be more efficient in protecting agricultural trade, a company's brand, and traditional knowledge. It is also understood that agricultural and forestry product processing companies also prefer these other forms of IP, mainly due to the low barrier of entry and the high strength of legal protection that they confer.

12.3 The Concept of 'Light IP'

Through a theoretical study of the relationship between IP and regional industrial economic structure, we have found that invention patents have a significant positive effect on heavy chemical, pharmaceutical, and sophisticated machinery manufacturing industries, while other forms of IP not only efficiently drive the development of the agricultural and forestry product processing industries and other light industries, but also promote the protection of the natural environment and traditional culture. Considering the properties and applications of these other forms of IP, we have proposed the new concept of 'light IP', which represents a new path to growth, and a new opportunity to apply the government's IP development strategies to develop regional light industry.

Light IP rights can be considered as a form of IP rights providing protection when industrial external-design,[3] regional traditional resources (including natural resource and human culture) are to be commercially exploited. The scope of light IP includes the main forms of IP, other than invention patents. Namely, these are

[3]Industrial external-design means the IP highly related to product trade, and which makes the product visually appealing to the customer. This IP can include utility model patents, design patents, trademarks, and software copyrights, etc.

design patents, geographical indications, trademarks (including community trademarks and certification marks), copyright, trade secrets, utility model patents, and new plant varieties.

The name 'light IP' was chosen because the targets to be covered and protected by light IP are those found in the light industries, traditional knowledge, and the natural resource and forestry processing industry, and not in heavier industries with higher technological advancement entry barriers. In terms of the application and grant procedures, light IP applications generally do not require a particularly substantive examination. Furthermore, in terms of resource usage, light IP typically requires less investment in manpower and material resources to fund product and service research and development and enable IP protection. Light IP is different to invention patents, as the latter concern high technology, strong innovation and large investment into R&D. Invention patents are more embodied in physical technology and innovation equipment, while light IP, such as copyright and trademarks etc., is reflected in ideas, signs and through other mediums.

In general, light IP reflects the attributes of lower investment into R&D, in terms of typically shorter examination timelines, and the relative ease of identifying infringement compared with invention patents. As such, they are typically easier to protect under the law. The agricultural and forestry product processing industries, as well as some other light industries, are dominated by small and medium-size enterprises. Therefore, these enterprises with typically low R&D investment, will favor light IP, which will help to protect their intangible assets.

Based on the typical path of development of enterprises in regions that are rich in natural resources and less heavily industrialized, we propose the concept of light IP. In districts specializing in the heavy industries, particularly those mentioned in Sect. 12.2.1, IP strategy tends to involve invention patents and utility model patents. This 'technical IP' is useful in renewing technical equipment, promoting the application of technology, and in exploiting new products. In contrast, in districts that are less heavily industrialized and have limited heavy large-scale industrial capability but are rich in natural resources, the regional IP strategy has to rely on light IP. This includes trademarks, copyright, geographical indications, design patents, new plant varieties, and perhaps utility models patents, and aligns with the demand of regional industries, and will help drive regional industrial development and protection of the environment.

12.4 IP-Conditioned Government Incentives in China's System of Economic Decentralization

According to geographical location and culture, China is divided into three regions: the east, middle, and west regions. Regional divisions also exist when considering economic development. In first position, the per capita GDP of Tianjin City reached 116,700 RMB in 2014, which is twice that of 11th-placed Jilin Province with

50,200 RMB, approximately three times that of 21st-placed Heilongjiang Province with 39,200 RMB, and more than four times that of 31st-placed Gansu Province with 26,430 RMB.[4] In addition, differences in natural resources, and historical and cultural factors have exacerbated the imbalance in regional economic development.

It is difficult for the Chinese central government to issue a uniform science and technology policy that is fit for every region, due to the large territory of the country, different economic levels, and different domestic cultures. This has resulted in the creation of a system of economic decentralization, whereby regional governments can often decide how exactly they want to implement the industrial policies made by the central-government, amending and adjusting them to their own local needs and capabilities. Nonetheless, some local governments simply blindly follow central-level government IP policy, ignoring local science and technology capacity, industrial development and the cultural environment in their region, which can lead to a sub-optimal and even negative influence upon the harmonious development of the economy and society.

In order to guide the development of a national innovation system, the National IP Strategy 2014–2020 was recently issued by the central government. The expected targets of the National IP Strategy were set, with the predominant aim of improving the number of invention patents. However, that being said, geographical indications, trademarks, new plant varieties, copyright, and design patents are also generally suggested as tools to drive the development of modern agriculture and an upgrading of the industry. The central government has advised regional governments that in order to implement the National IP Strategy 2014–2020, they should undertake appropriate measures to create, manage, utilize, and enforce IP in order to develop local industry.

Lishui Prefecture, which is one of cities in Zhejiang Province and rich in natural resources, traditional knowledge and ethnic culture, has issued many policies directed and tailored to its own local needs to promote light IP by using tax reduction, fiscal subsidies, and public preferential procurement. For example, in order to protect rare mushroom resources, the local government actively provides support to local industry associations so that they can apply for a national famous trademark and a geographical indication designation. Local government and IP offices have garnered support from SIPO to obtain for the prefecture the title of 'National IPR Model Pilot County of Traditional Knowledge' in relation to famous traditional arts and crafts, such as 'Longquan celadon' and swords. We use the light IP strategy of Lishui Prefecture as a case study to demonstrate that local governments can and should choose an IP strategy that is appropriate and tailored to local

[4]There are 31 provinces in China. In order to easily analyze the economic decentralization, the provinces of China are divided into three groups according to their per capital GDP. The high-income group covers the top ten provinces of Tianjin, Beijing, Shanghai, Jiangsu, Inner Mongolia, Liaoning, Fujian, Guangdong and Shandong; the middle-income group includes Jilin, Chongqing, Hubei, Shaanxi, Ningxia, Xinjiang, Hunan, Hebei, Qinghai, Hainan; the third income group consists of Heilongjiang, Henan, Shanxi, Sichuan, Jiangxi, Anhui, Guangxi, Xizang, Yunnan, Guizhou and Gansu.

circumstances to drive regional industrial development, rather than simply blindly following central government policy that is not completely suited to local conditions.

12.5 Methodology

It is difficult to analyze the relationship between light IP and the regional development of certain industries, such as agriculture, forestry, tourism and leisure, furniture, arts and handicrafts, and small-scale processing industries in China, from a macro perspective. Given that China covers a vast geographical area, using national-level data to analyze the relationship between light IP and industry-driven prosperity inevitably ignores the regional economic disparities in China and will lead to improperly informed conclusions. A reasonable method to robustly analyze the relationship between light IP and industrial development is to identify a specific region for case study analysis, taking account of socioeconomic and eco-environmental factors. In light of these considerations, Lishui Prefecture was selected as the basis for the case study in this chapter.

More specifically, Lishui Prefecture was selected for two main reasons. Firstly, Lishui Prefecture is not heavily industrialized, and it has rich ecological resources and traditional knowledge. In line with the concepts discussed in Sects. 12.2 and 12.3 above, these circumstances make Lishui an ideal location in which to attempt a light IP-driven development strategy. Secondly, the Lishui Prefecture government adjusts the central government's science and technology policy to adapt to the needs of local industry and cultural development, while being mindful of the importance of avoiding significant environmental degradation. Some of these policies can be generally considered as forms of IP-conditioned government incentives, the topic of the book in which this chapter is published. In line with the concepts discussed in Sect. 12.4 above, taking advantage of the economic decentralization afforded to regional policymakers in such a way can help ensure the ultimate effectiveness of Lishui's regional development policy.

Company-level interviews and interviews with government officials at the local science and technology department in Lishui are used as the main data sources for our case study. We conducted more than 32 on-the-ground and in-depth interviews with local entrepreneurs and companies identified by the local government as operating in dominant industries and importantly contributing to economic and cultural development in Lishui. The semi-structured interviews focused on how managers use their IP strategy to promote enterprise development and which forms of IP play a crucial role in their business operations. These interviewees operated in the agricultural, furniture, arts and handicrafts and small-scale materials processing industries. The statistics in Sect. 12.6 provide more details on the importance of these industries and companies. We also interviewed more than 35 government officials in charge of science and technology policymaking and administration in

Lishui about regional IP strategy and the coordination of central government IP polices and the local economic situation.

In addition, a range of economic and IP statistics were collected from government databases. These were analyzed to provide a quantitative context to the case study.

12.6 Case Study Examining Light IP as a Driver of Green Growth in Lishui Prefecture

12.6.1 Current Status of Lishui Prefecture

When studying the relationship between IP and regional green economic development, we found that Lishui Prefecture, with the highest percentage of forest coverage and making up the largest area in Zhejiang Province, effectively uses light IP to facilitate green economic development. Nestled between the Oujiang River to the south and surrounded by mountains on all sides, Lishui is situated in the southwest of Zhejiang Province. Lishui Prefecture administers two cities, Lishui and Longquan; one district, Liandu; and seven counties, Qingtian, Jinyun, Yunhe, Qingyuan, Suichang, Songyang, and Jingning Autonomous County of the She minority people. In total, Lishui has a population of 2,506,600. The prefecture is bordered by Fujian Province to the south, and Wenzhou to the southeast. The region of Lishui is mainly covered by low mountains and rolling hills. Of the 17,298 km^2 making up Lishui, 88.42 % is mountainous, 5.52 % is farmland, and 6.06 % is comprised of roads, villages, and streams. The local area is rich in traditional culture, crafts, agricultural and forestry resources, and tourist-related natural resources.

In 2013, the GDP of Lishui Prefecture had reached 98.31 billion RMB, and the per capita GDP was close to 464,000 RMB. In terms of industrial structure, the shares of the primary, secondary and tertiary industries that make up the GDP are 8.6, 50.6 and 40.8 % respectively, and they have all been stable over recent years. The proportion of agricultural products in the primary industry is as high as 65.11 %. Furthermore, the scale of forestry products, animal husbandry and fishery products is 16.2, 16.1 and 1.8 %, respectively. Manufacturing enterprises have been transferred mainly from Wenzhou Prefecture of Zhejiang Province, and the industry is dominated by small and medium enterprises. The added value of tertiary industry has contributed up to 41 % of the city's GDP over the last 10 years. Tourists are mainly domestic, and represent 99.4 % of all tourists. The tourism industry has maintained its rapid growth, but the origin polarization effect also exists: domestic tourists spend 502.6 RMB per head while each foreign tourist spends 14,707.3 RMB.

The local government has enforced its development concept 'Nature is the true treasure'. The development of environmental industries has become important.

Table 12.1 The district distribution and the dominant industries of Lishui Prefecture in 2013

District distribution	Dominant industry
Liandu District	agricultural products, household chemicals, machinery processing, electronic equipment
Longquan City	tourism, wood processing, celadon swords, green food, pharmaceutical chemicals, metal auto parts
Qingtian County	tourism, stone carving, metal processing, shoes, electrical machinery, mineral products
Yunhe County	tourism, wooden toys, mushroom products, fruit products, small hydro, metal processing, bearing products
Qingyuan County	wood products, green food, pencils, water and electricity industries
Jinyun County	band sawing, special machinery and equipment industry, metal industry
Suichang County	wood products, metal auto parts, stainless steel, precision machinery, electric car & bike parts
Songyang County	tourism, tea industry
Jingning She Autonomous County	tourism, ethnic cultural products

Source Data collected from Lishui Prefecture Science and Technology Office

These industries specialize in agriculture, forestry, tourism and leisure, furniture, arts and handicrafts, and also include the small-scale processing industries. The main industries of each district of Lishui Prefecture can be seen in Table 12.1.

The dominant industries of each county were identified according to their contribution to the county's GDP, and can be seen in Table 12.1. Tourism is the important industry in supporting the regional economy of Longquan City, Yunhe County, Qingtian County, Songyang County and Jingning She Autonomous County. Typical products produced by Lishui Prefecture's primary and tertiary industries include wood, agricultural, and ethnic cultural products. Furthermore, we found that the most common dominant industries of every county are mainly those belonging to the natural tourist resource, the agricultural and forestry resource processing, and the traditional culture industries. While metal processing, machinery, and a few other industries are also important, they are only important to a lesser extent.

Figures 12.1 and 12.2 show the number of patent applications and granted patents over a recent three-year period. The total number of applications and granted patents (invention patents, utility model and design patents) is increasing, and the average rates of increase are 36.14 and 48.72 %, respectively. At less than 8 %, invention patents comprise a small proportion of the total number of patents, and an especially small proportion of the number of granted patents, which have experienced relatively no growth over the three-year period. Utility model patents make up the highest proportion of the total number of patents, which includes both applications and granted patents. From Figs. 12.1 and 12.2, we can calculate that design patents rank second to utility model patents, in terms of number. The average annual growth rate of most recently granted design patents (61 %) is higher

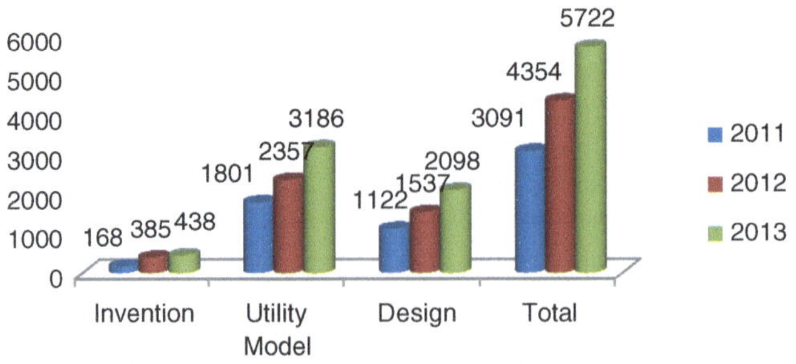

Fig. 12.1 The number of patent applications in Lishui Prefecture from 2011 to 2013. *Source* Data collected from Lishui Prefecture Science and Technology Office

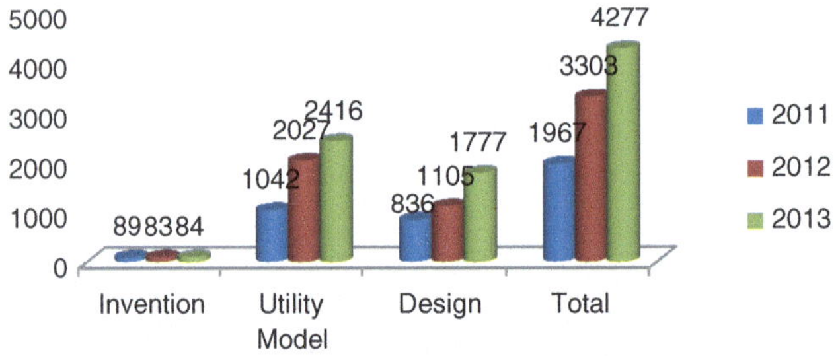

Fig. 12.2 The number of granted patents in Lishui Prefecture from 2011 to 2013. *Source* Data collected from Lishui Prefecture Science and Technology Office

than that of the most recently granted utility model patents (18 %), and much higher than the number of granted invention patents (only 1 %).

Comparing Table 12.1 with Figs. 12.1 and 12.2, the relationship between the dominant industries of each county and the number of patents can be identified. Utility model and design patents are two forms of patent that contain a comparatively low level of technological innovation. As important components of light IP, applications for utility model and design patents by local enterprises are suitable for economic needs. In addition, the number of utility model and design patents is also increasing with the development of light industry.

12.6.2 *Light IP Promotes Economic Development*

The prosperity of enterprises determines how investable they are, and is a good indicator of the regional economic development of Lishui Prefecture. Because enterprises are responsible for regional economic development and also for creations of the mind, IP can therefore provide an important guarantee for companies, and legal protection of their technological innovation. Amidst the arrival of the 'new normal' in China, market competition is increasing every day. IP is not only an effective tool for companies to use to defend themselves against third party misappropriation of their assets, but it can also be one of several important tools used by an enterprise to develop new products and compete, which is an essential part of a successful business operations strategy.

In considering an application to register IP, enterprises will fully take into account the costs and benefits that the IP may provide. To maximize profits, companies will apply for the most appropriate form of IP in order to enlarge their market share. In this regard, they will consider factors such as cost, how to best safeguard their rights, and their economic interests. In addition, IP rights are a form of intangible assets. When companies are awarded IP, they not only use their technical knowledge to manufacture and develop new products, but they should also maximize the economic benefit through a variety of methods, such as licensing and pledge financing, for example. Based on the research above, we conclude that the characteristics of light IP make it more fitting than invention patents to enterprise development in Lishui.

Because of variations in natural resources and industrial agglomeration, the IP strategies of different regions show differentiation. For the regions where light industry is dominant, light IP can be an important part of the regional strategy and can cultivate modern industry that is suitable for the demands of economic development.

Through our interviews, we have found that enterprises have improved their light IP strategy in order for it to be effectively utilized for developing products, participating in market competition, and gaining further market share. Companies with a high share of the export market tend to be more concerned about light IP in the course of their operations in the market, such as design rights and trademarks. The local government in Lishui gradually realized that IP should be suitable for the needs of local enterprises. With the support of the government in Lishui, some agricultural associations were founded to apply for geographical indications and collective trademarks, which contribute to the added value of products and improve market competitiveness. Both utility model patents and design patents play an important role in protecting production facilities and in making improvement to packaging for the trade of products.

When considering the protection of light IP, Lishui's enterprises adopt a variety of strategies, which can include collaboration concerning local technology and business administration. For electronic commerce tort violations, enterprises can make full use of light IP infringement characteristics. For example, such violations are easily found and identified, and cooperation with the business platform leads to safeguarding the legitimate rights and interests of enterprises.

Most of Lishui's small and medium enterprises specialize in light industry, such as services, forestry and agriculture, and resource manufacturing. The number of large enterprises with heavy industry and high-end equipment manufacturing is low due to dynamics in the economic base and natural resources. These reasons have led to particular IP applications and IP enforcement strategies being adopted by Lishui enterprises, which place more emphasis on the operational management of light IP. To analyze the operational IP situation, information on the business situation of the largest ten enterprises in Lishui Prefecture, in terms of the number of IP applications filed, were collected. Collectively, these represent 16.76 % all IP applications made in Lishui. As discussed above, design patents and trademarks are preferred by Lishui enterprises, which possess a low technical content and can be easily used to protect intangible assets. More details are shown in Table 12.2.

Most of our interviews focused on the role and importance of light IP to enterprises' revenue and growth strategy. In general, enterprises favor light IP, which is suitable for future strategy development, and is helpful in increasing operating income because the majority of companies in Lishui belong to the light industrial sector. The focus of local government and companies has turned to the application and protection of light IP. Our interviews indicated that light IP is an efficient protection tool to increase market sales of products produced by these industries, and has become key to gain market competitiveness, and is clearly a preferred option over invention patents. Light IP plays a foundational role in upgrading industry and in the regional economic development of Lishui Prefecture.

From Table 12.2, we can see that the number of IP applications made by enterprises far exceed those made by colleges. The number of design patents accounts for 65.85 % of all patent applications for the top ten enterprises. The main business interests of these enterprises belong to the agricultural, forestry and the small processing industries. Designs are important to the abovementioned industries, hence why the local government and enterprises prefer design patents.

In addition, nine geographical indications have been granted in total to Yunhe County Fungus, Longquan City Ganoderma Lucidum, Longquan City Celadon, Qingyun County Mushroom, Chuzhou[5] White Lotus, Jinyun County Sheldrake, Songyang County Tea, Jingning County Tea, and Suichang County Bamboo Charcoal. The nine geographical indications provide great impetus to the agricultural and forestry products trade, which are the foundation of the local resource-based industries. Indeed, from our interviews we identified that geographical indications are essential to product price and market competitiveness. Further, geographical indications help enable 'green' products to enter domestic and foreign markets.

As indicated in Table 12.2, most of the enterprises that are top patent filers in Lishui also obtained status as having national famous brands, provincial famous trademarks, and/or prefecture famous trademarks. These light IP rights were reported to be important tools in the marketing strategy of these companies to increase their competitiveness.

Our interviews identified that the enterprises in Lishui Prefecture that are important contributors to the local economy are able to use their light IP to good effect. Light IP allows them to charge increased product prices, enhance their corporate image, and more generally expand in the domestic market and, in some cases foreign markets. In addition to these key points above, enterprises may prefer

[5]Chuzhou is the ancient name of Lishui City.

Table 12.2 The top 10 enterprises in terms of number of IP applications in Lishui Prefecture in 2013

Ranking	IP applicant	Total patent applications (invention, utility model, designs)	Designs as percentage of total patent applications	Brand qualification	Main business	Product market	Company headquarters
1	Zhejiang Nice Group	405	94.81	Chinese famous brand, Lishui Prefecture famous trademark	daily use detergents	China	Liandu District
2	Lishui University	279	25.81	N/A	education	China	Liandu District
3	Zhejiang Start Children's Products company	238	85.29	China's top ten brand of children's shoes	children's clothing shoes and hats	China	Qingtian County
4	Yunhe County Wood Co., Ltd	233	93.56	Lishui Prefecture famous trademark	wooden toys	China, Europe, Southeast Asian	Yunhe County
5	Zhejiang Mulolo Toys Co., Ltd	210	59.52	N/A	wooden toys, crafts	North America, European	Yunhe County
6	Zhejiang Jiuchuan Bamboo & Wood Co., Ltd	198	47.47	Lishui Prefecture famous trademark	bamboo and wood products	China	Qingyuan County
7	Zhejiang Xinyun Wood Industry Group Co., Ltd	185	35.68	Zhejiang Province famous trademark, Lishui Prefecture famous trademark	wooden toys, crafts	China, elsewhere overseas	Yunhe County

(continued)

Table 12.2 (continued)

Ranking	IP applicant	Total patent applications (invention, utility model, designs)	Designs as percentage of total patent applications	Brand qualification	Main business	Product market	Company headquarters
8	Zhejiang Yearcon Company	173	97.11	Chinese famous brand, Zhejiang Province well-known company	leather shoes	China	Qingtian County
9	Lishui Vocational & Technical College	141	0.71	N/A	education	China	Liandu District
10	Zhejiang Suncha Bamboo Co., Ltd	134	85.82	Chinese famous brand, Zhejiang Province famous trademark	bamboo and wood products	China, Southeast Asian	Qingyuan County
Total		2196	65.85				

Source Data collected from Lishui Prefecture Science and Technology Office light IP in order to achieve a balance between light IP resource input and economic performance output, reasonably using both their own internal resources and external natural resources. Therefore by using light IP, enterprises are able to effectively promote and develop their product's marketing strategy while also contributing to regional eco-friendly economic development.

12.6.3 Government Policies for Promoting Light IP

The interviewees from the government held the belief that light IP is essential to their region's leading industries and companies' main business, and also benefit the local specialized economy as they have a low technology threshold requirement and are comparatively easy to protect. Therefore, they are suitable for the agricultural, forestry, tourism and leisure, furniture, arts and handicrafts, and small-scale processing industries.

According to the light IP requirements of local enterprises, Lishui Prefecture government has issued various policies to encourage the development of light IP, and especially to support local famous trademarks, geographical indications, and other types of IP. Some of the major polices are listed in Table 12.3. The related policies concerning trademarks include 'Lishui Prefecture Brand Trademark

Table 12.3 Key IP-related policies issued by Lishui Prefecture Government

Year issued	Title of administrative policy	Key points of policy
2005	Temporary measures of professional brand base recognition and management in Lishui Prefecture	Develop brand strategy, and foster economic development continuously and healthily
2009	Trademark pledge loan guidance in Lishui Prefecture	Implement city brand prospering strategy, and expand the financing sources
2011	Interim measures for the identification and management of IP demonstration enterprises in Lishui Prefecture	Improve the IP operation level of companies, and promote domestic innovation and industrial upgrading
2014	Temporary administration measures of new agricultural breeding varieties special fund in Lishui Prefecture	Promote agricultural, scientific and technical innovation, develop ecological agriculture, and strengthen environmental protection and ecological construction
2015	Implementation opinion on promoting protection of products of ecological origin in Lishui Prefecture	Take measures to protect products of ecological origin, promote special industrial upgrading and build own brands
2015	Implementation opinion on mass entrepreneurship to promote employment in Lishui Prefecture	Use the IP to pull mass entrepreneurship, promote transformation of science & technology achievement and activate entrepreneurial passion

Source Data collected from Lishui Prefecture Science and Technology Office

Development Strategic Planning', and 'Lishui Prefecture Famous Trademark Identification and Protection Measures', which integrate administrative and fiscal measures. Moreover, financial subsidies and tax exemptions are also used to encourage enterprises to apply for design patents.

Several other policies and programs have been instituted in order to encourage and to develop light IP in Lishui. Making full use of natural geographical resources, the government has applied for five geographical indications, which are granted by the State Quality Inspection Administration. In order to protect famous mushrooms, wooden toys, ethnic minority products and other special local products, the government encourages farmers and entrepreneurs to establish professional associations and strengthen the construction of local technical supporting stations. For the better protection of traditional knowledge and natural resources, the local government has set up a special steering group to monitor and report on the work of the 'National IPR Model Pilot County of Traditional Knowledge', the aim of which is to improve the management and level of protection of regional IP by SIPO. Furthermore, with the deterioration of the ecological environment and as the ecological crisis intensifies elsewhere in China, the government has invested more in publicizing the importance of the concept of light IP-driven regional green economic development.

Our interviews with entrepreneurs and government officials in Lishui in charge of monitoring the policies and programs mentioned above, generally indicated their belief that most of these policies were helpful for encouraging Lishui's enterprises to become more competitive domestically and even to expand abroad. The fact that the policies are specifically focused on developing light IP, which the entrepreneurs relied upon heavily in order to grow their business, rather than prioritizing the filing of invention patents, was identified as an important aspect of the policies. While future research should examine the different policies in more depth and consider how they function to encourage the development of light IP and whether they can be improved, the fundamental finding that light IP can increase the competitiveness of enterprises is a main takeaway from our research.

12.7 Conclusions and Policy Recommendations

Our analysis finds that Chinese localities with comparative advantages in lighter industries should consider primarily promoting light IP rights with their IP policies, including IP-conditioned government incentives, rather than blindly following central government-level policy advice to strongly promote invention patents. This does not necessarily mean these governments should discourage invention patenting. Rather, invention patents should not be as strongly promoted as part of these local governments' economic development strategies.

The traditional heavy chemical development model has led to a poor quality environment and rampant pollution in China. Therefore, using a development model that results in even further environmental pollution to promote economic development is no longer justifiable to lead China's future development. Regions such as Lishui that specialize in agricultural and forestry products, tourism and other light industries often have comparative advantages and capabilities in these industries. And light IP can be better suited than invention patents to developing these industries. Therefore, there is an opportunity to use government policies to support the development and utilization of light IP rights to enable both economic development and environmental protection in such regions. If light IP is developed strategically, it can contribute to sustainable economic development while protecting and optimizing environmental conditions. Our study of Lishui's development illustrates this paradigm.

In order to realize the greater effect of light IP on regional economic development, two approaches can be taken. First, enterprises in regions with economic and environmental conditions similar to Lishui should cultivate their knowledge and awareness of light IP, follow the 'Rules of Enterprises' IPR Management'[6] in order to perfect their light IP management system, and invest more resources into light IP operation.

Second, the government should realize the differentiated demand for different types of IP from different regions based on their local natural resources and industrial bases, and craft IP support policies accordingly. The number of invention patents, used as the key performance indicator of regional science and technology capacity, may be not appropriate, and may even have a negative effect on natural resource-intensive regions. Therefore, the central-level policy and advice should be replaced by IP strategies that better achieve balanced development among different regions. Such a strategy may include support for high-quality intermediary consulting services, increased government subsidies for light IP, improved pledge financing, and the establishment of an information service platform. However, these policies should of course be carefully formulated in order to ensure that they provide support to enterprises that truly need it, while at the same time limiting the possibility of potential adverse incentives created by inappropriately formulated policies.

References

Arora A (1997) Patents, licensing, and market structure in the chemical industry. Res Policy 26:391–403

Cecere G, Nicoletta C, Cédric G, Muge O (2014) Technological pervasiveness and variety of innovators in Green ICT: a patent-based analysis. Res Policy 10:1827–1839

Furman J, Poter M, Stern S (2002) The determinants of national innovative capacity. Res policy 31:899–933

Huang Z, Yu P (2007) The panel data study of technical innovation's effect on economic development of China in recent years. Sci Technol Manage Res 5:74–77

[6]Rules of Enterprises' IPR management are the first Chinese national standards concerning enterprises' IPR management, and were drafted and issued by SIPO in 2013 [http://www.cneip.org.cn/zt/gb/].

Jin Z, Liu H, Wei T (2012) Innovation performance of high-tech industry in China. J Beijing Inst Technol 21:9–16
Johnson WHA, Liu Q (2011) Patenting and the role of technology markets in regional innovation in China: an empirical analysis. J High Technol Manage Res 22:14–25
Karvonen M, Rahul K, Antti U, Ville O (2016) Technology competition in the internal combustion engine waste heat recovery: a patent landscape analysis. J Clean Prod 112:3735–3743
Li Y, Dong W (2009) The application of trademark and geographic indication in the development of agricultural industrialization. Rural Econ 7:47–49
Li Y, Ma L, Yuan X (2014a) The relationship among the patent number, knowledge variance and performance of enterprise. J Inf 2:194–200
Li Q, Zhao S, Yan X (2014b) Empirical study of agricultural economic development promoted by geographical indication in China. Econ Surv 3:26–30
Liu X, Buck T (2007) Innovation performance and channels for international technology spillovers: evidence from Chinese high-tech industries. Res Policy 36:355–366
Luthi R, Brice C (2015) Protection of inventions in medical chemistry. In: Wermuth CG, Aldous D, Raboisson P, Rognan D (eds) The practice of medicinal chemistry, 4th edn. Academic Press, Cambridge, pp 843–862
Malo S (2009) The contribution of (not so) public research to commercial innovations in the field of combinatorial chemistry. Res Policy 38:957–970
Petroni A, Panciroli B (2002) Innovation as a determinant of suppliers' roles and performances: an empirical study in the food machinery industry. Eur J Purchasing Supply Manage 3:135–149
Rassenfosse G, Potterie B (2009) A policy insight into the R&D-patent relationship. Res Policy 38:779–792
Rentocchini F (2011) Sources and characteristic of software patents in the European Union: some empirical considerations. Inf Econ Policy 1:141–157
Sui G, Shen M, Song J (2005) Study of high-tech industrialization based on the regional disparity of patent. Manag World 8:87–93, 169
Sukarmijian S, Sapong OV (2014) The importance of intellectual property for SMEs. Challenges and moving forward. UMK Procedia (international agribusiness marketing conference 2013), vol 1, pp 74–81
Sun Q (2012) Geographic logo products and county economic development. J Nanjing Agric Univ (Soc Sci Ed) 1:37–42
Tsai Y, Lin JY, Kurekova L (2009) Innovation R&D and option investment under uncertainty in high-tech industries: an implication for emerging economies. Res Policy 38:1388–1395
Wu M, Zhu J, Mo Y, Wang P (2003) Push regional tourism development by minority's traditional culture. J Lishui Teachers Coll 1:10–12, 71
Xia X, Li W, Zhang H (2012) An empirical study on the effect of different kinds of patents on technology progress of China. Sci Technol Manag Res 15:189–193
Yuan J, Liu J (2014) Empirical analysis of the influence of firm characteristic on patenting decisions. Stud Sci Sci 11:1652–1660
Zhou X, Wang D (2011) On the relationship between traditional culture and arts of minorities and regional tourism development. J Chengdu Univ (Soc Sci) 1:102–105
Zhu Y, Zhang Z (2005) Study on the regional disparity caused by technical innovation. China Soft Sci 11:92–98

The manufacturer's authorised representative in the EU is Springer Nature Customer Service Centre GmbH, Europaplatz 3, 69115 Heidelberg, Germany. If you have any concerns regarding our products, please contact ProductSafety@springernature.com

Printed and bound by CPI Group (UK) Ltd, Croydon, CR0 4YY
30/09/2026
02225440-0009